Toronto Blue Jays Official
25th Anniversary Commemorative Book

Toronto Blue Jays Official 25th Anniversary Commemorative Book

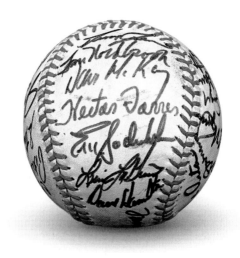

A Dan Diamond and Associates Book

Publisher

Dan Diamond and Associates, Inc.,
194 Dovercourt Road, Toronto, Ontario M6J 3C8 Canada
416/531-6535; FAX 416/531-3939 e-mail: dda.nhl@sympatico.ca

**Special thanks to the Toronto Blue Jays
Media Relations Department**

Howard Starkman, Jay Stenhouse, Mike Shaw,
Laura Ammendolia, Leanna England

Trade sales and distribution

North 49 Books, 35 Prince Andrew Drive,
Toronto, Ontario M3C 2H2 Canada
416/449-4000; FAX 416/449-9924

Dan Diamond and Associates, Inc.
194 Dovercourt Road, Toronto, Ontario M6J 3C8 Canada
416/531-6535; FAX 416/531-3939 e-mail: dda.nhl@sympatico.ca

ISBN 0-920445-76-4

Printed in Canada.
10 9 8 7 6 5 4 3 2 1

Managing Editor: Eric Zweig
Contributing Editors: Paul Bontje, Ralph Dinger, James Duplacey,
Jonathan Zweig
Copy Editor: Patricia MacDonald
Photo Research: Anne-Marie Beaton, Francine Bellefeuille,
Jean Bradshaw, Jillian Goddard, Andrea Gordon, Julie Kirsch,
Sue Pelton
Project Manager: Dan Diamond

Design and Page Composition: Joseph Gisini, Andrew Smith and
Kevin Cockburn of PageWave Graphics Inc., Toronto, Ontario
Photo CD Scanning: Moveable Type, Toronto, Ontario
Digital Image Scanning and Retouching: Stafford Graphics,
Toronto, Ontario
Printing: Transcontinental Printing Book Group
Production Management: Dan Diamond and Associates, Inc.,
Toronto Ontario

*(Preceding pages) A beaming Joe Carter, an exuberant Jimmy Key
and a relieved Jack Morris are among the faces in the Blue Jays victory
scrum following the final out of the 1992 World Series; a baseball
signed by Toronto Blue Jays, 1977. (Below) Awaiting the start of the
1993 World Series.*

I'm honoured to introduce the Toronto Blue Jays Official 25th Anniversary Commemorative Book.

Twenty-five years is an interesting amount of time; long enough to reach back to an earlier era in the city's sporting history and short enough to seem like "just the other day" for many of us. From snowy Exhibition Stadium in 1977, to back-to-back World Series championships in 1992 and 1993, to a sun-drenched Puerto Rican ballpark in 2001: every ballplayer, every big moment and every thrill in Blue Jays history is depicted here.

If baseball had a quadruple play, this would be it: great writers, more than 400 terrific photos, the best fans and a winning ballclub.

Thanks for being an important part of the first twenty-five years of Toronto Blue Jays baseball.

On we go!

Paul Godfrey,
President and CEO
Toronto Blue Jays

Contents

25 Great Moments

In the Beginning . . .

Neil MacCarl

Despite four pennants and two runner-up finishes in seven seasons (1954–1960), talk of major league baseball helped kill the Triple-A Maple Leafs of the International League. Maple Leafs owner Jack Kent Cooke was one of five founding fathers of the proposed Continental League — a rival third major league — in 1959. Cooke had plans drawn up to convert Exhibition Stadium for baseball, but city fathers expanded it for football instead. Soon, attendance for minor league baseball declined and the Maple Leafs were sold and moved following the 1967 season.

In the early 1970s, John Alevizos, an executive with the Boston Red Sox, sparked an interest in baseball in Metro Chairman Paul Godfrey and the provincial government. Though there was no stadium, Toronto's wide drawing area appealed to Alevizos, who hoped to buy the Cleveland Indians and move them. He was put in touch with businessman Syd Cooper and Labatt Breweries, while Paul Godfrey began campaigning major league executives at the World Series and All-Star Game.

Alevizos soon dropped out of the picture, but the Labatt group, which included R. Howard Webster and the Canadian Imperial Bank of Commerce, made an unsuccessful bid for the San Francisco Giants. Sights were then set on the American League, which awarded Toronto a franchise in March of 1976.

"It's like a combination of Anheuser Busch, the Rockefellers and the Bank of America," enthused one AL owner of the Labatt group.

Once the announcement of an expansion team was made, things moved quickly. In June, Peter Bavasi was picked as general manager. He hired Pat Gillick away from the New York Yankees to be in charge of player personnel. (Gillick was the chief architect at the November expansion draft.) A contest to name the team drew more than 30,000 entries, and on August 12, 1976, "Blue Jays" was selected. In September, Roy Hartsfield was hired as the club's manager.

Shortly before Hartsfield came on board, the Blue Jays had selected Dunedin, Florida, as their spring training site.

"I want somewhere we can put down roots," said Bavasi, "so people will know we will be there next year and 10 years down the road."

Twenty-five years later, the Blue Jays are still there.

It was in Dunedin in 1977 where, after more than 20 years of talk and months of expectations, we were about to get our first look at the collection of kids and castoffs the Blue Jays had selected in the expansion draft. Manager Roy Hartsfield and his coaches had already gathered in Dunedin in advance of the February 24 reporting date for pitchers and catchers. They had gotten together to discuss and prepare the training schedule, assign areas of responsibility and devise how-to sessions on pitching and fielding.

February, 1977: Dunedin gets ready to welcome the Blue Jays to their winter home.

Despite media speculation on an assortment of bigger names, Hartsfield — a 51-year-old former infielder with 15 years experience managing in the minors — got the Blue Jays job. Little did we know at the time that Bavasi had a friendship with Hartsfield from their days in the Dodgers organization when Bavasi was a fledgling front office employee. He had promised "Hartsy" that he would call if he was ever in a position to hire a manager for a major league team — and he did.

Like Hartsfield, the rest of the coaching staff was mostly from the minor league ranks. Harry Warner had spent 15 years managing in the Minnesota Twins organization. Jackie Moore, who had played briefly in Toronto and was actually named the manager of the Maple Leafs in the final weeks of the team's last season, had coached for seven years for the Texas Rangers. Don Leppert had nine years experience with the Pittsburgh Pirates. Bob Miller, the pitching coach, was much travelled, having worn 10 different major league uniforms. The best-known of the Blue Jays' new coaches was Bobby Doerr. The longtime second baseman with the Boston Red Sox and future Hall of Famer had been hired as a part time hitting instructor.

In many of his initial hirings, Peter Bavasi sought out Canadians. He got Bobby Prentice from the Detroit Tigers to head up the Blue Jays' Canadian scouting department and hired Howie Starkman as the director of public relations. Starkman had experience in a similar job with the hockey Maple Leafs. Another hockey veteran was trainer Ken Carson, who had spent 17 years in the game, the last nine with the Pittsburgh Penguins.

"They came to me, but I turned them down several times," said Carson, now director of the team's Florida operations. He finally went down to the Pirates' instructional league for a month, where trainer Tony Bartirome helped him make the switch. In hockey, he mostly had to deal with cuts, bruises and groin pulls. In baseball, it was shoulders, elbows and hamstrings. Veteran pitcher Bill Singer gave Carson plenty of help. Throughout his career, he'd been plagued by broken fingers, bone chips in his elbow and problems in his back and shoulder.

By the end of February, the entire team had reported to Dunedin. The clubhouse was crowded — too many players and too little space. There was no heat or air conditioning and uniforms were hung in the offices to dry at night.

"Basically, we were all trying to survive," recalled Garth Iorg. "The field was rough and it had lots of ant hills. I remember Doug Ault diving for a ball and coming up covered in ants. If you stood too long in one spot in the outfield, you were going to get bit."

One position where the early Blue Jays were well set was at catcher. Alan Ashby and Rick Cerone had both been acquired in deals with the Cleveland Indians, and veteran Phil Roof had been obtained as insurance. There was also rookie Ernie Whitt, but he needed more seasoning.

Ashby had been acquired in an arranged deal that saw Pat Gillick select Al Fitzmorris from Kansas City in the expansion

(Left to right) Catchers Phil Roof, Rick Cerone, Alan Ashby and Ernie Whitt (#12) read up on how to do things the Blue Jay way.

draft and then send him to Cleveland for the switch-hitting catcher. He obviously had not turned to switch hitting to take advantage of his speed.

"I grew up in the L.A. area watching the Dodgers," Ashby explained. "They had an infield of four switch-batters — Wes Parker, Jim Lefebvre, Maury Wills and Junior Gilliam. I thought that's what you had to do, so I would throw a ball against the garage door and take 10 swings right and then 10 swings left."

The most impressive young player at spring training was Bob Bailor. Bailor was the Blue Jay' first pick in the expansion draft (second overall behind Ruppert Jones). Bailor could run and steal bases. He was a spray hitter who liked to swing the bat — seldom striking out, but drawing bases-on-balls even less frequently. He was a shortstop, but he could also play the outfield.

"Just because you'd been drafted by an expansion team didn't make you a major leaguer," believed Bailor. "The challenge was to go out there everyday and prove you belonged."

After two weeks of long, hard days of practice and instruction, the Blue Jays were ready to begin the Grapefruit League schedule against the Philadelphia Phillies on March 10. Unfortunately, the weatherman didn't co-operate — the game was rained out — so the first time the Blue Jays took to the field as a team was against the New York Mets on March 11. They won that day and added victories over the Montreal Expos and the Cincinnati Reds in their first week.

It was pretty heady stuff, but Kansas City Royals manager Whitey Herzog helped put things in proper focus when he advised the media not to get carried away by a few wins.

"This team should always have a good record in the spring," said Herzog, "because nobody wants to bring their good players here and risk getting them injured on this field."

Not only were conditions cramped in the clubhouse and the press box, but also in the radio booth that was shared by Tom Cheek and his partner, Hall of Fame pitcher Early Wynn.

"We were both good sized men and we worked in a space about the size of a telephone booth," said Cheek, who has been the voice of the Blue Jays since Day One. "It was so small, our engineer had to sit outside our booth.

"On our first broadcast, our producer kept complaining about the sound of a baby crying that was being picked up by our field mike. He asked us to do something about it, but the players' wives were seated behind home plate and the baby belonged to Ernie Whitt's wife, Chris."

One of the media tagged her "the designated crier."

With the addition of the Blue Jays to the American League, it became necessary to play both the Canadian and U.S. national anthems prior to the start of all games. One day in Sarasota, Howie Starkman forgot to bring a tape of *O Canada*, so after the playing of the *Star Spangled Banner*, home plate umpire Jim McKean bent over to sweep off the plate. Then out of the stands came the sounds of *O Canada* being sung by the Canadians in the crowd. McKean, a Montrealer who had played in the Canadian Football League, halted proceedings until the anthem was finished.

While most of the spring travel was made up of shorter trips to nearby cities like Sarasota, the schedule did include an overnight road trip to Vero Beach (Dodgers) and Daytona Beach (Montreal). Players were ordered not to wear jeans on the trip — then Bavasi showed up sporting a jeans suit. Another team clothing rule saw everybody at first wearing black shoes with their uniforms. But midway through spring training, the Blue Jays acquired Ron Fairly and the veteran arrived with blue shoes. Soon everyone on the team wore blue shoes.

The overall record for the Blue Jays in spring training in 1977 was eight wins against 16 losses, but the most important thing was sorting out who to keep and who to send out for more experience. Lacking a farm system, the Blue Jays had an arrangement with the Indians to place some players with their affiliates.

> *The overall record for the Blue Jays in spring training in 1977 was eight wins against 16 losses, but the most important thing was sorting out who to keep and who to send out for more experience.*

Pitchers Jim Clancy and Jeff Byrd were sent to Jersey City, while Garth Iorg and Ernie Whitt went to Charleston, West Virginia.

Because Gillick had opted for youngsters in the expansion draft, the Blue Jays had five good-looking young arms — Byrd, Mike Darr and Butch Edge, all just 20, and Clancy and Jerry Garvin, both 21. Garvin was the most impressive of the kid pitchers. A lefty with a high leg kick and a great pickoff move, he didn't throw hard, but he threw strikes. Garvin was Mormon, and he had called the Blue Jays in February to ask permission to get married so that he could bring his wife to spring training. Garvin made the team as a starter along with Bill Singer, Dave Lemanczyk, Jesse Jefferson and Pete Vuckovich — although Hartsy wasn't sure whether to use "Vucko" as a starter or as his closer.

A bigger challenge facing Hartsfield in the spring of 1977 was the team's obvious lack of power.

"You just can't go down to the corner drug store and buy one of those [power hitters]," the manager pointed out.

One potential power source the Blue Jays dealt away was John Lowenstein. He and Hartsfield were never on the same page and Lowenstein did a lot of complaining before being shipped back to Cleveland for Hector Torres. The big surprise among the hitters was Sam Ewing, a lefthanded bat who was most likely to be used as a designated hitter and pinch hitter.

"He has a way of attracting my attention with his bat," observed Hartsy. Ewing led the team in home runs (four) and runs batted in (11) in Florida.

Then the team headed north, and baseball was back in town.

The only surprise in the opening day lineup was catcher Rick Cerone, who had a spring time average of .048 on only one hit in 21 at-bats. But he batted right and the White Sox were starting lefty Ken Brett. Bob Bailor was out of the lineup. He had cut his thumb on a can of oysters and had to be replaced at shortstop by Hector Torres.

Despite the fact the field was covered in snow, Exhibition Stadium was packed. The start of the game was delayed while the Zamboni tried to clear the snow, but when asked if there was going to be a game, umpire crew chief Nestor Chylak said: "There are 40,000 people out there who came to see a game and I'm not going to disappoint them." Neither did the Blue Jays. Led by instant hero Doug Ault, who hit a pair of home runs, the Jays took flight with a 9–5 victory.

For Hartsfield, now 75, his favourite recollection of three years in Toronto is "all those fans sitting there waiting for the snow to be cleared."

"Those fans in Toronto were wonderful."

1977

54–107 .335 7th -45.5

Baseball came to Toronto on April 7, 1977 as the Blue Jays defeated the White Sox 9–5. Bob Bailor hit .310, the highest mark for a player on an expansion team. Ron Fairly (19 HR) became the first player since Stan Musial to play more than 1,000 games in both the infield and the outfield. Dave Lemanczyk set an expansion club record with 13 wins, while Jerry Garvin (10 wins) and Roy Howell (.316, 44 RBI) both made impressive contributions.

Bill Singer delivers the first pitch in Blue Jays history.

(Above) Spring Training: Dunedin Florida, 1977.

Famous Firsts and Records [#]1

MARCH 11, 1977 • *Blue Jays 3, NY Mets 1*

Having been vigorously pursued by vice mayor Cecil P. Englebert, the Toronto Blue Jays announced in August of 1976 that they had chosen the city of Dunedin, Florida, to be their spring training home. Pitchers and catchers first reported to Dunedin on February 24, 1977. The remainder of the squad arrived four days later, and on March 1, 1977, Roy Hartsfield addressed the troops.

"Good morning, men," the manager said. "I want to welcome all of you to sunny Florida and the Toronto Blue Jays. For the one and only time in the history of the club, every position out there is open."

The Blue Jays played their first exhibition game against the New York Mets on March 11, 1977. Bill Singer was the starting pitcher that day. He allowed the Mets to break on top with a run in the top of the first, but the Blue Jays tied it on an RBI single by Gary Woods in the fifth. They won it in the eighth when Sam Ewing socked a two-run double. Dennis DeBarr earned the victory.

Singer, of course, would get the start when the Blue Jays began things for real on April 7. Gary Woods was the center fielder that day. Both he and Sam Ewing would be members of the team in 1977 and 1978. DeBarr would make 14 appearances for Toronto during the 1977 season, but never pitched in the major leagues again.

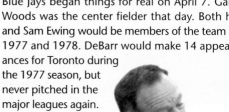

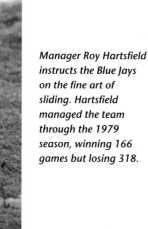

Manager Roy Hartsfield instructs the Blue Jays on the fine art of sliding. Hartsfield managed the team through the 1979 season, winning 166 games but losing 318.

Great Moments #1

APRIL 7, 1977 • *Blue Jays 9, White Sox 5*

The Blue Jays of 1977 left their first spring training camp in Dunedin on April 4 and arrived in Toronto three days before Opening Day. Most of the players saw Exhibition Stadium for the first time on April 5. It was cold and rainy and the wind howled off Lake Ontario. One day later, the city held a civic parade to officially welcome the team to town. It snowed. The morning of April 7 dawned cold and grey. By noon it had started to snow again. The game was scheduled for 1:30 p.m. It would start late, but no serious thought was ever given to a postponement.

A Zamboni-type machine cleared snow off the field as game time approached. Jack Brohamer of the visiting White Sox (left) strapped a pair of catcher's shin pads to his cleats and used bats as poles to cross-country "ski" across the infield. The 48th Highlanders marched onto the field and Anne Murray sang the national anthem. Finally, at 1:50 p.m., Bill Singer delivered the first pitch in Blue Jays history. White Sox lead-off man Ralph Garr took it. Home plate umpire Nestor Chylak called it a strike. The ball was then removed from the game and sent to the Baseball Hall of Fame in Cooperstown, New York.

Dave McKay, Alan Ashby, Chuck Hartenstein, Bob Bailor, Otto Velez and Pedro Garcia try to stay warm before Opening Day. The boy on Ashby's lap is Timmy Flynn, son of Etobicoke mayor Dennis Flynn.

Garr eventually worked Singer for a walk. The next two men were retired, but then Richie Zisk homered and the White Sox led 2–0. The first batter to come to the plate for the Blue Jays was left fielder John Scott. He struck out. So did shortstop Hector Torres. With two out, Doug Ault came to the plate and wrote his name into the history books by taking Ken Brett deep for the team's first home run. Two innings later, Ault became a Blue Jays legend when he slugged another home run. Ault's second blast was a two-run shot that tied the game 4–4. Dave McKay put the Blue Jays ahead 5–4 in the fourth. A few batters later, Doug Ault came to the plate again. The bases were loaded, but instead of belting a grand slam, Ault grounded into a double play. No matter. His place in the annals of Blue Jays history was already assured. Another historic moment occured in the bottom of the fifth when Alvis Woods came to the plate to bat for right fielder Steve Bowling. It was his major league debut, and he became just the 11th player in baseball history to launch a pinch-hit homer in his first career at-bat.

The score was now 7–4 for the Blue Jays. It would wind up 9–5. Jerry Johnson picked up the win. He had come on in relief of Bill Singer with one out in the fifth. Pete Vuckovich worked the final two innings to record the save. Only a handful of the 44,649 fans who had been in attendance were still around when Vuckovich retired Oscar Gamble for the game's final out. The Blue Jays were in first place and would stay there . . . for a couple of days. It was pretty heady stuff for a team that would eventually finish the season 54–107, 45½ games behind the New York Yankees.

Chicago	AB	R	H	RBI	Toronto	AB	R	H	RBI
Garr, lf	5	2	3	0	Scott, lf	5	1	1	0
Bannister, ss	5	0	1	1	Torres, ss	2	1	1	0
Nyman, ph	1	0	0	0	Mason, ph-ss	1	1	0	0
Nordbrook, ss	0	0	0	0	Ault, 1b	4	2	3	4
Orta, 2b	4	0	0	1	Velez, dh	4	1	2	0
Zisk, rf	6	2	4	2	G. Woods, cf	5	1	1	0
Spencer, 1b	6	0	2	0	Bowling, rf	2	0	0	0
Gamble, dh	3	0	0	0	A. Woods, ph-rf	3	1	1	2
Soderholm, 3b	5	0	2	1	Garcia, 2b	4	1	3	1
Lemon, cf	4	0	0	0	McKay, 3b	4	0	2	1
Downing, c	4	1	3	0	Cerone, c	4	0	2	0
Totals	**43**	**5**	**15**	**5**	**Totals**	**38**	**9**	**16**	**8**

Chicago				220	001	000 –	5
Toronto				112	120	02x –	9

Chicago	IP	H	R	ER	BB	SO
Brett (L. 0-1)	3	9	5	5	0	4
Barrios	3	3	2	2	3	1
Hamilton	1	3	2	2	0	1
LaGrow	1	1	0	0	0	1

Toronto	IP	H	R	ER	BB	SO
Singer	4⅓	11	4	3	3	5
Johnson (W. 1-0)	2⅔	3	1	1	3	3
Vuckovich (S1)	2	1	0	0	1	3

Brett pitched to three batters in fourth.
Hamilton pitched to three batters in eighth.

E – Cerone, McKay, Scott. DP – Chicago 2. LOB – Chicago 19, Toronto 8. 2B – Zisk, Garcia, Cerone, Scott. HR –Zisk (1), Ault 2 (2), A. Woods (1). SB – Garr, G. Woods, Velez. SF – Orta.
T – 3:22. A – 44,649.

Famous Firsts and Records #2

JUNE 27, 1977 • *Blue Jays 7, Yankees 6*

The New York Yankees made their first appearance at Exhibition Stadium to face the Blue Jays on June 27, 1977. A crowd of nearly 30,000 fans showed up to see the Bronx Bombers on a hot and humid Monday night. On the mound for Toronto was Jesse Jefferson. Opposing him was Ron Guidry. The future Yankees star had almost become a Blue Jay earlier in the year. Pat Gillick had worked out a deal that would have brought Guidry to Toronto in exchange for Bill Singer, but the trade was vetoed by club president Peter Bavasi. Bavasi felt the Blue Jays needed a "name" pitcher, and Singer was a former 20-game winner with the Los Angeles Dodgers.

Guidry was perfect through four innings against the Blue Jays that night, and the Yankees had a 1–0 lead. In the bottom of the fifth, Guidry finally lost his control. He walked Doug Rader, Doug Ault and Alan Ashby to load the bases for Hector Torres with nobody out. Torres worked the count to 2-and-2, then ripped the ball into the left field seats for the first grand slam in Blue Jays history. Toronto went on to win the game 7–6.

Hector's heroics at the plate came just one day after another historic Blue Jays first. On June 26 in Baltimore, Pete Vuckovich had outdueled Jim Palmer to toss the team's first shutout with a 2–0 victory over the Orioles. Though he was used primarily as a reliever during the 1977 season, Vuckovich went the distance on a six-hitter, walking only one and striking out 12. Though later tied several times, no Blue Jays pitcher would strike out more than 12 batters until Pat Hentgen K'd 14 in 1994. Entering the 2001 season, Hentgen and Roger Clemens (16 and 18) are the only pitchers in club history to have more strikeouts in a game than Pete Vuckovich.

(Above) Doug Rader, Otto Velez and Alan Ashby greet Hector Torres after the first grand slam in Blue Jays history. (Below) With his high leg kick and deceptive move, Jerry Garvin picked off 22 runners in 1977. He pitched with the Blue Jays until 1982.

Bad Breaks, Near Misses and Disappointments #1

JULY 4, 1977 • *Red Sox 9, Blue Jays 6*

The Toronto Blue Jays made their first trip to Boston's Fenway Park in early July of 1977. The series opened with a Monday afternoon game on U.S. Independence Day, and the Red Sox celebrated with their own amazing fireworks display. Snapping off a nine-game losing streak at Toronto's expense, Boston batters belted eight home runs, tying what was then a record that would last another decade before the Blue Jays slugged 10 homers in a single game in 1987.

Jerry Garvin had opened the season with five straight wins, but his record had slipped to 7–7 as he took to the mound to face the Red Sox. Through six innings, Fred Lynn and George Scott had both taken him deep, but the Blue Jays enjoyed a 6–3 lead. Instead of sending Garvin back out in the seventh, manager Roy Hartsfield brought in Chuck Hartenstein, a sidewinding right-hander who had been on the disabled list for seven weeks. He retired the first two Red Sox he faced, then gave up back-to-back homers to Butch Hobson and Bernie Carbo. With one out in the eighth, Hartenstein served up consecutive solo shots to Lynn and Jim Rice to give Boston a 7–6 lead. Mike Willis was summoned from the bullpen to keep the game close, but he was touched up for taters by Carl Yastrzemski and George Scott. Jerry Johnson finally got the Blue Jays out of the eighth inning, but the game was already as good as over.

The Blue Jays' first choice in the Expansion Draft, Bob Bailor forces out former Montreal Expos star Rusty Staub.

SEPTEMBER 10, 1977 • *Blue Jays 19, Yankees 3*

The Toronto Blue Jays enjoyed surprising success against the New York Yankees in 1977, particularly on the Yankees' home turf. The Blue Jays made their first visit to Yankee Stadium on April 18, 1977, and beat New York 5–1. Dave Lemanczyk pitched a complete game and former Yankee Otto Velez homered. The next day, Jerry Garvin pitched a complete game as the Blue Jays scored an 8–3 victory. Toronto was actually four games ahead of New York in the standings then, but by the time September rolled around, the Blue Jays trailed the first-place Yankees by almost 40 games. Toronto had lost 13 of its last 14 — and had scored just 14 runs in their last nine games — when the Yankees blanked them 2–0 on September 9, but the Blue Jays were about to break out of their slump in record fashion.

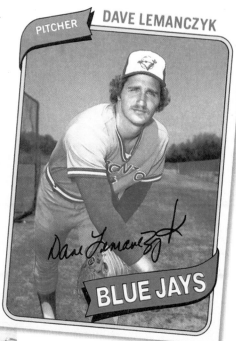

PITCHER — DAVE LEMANCZYK

BLUE JAYS

Dave Lemanczyk (left) pitched 252 innings for the Blue Jays in 1977 and posted a record of 13–16. Although he won only 14 more games for the team over the next three seasons, he tossed the Jays' first one-hitter against the Texas Rangers on April 24, 1979. (Below, left) Roy Howell, Tom Murphy, Steve Staggs and Alan Ashby sample the spread in the visiting clubhouse.

Catfish Hunter was on the mound for the Yankees and the Blue Jays got to him early. With one out in the top of the first, Al Woods doubled and scored when Roy Howell followed with another two-bagger. Ron Fairly then drove in Howell for his 1,000th career RBI. In the third inning, Howell and Fairly hit back-to-back homers to up Toronto's advantage to 4–0.

The score was 6–2 through five innings when the Blue Jays broke things open in the top of the sixth. Steve Bowling led off with a single against Ken Clay and advanced all the way to third

when Chris Chambliss threw away Rick Cerone's attempted sacrifice bunt. He then scored on a Willie Randolph error. After a walk and a single drove in another run, Howell plated Tim Nordbrook and Steve Staggs to highlight a five-run uprising. Howell launched a three-run homer in the seventh inning as Toronto scored five again, upping the lead to 16–3. The Blue Jays rounded out the scoring with three more runs in the top of the ninth. Howell's second double scored Staggs and Woods before a Doug Ault grounder cashed him in with the final run.

Jim Clancy went the distance to get the win for Toronto, while Blue Jays batters touched up five New York pitchers for 20 hits. The 19 runs they scored were the most surrendered by Yankee hurlers since Ty Cobb had led the Detroit Tigers to a 19–1 victory on June 17, 1925. Roy Howell was the big hero for the Blue Jays with five hits in six at-bats. He had two homers, two doubles, four runs scored and nine RBIs.

"We don't have anything to gain by winning but our self-pride," said the red-headed third baseman, "but knocking off the Yankees is a special treat."

Toronto	AB	R	H	RBI	New York	AB	R	H	RBI
Staggs, 2b	5	3	3	1	Rivers, cf	4	0	1	0
AWoods, lf	6	4	4	2	Blair, cf	0	0	0	0
Howell, 3b	6	4	5	9	Nettles, 3b	4	0	1	0
Fairly, dh	6	1	4	2	Klutts, 3b	0	0	0	0
Ault, 1b	6	0	0	2	Munson, c	3	0	0	0
GWoods, cf	6	0	0	0	Hendrick, c	1	0	0	0
Bowling, rf	4	3	2	0	Jackson, dh	4	0	0	0
Cerone, c	5	1	0	0	Chambliss, 1b	2	1	1	0
Nordbrook, ss	5	3	2	1	Zeber, 2b	1	0	0	0
					Piniella, rf	3	1	2	0
					May, rf	1	0	0	0
					White, lf	4	0	1	0
					Randolph, 2b	2	0	2	1
					Bergman, 1b	1	0	0	1
					Dent, ss	2	1	0	0
					Alston, ph	1	0	0	0
					Stanley, ss	1	0	0	0
Totals	**49**	**19**	**20**	**17**	**Totals**	**34**	**3**	**8**	**2**

Toronto	202	205	503 — 19
New York	001	101	000 — 3

Toronto	IP	H	R	ER	BB	SO
Clancy (W. 3-6)	9	8	3	3	1	3

New York	IP	H	R	ER	BB	SO
Hunter (L. 9-9)	3⅓	7	6	6	1	1
Clay	1⅔	5	5	2	1	0
Thomas	1⅓	3	3	1	0	0
McCall	⅔	2	2	1	0	0
Holtzman	2	3	3	2	0	0

Clay pitched to five batters in sixth

E – Chambliss, Randolph, Nettles, McCall. DP – New York 2. LOB – Toronto 5, New York 6. 2B – AWoods, Howell 2, Staggs, White. HR – Fairly (18), Howell 2 (6). SB – Nordbrook. SF – Bergman. WP – Holtzman. PB – Hendrick. T – 2:47. A – 20,296.

Oddities and Others #1

SEPTEMBER 15, 1977 • *Blue Jays 9, Orioles 0*

New York, Boston and Baltimore were all involved in a tight pennant race when the Orioles arrived in Toronto for a four-game midweek series in mid-September. The Birds were just 2½ games back of the Bronx Bombers after taking the first three games from the Blue Jays, and though they trailed the fourth game 4–0 in the fifth, there was still time for a comeback.

A light rain had been falling for about 20 minutes as Jim Clancy prepared to face the Orioles in the fifth, so the ground crew placed a tarpaulin over the two mounds in the Blue Jays bullpen. Baltimore manager Earl Weaver wasn't happy. The bullpen was just a few feet inside foul territory, so the tarp could easily become an obstacle for one of his players. Weaver brought this point to the attention of umpire Marty Springstead, but he would only agree to remove the plastic covering from the mound closest to fair territory. Weaver argued the point for some 20 minutes, then pulled his players off the field. By removing his team, the Orioles manager had forfeited the game and the Blue Jays were awarded a 9–0 victory.

"I realize this one game could cost us the championship," Weaver thundered afterwards, "but we've got 16 games left and I want to go the rest of the way with all of our guys. I wasn't going to take a chance on one of my players slipping on the tarp or catching a cleat. I might have saved somebody's career tonight."

The Orioles ended the season exactly where they were in the standings that night: 2½ games behind the division-winning Yankees.

Veteran Ron Fairly was well known to Blue Jays fans from his years with the Dodgers and the Expos. The 1977 campaign was to be Fairly's only year of service with the Jays, but he left a lasting impression on the young ball players he took under his wing.

Selected from Texas in the Expansion Draft, Jim Clancy (left) began the 1977 season at Double-A Jersey City. He made his major league debut for the Blue Jays on July 26. Rick Cerone (right) was a Blue Jay from 1977 to 1979. His entire career stretched from 1975 to 1992 and took him to eight teams.

1978

59–102 .366 7th -40

Rico Carty and John Mayberry joined the Jays for the 1978 season, combining to hit 42 home runs and drive in 138 runs. Rookie centerfielder Rick Bosetti nailed 17 opposition runners while the infield was anchored by third baseman Roy Howell (8 HR, 61 RBI) and Bob Bailor (52 RBI). On the mound, Jim Clancy was the top starter, winning 10 games with a modest 4.02 ERA while Victor Cruz converted nine saves.

Roy Howell slides safely into third during the Blue Jays' 24–10 romp over the Baltimore Orioles.

Famous Firsts and Records #3

APRIL 22, 1978 • *First Triple Play*

Though they have not pulled one off since 1979, the Blue Jays have turned three triple plays in club history. Two of them occured within a two-week span in September of 1979, and both involved hitters who would later play for the team. Ted Cox (who was a Blue Jay in 1981) grounded into a triple play on September 7, while Damaso Garcia's line drive turned into three New York Yankees outs on September 21.

The first triple play in Blue Jays history happened on April 22, 1978. It was a sunny spring Saturday and, with a game-day giveaway of team jackets to the youngsters in attendance, a crowd of 44,327 fans had turned out. (Outside of Opening Day in 1977, this would be the largest attendance for a Blue Jays game at Exhibition Stadium until the summer of 1983.) Jim Clancy was on the mound for Toronto and had just served up a solo home run to Bobby Bonds, leading off the White Sox half of the second inning. Lamar Johnson followed up with a double, and stayed at second on an infield single by Ron Blomberg.

Junior Moore came to the plate next and attempted to advance the Chicago runners with a bunt. Instead of laying it down, he popped up the first pitch. Clancy grabbed the ball out of the air and fired to John Mayberry at first base, doubling off Blomberg. Mayberry then whipped the ball to shortstop Luis Gomez who caught it at second base before Johnson could scramble back to the bag, completing the triple play.

(Above) Prime Minister Pierre Trudeau threw out the first pitch on April 22, 1978 — the day the Jays turned their first triple play.
(Left) Briefly a Blue Jay (six games in 1978), Butch Alberts signs an autograph for three optimistic young fans.

(Right) The National League batting champion in 1970, Rico Carty was drafted by the Blue Jays in 1977, but was traded before he ever played a game. "The Beeg Mon" returned to Toronto in 1978 and slugged 20 home runs before being traded to Oakland on August 15. He was back with the Blue Jays again in 1979 for his 15th and final big league season.
(Far right) Shortstop Luis Gomez was the first free-agent acquisition in Blue Jays history, signing with the team on November 11, 1977. He lost his job to Alfredo Griffin in 1979.

1978

Great Moments #3

JUNE 26, 1978 • *Blue Jays 24, Orioles 10*

Tom Underwood was a hard-luck pitcher in two seasons with the Toronto Blue Jays. In 1979, he lost his first nine decisions and ultimately posted a 9–16 record despite an ERA of just 3.69. The year before, Underwood had been 6–14, but the Blue Jays defense allowed more unearned runs behind him than any other Toronto pitcher, and the offense failed to score more than three runs in 10 of his 14 losses. Yet on the night of June 26, 1978, Tom Underwood received more support than any other pitcher in team history as the Blue Jays crushed the Baltimore Orioles by a score of 24–10.

There was little reason to expect anything special that night, and only 16,184 fans showed up. The Blue Jays had lost seven of their last eight games and would be facing one of the game's top pitchers in Mike Flanagan. He was already 11–4, while Underwood was just 3–7. Underwood allowed the Orioles to break on top with a run in the first inning, but the Blue Jays stormed back in the bottom of the second, sending 13 men to the plate and scoring nine runs on nine hits. Otto Velez and Dave McKay both socked a pair of doubles during the onslaught, tying a record that had been set, coincidentally, by Orioles shortstop Mark Belanger back in 1969.

The Blue Jays crammed all of their scoring that night into just four innings, following up the nine-run second with a four-run third, a six-run fourth and a five-run fifth. By the end of the fourth inning, the game had been so far out of hand that Orioles manager Earl Weaver brought in outfielder Larry Harlow to pitch. With a doubleheader the following night, Weaver wanted to protect his staff. Blue Jays manager Roy Hartsfield protested, but there was nothing in the rules to prevent such a move. Unfortunately for the Orioles, Harlow lasted just two-thirds of an inning, walking four batters and surrendering five runs. Catcher Elrod Hendricks fared much better, tossing 2.1 innings of scoreless, one-hit ball. "Toronto got 19 runs off my regular pitchers and only five off the other guys," Weaver pointed out after the game. "I brought them in because they had pitched the best in batting practice."

In addition to Velez and McKay, hitting heroes for the Blue Jays that night included John Mayberry, who had been on the bench when the game began. He pinch hit for Doug Ault during the nine-run second and slugged a two-run homer. He later added another home run and a double and finished the night with a career-best seven RBIs. Catcher Brian Milner, playing just his second major league game, was 3-for-5 with a triple and two runs batted in. The Blue Jays had signed Milner on June 17, and the 18-year-old had insisted that he make his professional debut with the club. He was farmed out to Medicine Hat the day after Toronto's 24–10 victory and never returned to the major leagues. His career record stands at four hits in nine at-bats for a lifetime average of .444.

Brian Milner was signed by the Blue Jays just hours after playing in the Texas High School All-Star Game. He was only 18 when he made his major league debut against Cleveland on June 23 and remains the youngest player in Blue Jays history.

Baltimore	AB	R	H	RBI	Toronto	AB	R	H	RBI
Garcia, ss	5	0	1	2	Upshaw, lf	5	1	2	1
Dauer, 3b	4	2	2	1	Bailor, cf	5	4	2	1
Murray, 1b	5	0	2	1	Howell, 3b	5	3	2	4
Singleton, rf	4	0	0	0	Carty, dh	6	2	2	3
May, dh	5	2	4	3	Velez, rf	3	4	3	2
Mora, lf	5	0	0	0	Ault, 1b	1	1	1	0
xLopez, cf	4	2	1	0	Mayberry, ph-1b	5	3	3	7
Smith, 2b	4	2	1	2	McKay, 2b	5	1	3	3
Dempsey, c	2	2	1	0	Gomez, ss	2	1	1	1
					Johnson, ss	4	1	2	0
					Milner, c	5	3	3	2
					Ashby, c	1	0	0	0
Totals	**38**	**10**	**12**	**9**	**Totals**	**47**	**24**	**24**	**24**

Baltimore . . . . .101 310 031 – 10
Toronto .094 650 00x – 24

Baltimore	IP	H	R	ER	BB	SO
Flanagan (L. 11-5)	1	6	6	6	1	1
Kerrigan	1⅓	9	7	7	0	0
TMartinez	1⅔	5	6	6	2	3
Harlow	⅔	2	5	5	4	1
Hendricks	2⅓	1	0	0	1	0
Stanhouse	1	1	0	0	0	1

Toronto	IP	H	R	ER	BB	SO
Underwood (W. 4-7)	5	6	6	5	4	0
Murphy	4	6	4	4	1	3

Flanagan pitched to six batters in second

x – Awarded first base on catcher's interference. E – Milner, Bailor. DP – Toronto 1. LOB – Baltimore 7, Toronto 8. 2B – Murray, Bailor, Velez, McKay 2, May, Howell, Garcia, Mayberry. 3B – Howell, Milner. HR – Mayberry 2 (12), May 2 (15), Smith (4). SF – Upshaw. WP – Harlow, Murphy. PB – Milner 2.
T – 2:58. A – 16,184.

Oddities and Others #2

September 20, 1978 • *Blue Jays 8, Yankees 1*

Pitcher Ron Guidry enjoyed one of the greatest years in modern baseball history when he went 25–3 with a 1.74 ERA for the New York Yankees in 1978. His worst outing by far that season came at the hands of the game's worst team — the Blue Jays.

Guidry took a record of 22–2 to the mound for the Yankees in the opener of a doubleheader at Exhibition Stadium. Opposing him was Mike Willis, who had a record of just 2–6 and was making his first start of the season after 42 appearances out of the bullpen. Guidry's only two losses so far that season had come against pitchers named Mike — Milwaukee's Mike Caldwell and Boston's Mike Torres — but there was little reason to think that "Louisiana Lightning" would be anything but dominant against a team that trailed the Yankees by 33½ games in the standings. But things went bad for Guidry right from the start.

Rick Bosetti led off the bottom of the first with a single, and Bob Bailor did the same. Roy Howell then laid down a bunt, which Guidry fielded — and promptly threw away! Both runners scored on the error and Toronto had a 2–0 lead. Guidry recovered to retire the next three batters, then got two quick outs to begin the Blue Jays second before Rick Cerone and Luis Gomez singled. When Bosetti and Bailor followed with back-to-back triples, Guidry was gone after just 1.2 innings.

As for Mike Willis, he pitched "the greatest game of my life" that night, tossing the only complete game of his career in an 8–1 victory. He allowed the Yankees just six hits, the only run coming when Cliff Johnson took him deep in the seventh inning. The Blue Jays had the Yankees in trouble again with a 2–0 lead through eight innings in the nightcap, but the Bronx Bombers rallied to score three in the ninth against Tom Underwood and Victor Cruz.

Mike Willis was a member of the Blue Jays from 1977 to 1981. Used mostly out of the bullpen, just six of his 144 appearances came as a starter. Willis had a record of 7–21 with 15 saves as a Blue Jay and is best remembered for his victory over Ron Guidry.

The pitching motion of Victor Cruz was heavily influenced by his idol, Luis Tiant. Cruz posted a sterling 7–3 record with nine saves and a 1.71 ERA in 1978. Acquired from St. Louis with Tom Underwood for Pete Vuckovich, Cruz was later traded to the Cleveland Indians for a young infielder named Alfredo Griffin.

1979

53–109 .327 7th -50.5

Rick Cerone became the club's number-one catcher in 1979, appearing in 136 games and driving home 61 runs. Shortstop Alfredo Griffin (.287, 179 hits and 21 stolen bases) earned a share of the American League's Rookie-of-the-Year Award. John Mayberry (21 HR, 74 RBI), Roy Howell (15 HR, 72 RBI) and Otto Velez (.288, 15 HR, 48 RBI) fueled the offense. Tom Underwood (9–16) and Dave Stieb (8–8), were the mainstays of the pitching staff.

Rookie-of-the-Year shortstop Alfredo Griffin pivots to avoid a sliding Tom Veryzer of the Cleveland Indians and fires to first base to complete another Blue Jays double-play during the 1979 season.

Oddities and Others #3

MAY 31, 1979 • *Tigers 1, Blue Jays 0*

The Detroit Tigers were looking to complete a four-game sweep of the Blue Jays at Exhibition Stadium when they sent Pat Underwood to the mound in his major league debut. Opposing him for Toronto that night was Tom Underwood — Pat's older brother.

Though Tom was 0–6 on the season and Pat was a raw rookie, the Underwood brothers battled each other in one of the greatest pitching duels in Blue Jays history. Both kept putting zeroes on the scoreboard until the top of the eighth, when Jerry Morales touched Tom for a solo homer. It was one of only six hits he gave up during his complete-game effort, but the Blue Jays had reached Pat for just two — a Danny Ainge single and a Rico Carty double.

Pat Underwood carried his two-hit shutout into the bottom of the ninth. He retired Bob Robertson for the first out, but when Alfredo Griffin doubled to put the tying run in scoring position, manager Les Moss (who was soon to be replaced by Sparky Anderson) decided he'd seen enough. Dave Tobik came on to retire Bob Bailor, then John Hiller struck out Roy Howell to preserve the Tigers' 1–0 victory.

Originally drafted by the Blue Jays as an outfielder, Dave Stieb was transformed into a pitcher and fast-tracked through the minors. On June 26, 1979, with only 19 minor league appearances under his belt, Stieb made his major league debut.

(Above) Brothers with Arms: Tom (left) and Pat Underwood went head-to-head against each other on May 31, 1979. Tom was named the Blue Jays' Pitcher of the Year in 1979 with a 9–16 record and a 3.69 ERA. (Below) Catcher Rick Cerone limbers up with team mascot B.J. Birdy prior to a game at Exhibition Stadium. Although Cerone established himself as the Jays' number-one pivot in 1979, appearing in 136 games with seven homers and 61 RBIs, he was traded to the New York Yankees in the deal that brought Damaso Garcia to Toronto.

Fireballing right-hander Jesse Jefferson compiled a 2–10 record with a lofty 5.51 ERA for the Jays in 1979. He was one of the pitchers victimized by the California Angels when they pummelled the Jays 24–2 on August 25, 1979.

1979

Bad Breaks, Near Misses and Disappointments #2

AUGUST 25, 1979 • *Angels 24, Blue Jays 2*

After two years of modest improvement, the Blue Jays suffered through the worst season in franchise history in 1979. The team's record was a woeful 53–109 and they finished 50½ games behind the first-place Baltimore Orioles. The worst defeat in the team's worst season came on a Saturday afternoon at Exhibition Stadium when the California Angels — led by manager Jim Fregosi — beat the Blue Jays 24–2.

Balor Moore, who split the 1979 season between the bullpen and the starting rotation, got the start for the Blue Jays against the Angels that day. He was shaky from the very beginning, allowing the first three batters to reach base. Don Baylor, who would be named the American League MVP for 1979, then slugged a grand slam to give California an early 4–0 lead. Baylor would knock in eight runs on the day, bringing his season total to 118.

As the game wore on, Jesse Jefferson and Jackson Todd were summoned from the Blue Jays bullpen, but neither could stop the Angels onslaught. By the end of four innings, the score was 16–2. In the sixth, the Angels led 22–2 when manager Roy Hartsfield summoned backup infielder Craig Kusick to the mound. Hartsfield had protested when Earl Weaver made a similar move during Toronto's 24–10 pounding of the Orioles the year before, but now the thought of resting his pitching staff made a lot of sense. And Kusick pitched better than anyone else that day.

Kusick entered the game like Al Hrabosky, the Kansas City relief ace known as "the Mad Hungarian." He stomped around behind the mound and slammed the ball into his glove. Then he retired two batters to close out the sixth. Kusick retired the side in order in the seventh, but was touched up for a two-run homer in the eighth. He set down the Angels again in the ninth and left the field to a rousing ovation.

Craig Kusick spent the second half of his seventh and final major league season with the Blue Jays in 1979. He appeared in 24 games, most of them at first base – but he'll be best remembered as the only effective pitcher during the Blue Jays' most lopsided defeat.

Famous Firsts and Records #4

NOVEMBER 26, 1979 • *Alfredo Griffin*

Amid all the losing that came during a disappointing 1979 season, there were two bright spots. One was the pitching of Dave Stieb, who joined the team late in June. The other was the play of Alfredo Griffin. When it came time for Major League Baseball to hand out the hardware after the season, Griffin was named co-winner of the American League Rookie of the Year.

Griffin was acquired from the Cleveland Indians in a deal for popular relief pitcher Victor Cruz. After a slow start in April, he caught fire in May and was named Labatt's Player of the Month, an honour he would garner again in August and September. Alfredo was also named American League Player of the Month in September, batting .347 during the final month of the season. For the year, Griffin hit .287 to lead all AL shortstops and established new club records with 179 hits, 81 runs, 10 triples and 21 stolen bases.

When it came time to select the Rookie of the Year, voters had a hard time choosing among a strong rookie crop. In the end, Griffin and Minnesota Twins third baseman John Castino both received seven of a possible 28 votes, marking the first time that the American League rookie honour was shared. California Angels reliever Mark Clear was named on five ballots, while Yankees pitcher Ron Davis, White Sox hurler Ross Baumgarten and Texas first baseman Pat Putnam received three votes apiece.

Griffin would never again match the offensive totals he put up during his rookie season, but his aggressive play on defense and obvious joy in playing the game forever endeared him to Blue Jays fans.

Former New York Yankees shortstop and Blue Jays broadcaster Tony Kubek (above) presents Alfredo Griffin with the American League Rookie-of-the-Year Award that he shared with Minnesota third baseman John Castino in 1979. Alfredo Griffin (left), whose ready smile, accurate arm and acrobatic fielding made him an instant fan favourite, was one of the most popular Blue Jays of all-time. In 1992, Griffin returned to Toronto and was a key cog in the Jays' first World Series championship.

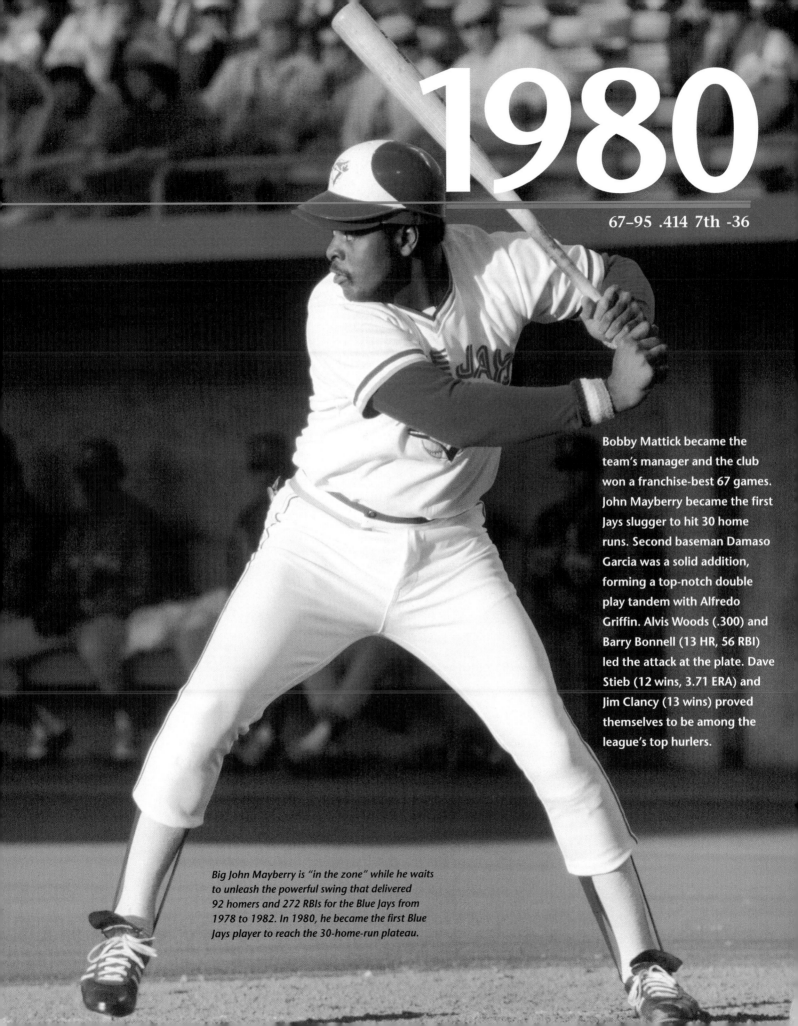

1980

67–95 .414 7th -36

Bobby Mattick became the team's manager and the club won a franchise-best 67 games. John Mayberry became the first Jays slugger to hit 30 home runs. Second baseman Damaso Garcia was a solid addition, forming a top-notch double play tandem with Alfredo Griffin. Alvis Woods (.300) and Barry Bonnell (13 HR, 56 RBI) led the attack at the plate. Dave Stieb (12 wins, 3.71 ERA) and Jim Clancy (13 wins) proved themselves to be among the league's top hurlers.

Big John Mayberry is "in the zone" while he waits to unleash the powerful swing that delivered 92 homers and 272 RBIs for the Blue Jays from 1978 to 1982. In 1980, he became the first Blue Jays player to reach the 30-home-run plateau.

Great Moments #4

MAY 4, 1980 • *Blue Jays vs. Indians*

Otto Velez was one of the early favourites among Blue Jays fans. He spent six years with the team from 1977 to 1982, enjoying his best season in 1980 when he led all American League designated hitters with a career-high 20 home runs. Four of those blasts

came on a single Sunday in May as Velez provided the team with one of its truly memorable moments in a doubleheader sweep of the Cleveland Indians.

Velez had swung the bat well in batting practice that day, prompting hitting coach Bobby Doerr to remark that he looked like a guy who was about to break loose. Otto proved Doerr prophetic in his very first at-bat when he came to the plate with the bases loaded in the bottom of the first and took Dan Spillner deep for a grand slam.

Otto Velez selects a new piece of lumber from the bat rack.

The Blue Jays led 4–0 after one inning, 5–0 after two and 6–0 after four, but the Indians began to chip away and had closed the gap to 6–5 after a three-run outburst in the top of the eighth. In the bottom of the inning, Velez stepped in against Wayne Garland and launched his second homer of the game, a two-run shot. But again the Indians fought back, scoring three times in the top of the ninth to tie the game 8–8. It was still tied when Otto came to the plate again to lead off the bottom of the tenth. No Blue Jays player had hit three home runs in a game before, but Velez took Sid Monge over the fence in right field to win the game 9–8. Otto's heroics had overcome five Cleveland homers, including a pinch-hit blast by future Blue Jay Cliff Johnson — who had once hit three home runs in a game for the Yankees against Toronto at Exhibition Stadium in June of 1977.

The crowd of 26,114 fans had barely stopped buzzing about Otto's performance in the opener when he came to the plate in the first inning of game two with two runners on base. This time, Velez took Bob Owchinko downtown for a three-run blast, giving him 10 RBIs on the afternoon and

completing his home run "cycle" (solo, two-run, three-run and grand slam). Otto had tied the American League record for home runs in a doubleheader, and had also taken over the league lead in homers and RBIs, with seven and 20. The Blue Jays went on to a 7–2 victory and a share of first place in the division with a record of 12–9.

"Quite a day," said manager Bobby Mattick. "Otto's strong. He can hit anytime."

"I think it helps me that I get to play every day now," said the slugger. "I guess I got lucky today."

Cleveland	AB	R	H	RBI	Toronto	AB	R	H	RBI
Orta, cf	6	1	2	1	Griffin, ss	4	0	2	1
Kuiper, 2b	6	1	1	0	Bailor, 3b	5	1	1	0
Hargrove, 1b	4	1	2	2	Bonnell, rf	3	1	0	0
Hassey, c	4	0	0	0	Mayberry, 1b	2	1	0	0
Johnson, ph	1	1	1	1	Cannon, pr	0	1	0	0
Diaz, c	0	0	0	0	Upshaw, 1b	1	0	0	0
Harrah, 3b	5	2	3	1	Velez, dh	5	3	3	7
Monge, p	0	0	0	0	Woods, lf	4	0	1	0
Charboneau, lf	3	1	1	0	Garcia, 2b	4	0	0	0
Alexander, dh	3	1	1	2	Ainge, cf	4	0	1	0
Dybzinski, 3b	0	0	0	0	Davis, c	0	0	0	0
Pruitt, rf	5	0	1	1	Whitt, c	2	2	1	0
Veryzer, ss	5	0	1	0	Bosetti, cf	0	0	0	0
Totals	**42**	**8**	**13**	**8**	**Totals**	**34**	**9**	**9**	**8**

```
Cleveland ............................000 011 033 0 – 8
Toronto ..............................410 100 020 1 – 9
    No outs when winning run scored
```

Cleveland	IP	H	R	ER	BB	SO
Spillner	4	6	6	5	3	1
Garland	4	2	2	2	1	3
Monge (L. 0-1)	1	1	1	1	2	1

Toronto	IP	H	R	ER	BB	SO
Clancy	7	9	5	5	3	2
McLaughlin	1	2	2	2	0	0
Garvin	0	1	1	1	0	0
Buskey (W. 2-0)	2	1	0	0	1	0

```
    Clancy pitched to three batters in eight
    McLaughlin pitched to two batters in ninth
Garvin pitched to one batter in ninth
    Monge pitched to one batter in tenth
```

E – Hargrove, Griffin. DP – Cleveland 1, Toronto 2. LOB – Cleveland 9, Toronto 5. 2B – Bailor. 3B – Griffin. HR – Velez 3 (6), Orta (2), Harrah (1), Alexander (1), Hargrove (3), Johnson (1). SB – Harrah. S – Griffin. HBP – by Clancy (Hargrove).
T – 2:44.

Cleveland	AB	R	H	RBI	Toronto	AB	R	H	RBI
Orta, cf	5	1	2	0	Griffin, ss	4	1	2	0
Kuiper, 2b	5	0	1	1	Bosetti, cf	4	1	3	1
Hargrove, 1b	4	0	1	1	Bonnell, lf	3	1	1	1
Hassey, c	2	0	0	0	Velez, dh	4	1	1	3
Johnson, ph	1	0	0	0	Garcia, 2b	4	2	2	0
Diaz, c	0	0	0	0	Mayberry, 1b	4	0	2	2
Harrah, 3b	3	0	2	0	Macha, 3b	3	0	0	0
Charboneau, lf	4	0	0	0	Upshaw, ph	1	0	0	0
Alexander, dh	3	0	0	0	Ainge, lf	0	0	0	0
Mora, rf	4	0	0	0	Bailor, lf	4	0	1	0
Dybzinski, ss	4	1	2	0	Davis, c	1	1	0	0
Totals	**35**	**2**	**8**	**2**	**Totals**	**32**	**7**	**12**	**7**

```
Cleveland .............................002 000 000 – 2
Toronto ..............................300 001 21x – 7
```

Cleveland	IP	H	R	ER	BB	SO
Owchinko (L. 0-3)	6	8	4	4	1	1
Stanton	1⅓	2	2	2	1	0
Cruz	1⅓	2	1	1	0	1

Toronto	IP	H	R	ER	BB	SO
Jefferson (W. 1-1)	5⅔	6	2	2	4	3
Garvin	⅔	1	0	0	0	1
McLaughlin (S2)	2⅔	1	0	0	0	2

E – Macha 2. DP – Cleveland 1, Toronto 1. LOB – Cleveland 10, Toronto 4. 2B – Orta, Bosetti, Garcia. 3B – Garcia. HR – Velez (7). SF – Bonnell.
T – 2:31. A – 26,114.

Former college basketball player Danny Ainge was a two-sport star who tried to make a go of it as a major league baseball player in Toronto from 1979 to 1981. A .220 average in 211 games convinced him to join the Boston Celtics of the NBA.

Oddities and Others #4

AUGUST 4, 8, 16, 1980 • *Bob Bailor*

Though he hit .310 for the Blue Jays in 1977, Bob Bailor's true value to the team was his versatility.

Over four seasons in Toronto, Bailor played third base, shortstop and the outfield. He even made three appearances as a pitcher during the 1980 campaign.

Bailor was summoned to the mound for the first time during a game in Cleveland on August 4. The Indians had chased starter Paul Mirabella with six runs in just 3.1 innings and, by the seventh, were in the process of roughing up reliever Tom Buskey for the second inning in a row. After Bo Diaz and Rick Manning had reached him for back-to-back homers, Buskey threw three brushback pitches to Miguel Dilone and was ejected from the game. With the score 11–3, manager Bobby Mattick moved Bailor to the mound from shortstop. He was known to have a pretty good knuckleball, and Bailor used it to retire all four batters he faced over 1.1 innings.

Four nights later, the Kansas City Royals pounded Jim Clancy and Joey McLaughlin for a 9–0 lead through eight innings in the first game of a doubleheader at Exhibition Stadium. Looking to conserve his bullpen for the nightcap, Mattick turned to Bailor again to pitch the ninth. This time he surrendered two hits, but still managed to get out of the inning without giving up a run. However, his shutout string would come to an end in his third and final relief appearance the following week in Kansas City.

The score was 9–3 for the Royals when Bailor replaced Joey McLaughlin to start the seventh inning. He was greeted with back-to-back doubles from Clint Hurdle and Rance Mulliniks, then walked U.L. Washington and was pulled from the game. When Mulliniks later came in to score, Bailor's lifetime ERA had ballooned to a mark of 7.71.

Bob Bailor (above and right) proved that he was deserving of the nickname "Mr. Versatility," when he was called upon to pitch three times in 12 days during the dog days of August in 1980. Bobby Mattick (left) had spent a lifetime in baseball, but most of it as a scout before he became a 64-year-old rookie manager in 1980. His knowledge of the game helped many young Blue Jays develop into stars.

Oddities and Others #5

Until the introduction of inter-league play in 1997, the Blue Jays had never had a pitcher come to the plate in a regular-season game. A check of the records for the 1980 season will indicate that Dave Stieb had one turn at bat that year, but Stieb was actually playing in the outfield at the time. This was the result of a suspended game.

Prior to the 1982 season, the Blue Jays were only scheduled to play afternoon games during the Canadian National Exhibition, allowing Exhibition Stadium to be used for concerts at night. In order to ensure that there would be no delays, Blue Jays games were scheduled for 1:00 p.m. with a curfew stating that no complete inning could begin after 5 o'clock. As a result, when the Twins and Blue Jays were deadlocked at 5–5 through 14 innings on the afternoon of August 28, 1980, the completion of the game had to be put off until noon the following day. That evening, Otto Velez fractured his right cheekbone in a minor automobile accident. With Al Woods already ailing and Rick Bosetti and Barry Bonnell on the disabled list, the Blue Jays were desperately short of players. When the game resumed, Stieb — who had been an outfielder in college — was forced to go into left field.

Stieb fielded the only ball that came his way (a Dave Edwards single in the top of the 15th), but the Twins scored two runs to take a 7–5 lead. In the bottom of the inning, Stieb came to the plate against Al Williams with nobody out and Damaso Garcia at first base. He lined out to center fielder Ken Landreaux. Two batters later, Roy Howell grounded into a game-ending double play. When the regularly scheduled game got under way a short time later, Stieb was out on the mound as the starting pitcher. He took the loss in a 5–2 Twins victory.

Only weeks after Bob Bailor had been called upon to pitch, Dave Stieb was forced to play the outfield in the top of the 15th inning of a game against Minnesota. At least he was familiar with the position, since he was originally an outfielder in both college and the minors.

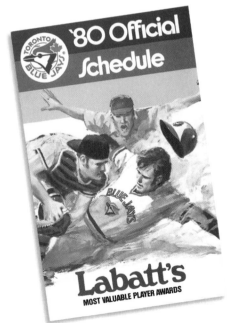

Outfielder Alvis Woods, who put his name in the record books by hitting a pinch-hit homer in his first major league at-bat in 1977, was on the shelf with an injury the day Stieb was forced to play left field. Woods hit .300 in 1980.

1980

1981

Split season
16–42 .276 7th -19
21–27 .438 7th -7.5

In a season split by a strike, the Jays combined the worst start and the strongest finish in the club's five-year history. Dave Stieb (11–10) was the first starter to have more wins than losses and Luis Leal (7–13, 3.19 ERA) continued to improve. Joey McLaughlin (10 saves, 2.85 ERA) and Roy Lee Jackson (seven saves, 2.61 ERA) anchored the bullpen. George Bell, Jesse Barfield, Lloyd Moseby, Ernie Whitt and Garth Iorg all made appearances during this campaign.

Garth Iorg dances away from a sliding John Wathan while turning a twin killing for the Jays. Iorg remains a member of the Blue Jays family, serving as the team's first base coach during the 2001 season.

Bad Breaks, Near Misses and Disappointments #3

MAY 15, 1981 • *Indians 3, Blue Jays 0*

It was a cool and damp evening in Cleveland, and though the perennially poor Indians were in first place at the time, only 7,290 fans were on hand at cavernous Municipal Stadium to watch the home team take on the last-place Blue Jays. Ten days before, Indians pitcher Bert Blyleven had no-hit Toronto through eight innings at Exhibition Stadium. This night, Len Barker would go him one inning better — and then some!

Barker set down Alfredo Griffin, Lloyd Moseby and George Bell in the first inning and then was staked to a 2–0 lead when the Indians scored a pair of unearned runs off Luis Leal. Barker retired John Mayberry, Willie Upshaw and Damaso Garcia in the second, then got Rick Bosetti, Danny Ainge and Buck Martinez in the third. The American League strikeout leader in 1980 had yet to record a single K, but the often erratic Barker was displaying unusual control. He finally fanned his first two Blue Jays in the fourth, then struck out two again in each of the fifth, sixth, seventh and eighth innings. After Jorge Orta socked a solo homer to make the score 3–0 in the bottom of the eighth, Barker returned to the mound one last time. Not a single Blue Jays batter had reached base against him all night. Few had even come close. In the fourth inning, Lloyd Moseby had ripped a ball down the right field line but it went foul. In the seventh, second baseman Duane Kuiper ranged far to his left to rob Alfredo Griffin of a base hit.

First to face Barker in the top of the ninth was Bosetti, who lifted a foul pop fly to third baseman Toby Harrah. Al Woods was sent up to pinch hit for Ainge and he struck out on three pitches. Now just one batter stood between Barker and baseball immortality. Buck Martinez was the scheduled hitter, but manager Bobby Mattick lifted him for Ernie Whitt. With the count 0-and-1, Whitt lifted a fly ball into shallow center field. It was the first time since the third inning that a Blue Jays batter had even managed to get the ball out of the infield, but when Rick Manning squeezed it for the final out, the 12th perfect game in major league history was in the books. Barker had needed just 103 pitches (74 strikes/29 balls) to retire 27 straight Blue Jays and all 11 of his strikeout victims went down swinging.

ALVIS WOODS

Coincidence? Less than a month after becoming one of Len Barker's ninth-inning victims during the Cleveland hurler's perfect game, Rick Bosetti was traded to the Oakland Athletics for "future considerations."

Al Woods, who struck out only 176 times in almost 2,000 career at-bats with the Blue Jays, whiffed on three pitches to become the second out in the ninth inning during Len Barker's perfect gem.

Buck Martinez, who became the 11th manager of the Toronto Blue Jays on November 3, 2000, was granted clemency from an inglorious spot in baseball infamy when manager Bobby Mattick pinch hit for him with two out in the bottom of the ninth inning. Ernie Whitt wasn't so fortunate.

Bad Breaks, Near Misses and Disappointments #4

JUNE 12, 1981 • *Players Strike*

The 1981 season marked the second straight year in which baseball fans endured the threat of a players strike. An 11th hour agreement had seen the season saved in 1980, but there would be no such luck in 1981. The players walked off the job on June 12 and continued to strike until a deal was finally reached in the early hours of July 31. Clubs then opened a week-long "training camp" on August 1 before the season resumed with the All-Star Game on August 9. The regular schedule picked up again on August 10.

For baseball fans in Toronto, the strike had been like a blessing in disguise. The team had lost 11 in a row from May 31 to June 11 and had a dismal record of 16–42. The team batting average was a woeful .218, and not a single player was hitting above the .247 clip of utility infielder Garth Iorg. Among the regulars, Barry Bonnell (.238) and Lloyd Moseby (.235) were leading the way, while John Mayberry topped the team with just nine home runs. (He and Bonnell had 25 RBIs.) Luis Leal had a record of 3–8 despite an ERA of 2.78, while Dave Stieb's ERA of 3.31 produced a team-leading four victories — and seven losses.

The Blue Jays losing streak reached 12 games when they dropped a 4–3 decision to the Tigers to start the second half of the season, but then things finally started to click. The team that had shown so much improvement under new manager Bobby Mattick in 1980 rattled off four straight wins and moved to the top of the second-half standings. The Blue Jays were still playing better than .500 ball as late as September 20, and though they had fallen into sixth place, they were just 3½ games out of first and were actually given permission to print playoff tickets for the division series that would pit the first-half champions against the winners of the second half. Though nine losses in their last 11 games ended any hopes for the playoffs, Blue Jays fans had finally seen a glimpse of the better days that lay ahead.

Although the Jays were a fairly dismal outfit throughout the first half of the 1981 season, Lloyd Moseby, Barry Bonnell John Mayberry (seen here crossing home plate) and Damaso Garcia did turn in some above-average performances.

Roy Lee Jackson was a steadying influence on a surprisingly strong Blue Jays bullpen in 1981, collecting seven saves with a tidy 2.61 ERA.

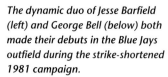

The dynamic duo of Jesse Barfield (left) and George Bell (below) both made their debuts in the Blue Jays outfield during the strike-shortened 1981 campaign.

Although it was often called "the Mistake by the Lake," Exhibition Stadium was a cozy ballpark that supplied more than a decade of diamond dreams to ball fans in Toronto.

1982

78–84 .481 T6th -17

Willie Upshaw and Damaso Garcia lead the cheers as the Blue Jays salute their fans following the final home game of the 1982 season. The Jays won a franchise-record 78 games that year and tied for last place.

New manager Bobby Cox was an expert strategist who used a platoon system at third base and behind the plate. Willie Upshaw (21 HR, 75 RBI) and Damaso Garcia (54 steals, .310) were the stars at the plate while Luis Leal (12–15, 3.95), Jim Clancy (16–14, 3.71) and Dave Stieb (17–10, 3.25) all established themselves as top-notch hurlers. Dale Murray (11 saves) and Jesse Barfield (15 outfield assists) were other keys to the Jays' success.

Bad Breaks, Near Misses #5 and Disappointments

SEPTEMBER 28, 1982 • *Blue Jays 3, Twins 0*

One in Hand, but Two in Bush: Jim Clancy prepares to fire another strike past a Minnesota Twins hitter during his near perfecto on September 28, 1982. Clancy lost his bid for a perfect game when Randy Bush blooped a single beyond the reach of Damaso Garcia to lead off the ninth.

Jim Clancy had already established a new career high with his 14th victory six days before. Now he was on the mound again, trying to nudge his season record over .500. It was the first game of a doubleheader against Minnesota on a Tuesday evening, and only a few thousand fans were on hand (the attendance would be just 11,124) as Clancy retired the Twins three up and three down the first time through the order.

Like Clancy, Twins rookie starter Frank Viola had shut out the Blue Jays through three innings, but after Clancy blanked the Twins again in the fourth, Garth Iorg and Jesse Barfield reached Viola for a pair of solo homers. That was when Clancy began to think about a no-hitter. After he set the Twins down in order again in the fifth, everyone was beginning to take notice. Following three more outs in the sixth, the fans cheered Clancy when he headed back to the dugout. The cheers grew louder when Clancy retired the side in order again in the seventh. He'd needed some defensive help that inning when Twins leadoff hitter Bobby Mitchell smashed a ball that deflected off his leg. "I thought for sure it was up the middle," Clancy said afterward, but Alfredo Griffin made the play. Clancy then set the Twins down in order again in the eighth. "He was in total command," said Buck Martinez, "and the fans sensed it." No pitcher in Blue Jays history had ever taken a no-hitter into the ninth inning before, and Clancy didn't just have a no-hitter, he had a perfect game!

Leading off the ninth inning for the Twins was designated hitter Randy Bush. Clancy had thrown just 78 pitches when he broke Bush's bat with a 2-and-2 offering. Still, Bush managed to lift a little looper into shallow center field. Damaso Garcia raced after the ball with his back to the infield, but he just couldn't reach it. Bush had a base hit.

The perfect game was over.

Clancy promptly erased Bush with a double-play ball, but then issued his only walk of the evening. When he got Bobby Mitchell on a fielder's choice grounder, a superb one-hit shutout was in the books.

Rookie right-hander Jim Gott proved to be a pleasant surprise in the Blue Jays' starting rotation, collecting five wins with a respectable 4.43 ERA during the 1982 campaign.

OK Blue Jays: The Blue Jays Theme Song

First Verse

You've got a diamond, You've got nine men.
You've got a hat and a bat and that's not all.
You've got the bleachers, Got 'em from spring 'till fall,
You got a dog and a drink and the umpire's call,
Waddaya want? Let's play ball!

Chorus

OKAY (Okay), BLUE JAYS (Blue Jays),
LET'S (Let's) PLAY (Play) BALL!

Oddities and Others #6

OCTOBER 3, 1982 • *Blue Jays 5, Mariners 2*

The 59-day strike that split the 1981 season stands as a turning point in the history of the Toronto Blue Jays. At the time of the strike, the Blue Jays had played four-and-a-half seasons and had a franchise record of 249–455 for a .354 winning percentage and an average of just 57 wins per year. Over the next four-and-a-half seasons, the team was 376–319 for a .541 percentage and an average of 88 wins per year, culminating in their American League East Division title in 1985.

The Blue Jays had come on strong in the second half of 1981, but still finished in last place. Finally, in 1982 the team escaped the cellar for the first time — finishing tied with the Cleveland Indians for sixth place in the division with a record of 78–84. While this hardly seems like cause for a celebration, it was the way the Blue Jays finished the year that had their fans excited about the future.

Players like Willie Upshaw and Damaso Garcia had begun to flourish under new manager Bobby Cox in 1982, as did platoon partners Garth Iorg and Rance Mulliniks, and Buck Martinez and Ernie Whitt. The Blue Jays posted a record of 44–37 after the All-Star break and won nine of their final 12 games, including a sweep of the Seattle Mariners to close out the season.

In order to pull out of last place, the Blue Jays had needed to beat Seattle on the last day of the season. They entered the eighth inning in a 2–2 tie, but an Upshaw triple triggered a three-run rally against Mariners relief ace Bill Caudill.

When Jim Clancy completed the game in the top of the ninth, the fans gave him — and the team — a raucous standing ovation. Clancy fired his hat and glove into the seats, as did several other players. Alfredo Griffin brought a bag of balls out of the dugout and began tossing them into the stands.

"We're Number Six!" shouted the fans.

It wouldn't be too much longer before the team was finally Number One.

American League pitchers would soon become very familiar with the steely-eyed stare of Willie Upshaw.

This lineup card from the Jays' final game of the 1982 season clearly shows the freewheeling, substitution-happy managerial style of Bobby Cox.

37

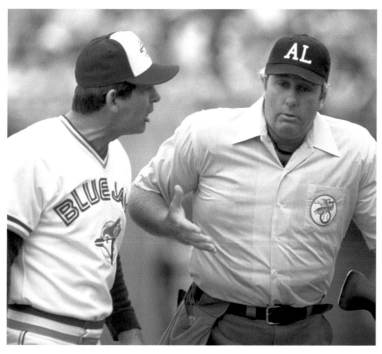

The Puppet Master: Bobby Cox pulled all the right strings in 1982. He implemented an efficient and successful platoon system at both third base and behind the plate — and wasn't afraid to tell umpires (in this case Montreal's Jim McKean) when they were wrong.

The Ace: Dale Murray became the ace of the Jays bullpen in 1982, winning eight games while collecting a team-record 11 saves.

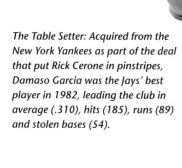

The Table Setter: Acquired from the New York Yankees as part of the deal that put Rick Cerone in pinstripes, Damaso Garcia was the Jays' best player in 1982, leading the club in average (.310), hits (185), runs (89) and stolen bases (54).

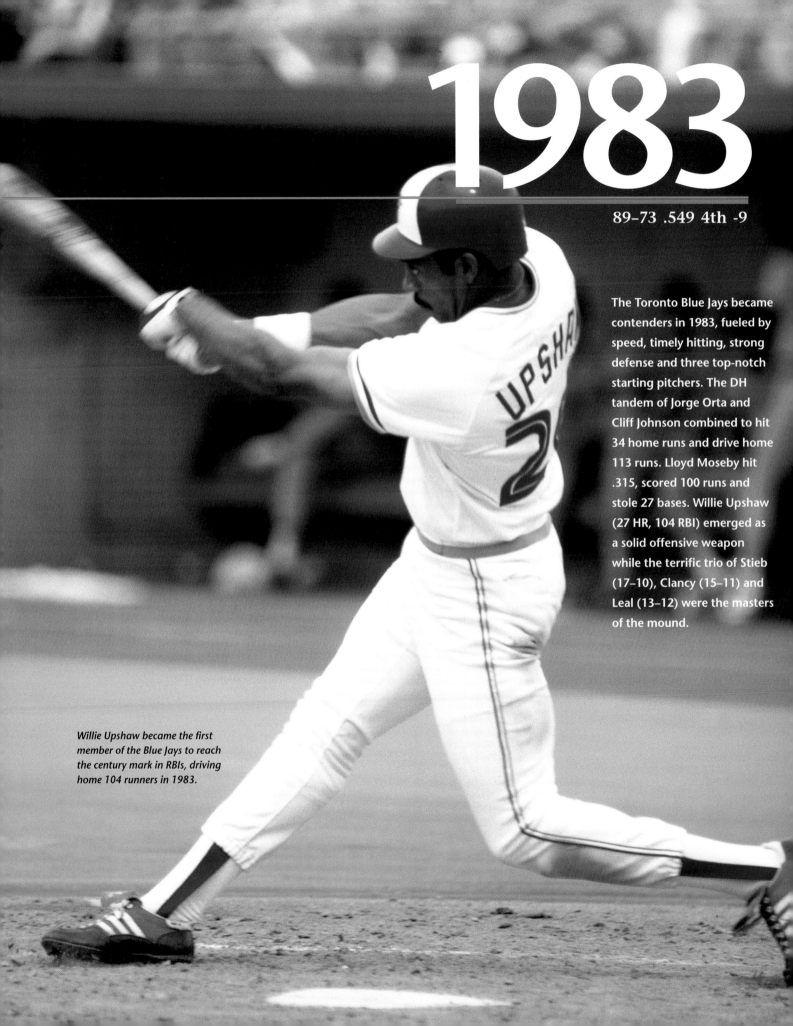

1983

89–73 .549 4th -9

The Toronto Blue Jays became contenders in 1983, fueled by speed, timely hitting, strong defense and three top-notch starting pitchers. The DH tandem of Jorge Orta and Cliff Johnson combined to hit 34 home runs and drive home 113 runs. Lloyd Moseby hit .315, scored 100 runs and stole 27 bases. Willie Upshaw (27 HR, 104 RBI) emerged as a solid offensive weapon while the terrific trio of Stieb (17–10), Clancy (15–11) and Leal (13–12) were the masters of the mound.

Willie Upshaw became the first member of the Blue Jays to reach the century mark in RBIs, driving home 104 runners in 1983.

Famous Firsts and Records #5

MAY 15, 22, 29, 1983 • *Leal, Stieb, Moseby*

A strong finish to the 1982 season had Blue Jays fans looking for better things in 1983, and the month of May proved to everyone that the team could indeed contend in the American League East. Winning a club-record 18 games against just nine losses, the Blue Jays took over first place by the end of the month. Heroes for May included Luis Leal, Dave Stieb and Lloyd Moseby, each of whom earned recognition as the American League Player of the Week.

Leal took the honours for the week of May 9–15, posting a 2–0 record with an ERA of 0.64. He threw a three-hitter for a 6–1 victory over the White Sox on May 9, then beat the Indians 8–1 on May 14 after firing five innings of no-hit ball. Dave Stieb was rewarded for the week of May 16–22 when he pitched a pair of complete games, beating the Brewers 2–1 in 10 innings, then shutting out the Orioles 6–0. The win over Baltimore was Stieb's fifth victory in May. He would be named the American League Pitcher of the Month.

Completing the Toronto trifecta of weekly award winners was Lloyd Moseby. During the week of May 23–29, "the Shaker" batted .556 (10-for-18) with two doubles, three homers and five RBIs. Leal, Stieb and Moseby became just the second set of teammates to earn three consecutive Player-of-the-Week honours in the American League, joining the Yankees trio of Graig Nettles, Goose Gossage and Ron Guidry in 1978.

Another example of the Cox managerial system: numerous substitutions — in this case Iorg for Mulliniks, Martinez for Whitt, Johnson for Orta and Bonnell for Collins.

A 13-game winner in 1983, Luis Leal was the AL Player of the Week for May 9–15.

Famous Firsts and Records #6

JULY 4, 1983 • *First Place*

Blue Jays fans were optimistic entering the 1983 season and the team began successfully with a 7–1 victory over the Red Sox at Fenway Park. It was the first time since 1977 that the Blue Jays had begun the year with a victory, and the first time they had ever won an opening day game on the road. However, through the first ten games, the Blue Jays won just three more times. Then, trailing the Indians 7–5 with two out in the bottom of the ninth on April 19, Cliff Johnson and Lloyd Moseby both hit two-run homers to pull out a 9–7 victory. From that point on, the Blue Jays won 22 of 35 games. They moved into first place all alone in the American League East on May 24.

Toronto, Baltimore, New York and Milwaukee were all in a tight battle for the division lead throughout the month of June. The Blue Jays dipped down as far as third place, but were never more than four games behind the leader and reclaimed top spot for themselves on June 29. When the first half of the season ended on July 4, the Blue Jays had a record of 43–33 and were one game ahead of the Orioles in the tightly packed American League East. Not only was it the first time the Blue Jays had been in first place at the All-Star break, it was the first time they had been anywhere other than last place!

Players like Lloyd Moseby, Willie Upshaw and Damaso Garcia were finally beginning to come into their own (George Bell was tearing it up in Syracuse and would soon be summoned back to Toronto), but the real strength of the team through the first half of 1983 was pitching — especially Dave Stieb, who had 10 wins and a 2.54 ERA at the break.

1983

Buck Martinez, who was freely platooned with Ernie Whitt, tied a career high with 10 homers in 1983.

Famous Firsts and Records #7

JULY 6, 1983 • *All-Star Game*

Dave Stieb had pitched in the All-Star Game before, making appearances in both 1980 and 1981. But this time it would be different. This time the ace of the Blue Jays staff was going to be the starting pitcher in the 50th Anniversary All-Star Game at Comiskey Park — the place where the game had started back in 1933.

Many had expected American League manager Harvey Kuenn to name Texas lefty Rick Honeycutt as his starter. His record was 11–4 with a stingy 1.52 ERA, but the Milwaukee skipper wanted to use a righty against the National League's strong right-handed lineup. "Stieb is an outstanding pitcher," said Kuenn. "I know he's lost some games lately [Stieb's record had fallen from 10–4 to 10–7 in his last three starts] but I know that he hasn't pitched badly."

Stieb called the start "something I will cherish as long as I live," but in the first inning it sure didn't look like it would be a night to remember. Steve Sax led off with a bouncer back towards the mound. Stieb fielded it, but tossed it over Rod Carew's head. Then Tim Raines hit a grounder back to Stieb. This time the throw to first base was on the money — but Carew lost it in the setting sun. Second baseman Manny Trillo chased down the ball and threw to the plate in time to get Sax — but Ted Simmons let the throw get away from him. Sax scored an unearned run and Raines went all the way to third.

"I didn't want to be the guy to blow the game in the first inning," said Stieb later, and he settled down to strike out Andre Dawson. After a walk to Al Oliver, Stieb fanned Dale Murphy and Mike Schmidt to come out of the inning. He then had a three-up, three-down top of the second. Stieb came to the plate in the bottom of the second and laid down a bunt that helped the American League take a 2–1 lead. After Stieb again retired the side in order in the top of the third, the AL got a grand slam from Fred Lynn (the first in All-Star history) to highlight a seven-run inning. The American League went on to its first win since 1971 and Stieb was credited with the victory in a 13–3 blowout.

Dave Stieb shared the cover of Sports Illustrated magazine with Montreal Expos star slugger Andre Dawson to commemorate the fact that both of Canada's major league ball clubs were in first place at the midseason break.

Barry Bonnell's sweet swing and keen eye allowed him to hit a team-high .318 over the course of the 1983 season.

Dave Stieb cemented himself as the ace of the Jays' starting rotation in 1983, tying his own team record with 17 victories while recording an impressive 3.04 ERA.

Oddities and Others #7

JULY 18, 1983 • *Blue Jays 8, Royals 2*

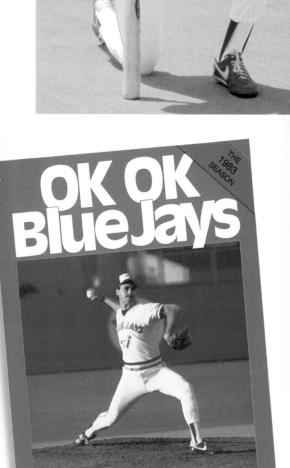

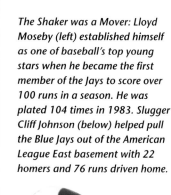

The Shaker was a Mover: Lloyd Moseby (left) established himself as one of baseball's top young stars when he became the first member of the Jays to score over 100 runs in a season. He was plated 104 times in 1983. Slugger Cliff Johnson (below) helped pull the Blue Jays out of the American League East basement with 22 homers and 76 runs driven home.

The Blue Jays were finally earning our respect in the summer of 1983. Canadian sports fans were beginning to look to them, not the Expos, as the country's most popular baseball club, and Torontonians were beginning to put them on a par with the Argonauts, who were en route to their first Grey Cup championship in 31 years. Even Americans were beginning to take notice. When the Blue Jays charged out of the All-Star break with eight wins in their first ten games, *Monday Night Baseball* came to Toronto to feature the Blue Jays as their lead game for the first time. With Howard Cosell waxing poetic about the team's carefully constructed rise to power, the Blue Jays destroyed the Kansas City Royals.

Toronto broke on top 1–0 in the bottom of the first when Garth Iorg singled in Lloyd Moseby, then broke a 1–1 tie in the third when Moseby tripled in Damaso Garcia and came in to score on a sacrifice fly by Barry Bonnell. They broke the game open with a five-run third, highlighted by a two-run homer from Buck Martinez and a two-run double from Cliff Johnson.

But even with all the offensive fireworks, the real hero of the game was Alfredo Griffin, who turned in four brilliant plays in the field. After just missing Amos Otis at first base on a play early in the game, Alfredo later threw out the fleet-footed Willie Wilson on a tough ground ball, snared a liner off the bat of U.L. Washington, and crossed the bag at second base to steal a sure single from Frank White. Griffin's greatest play came in the sixth inning when he raced deep into the hole to field a hot smash off the bat of Willie Aikens. With no time to set himself, Alfredo twisted, turned and tossed without stopping. His looping throw was right on the money. Aikens was out and the fans went wild.

OK OK Blue Jays

THE 1983 SEASON

THE STORY OF THE AMAZING JAYS

1983

Great Moments #5

AUGUST 2, 1983 • *Blue Jays vs. Yankees*

The race for first place in the American League East was incredibly tight, with five teams entering August bunched within 3½ games of top spot. The Blue Jays, who had led the division for most of July, had now fallen into fourth place, but were just three games back of the front-running Orioles, 2½ behind second-place Detroit and mere percentage points behind third-place New York. The atmosphere was electric when the Yankees came to town for a doubleheader that opened a four-game series.

A record crowd of 45,102 jammed Exhibition Stadium that night, with the fans in the north grandstand extending well beyond center field and all the way down to the football end-zone. They watched the Blue Jays break on top early when Lloyd Moseby and Willie Upshaw slugged back-to-back homers in the first inning, but the Yankees scored a run in the second and then five in the third. Moseby blasted another home run in the fourth and the Blue Jays scratched their way back into a 7–6 lead with two runs in the fifth and two more in the sixth. Now it was the Yankees' turn to come back, and they scored two in the seventh and one in the eighth against starter Luis Leal and relievers Dave Geisel and Joey McLaughlin. Jorge Orta got one run back for the Blue Jays with a sacrifice fly off Goose Gossage in the bottom of the eighth, but the intimidating Yankees stopper was back in the ninth to protect a precarious 9–8 lead.

Gossage retired Rance Mulliniks leading off, but the Blue Jays reached him for consecutive singles by Lloyd Moseby, Willie Upshaw and Cliff Johnson to load the bases with only one out. The huge crowd was going wild as Ernie Whitt strode to the plate. He launched a sacrifice fly and the game was tied. Roy Lee

The old band box that was Exhibition Stadium caught pennant fever in 1983 as 1,930,415 fans jammed the yard to watch the Jays finish over .500 for the first time with an 89–73 record.

Jackson came on to pitch in the top of the tenth, and though the Yankees reached him for a couple of hits, the Blue Jays escaped the inning unscathed. Dale Murray was now on the mound for New York, and Garth Iorg worked him for a leadoff walk. Damaso Garcia bunted him into scoring position and when Dave Collins ripped a single into right field, the Blue Jays had a thrilling 10–9 victory!

Matt Williams was fresh up from Syracuse to make his major league debut in the nightcap, and the Blue Jays made his job a little easier when they knocked Yankees starter Bob Shirley out of the box with four runs in the second inning. Though the Bronx Bombers battled back against the Blue Jays rookie, a five-run fifth inning put the game out of reach. Dave Geisel pitched a solid 3.1 innings out of the bullpen and Toronto completed the doubleheader sweep with a 13–6 victory. It was the first time in franchise history that the Blue Jays had swept a doubleheader from the Yankees and they made it three wins in a row with a 6–2 victory the following night. The key play in that game came in the sixth inning when Jesse Barfield nailed Ken Griffey Sr. at the plate on a picture perfect throw from right field.

A versatile performer with a crafty ability to slap the ball past opposing infielders and find the gaps in the outfield, Dave Collins was one of the most exciting players to ever wear the Jays uniform. Collins tore up the basepaths during his two-year tenure with the team, swiping 91 bags, including a club-record 60 steals in 1984.

New York	AB	R	H	RBI
Mattingly, 1b	5	2	3	1
Nettles, 3b	5	1	1	1
Gamble, rf	3	1	1	0
Winfield, ph-lf	2	0	1	1
Griffey, dh	5	0	1	1
Wynegar, c	4	1	1	0
Kemp, lf	5	1	1	3
Smalley, ss	4	2	2	2
Milburne, 2b	1	0	1	0
Mumphrey, cf	5	1	1	0
Robertson, 2b-ss	4	0	0	0
Totals	**43**	**9**	**13**	**9**

Toronto	AB	R	H	RBI
Collins, lf	5	0	1	1
Mulliniks, 3b-ss	5	1	2	0
Moseby, cf	5	2	3	2
Upshaw, 1b	5	1	1	1
Johnson, dh	5	1	2	0
Whitt, c	3	2	1	1
Bonnell, rf	4	1	2	0
Iorg, 2b-3b	4	2	3	2
Griffin, ss	3	0	0	0
Orta, ph	0	0	0	1
Garcia, 2b	0	0	0	0
Totals	**39**	**10**	**15**	**8**

```
New York .................015 000 210 0 – 9
Toronto .................200 122 011 1 – 10
        One out when winning run scored
```

New York	IP	H	R	ER	BB	SO
Keough	5	6	6	4	1	1
Frazier	2⅓	5	2	2	1	1
Gossage	1⅓	3	1	1	0	1
Murray (L. 2-2)	⅓	1	1	1	1	0

Toronto	IP	H	R	ER	BB	SO
Leal	6⅓	7	7	7	1	4
Geisel	⅓	1	1	1	0	0
McLaughlin	2⅓	3	1	1	0	1
Jackson (W. 8-1)	1	2	0	0	0	1
Keough pitched to one batter in sixth						

GW-RBI – Collins (4). E – Smalley. DP – New York 1. LOB – New York 5, Toronto 8. 2B – Johnson, Iorg. HR – Moseby 2 (13), Upshaw (19), Smalley 2 (13), Mattingly (2), Nettles (14), Kemp (10). SB – Iorg (4). S – Bonnell, Garcia. SF – Orta, Whitt. T – 3:00.

New York	AB	R	H	RBI
Mattingly, 1b	5	0	1	0
Nettles, 3b	5	1	2	1
Winfield, cf	4	2	2	2
Gamble, rf	2	0	0	0
Piniella, rf	2	0	1	0
Kemp, lf	4	1	1	1
Baylor, dh	5	1	1	2
Cerone, c	4	0	1	0
Milburne, 2b	3	0	0	0
Robertson, ss	0	0	0	0
Smalley, ss	3	1	1	0
Totals	**37**	**6**	**10**	**6**

Toronto	AB	R	H	RBI
Garcia, 2b	3	3	3	3
Moseby, cf	4	1	2	1
Iorg, 3b	3	1	1	0
Mulliniks, 3b	2	0	2	4
Johnson, dh	2	0	0	0
Orta, lf	3	0	0	0
Bonnell, lf-rf	5	3	2	0
Barfield, rf	1	1	0	0
Collins, lf	3	0	0	0
Upshaw, 1b	3	1	2	1
Martinez, c	1	0	0	1
Whitt, c	2	1	0	0
Griffin, ss	3	2	1	2
Totals	**35**	**13**	**13**	**12**

```
New York ...............002 031 000 – 6
Toronto .................042 050 20x – 13
```

New York	IP	H	R	ER	BB	SO
Shirley (L. 3-6)	2	5	4	4	1	1
Murray	2⅔	3	5	3	3	2
Howell	3⅓	5	4	4	2	4

Toronto	IP	H	R	ER	BB	SO
Williams (W. 1-0)	5	5	5	5	4	3
Jackson	2⁄3	3	1	1	0	0
Geisel (S2)	3⅓	2	0	0	0	3

GW-RBI – Martinez (4). E – Gamble. LOB – New York 9, Toronto 7. 2B – Garcia 2, Bonnell 2, Kemp, Mulliniks. HR – Nettles (15), Winfield (19), Baylor (14). SB – Griffin (7), Bonnell (9), Garcia (25). S – Upshaw. SF – Martinez. HPB – by Williams (Robertson), by Howell (Garcia). T – 2:41. A – 45,102.

Oddities and Others #8
AUGUST 4 1983 • *Fowl Play*

After dropping the first three games of a four-game set with the Blue Jays, the New York Yankees managed to salvage something from the series with a 3–1 win in the finale. During the game, Yankees right fielder Dave Winfield had been warming up between innings, tossing a ball with a ball boy. As the inning was about to start, Winfield took his final toss — and struck a seagull.

Gulls from the lakeshore had long been attracted to the Exhibition Stadium. It became a familiar sight in late innings to see the birds gathering along the bench seats in right field. They were waiting for the fans to leave so they could eat their fill of the food that had spilled into the stands. Sometimes they strayed onto the field, but never before had one been killed in action! The game was delayed for a few minutes while a ball boy wrapped the fowl in a towel and carried it away.

Little more thought was given to the incident until after the game when Winfield was arrested. Police believed he had killed the bird on purpose.

"They wouldn't say that if they'd seen the way he's been throwing," said Yankees manager Billy Martin. "He hasn't hit the cutoff man all year."

Be that as it may, Winfield was charged with a violation of the Animal Protection Act and hauled off to a nearby police station to be interrogated. The next day, embarrassed city officials dropped the charges. Winfield would later make the best of a bad situation, commissioning a portrait of a seagull that was auctioned off at the annual Easter Seals dinner in Toronto and brought in $32,000 for charity.

A Blue Jays ball boy prepares to drape a towel over a gone-to-meet-its-maker seagull that was robbed of its chance for a decent postgame meal by a deadly accurate throw from the arm of Yankees outfielder Dave Winfield. The whole affair became known as "Gull-Gate."

Bad Breaks, Near Misses and Disappointments #6
AUGUST 24, 1983 • *Orioles 7, Blue Jays 4*

The Blue Jays were just 2½ games behind first-place Milwaukee and only two back of Baltimore when they arrived at Memorial Stadium to begin a key three-game series with the Orioles on August 23. They crept closer with a 9–3 victory that night and seemed poised to pull even with the Orioles when they took a 3–1 lead into the bottom of the ninth on August 24.

Jim Clancy retired John Lowenstein on a fly ball to center for the first out, but John Shelby reached base with a bunt single. It was just the third hit Clancy had surrendered in the game, and he bounced back by striking out pinch hitter Gary Roenicke. Then Clancy issued his sixth walk of the evening, and with the tying runs now on base, manager Bobby Cox turned to the bullpen to nail down the final out. Lefty Dave Geisel was summoned to face catcher Joe Nolan, but Earl Weaver lifted him for right-handed hitter Benny Ayala — who delivered a run-scoring single. When Al Bumbry followed with another base hit, the game was tied. Joey McLaughlin came on to put out the Baltimore fire, but the game was now headed into extra innings.

Because he had pinch hit for Nolan, who had already come on to replace Rick Dempsey, Earl Weaver found himself without a catcher for the top of the tenth. He decided to send utility infielder Lenn Sakata behind the plate. The move appeared to be little more than a footnote to the game story when Cliff Johnson led off with a towering home run off Tim Stoddard. When Barry Bonnell followed with a single, Weaver brought in Tippy Martinez. And that's when the trouble started. Bonnell was eager to run on the unproven catcher, but Martinez threw over to first base and the Blue Jays outfielder was trapped in a rundown. Eddie Murray tagged him out. Next, Dave Collins drew a walk. He also tried to run on Sakata, but Martinez picked him off. Then Willie Upshaw reached base with a single — and Martinez picked him off too. Still, the Blue Jays did have a 4–3 lead heading into the bottom of the tenth.

It didn't last long.

Cal Ripken batted first and he homered off McLaughlin. Then Joey walked Eddie Murray. After a ground ball moved Murray to second, McLaughlin was ordered to walk John Shelby. Randy Moffitt came on to strike out Roenicke, then Lenn Sakata came to the plate. The emergency catcher launched a three-run homer and the Orioles had a stunning 7–4 victory.

1983

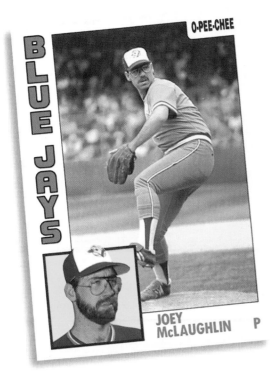

BLUE JAYS

O·PEE·CHEE

JOEY McLAUGHLIN   P

Reliever Joey McLaughlin (left) and Dave Collins (below) watched the Blue Jays' chances of a 1983 American League East title go by the boards during a devastating weekend series against their divisional arch-rivals, the Detroit Tigers. McLaughlin was more goat than hero as the Tigers feasted on their feathered cousins from down the 401.

Bad Breaks, Near Misses and Disappointments #7

AUGUST 28, 1983 • *Tigers 4, Blue Jays 2*

In the next game after their tough loss to the Orioles, Dave Stieb blanked Baltimore through nine brilliant innings. Unfortunately, Storm Davis and Tippy Martinez had combined to pitch shutout ball as well. Barry Bonnell finally got the Blue Jays on the board with a home run in the tenth, and Bobby Cox sent Roy Lee Jackson to the mound to wrap up the victory. He didn't. After recording the first out, Jackson gave up back-to-back singles, then a Dan Ford double past Lloyd Moseby in center to give the Orioles a 2–1 victory.

Having been burned by his bullpen again, Cox left starter Jim Gott on the mound to pitch the tenth inning of a 3–3 tie in Detroit the following night. With two out, Alan Trammell smacked a game-winning homer. Doyle Alexander got the team back on the winning track on Saturday with his first victory as a Blue Jay, but on Sunday afternoon disaster struck the bullpen once again.

The Blue Jays were clinging to a 2–1 lead when the Tigers came to bat in the bottom of the ninth. The relief crew had managed to preserve the slim advantage since Luis Leal had been lifted with a sore shoulder in the seventh, but with one out in the ninth, Dave Geisel walked Lance Parrish. Randy Moffitt came on and retired Glenn Wilson on a loud line drive to center. Then Joey McLaughlin was summoned to the mound. First to face him was Rick Leach, who singled on the second pitch. Chet Lemon needed three pitches before he launched a three-run homer to left field. Detroit had a 4–2 victory.

While Tigers fans cheered, a dazed McLaughlin stood on the mound, hands on his hips, staring at the ground. In the space of just five days, the Blue Jays had lost four games in the other team's last at-bats. They had fallen five games off the pace in the American League East and would never come any closer the rest of the season.

TORONTO
DETROIT

Famous Firsts and Records #8
SEPTEMBER 20, 1983 • *Blue Jays 7, Mariners 3*

Lloyd Moseby and Willie Upshaw were the dynamic duo that led the Blue Jays offense in 1983, and though the team fell out of contention in September, fans in Toronto still had the excitement of watching them go after a pair of major milestones. On September 19, Moseby became the first player in franchise history to score 100 runs in a season. One night later, Upshaw became the first Blue Jay to reach 100 RBIs.

Upshaw entered the game against Seattle with 99 RBIs and came to the plate in the first inning with two out and his pal Moseby at first base. Upshaw doubled into right field and Moseby came around to score when the throw home from Ricky Nelson bounced off the first-base bag. But the play was ruled an error and Upshaw was not credited with an RBI. The historic moment would have to wait.

The next time Upshaw came to bat was in the third inning. Dave Collins and Rance Mulliniks were on base with walks, and a long fly ball from Moseby had put them both in scoring position. When Upshaw singled to right, Collins and Mulliniks crossed the plate and Upshaw had passed the century mark.

Upshaw would finish the season among the American League leaders in several categories, including average (.306), homers (27) and RBIs (104). Moseby's .315 average ranked sixth in the league, while his 104 runs scored were fifth. Fittingly, the two good friends shared the honours as Blue Jays Player of the Year.

While the Blue Jays failed in their first serious attempt to win a division crown, it was a career year for first baseman Willie Upshaw (left). The lanky slugger tied for the team lead with 27 homers, and topped the club with 104 RBIs, 177 hits and 579 at-bats.

1983 Media Guide

1984

89–73 .549 2nd -15

Alfredo Griffin bends away from some nasty chin music orchestrated by Baltimore pitcher Jim Palmer. Griffin was dispatched to Oakland after the season in the deal that delivered Bill "Cuffs" Caudill to Toronto.

The Tigers were too tough in 1984. George Bell (26 HR, 87 RBI) established himself as the team's offensive leader while speed demon Dave Collins set a club record with 60 stolen bases. Lloyd Moseby (18 HR, 92 RBI) and Doyle Alexander (17–6, 11 complete games) were the other leaders. Dave Stieb, Luis Leal and Jim Clancy all reached double digits in victories and southpaw Jimmy Key set a Jays rookie record with 10 saves.

Bad Breaks, Near Misses and Disappointments #8

APRIL 4, 1984 • *Mariners 3, Blue Jays 2*

For the first time in franchise history, the Toronto Blue Jays prepared for the new baseball season as serious pennant contenders. After recording a club-record 89 wins in 1983, the team seemed poised to take the next step and move up the ladder. The first order of business was to shore up the shaky bullpen. Desperate to acquire a top closer for the 1984 season, general manager Pat Gillick made an impassioned effort to sign the Yankees' Rich Gossage, one of baseball's best bullpen aces. When "the Goose" flew the coop for San Diego, Gillick turned to Dennis Lamp.

A starter for much of his four-year stay with the Chicago Cubs, Lamp had then pitched mostly middle relief in two seasons with the White Sox. Converted to closer in the second half of 1983, Lamp had finished the year with 15 saves. When he signed with the Blue Jays in 1984, he was regarded as the club's savior. Unfortunately, the bullpen would prove to be the team's weak link once again — a point that was made painfully obvious in the very first game of the new season.

Jim Clancy took the ball for the Blue Jays on opening day in Seattle and held off the Mariners with seven-plus innings of solid work. Lamp entered the game with two on and two out in the eighth and needed only one pitch to escape the jam, but in the bottom of the ninth Gorman Thomas led off with a double and Ken Phelps reached Lamp for a game-tying single. In the tenth, Lamp walked leadoff man Spike Owen, who advanced on a sacrifice bunt. When Phil Bradley followed with a single, Seattle had rallied for a 3–2 victory. "Being a relief pitcher is a challenge," said Lamp, "and it's a very humbling position."

Toronto's relievers continued to be humbled throughout the rest of the season-opening 10-game road trip. By the time the team returned to Toronto for the home opener, the bullpen was being called the "grenade brigade" and Lamp was dubbed "Dennis the Menace." By the end of August, he was moved into the starting rotation. Lamp would finally find his niche in middle relief — but not until 1985.

Interchangeable Parts: Third baseman Rance Mulliniks, part of what was known as Mullinlorg because of his platoon partnership with Garth Iorg, was best known for his defensive abilities. In 1984, however, he became a terror at the plate, hitting .324 with 42 RBIs in only 343 at-bats.

After being plucked off the waiver wire midway through the 1983 season, a crafty "Dour" Doyle Alexander surprised most of the scribes and armchair managers by becoming the team's steadiest pitcher in 1984, compiling a 17–6 record with a nifty 3.03 ERA.

1984

Bad Breaks, Near Misses and Disappointments #9

JUNE 4, 1984 • *Tigers 6, Blue Jays 3*

Even though they were still without a reliable bullpen closer, the Blue Jays were flying high in 1984. Through the first 40 games of the season, the team had a record of 26–14, which easily marked the best start in franchise history. Unfortunately, the Detroit Tigers were enjoying the best start in *baseball* history. With an amazing mark of 35–5, Detroit was already eight games ahead of second-place Toronto. But the Blue Jays kept chipping away. By the time they arrived in Detroit on June 4 to play the Tigers for the first time, their record was an impressive 34–16 and the deficit had been reduced to just 4½ games. With Howard Cosell and ABC TV's *Monday Night Baseball* crew on hand, all eyes were on Tiger Stadium for the opener of the four-game "Showdown in Motown."

The Blue Jays got on the scoreboard first when Willie Upshaw homered into the upper deck in the second inning. Upshaw scored again when George Bell homered in the sixth to give the Blue Jays a 3–0 lead. The Tigers didn't get to Dave Stieb until the seventh. With two out, Stieb hit Chet Lemon, then allowed a single to Dave Bergman before Howard Johnson launched a three-run homer to tie the game. The score was still 3–3 when Lance Parrish led off the tenth inning with a single against rookie reliever Jimmy Key. Dwight Evans sacrificed him to second, then Roy Lee Jackson entered the game. He retired Rusty Kuntz for the second out, but then walked Chet Lemon.

If ever an entire season can rotate on the result of a single at-bat, the epic ten-minute struggle between Roy Lee Jackson and Dave Bergman would be it. Bergman fouled off the first five pitches Jackson threw before taking two balls. After fouling off another pitch, Jackson ran the count full with a low fastball. Bergman then fouled off three more pitches before depositing the reliever's 13th offering into the upper deck for a 6–3 Detroit win.

"Best game I've ever been involved in," expounded Tigers manager Sparky Anderson, although he has been known to exaggerate. That one Tigers victory proved that while the Jays could compete, they were still missing the vital ingredients that would put them over the top.

Long thought of as the organization's top prospect, Tony Fernandez was called up to Toronto in September of 1983. A slick fielder, he began pushing Alfredo Griffin for playing time in 1984 and won the job with a .270 average in 88 games.

Oddities and Others #9

JULY 20, 1984 • *Blue Jays 12, Mariners 7*

The Blue Jays were trailing 3–1 through eight innings at the Seattle Kingdome. Manager Bobby Cox, pitching coach Al Widmar and third base coach Jimy Williams had all been ejected from the game by home plate umpire Durwood Merrill. Hitting coach Cito Gaston was in charge of the team. Maybe that had something to do with the way in which the bats came to life, as the Blue Jays sent 16 men to the plate and scored a club-record 11 runs.

In the big inning, Lloyd Moseby tripled off Mike Stanton. Willie Upshaw struck out, but when Willie Aikens scored "the Shaker" with a single, the Mariners went to the bullpen for former Blue Jay Paul Mirabella. Pinch hitter Cliff Johnson then singled pinch runner Alfredo Griffin to second base. Griffin moved to third on a George Bell single, then was waved home with the tying run when Mariners third baseman Jim Presley was charged with obstruction. Jesse Barfield hit a single to load the bases and Tony Fernandez followed with another single to score two more runs and put the Blue Jays ahead 5–3.

Edwin Nunez was summoned to the mound to quell the uprising, but Damaso Garcia greeted him with a single to score Barfield. When Dave Collins walked to reload the bases, Nunez was replaced by another former Blue Jays hurler, Dave Geisel. But the onslaught continued. Moseby came up to the plate for the second time in the inning and singled in a pair of runs to make the score 8–3. Upshaw then singled in Collins before Griffin cashed Moseby for the ninth run of the inning.

Ten straight batters had now reached base safely, but the streak ended when Garth Iorg hit into a fielder's choice. Bell then walked to load the bases again, and Barfield singled in two more runs to make the score 12–3. When Tony Fernandez struck out, the side was finally retired. The line for the inning read 11 runs on 11 hits, one error, two walks and two left on base. Incredibly, Seattle managed to score four runs of their own in the bottom of the ninth and the two teams combined to set an American League record by plating 15 runs in a single inning.

Famous Firsts and Records #9
AUGUST 5, 1984 • *Blue Jays 4, Orioles 3*

Memorial Stadium in Baltimore was never very accommodating to the Blue Jays, particularly not in the early years of the franchise. In fact, through 1983, the team had just nine wins and 36 losses to show for six years of visits to Baltimore. The 1984 season marked the first time Toronto escaped Memorial Stadium with more wins than losses, notching their fourth win in six games thanks to a series sweep on a record-setting Sunday afternoon in August. The Blue Jays had a team-high seven stolen bases, including four by Dave Collins, but the big story belonged to Cliff Johnson.

Toronto trailed the game 2–0 until scoring three runs in the top of the seventh, but then allowed the Orioles to tie the score in the bottom of the inning. In the eighth, Johnson came off the bench to pinch hit for Willie Aikens. "Heathcliff" was one of baseball's best clutch hitters and, as he would say after the game, "Bobby [Cox] wasn't looking for a single." He took Tippy Martinez deep for a home run that gave the Blue Jays a 4–3 victory.

For Johnson, the blast was the 19th pinch-hit homer of his career, establishing a new major league mark. The 18-year veteran had forged his record while playing for six different teams and against 17 different pitchers. The only one he had victimized twice was Martinez, who had served up Johnson's 18th pinch homer one year before, allowing him to tie the record previously held by Jerry Lynch. Johnson later pushed his record to 20 pinch-hit home runs when he took Detroit's Willie Hernandez deep to lead off the eighth inning at Exhibition Stadium on June 13, 1986.

Best known for his abilities on the gridiron as the starting quarterback for the University of Michigan, Rick Leach (right) turned his attention to professional baseball after graduation and was a mainstay with the Blue Jays for six seasons. (Below) Cliff Johnson, hugging Pete Rose during the annual Pearson Cup game between the Expos and the Blue Jays early in the season, set a major league record with his 19th pinch-hit home run later in 1984.

Oddities and Others #10
AUGUST 15, 1984 • *Indians 16, Blue Jays 1*

When Rick Leach climbed the mound in the eighth inning at Cleveland it had been almost four years to the day since a Blue Jays position player had last been used to pitch. The Blue Jays were trailing the Indians 13–1 in the first game of a doubleheader. Cleveland had already rocked starter Luis Leal for 10 runs on 13 hits in 5.2 innings. They had cuffed Jimmy Key for three more runs in the seventh. The former Michigan quarterback didn't fare much better.

Leach walked Brook Jacoby leading off the eighth, then served up a two-run homer to Jerry Willard. After retiring Tony Bernazard on a ground ball to short, Leach walked Brett Butler and watched him move to third when Mike Fischlin doubled to left. Mike Hargrove's ground ball to first plated Butler, and the inning finally came to an end when pinch hitter Carmen Castillo grounded to short. Leach left the mound with a lifetime ERA of 27.00.

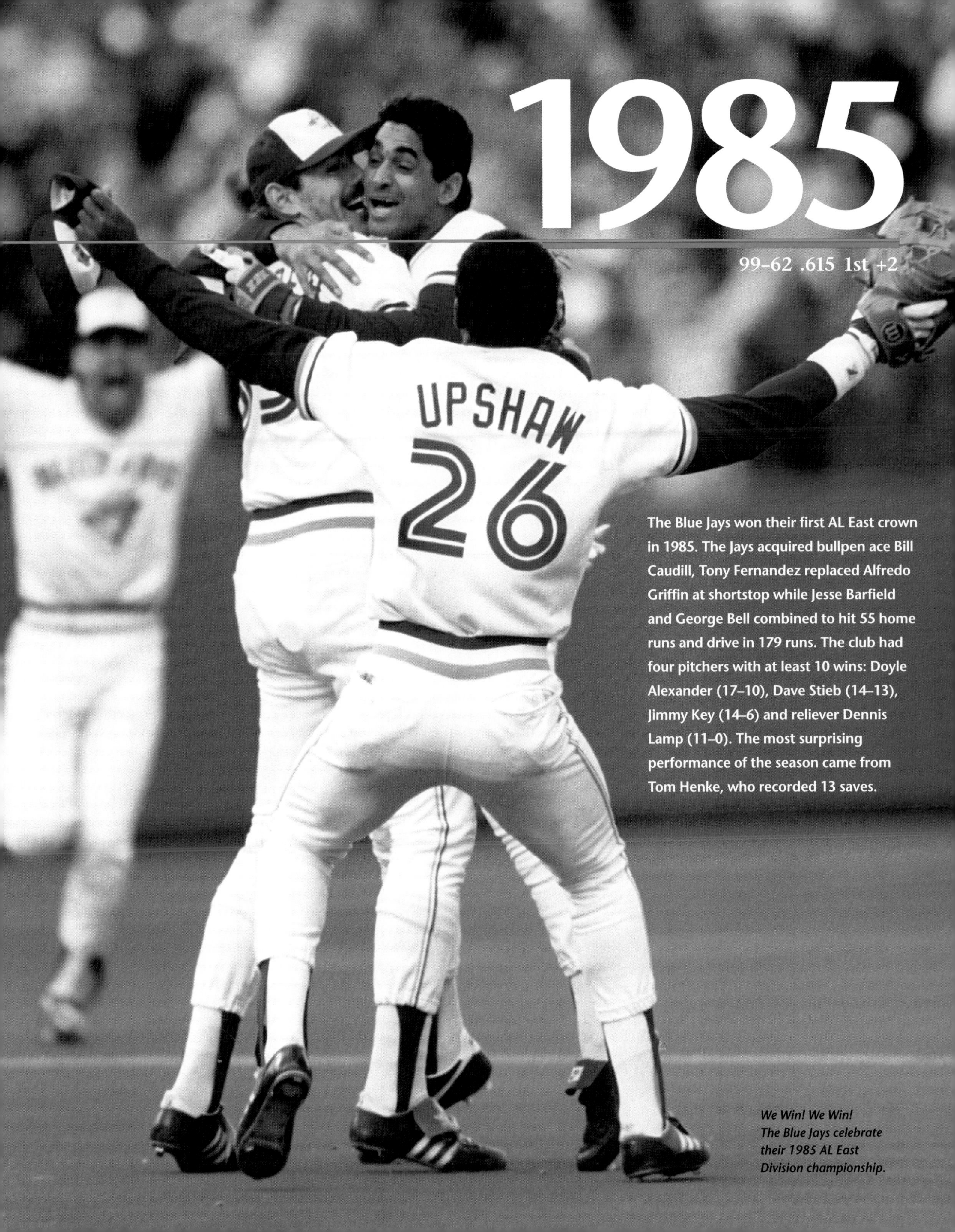

1985

99–62 .615 1st +2

The Blue Jays won their first AL East crown in 1985. The Jays acquired bullpen ace Bill Caudill, Tony Fernandez replaced Alfredo Griffin at shortstop while Jesse Barfield and George Bell combined to hit 55 home runs and drive in 179 runs. The club had four pitchers with at least 10 wins: Doyle Alexander (17–10), Dave Stieb (14–13), Jimmy Key (14–6) and reliever Dennis Lamp (11–0). The most surprising performance of the season came from Tom Henke, who recorded 13 saves.

We Win! We Win!
The Blue Jays celebrate
their 1985 AL East
Division championship.

Great Moments #6

Though they eventually finished 15 games behind the Detroit Tigers, Toronto's record of 89–73 in 1984 proved that the Blue Jays had the tools to ascend to the top of the American League East. Expectations were high in 1985, and the Blue Jays met them. They climbed into first place on the last day of April and were beginning to pull away by the end of May.

As June began, the Blue Jays were five games ahead of second-place Baltimore, but Toronto's success so far in 1985 had come mostly at the expense of the weaker West Division. Beginning on June 6, Toronto would play 27 straight games against East Division clubs. The opponents that night were the Detroit Tigers. Detroit was in third place, 6½ games back, but they were the defending World Series champions and the 1984 season had turned the Tigers into the Blue Jays' fiercest rival.

Some 36,000 fans were in attendance that Thursday night to see Jimmy Key battle Detroit's Dan Petry. What they witnessed was one of the greatest pitching performances in franchise history. Using his assortment of off-speed curves, change-ups and pinpoint control, Key kept the Tigers completely off balance. He carried a perfect game into the sixth inning, and still had a no-hitter intact through eight. Unfortunately, Petry was equally strong and the game was still scoreless. Key saw his bid for a no-hitter vanish when Tom Brookens lined a clean single in the ninth, but he maintained his shutout and a chance to win. So did Petry. Both pitchers wound up going 10 innings, with Key allowing two hits and Petry six. Relievers Gary Lavelle and Jim Acker got the Blue Jays through the 11th and 12th. Closer Willie Hernandez pitched the 11th for Detroit, but hurt himself fielding a bunt and Aurelio Lopez came out to work the bottom of the 12th.

George Bell was the first Blue Jays batter to face "Senor Smoke" and he was hit by a pitch. After Len Matuszek was retired, Buck Martinez came to the plate. He was hitting just .134 at the time, and quickly fell behind 1-and-2 in the count. Then he connected with a Lopez breaking ball and slammed it into the seats in the north grandstand. The Blue Jays had a confidence-building 2–0 victory.

(Above) Mr. Consistency: Jimmy Key, the Jays' smooth left-hander, won 14 games in 1985. (Below) Right fielder Jesse Barfield keeps his eye on the prize with a crazy catch.

Detroit	AB	R	H	RBI	Toronto	AB	R	H	RBI
Whitaker, 2b	3	0	0	0	Garcia, 2b	5	0	0	0
Trammell, ss	4	0	0	0	Mulliniks, 3b	4	0	1	0
Gibson, rf	5	0	0	0	Iorg, ph-3b	1	0	1	0
Parrish, c	5	0	0	0	Moseby, cf	5	0	0	0
Lemon, cf	5	0	0	0	Upshaw, 1b	4	0	0	0
Evans, 1b	2	0	0	0	Bell, lf	4	1	2	0
Sanchez, pr	0	0	0	0	Matuszek, dh	5	0	0	0
Bergman, 1b	1	0	1	0	Whitt, c	3	0	1	0
Herndon, lf	5	0	1	0	Lee, pr	0	0	0	0
Garbey, dh	5	0	1	0	Martinez, c	1	1	1	2
Brookens, 3b	3	0	1	0	Barfield, rf	4	0	1	0
					Fernandez, ss	3	0	1	0
Totals	**38**	**0**	**4**	**0**	**Totals**	**39**	**2**	**8**	**2**

```
Detroit .......................... 000 000 000 000 – 0
Toronto .......................... 000 000 000 002 – 2
    One out when winning run scored
```

Detroit	IP	H	R	ER	BB	SO
Petry	10	6	0	0	3	5
Hernandez	1	1	0	0	0	0
Lopez (L, 0-4)	⅓	1	2	2	0	0

Toronto	IP	H	R	ER	BB	SO
Key	10	2	0	0	2	6
Lavelle	1	1	0	0	1	0
Acker (W, 2-0)	1	1	0	0	1	0

GW RBI – Martinez E – Fernandez, Whitaker. DP – Detroit 3, Toronto 1. LOB – Detroit 8, Toronto 7. 2B – Mulliniks. HR – Martinez (4). SB – Brookens, Fernandez, Bell, S – Whitaker, Brookens. HBP – by Lopez (Bell). T – 3:25. A – 36,384.

Oddities and Others #11

JUNE 23, 1985 • *Blue Jays 8, Red Sox 1*

George Bell was an emotional player at the best of times, but brushback pitches really set him off. Having been seriously injured by a beanball in the minors, Bell always took exception when a pitcher came too close to him. Bruce Kison, on the other hand, was a pitcher who did whatever it took to win. In the fourth inning of a Sunday game with the Blue Jays, Kison felt that meant coming inside on George Bell.

The Blue Jays were leading 2–0 when Kison's pitch hit Bell on the shoulder. George hesitated for a split second, then charged the mound, where the Boston pitcher stood defiantly. Bell leaped at him, delivering a karate-style kick that connected with Kison's hip. Then he turned around and delivered a 1–2 combination to the forehead of Red Sox catcher Rich Gedman, who had followed him out to the mound. Bell then retreated to the Blue Jays dugout as a full-scale brawl broke out. Few baseball fights ever turn ugly, but this one did — especially after Red Sox first baseman Bill Buckner kicked Blue Jays coach John Sullivan in the face. When order was finally restored, Bell was thrown out of the game for charging the mound, but Kison was allowed to continue pitching.

Earlier in the game, the Red Sox hurler had sailed a pitch over Ernie Whitt's head. In the sixth inning, with Toronto still leading 2–0, the Blue Jays catcher was at bat again with the bases loaded. He turned on Kison's first delivery and drove the ball over the right field fence. It was his first career grand slam, and the whole way around the bases Whitt never took his eyes off Kison, shouting at him as he ran.

"We couldn't hear what he was saying because the crowd was going berserk," Buck Martinez would later write, "[but] it was very gratifying revenge for all of us." As for Whitt, he offered no comment to reporters. "You couldn't print it anyway."

Many expected his career was over when Buck Martinez broke his leg in 1985 but, with hard work, he came back in 1986 to play one more season.

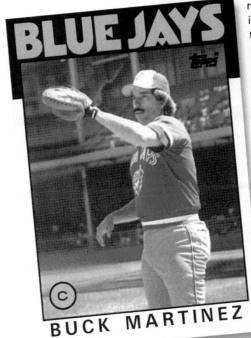

BLUE JAYS

BUCK MARTINEZ

Oddities and Others #12

JULY 9, 1985 • *Blue Jays 9, Mariners 4*

The team was in Seattle for a midweek game in the middle of a western road swing. There was no television coverage in Toronto that night, so few Blue Jays fans saw a play that remains one of the most amazing in baseball history. It came in the third inning of a game that marked pitcher Tom Filer's Blue Jays debut. Jesse Barfield had already bailed him out by nailing a runner at the plate in the second. Now, he was about to do it again.

The Mariners had Phil Bradley on second base with slugger Gorman Thomas at the plate. Thomas slashed a single through the right side that Barfield fielded and delivered on a line to the plate. Buck Martinez snagged the throw and pivoted to make the tag on the oncoming Bradley, a former quarterback at the University of Missouri. Using some of those football skills, Bradley crashed into Martinez in an attempt to jar the ball loose. What he did was tear the tendons in Martinez's ankle and break his right leg.

Martinez might have been down, but Bradley was out. Thomas, who had gone to second on the throw to the plate, decided to continue to third base.

Obviously injured, but still alert, Martinez saw Thomas attempting to advance and fired the ball toward third. The toss sailed wide of the bag, but George Bell backed up the play and returned the ball on one hop to home plate. Though almost flat on his back, somehow Martinez caught the ball and tagged out Thomas before collapsing in a heap. In what Blue Jays vice president Bobby Mattick called the "greatest play I've ever seen," Martinez had completed the first, and only, 9-2-7-2 double play in club history.

Martinez, who had been a pivotal part of the Blue Jays organization since 1981, was removed from the field on a stretcher and would not play again that season. Through hard work and rehabilitation, he managed to return in 1986 and played one final year before moving into the broadcast booth.

Kung Fu Fighting: Fiery Jays outfielder George Bell manages to avoid Red Sox catcher Rich Gedman's advances moments after delivering a Bruce Lee-like karate kick to the midsection of Boston hurler Bruce Kison.

Famous Firsts and Records #10

JULY 29, 1985 • *Blue Jays 4, Orioles 3*

After he left successive late-July starts against Oakland and California with a sore neck and a sore right shoulder respectively, the Blue Jays placed Jim Clancy on the disabled list for the second time in the 1985 season. To fill his spot on the roster, the contract of Tom Henke was purchased from Syracuse on July 28.

The Blue Jays had acquired Henke from the Texas Rangers in the off-season as compensation for their signing of free agent Cliff Johnson. Henke had not shown much in parts of three seasons with the Rangers, but he had impressed the Blue Jays at spring training. Still, with the acquisition of Bill Caudill and Gary Lavelle for the bullpen, Henke had been ticketed for Triple-A. In 39 games with Syracuse, Henke had a 2–1 record with 18 saves. In 51⅓ innings he had allowed just five runs on 13 hits for an amazing 0.88 ERA. With Caudill struggling despite his 13 saves, it was time to see what Henke could do against major league hitters.

Henke made his first appearance for the Blue Jays in a game against Baltimore one day after joining the team. The score was tied 3–3 when Henke took over from Jimmy Key in the bottom of the ninth. He retired the side in order and when Damaso Garcia homered off Mike Boddicker in the top of the tenth, Henke was sent back out to protect the lead. After recording the first out, Henke walked pinch hitter Larry Sheets, then got John Shelby on a pop up to short. With two out, Cal Ripken Jr. came to the plate and ripped a fastball to deep center field. Just when it looked like yet another Blue Jays reliever was going to let a game slip away, Jesse Barfield (playing in place of Lloyd Moseby) caught the ball with his back against the wall.

"I thought it was out of here," said a relieved manager Bobby Cox, but Henke said he never doubted himself. "It's just a great feeling knowing that Bobby has the confidence to use me in a tight game." For Cox, it must have been an even greater feeling to know he finally had a closer he could count on.

Long and lanky fireballer Tom Henke (above) was the surprise of the 1985 Blue Jays' pennant-winning season, arriving from Syracuse midway through the year with a zipping fastball, a nasty splitter and a cool and calm countenance. The Missouri native still holds the Blue Jays' all-time save mark by preserving the lead in 217 Toronto victories.

Famous Firsts and Records #11

AUGUST 23–25, 1985 • *Blue Jays vs. White Sox*

George Bell was a streak hitter who was capable of carrying an entire team on his shoulders when his bat got hot. Never was Bell's bat hotter than during a steamy August weekend at Comiskey Park.

The Blue Jays and White Sox opened the series with a Friday night doubleheader to make up for a rainout in May. The Blue Jays swept it, winning 6–3 and 10–3. In the nightcap, Bell took a pitch from Dave Wehrmeister and slammed it into the center field bleachers for a home run that measured 455 feet. Bell became just the sixth player in baseball history to reach the center field seats in old Comiskey. On Saturday night, Bell took Tom Seaver high and deep over the roof in left field, making him just the 15th non-White Sox player to clear the park. The Blue Jays won the game 6–3. Dave Stieb had taken a no-hitter into the ninth inning before Rudy Law and Bryan Little roughed him up with back-to-back home runs.

Homers were still in the air on Sunday afternoon, and though the White Sox salvaged the final game of the series with a 5–3 victory, George Bell once again displayed his prodigious power. This time he hit a Floyd Bannister offering over the roof in left field, making him the first player to reach the roof twice in a single series. In fact, Bell joined Hall of Famers Jimmy Foxx and Ted Williams as the only non-White Sox players to reach the roof twice in their careers.

On Monday, the Blue Jays were in Minnesota and Bell hit yet another home run. His blast off Bert Blyleven led Toronto to a 4–3 victory and made him the first player in club history to hit home runs in four consecutive games. It's a feat matched only by Joe Carter, Shawn Green, Jose Canseco and Carlos Delgado (twice).

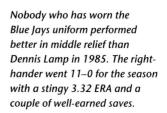

Nobody who has worn the Blue Jays uniform performed better in middle relief than Dennis Lamp in 1985. The right-hander went 11–0 for the season with a stingy 3.32 ERA and a couple of well-earned saves.

Bad Breaks, Near Misses and Disappointments #10

SEPTEMBER 12, 1985 • *Yankees 7, Blue Jays 5*

On the fourth day of August, the Blue Jays' lead in the American League East was 9½ games. By the time they headed to New York for a four-game series five weeks later, the lead was down to 2½. It wasn't that the Blue Jays were slumping — they had posted a record of 21–12. It was that the Yankees never seemed to lose. They were always coming up with the big inning just when they needed it and had just seen an 11-game winning streak come to an end.

Dave Stieb was on the mound for the Blue Jays against Ron Guidry for the series opener in New York. Guidry was 18–5 at the time. Stieb was just 13–10 but boasted the American League's best ERA at 2.47. A crowd of 52,141 rabid Yankees fans was on hand and they began the evening by booing the Canadian national anthem. The mood in the Bronx only got uglier as the Blue Jays built up a 4–1 lead through six innings. Ernie Whitt led the offense with a two-run homer, while Stieb, though wild, dominated the New York batters.

With one out in the bottom of the seventh, Yankees second baseman Willie Randolph worked Stieb for his sixth walk of the evening. Shortstop Bobby Meacham was up next and he slapped a ground ball to his Blue Jays counterpart for what looked like an inning-ending double play. Tony Fernandez fielded the ball cleanly and appeared to indicate that he would make the play at second base himself. Damaso Garcia cleared away, but Fernandez suddenly flipped the ball to the vacated bag. Everyone was safe. When Stieb followed with a walk to Rickey Henderson, the Yankees had the bases loaded.

Gary Lavelle came in to face Ken Griffey Sr. and he induced a ground ball to third. Garth Iorg threw to second for the force out, but Henderson's great speed caused Garcia to rush his throw and Griffey was safe at first. The score was 4–2 and the Yankees still had runners on the corners. A Don Mattingly single then made it 4–3. Dennis Lamp came in to face Dave Winfield, but when Fernandez misplayed his ground ball the score was tied. Catcher Ron Hassey was up next, and he crushed a 2-and-1 offering into the right field stands.

The Yankees won the game 7–5.

They had cut the lead to a game-and-a half.

But New York was not about to beat the Blue Jays overall.

(Above) Center fielder Lloyd Moseby and infielders Garth Iorg and Tony Fernandez come together behind second base during the September Showdown with the Yankees. (Right) The right-handed half of the third-base platoon, Garth Iorg established career highs with a .313 average and seven home runs in 1985.

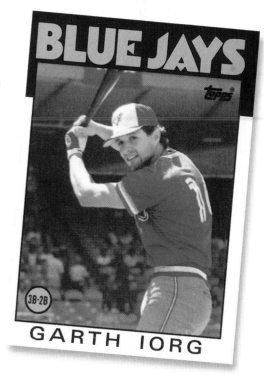

BLUE JAYS

GARTH IORG

Great Moments #7

September 13–15, 1985 • *Blue Jays vs. Yankees*

Fans wondered how the team would respond after the disappointing loss in the series opener — especially with first baseman Willie Upshaw and second baseman Damaso Garcia both now sidelined with injuries. But the Blue Jays responded like champions. They won the next three in a row to take a four-game set that was played in front of more than 200,000 New York fans.

The Blue Jays restored their 2½ game advantage atop the AL East when they bounced back from Thursday's loss with a 3–2 win. Heroes on Friday night were Al Oliver and the Blue Jays bullpen. "Scoop" drove in all three runs against Yankees starter Phil Niekro, who gave up only eight hits in going the distance. Gary Lavelle bailed out Jim Clancy with one out in the fifth and pitched three innings of shutout ball. He then turned it over to Tom Henke, who closed out the game with three strikeouts.

Yankee fans had booed the Canadian national anthem prior to the first game of the series and, despite an announcement pleading for the proper respect to be shown in game two, there was still a smattering of boos. Then the anthem situation hit an all-time low. A local New York performer named Mary O'Dowd was the singer on Saturday night. Not only did she forget the words to *O Canada*, she also mangled the tune! Even after she was given the lyrics on a sheet of paper, she couldn't get it right.

Canadian pride might have taken a beating, but it was Yankee pitchers who were battered when the Blue Jays scored five runs in the sixth to break open a 2–2 tie. Jimmy Key went the distance in a 7–4 Toronto victory, while the Yankees used five pitchers. Manager Billy Martin even summoned closer Dave Righetti from the bullpen to try to keep the game close in the pivotal sixth. Rance Mulliniks and Lloyd Moseby both reached him for key hits, while Cliff Johnson closed out the inning with a two-run single off Brian Fisher. Earlier in the game, Jesse Barfield had touched up starter Bob Shirley for a booming double

(Above) A contented flock of Blue Jays leaves the field after winning three straight pressure-packed games in Yankee Stadium during the pennant race of 1985.

and a long home run. Garth Iorg, subbing for Garcia at second, went 3-for-4.

The Blue Jays had been hoping for at least a split of the series, but as Iorg said: "It's comforting to have won two games here, but I figure we should have won all three. That first game was a ridiculous loss and some people may have started questioning us, but we've been bouncing back from losses like that all year."

A crowd of 54,699 — the largest of the series — jammed Yankee Stadium on Sunday afternoon, now hoping their team could salvage a split. That hope disappeared early as the Blue Jays scored six runs in the third inning. Doyle Alexander allowed only one hit through the first six innings, and though the Yankees later got to him and the bullpen, the Blue Jays coasted to an 8–5 win. Toronto's lead was up to 4½ games with just three weeks to go in the season.

Game 1

Toronto	AB	R	H	RBI	New York	AB	R	H	RBI
Fernandez, ss	5	0	1	0	Henderson, cf	4	0	2	0
Moseby, cf	4	2	0	0	Griffey, lf	4	0	0	0
Mulliniks, 3b	3	1	0	0	Mattingly, 1b	3	0	2	1
Bell, lf	4	0	0	0	Winfield, rf	4	0	1	0
Oliver, dh	4	0	2	3	Hassey, c	4	0	1	0
Upshaw, 1b	2	0	1	0	Sample, pr	0	0	0	0
Leach, 1b	2	0	0	0	Espino, c	0	0	0	0
Whitt, c	3	0	1	0	Pasqua, dh	2	0	0	0
Barfield, rf	3	0	1	0	Baylor, dh	2	0	0	0
Iorg, 2b	4	0	2	0	Pagliarulo, 3b	3	0	0	0
					Randolph, 2b	3	0	0	0
					Meacham, ss	3	1	2	1
					Wynegar, ph	1	0	0	0
Totals	**34**	**3**	**8**	**3**	**Totals**	**33**	**2**	**9**	**2**

| Toronto | | | | | | 002 | 010 | 000 | — 3 |
| New York | | | | | | 010 | 010 | 000 | — 2 |

Toronto	IP	H	R	ER	BB	SO
Clancy	4⅓	6	2	2	1	5
Lavelle (W. 5-7)	3	2	0	0	1	0
Henke (S12)	1⅔	1	0	0	0	3

New York	IP	H	R	ER	BB	SO
Niekro (L. 15-10)	9	8	3	0	4	5

GW RBI – Oliver. E – Mattingly, Hassey. DP – Toronto 1, New York 2. LOB – Toronto 6, New York 7. 2B – Upshaw, Meacham, Whitt. 3B – Oliver. SB – Iorg, Moseby. SF – Mattingly. WP – Niekro. PB – Hassey.
T – 3:13. A – 53,303.

Game 2

Toronto	AB	R	H	RBI	New York	AB	R	H	RBI
Fernandez, ss	5	1	1	0	Henderson, cf	3	2	1	1
Moseby, dh	5	1	3	2	Mattingly, 1b	4	0	1	0
Johnson, dh	4	0	2	2	Winfield, rf	4	0	0	1
Bell, lf	5	0	1	0	Baylor, dh	4	0	0	0
Barfield, rf	5	2	1	1	Sample, lf	4	1	1	0
Fielder, 1b	3	0	1	0	Robertson, 3b	4	0	1	0
Leach, 1b	2	0	0	0	Wynegar, c	3	0	0	0
Iorg, 2b	4	1	3	1	Hudler, 2b	3	1	2	1
Whitt, c	3	1	1	1	Meacham, ss	3	0	0	1
Mulliniks, 3b	4	1	1	1					
Totals	**40**	**7**	**14**	**7**	**Totals**	**32**	**4**	**6**	**4**

| Toronto | | | | | | 010 | 105 | 000 | — 7 |
| New York | | | | | | 110 | 000 | 020 | — 4 |

Toronto	IP	H	R	ER	BB	SO
Key (W. 13-6)	9	6	4	4	1	4

New York	IP	H	R	ER	BB	SO
Shirley	4⅓	7	2	2	1	3
Bordi (L. 5-7)	1	1	1	1	0	0
Righetti	0	3	4	4	1	0
Fisher	⅔	1	0	0	0	2
Allen	3	2	0	0	0	2

Righetti pitched to four batters in sixth

Game-winning RBI – Mulliniks. E – Robertson. DP – Toronto 1, New York 2. LOB – Toronto 8, New York 2. 2B – Mulliniks, Barfield, Iorg, Sample. 3B – Hudler. HR – Barfield (23), Henderson (21).
SB – Henderson 2.
T – 2:51. A – 54,367.

Game 3

Toronto	AB	R	H	RBI	New York	AB	R	H	RBI
Fernandez, ss	4	1	1	0	Henderson, cf	3	1	0	0
Moseby, cf	5	1	3	0	Griffey, lf	5	2	2	2
Mulliniks, 3b	4	2	2	1	Mattingly, 1b	5	0	0	0
Bell, lf	5	2	1	1	Winfield, rf	5	1	2	1
Oliver, dh	4	0	1	0	Hassey, c	2	0	1	0
Johnson, dh	4	0	2	3	Robertson, ph	1	0	0	0
Whitt, c	5	0	0	0	Espino, c	0	0	0	0
Leach, 1b	5	1	3	1	Pasqua, dh	2	0	0	0
Barfield, rf	4	1	2	1	Baylor, ph	1	1	1	1
Iorg, 2b	4	0	0	0	Pagliarulo, 3b	3	0	1	0
					Berra, ph-3b	1	0	1	1
					Hudler	2	0	0	0
					Bradley, ph	1	0	0	0
					Bonilla, 2b	1	0	0	0
					Meacham, ss	2	0	0	0
Totals	**41**	**8**	**14**	**7**	**Totals**	**34**	**5**	**8**	**5**

| Toronto | | | | | | 006 | 000 | 200 | — 8 |
| New York | | | | | | 000 | 000 | 032 | — 5 |

Toronto	IP	H	R	ER	BB	SO
Alexander (W. 16-8)	7⅓	5	2	2	5	4
Lavelle	1	3	3	3	1	1
Henke	⅔	0	0	0	0	0

New York	IP	H	R	ER	BB	SO
Whitson (L. 10-8)	2	7	4	4	0	0
Rasmussen	⅔	3	2	2	0	0
Bordi	3⅓	3	2	1	1	3
Scurry	2	1	0	0	1	4
Armstrong	1	0	0	0	0	1

Whitson pitched to four batters in third
Bordi pitched to three batters in seventh

GW RBI – Mulliniks. E – Griffey, Meacham, Bell, Pagliarulo. DP – Toronto 1, New York 1. LOB – Toronto 8, New York 8. 2B – Bell, Barfield, Griffey, Baylor. HR – Griffey (8).
SB – Moseby, Henderson.
T – 3:13. A – 54,699.

1985

Great Moments #8

OCTOBER 5, 1985 • *Blue Jays 5, Yankees 1*

One week after the big series in New York, the Blue Jays had built up their lead over the Yankees to seven games. But another week later, the Yankees had pulled back to within four. The Blue Jays opened the final week of the 1985 season in Detroit and, with a little luck, could have clinched the American League East Division title there. Instead, they were swept by the Tigers. Fortunately, Milwaukee Brewers rookie Teddy Higuera shut out the suddenly red-hot Yankees 1–0 on Wednesday night. That loss meant that when New York arrived in Toronto on Friday to begin the final weekend, the Blue Jays could clinch the division with just a single win.

An Exhibition Stadium-record crowd of 47,686 was hopeful of watching the Blue Jays win it all in the series opener. The game was scoreless until the fourth when the Yankees put two runs on the board. After a 59-minute rain delay, Toronto evened the score in the bottom of the inning. The team later carried a 3–2 lead into the ninth with the rain coming down again. The Blue Jays were just one strike away from clinching when Butch Wynegar yanked a Tom Henke pitch over the fence in right field. Rusty Meacham followed with a single and Rickey Henderson drew a walk. Don Mattingly then lifted a lazy fly ball into center field. The usually sure-handed Lloyd Moseby dropped it and the Yankees had a 4–3 victory.

New York	AB	R	H	RBI	Toronto	AB	R	H	RBI
Henderson, cf	4	0	0	0	Garcia, 2b	5	0	1	1
Griffey, lf	4	1	1	0	Moseby, cf	2	1	1	1
Mattingly, 1b	4	0	1	0	Upshaw, 1b	4	1	2	1
Winfield, rf	4	0	1	1	Oliver, dh	2	1	1	0
Hassey, c	4	0	0	0	Johnson, dh	2	0	1	0
Baylor, dh	3	0	1	0	Mulliniks, 3b	1	0	0	0
Pagliarulo, 3b	3	0	0	0	Iorg, ph-3b	3	0	2	0
Randolph, 2b	3	0	1	0	Bell, lf	3	0	0	1
Meacham, ss	2	0	0	0	Whitt, c	4	1	1	1
Pasqua, ph	1	0	0	0	Barfield, rf	4	0	1	0
Smith, ss	0	0	0	0	Fernandez, ss	4	1	2	0
Totals	**32**	**1**	**5**	**1**	**Totals**	**34**	**5**	**12**	**5**

New York .... .000 100 000 – 1
Toronto .... .013 100 00x – 5

New York	IP	H	R	ER	BB	SO
Cowley (L. 12-6)	2⅓	4	3	3	1	0
Shirley	0	2	1	1	0	0
Bordi	1	2	1	1	1	0
Rasmussen	⅓	0	0	0	0	1
Allen	4⅓	4	0	0	0	0

Toronto	IP	H	R	ER	BB	SO
Alexander (17-10)	9	5	1	1	0	0

..... Shirley pitched to two batters in third

GW RBI – Whitt. E – Hassey. DP – New York 1. LOB – New York 4, Toronto 8. 2B – Barfield, Oliver, Griffey, Fernandez. HR – Whitt, (19), Moseby (18), Upshaw (14). SB – Moseby, Winfield. SF – Bell. WP – Allen.
T – 2:38. A – 44,608.

After the heartbreaking loss on Friday night, the Blue Jays turned to Doyle Alexander on a cool and breezy Saturday afternoon. Pat Gillick had rescued him from the Yankees scrap heap late in the 1983 season and he had become the Blue Jays' winningest pitcher. Alexander had worked big games before, and he was not about to let the pressure faze him. The offense staked Doyle to an early lead when Ernie Whitt homered off Yankees starter Joe Cowley in the second inning. When Lloyd Moseby and Willie Upshaw went deep back-to-back in the third, Alexander had all the support he would need.

Saturday's game may have lacked the drama of Friday night's thriller, but the excitement was certainly building as the Blue Jays got closer and closer to finally clinching. The score was 5–1 as the game entered the ninth. Alexander was still on the mound. He was pitching a gem, having allowed only five hits and not a single walk.

With two out, Ron Hassey came to the plate.

He lifted the first pitch into left field.

George Bell drifted under it.

And made the catch!

Bell fell to his knees in celebration as the players raced from the dugout. They hoisted Alexander onto their shoulders and carried him off the field while fans streamed out of the stands to share in the celebration.

The Blue Jays had won the American League East.

An overflow of feverish fans on the field (above) and bubbly in the dressing room (left) can only mean one thing — the Blue Jays were the champions of the AL East.

Playoff Moments #1

OCTOBER 8, 1985 • *Blue Jays 6, Royals 1*

The American League Championship Series opened in Canada for the first time when the Blue Jays took on the Kansas City Royals at Exhibition Stadium in Game One of the newly expanded best-of-seven series. Since its inception in 1969, only three victories had been required to win the Championship Series. Now it would take four.

Throwing out the ceremonial first pitch that night was Prime Minister Brian Mulroney. On the mound for the Blue Jays in the series opener was Dave Stieb. Stieb had won 14 games in 1985 but had been beaten 13 times despite leading the American League with a 2.48 ERA. Opposing him was Charlie Leibrandt (17–9), whose ERA of 2.69 had been the AL's second best. Toronto's record of 99–62 was 8½ games better than Kansas City's mark of 91–71, but the Blue Jays had won just five of 12 games against the Royals during the season, so the series promised to be close. Game One, however, turned out to be anything but.

Stieb had total command of his pitches from the very start, relying more on his fastball than his nasty slider to attack the Royals hitters. In eight innings, he allowed just three singles and one base on balls. No Kansas City player advanced past second base on the Blue Jays ace. Meanwhile, after a scoreless first inning, Toronto had gotten on the board in the bottom of the second with RBI singles from Ernie Whitt and Tony Fernandez, the team's eighth and ninth hitters. The bottom of the lineup was at it again in the third inning when the Jays knocked out Leibrandt. With the bases loaded and nobody out, Royals manager Dick Howser lifted his lefty starter for right-handed reliever Steve Farr. Bobby Cox countered by inserting Rance Mulliniks for his platoon partner Garth Iorg, and Mulliniks promptly plated the game's third run. Whitt followed with a bases-loaded walk, and Fernandez capped the inning with a sacrifice fly that scored Willie Upshaw. The Blue Jays stretched the lead to 6–0 in the bottom of the fourth when George Bell's hustle forced Steve Balboni to throw the ball over George Brett's head on a play at third base. Bell scored easily.

Stieb had been masterful through eight innings, and manager Bobby Cox decided to give relief ace Tom Henke a pressure-free postseason debut in the top of the ninth. Henke struggled, giving up a run on a Pat Sheridan ground out that followed a Willie Wilson single and a George Brett double (his third hit of the game), but the Blue Jays wrapped up a 6–1 victory and took a 1–0 lead in the series.

(Above) Prime Minister Brian Mulroney and Ernie Whitt. (Top) The flock of Blue Jays faithful at Exhibition Stadium.

Playoff Moments #2

OCTOBER 9, 1985 • *Blue Jays 6, Royals 5*

After the one-sided victory in Game One, Game Two of the American League Championship Series proved to be a tense, dramatic affair with Toronto eking out a 6–5 victory in 10 innings. Al Oliver was the hero as the Blue Jays scooped up a victory they had almost let get away.

Jimmy Key was the Blue Jays starter on a damp afternoon at Exhibition Stadium. In his first season as a starting pitcher, Key had put up an impressive record of 14–6 with an ERA of 3.00, but he did not have his good stuff on this day. He lasted just 3.1 innings, giving up three runs on seven hits, including Willie Wilson's two-run homer that opened the scoring in the top of the third. Dennis Lamp, the man who had posted an 11–0 record in 1985, retired all 11 men he faced this day after entering the game in the fourth inning. Lamp's heroics on the mound allowed the Blue Jays bats to get back in the game, and Toronto tied the score at 3–3 in the bottom of the sixth when Jesse Barfield bounced a ball up the middle off Royals starter Bud Black.

The game was still 3–3 when Bobby Cox brought in Gary Lavelle to face George Brett to open the top of the eighth. When the slugging Royals third baseman drew a walk on five pitches, Cox went to Tom Henke who got out of the inning with no further damage. In the bottom of the eighth, George Bell delivered a sacrifice fly off Royals relief ace Dan Quisenberry. Henke was now in position to nail down the victory for the Blue Jays.

Leading off the top of the ninth, the Royals sent up Pat Sheridan to pinch hit for right-handed hitter Darryl Motley. Henke got ahead of him with two inside fastballs, but then left a forkball out over the plate. Sheridan deposited it over the right field fence and the game was tied 4–4. Quisenberry shut down the Blue Jays in the bottom of the ninth and the game headed for extra innings. With Henke still on the mound in the top of the tenth, Frank White batted for the Royals with two out and Willie Wilson at second base.

White lined Henke's first pitch into center field, where a hard-charging Lloyd Moseby appeared to make a shoestring catch. When second base umpire Ted Hendry looked to right field umpire Davey Phillips for help on the call, Phillips ruled that Moseby had trapped the ball. Wilson scored easily on the play and the Royals had a 5–4 lead.

Tony Fernandez led off the bottom of the tenth for the Blue Jays and beat out an infield single when shortstop Onix Concepcion double-clutched on his throw. After a Damaso Garcia grounder moved Fernandez to second, Lloyd Moseby pulled a single into right field. Fernandez ran through Jimy Williams's stop sign and scored the tying run. Moseby advanced to second on the throw to the plate. After George Bell was retired, Al Oliver placed an opposite-field single into left and Moseby raced home with the winning run.

(Left) Lloyd Moseby pleads his case after trapping a line drive in the tenth inning of game two. (Below) Al Oliver accepts his accolades.

Playoff Moments #3

OCTOBER 11, 1985 • *Royals 6, Blue Jays 5*

George Bell is a dead duck at third base during Kansas City's series-turning victory in Game Five of the 1985 ALCS.

Before the 1985 Championship Series had started, Blue Jays manager Bobby Cox had been adamant that George Brett was not going to beat them. But even Cox had to grudgingly admire Brett's performance in Game Three. The Blue Jays had 17-game winner Doyle Alexander on the mound that night. He was opposed by Kansas City's 20-game winner Bret Saberhagen, who would later be named the American League's Cy Young Award winner. But Game Three would be no pitchers' duel.

Brett got the Royals on the scoreboard in the bottom of the first inning when he pulled an Alexander changeup deep to right field for a home run. His next time up, he slammed a slider off the right field fence for a double. He then scored on a Frank White single and Kansas City was ahead 2–0 after four.

Saberhagen had not been sharp up to this point, but he had been good enough to keep the Blue Jays off the scoreboard. That changed in the top of the fifth when a two-run homer by Jesse Barfield tied the game. After Tony Fernandez was retired, Damaso Garcia laced a double and came around to score on a Lloyd Moseby single. When Rance Mulliniks followed up with the second two-run shot of the inning, the Blue Jays had a 5–2 lead and Saberhagen took an early shower.

The Royals narrowed the gap to 5–3 on a Jim Sundberg homer in the bottom of the fifth. A Willie Wilson single leading off the sixth then brought George Brett to the plate representing the tying run. This time, Alexander fed him a fastball on the outside part of the plate. Brett lifted it to left field, and when it carried over the fence he was 3-for-3 with three runs scored and three RBIs. More importantly for the Royals, the game was now 5–5.

Steve Farr had entered the game for Kansas City with two out in the fifth inning and he silenced the Blue Jays bats. Dennis Lamp had come in for Alexander and shut out the Royals for two innings before turning over the ball to Jim Clancy in the bottom of the eighth. Clancy had missed much of the 1985 season, first with a case of appendicitis that flared up near the end of spring training, then with a bout of tendinitis in his right shoulder that kept him sidelined for six weeks in the summer. Still, he had started 23 games for the Blue Jays and posted a respectable 9–6 record. But he had not made an appearance as a relief pitcher since 1979. Waiting to face Clancy as he came out of the bullpen was none other than George Brett, who promptly singled for his fourth hit of the night. After a Hal McRae sacrifice bunt put Brett in scoring position, Clancy retired Frank White then walked left-handed hitter Pat Sheridan to face rotund right-hander Steve Balboni. Balboni's 36 home runs had ranked third in the American League in 1985, but his looping single proved just as effective as it chased home Brett with the run that gave the Royals a 6–5 victory.

Playoff Moments #4

OCTOBER 12, 1985 • *Blue Jays 3, Royals 1*

Once again it was Al Oliver to the rescue as the Blue Jays moved to within one game of a berth in the World Series with a dramatic come-from-behind victory against the Royals in Game Four of the American League Championship Series. Oliver delivered the key hit as the Blue Jays scored a 3–1 victory, with all three runs in the top of the ninth inning.

Game Four featured a rematch of the Game One pitching matchup as Dave Stieb once again faced Charlie Leibrandt. Stieb was not as sharp on this night, walking seven Royals in just 6.2 innings. However, by allowing only two hits, he was able to limit the damage to just one run in a gutsy pitching performance. Unfortunately, through eight innings, the Blue Jays had not been able to score any on Leibrandt. The crafty, soft-tossing left-hander — the type of pitcher that always gave Toronto batters fits — had moved the ball in and out all night, allowing just four hits and a single walk. He struck out only one batter, but kept his infielders busy with his effective sinker.

Blue Jays leadoff hitter Damaso Garcia came to the plate to begin the top of the ninth. A .300 hitter in both 1982 and 1983, Garcia was still a dangerous batter who could slash singles with the best of them, but he was not known for his discerning eye. Indeed, he had hit .282 in 1985 but had walked just 15 times in more than 600 plate appearances. Yet leading off the top of the ninth, Garcia coaxed four balls from Leibrandt and the Blue Jays had the tying run on board. Lloyd Moseby was up next and drove a fastball deep into the right field power alley. Garcia scored easily on the booming double and the game was back to square one.

Leibrandt's night was over as Dick Howser turned to his relief ace, Dan Quisenberry. First to face him was George Bell, who looked awkward on the first two pitches before looping a line drive over Frank White's head. Moseby had to hold up to make sure the ball was not caught by the second baseman and could only advance to third. Due up next was designated hitter Cliff Johnson, but, sticking with the platoon system that had worked so well for him, Bobby Cox sent up Al Oliver to pinch hit. Oliver did not waste any time, ripping the first pitch down the right field line just fair and into the corner. Moseby scored easily, and a hustling Bell beat the relay throw to the

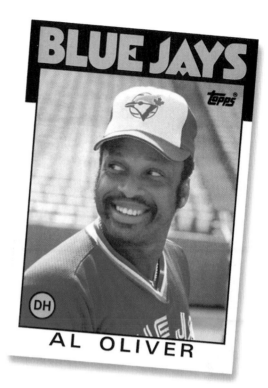

plate as Oliver cruised into second base with a two-run double.

But the game was not over yet. Tom Henke had picked up Stieb in the bottom of the seventh and had retired all four men he had faced heading into the bottom of the ninth. The next three outs would prove more difficult as Henke walked a pair of Royals batters before finally nailing down the win. The Blue Jays had pulled out a thrilling 3–1 victory and now led the series three games to one. Until this year, it would have been enough to send them to the World Series.

(Above) A .303 hitter in his career, Al Oliver batted just .251 in 61 games for the Jays in 1985, but delivered two key hits in the postseason. (Below) Aggressive baserunning and perfectly executed fundamentals were the keys to the Royals' series win over the Jays.

Playoff Moments #5

OCTOBER 16, 1985 • *Royals 6, Blue Jays 2*

A wind-blown triple. Three runs scored. It was only the sixth inning, but everyone knew the game was over. The series was over. The Blue Jays had their chances to wrap up the series in Game Five. They had their chances in Game Six. Game Seven was such a disappointment.

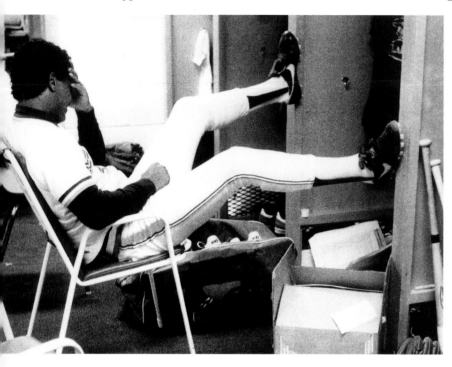

Game Five had been a matchup of young left-handers: Danny Jackson and Jimmy Key. Key allowed a run in both the first and second innings, but the Blue Jays had their chances to get back in it. They kept leaving runners on base. Jackson got stronger as the game went on, and wound up with an eight-hit shutout. The Royals scored a 2–0 victory. The Blue Jays had left eight runners on base. After an off day, the series returned to Toronto for Game Six. Doyle Alexander was on the mound for the Blue Jays, but he had suffered a slight hamstring injury in his Game Three start and was not at his usual effectiveness. Kansas City scored a 5–3 victory. George Brett's solo homer in the fifth had given the Royals a lead they would never relinquish. This time, Toronto had stranded nine baserunners. A few

(Above) George Bell reflects on what might have been.
(Right) 10/16/85. 11:28 p.m. The End.

calls had seemed to go against the Blue Jays, and after the game George Bell said he thought the umpires were anti-Canadian.

Dave Stieb was back on the mound for the Blue Jays in Game Seven, making his third start of the series in just nine days. Opposing him would be Bret Saberhagen, though the 1985 Cy Young Award winner would only last three innings before being knocked out with an injury and turning the ball over to Charlie Leibrandt. At the time, the Royals led 1–0 on Jim Sundberg's second-inning single. The Royals upped their advantage to 2–0 on Pat Sheridan's fourth-inning homer. The Blue Jays cut the lead to 2–1 in the bottom of the fifth, but with two out in the top of the sixth inning, Jim Sundberg came to the plate with Hal McRae, Sheridan and Steve Balboni on base via a pair of walks and a hit batsman. Sundberg lofted a Stieb offering into right field. At first it looked like a routine fly out, but the ball kept drifting. Jesse Barfield drifted with it, until his back was against the wall. He jumped, but the ball struck the top of the metal railing above the padded blue fence and bounced back into play. With two out, the runners had been off with the crack of the bat. All three scored easily on the only triple of the seven-game series. Frank White followed with a single, and the score was 6–1.

The game was all but over after that. The Blue Jays tried to stage a rally in the bottom of the ninth, but Dan Quisenberry came on to snuff it out. The game was over. Kansas City had a 6–2 victory. The Royals were going to the World Series. The Blue Jays were going home, having become just the fifth team in major league history to surrender a three-games-to-one lead. The Royals staged a similar rally against the St. Louis Cardinals in the World Series, while the Blue Jays would have to wait seven long years for their chance at glory in the Fall Classic.

SEE YOU IN '86

K. C. 6
TORONTO 2
INN 9
HEAVY HITTER
TECHNICS
STEREO
11:28

1985

1986

86–76 .531 4th -9.5

The Jays entered the 1986 season with Jimy Williams replacing Bobby Cox as manager. Jesse Barfield (40 HR) and George Bell (198 hits, 31 HR) had career years, setting a new club mark with 108 RBIs each. Tony Fernandez (.310) set a team record with 213 hits. Jimmy Key (14–11, 3.57 ERA), Tom Henke (27 saves) and Mark Eichhorn (14 wins, 1.72 ERA) anchored the pitching staff, which struggled throughout the season.

Buck up: A struggling Bill Caudill gets some advice from his catcher. Despite several great individual performances, the 1986 Blue Jays failed to live up to the expectations created by the 1985 campaign.

Bad Breaks, Near Misses and Disappointments #11

MAY 14, 1986 • *Athletics 9, Blue Jays 4*

While it was apparent that the Blue Jays would be doing some re-tooling and rebuilding after their loss to Kansas City in the 1985 AL playoffs, few expected that the first move would be to find a new manager. On October 25, only nine days after losing to the Royals, Bobby Cox announced he was leaving Toronto to assume general manager's duties with the Atlanta Braves. Jimy Williams, the Jays' third base coach since 1980, was appointed as the fourth field boss of the Blue Jays.

Williams inherited a team with a solid starting rotation, strength up the middle and one of the best outfield trios in the game. Unfortunately, nothing seemed to go right in 1986. Jimmy Key was winless in his first six games and Dave Stieb lost his first six decisions. The team fell into last place as early as April 18, and as the losses continued to pile up in May, the pressure continued to build. The situation finally erupted in Oakland on May 14 at the conclusion of an eight-game road trip.

Damaso Garcia had been unhappy since spring training when Williams had demoted him from the leadoff spot in the batting order. Though back in the top spot now, Garcia was 0-for-4 at the plate against the Athletics. In the field, he booted a routine ground ball, opening up a floodgate of unearned runs that led to a 9–4 loss. After the game, Garcia stormed into the bathroom of the Blue Jays clubhouse. He poured alcohol over his uniform and cap and set them on fire.

At first, the incident was treated almost like a joke, as if "Damo" had been attempting to lift some voodoo curse. But clearly the fans — and the media — were unhappy. Garcia was booed when the club returned home. The only positive side to the affair was that the incident appeared to take some of the pressure off the rest of the team. The Blue Jays did begin to play better, but after five years of improvement, the fourth-place finish in 1986 was a major disappointment. After the season, Garcia was traded to the Atlanta Braves.

A glum Damaso Garcia, his days as a productive member of the Toronto Blue Jays behind him, warms up (left) before a game during his last season with the club. The honeymoon between Garcia and the Blue Jays came to a bitter end during the 1986 season when the feisty second baseman, who was struggling to return to the form that had made him a fan favourite, burned his uniform following a disappointing loss to the Oakland A's.

Oddities and Others #13

JUNE 27, 1986 • *Blue Jays 14, Yankees 7*

Though the 1986 season was a disappointment overall, there were several great games and impressive individual performances throughout the year. Among the highlights was a sweep of the Yankees in New York in late June. The series began with Damaso Garcia tying a major league record when he hit four doubles in a single game.

The Blue Jays got to Ron Guidry early in this one, scoring two runs in their initial at-bat. Garcia's first double of the evening came leading off the third inning and sparked a four-run outburst that knocked Guidry from the mound. Unfortunately, Doyle Alexander was faring little better and the Yankees actually had a 7–6 lead after five. Things swung back in the Blue Jays' favour when Garcia led off the seventh inning with his second double of the night. After George Bell reached on an error, Jesse Barfield clubbed a three-run homer to put Toronto in front to stay. A 38-minute rain delay in the bottom of the seventh helped the cause considerably. The Yankees had the bases loaded when the skies opened up, but Tom Henke needed just one pitch to retire Rickey Henderson when play resumed.

Garcia's third double of the evening keyed another three-run rally that helped the Blue Jays put the game out of reach in the eighth inning. "Damo" launched his fourth double in the top of the ninth after Tony Fernandez kept the inning alive with a two-out, two-run homer. At the time, Garcia joined Roy Howell as the only Blue Jays players with four extra-base hits in a single game. On June 8, 2000, Shannon Stewart joined the club when he belted three doubles and a homer. On July 18, 2000, Stewart matched Garcia again when he hit four doubles against the New York Mets.

Despite the frustrations that plagued the 1986 Jays, there were two bright and shining lights. Mark Eichhorn (above) used a wacky submarine pitching motion and a sweeping slider to keep AL hitters off-balance for the entire season. Jesse Barfield (below) combined solid defense and the league's best outfield arm with a powerful home run stroke to become the first Blue Jays outfielder to win a Gold Glove and lead the league in homers.

Famous Firsts and Records #12

JULY 10, 1986 • *Blue Jays 8, Athletics 4*

Though he'd taken plenty of heat for his uniform-burning incident in May, there was no denying that Damaso Garcia was red hot in June and July. He had launched an 18-game hitting streak that was just three games short of the team record at the time (a mark he shared with Lloyd Moseby) and was batting .443 over a 20-game stretch after recording his second four-hit game of the season on July 10. Garcia's first hit that day made him the first player to reach 1,000 hits as a Blue Jay. The historic single came in the third inning against Oakland's Eric Plunk. His fourth hit of the afternoon keyed a five-run seventh inning that saw the Blue Jays break a 3–3 tie and go on to an 8–4 victory.

Famous Firsts and Records #13

JULY 28, 1986 • *Blue Jays 6, Royals 0*

As the Blue Jays celebrated their tenth season in 1986, only one player could claim that he had actually been a part of the team at the major league level in every one of those years. Garth Iorg and Ernie Whitt were also survivors of the team's original expansion draft on November 5, 1976, but only Jim Clancy had suited up with the Blue Jays in each one of their 10 years. On July 28, 1986, Clancy became the first Blue Jays pitcher to win 100 games.

Clancy recorded his 100th victory with a 6–0 win over Kansas City. He went the distance on a four-hitter to post his sixth consecutive victory and improve to 12–5 on the season. His lifetime record stood at 100 wins and 107 losses — but, of course, the Blue Jays themselves had not had a winning year until 1983, Clancy and the club's seventh season. Dave Stieb joined Clancy on the 100-win plateau later that year, pushing his lifetime record to 100–90 with a 3–1 win over Cleveland on September 3.

After hitting .311 in 30 games in 1985, Cecil Fielder batted just .157 in 1986. Not yet known as "Big Daddy," Fielder did manage to hit 31 homers and collect 84 RBIs in 506 at-bats with the Blue Jays through 1988.

CECIL FIELDER

O-Pee-Chee

Tony Fernandez was a smooth-fielding, line-drive hitting marvel who won the Gold Glove as the American League's top shortstop in 1986. He also batted .310 and became the first Blue Jay to reach the 200-hit plateau with 213 safeties.

Famous Firsts and Records #14

SEPTEMBER 22, 1986 • *200 Hits*

The Blue Jays finally began to play like defending champions after the All-Star break in 1986. From July 17 to August 31, the team went 25–15 and when the pennant race began in earnest on September 1, the Blue Jays found themselves sitting in second place just 3½ games behind Boston. Unfortunately, that was the closest the 1986 team was to get, as it seemed that every time the Blue Jays lost a game on the field in September, they also lost a game in the standings to the surging Red Sox. When the season finally limped to a close, Toronto sat in fourth place, 9½ games back of Boston with a record of 86–76.

Despite the disappointing results in the standings, a series of sensational individual performances highlighted the campaign. Mark Eichhorn won 14 games out of the bullpen and set a club record with a 1.72 ERA. Jesse Barfield led the major leagues with 40 home runs and earned himself a Gold Glove, a Silver Slugger award and a spot on both the American League and Major League All-Star teams. George Bell tied Barfield with 108 RBIs and reached career highs in homers (31) and batting average (.309).

Like Jesse Barfield, Tony Fernandez also won a Gold Glove and was voted to both the AL and Major League All-Star teams. Fernandez had enjoyed a remarkable season, playing in every single game for the second year in a row, and not only did he lead all American League shortstops in fielding percentage, he also established himself as the team's leadoff hitter and emerged as a major offensive threat with a .310 batting average. Having already shattered Damaso Garcia's club record of 185 hits, Fernandez became the first Blue Jay to collect 200 hits in a season on September 22. He finished the year with 213 hits, establishing a new major league record for shortstops.

1987

96–66 .592 2nd -2

George Bell (47 HR, 134 RBI) won the American League MVP award. Lloyd Moseby (26 HR, 96 RBI), Fred McGriff (20 HR) and Jesse Barfield (28 HR, 84 RBI) were the other offensive heroes. Rookie Jeff Musselman won 12 games while five other pitchers (Stieb, Key, Eichhorn, Clancy and John Cerutti) won at least 10 games. The highlight of the season came on September 14 when the Jays hit 10 home runs in a game against Baltimore.

Another slick-fielding prospect from the Dominican Republic, Nelson Liriano recorded his first major league hit in his first at-bat on August 25, 1987.

Oddities and Others #14

APRIL 9, 1987 • *Indians 14, Blue Jays 3*

Each of the Blue Jays' first three games of the 1987 season featured something that had never happened before. First, there was the home opener at Exhibition Stadium on Monday, April 6. Traditionally, as the home of baseball's oldest professional franchise, Cincinnati had the honour of playing the first game each season, but when Jimmy Key tossed the game's first pitch to Cleveland's Tony Bernazard at 12:52 p.m., the baseball season began in Canada for the first time. The Blue Jays were 7–3 winners that day, and when they followed up an off-day with a 5–1 victory on Wednesday, they had won two straight games to start the season for the first time. The winning streak ended with a 14–3 drubbing on April 9 in a game that featured yet another piece of baseball history.

Joey Johnson was on the mound for the Blue Jays, pitting his lifetime record of 17–13 against the 311–261 mark of Indians starter Phil Niekro. Youth certainly wasn't served that day, as Johnson allowed seven runs in just four innings and reliever John Cerutti coughed up five more through the sixth. Meanwhile, Niekro had battled through five innings and with the score now 12–3, the Indians removed him from the game before the Blue Jays batted in the sixth. When Steve Carlton emerged from the Cleveland bullpen, it marked his first relief appearance since 1971 and the first time in major league history that a pair of 300-game winners had worked for the same team in the same game. Carlton pitched the final four frames for the Indians and added his first save since 1967 to a lifetime record that then included 323 wins and 239 losses.

The Dominican Dynamo: George Bell uncoils from the powerful swing that allowed him to become the first — and only — Blue Jay to win the American League MVP Award in 1987. Bell led the club in homers (47), RBIs (134), runs (111), hits (188), doubles (32), slugging (.605) and sacrifice flies (8).

Famous Firsts and Records #15

JUNE 2–13, 1987 • *Eleven in a Row*

Despite a good start to the 1987 season, the Blue Jays had a hard time making headway in the American League East during the first two months of the schedule. The Milwaukee Brewers had burst out of the starting gate with a record 13 straight wins and the Blue Jays found themselves 5½ games out of first place despite a record of 12–8 in April. In May, Jim Clancy earned American League Pitcher-of-the-Month honours with a 5–1 record and 1.52 ERA. Offensively, George Bell set club records with 11 homers and 31 RBIs. The Blue Jays had improved to 28–19, and by June 1, the gap between Toronto and first place was down to just two games. It was the Yankees who the Blue Jays were chasing now, and they would catch them and then some during an 11-game winning streak from June 2 to 13.

The streak began at home with a pair of wins against Seattle that was followed by a three-game sweep of the Orioles. After that, it was on to New York for three at Yankee Stadium beginning on June 8. With the team now just a half-game out of top spot, first place was on the line that night and the Blue Jays grabbed it in convincing fashion with an 11–0 rout. Dave Stieb pitched seven-plus innings of two-hit ball, while George Bell clubbed two home runs, including a three-run shot in the seven-run fifth. He now had 20 homers and 50 RBIs on the season, but the big blast that night came from Fred McGriff. He launched a ball some 525 feet into the upper deck in right field. After a 7–2 win the following night, Jimmy Key improved his record to 8–3 as the Blue Jays completed the sweep with a 4–1 victory. Next, it was off to Baltimore, where Bell propelled the team to its record-tying ninth straight win with a grand slam and six RBIs in the series opener.

After two more wins, the Orioles finally snapped the Blue Jays' streak with an 8–5 victory on June 14. Eleven wins in a row is still a club record, matched only once when the Blue Jays won 11 straight in late August and early September of 1998.

Team mascot B.J. Birdy whoops it up with a young fan as the Jays got hot in June.

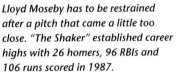

Lloyd Moseby has to be restrained after a pitch that came a little too close. "The Shaker" established career highs with 26 homers, 96 RBIs and 106 runs scored in 1987.

Bad Breaks, Near Misses and Disappointments #12

JUNE 29, 1987 • *Yankees 15, Blue Jays 14*

Though the 11-game winning streak at the beginning of June had vaulted the Blue Jays into first place in the American League East, inconsistent play over the next few weeks saw their lead evaporate. On June 29, 1987, the New York Yankees came to Toronto tied with the Blue Jays and looking for revenge after being swept at Yankee Stadium earlier in the month. The game that night is still one of the wildest in Blue Jays history.

In the first inning, Dave Winfield belted a two-run homer off John Cerutti to get the Yankees off to an early start. A Don Mattingly grand slam in the second upped the advantage as New York jumped out to an 11–4 lead by the sixth. The Blue Jays then got back in the game with four runs in the bottom of the inning, highlighted by a three-run homer from Lloyd Moseby. In the seventh, Tony Fernandez and Jesse Barfield each drove in a pair of runs as Toronto scored six times. The Blue Jays were now ahead 14–11, but the lead lasted less than half an inning.

The Yankees put three runners on base in the top of the eighth. With two outs, Winfield stepped in against Tom Henke and drove a towering shot to center field. The grand slam gave the Yankees a 15–14 lead they would not relinquish. Mattingly's and Winfield's bases-clearing blasts marked the first (and only) time in franchise history that an opposing team had two grand slams against the Blue Jays in one game.

The Yankees went on to sweep the three-game series at Exhibition Stadium, and by the time the Blue Jays climbed out of what became an eight-game losing streak, they were in third place, five games out of first. Though they would bounce back in July and August, the Blue Jays' streaky season would catch up with them in September.

Lefty John Cerutti, now a member of the Blue Jays' broadcast team, had a fabulous sophomore season in 1987, winning 11 games while recording a 4.40 ERA.

A Modern-Day Murderer's Row: Rance Mulliniks, George Bell, Lloyd Moseby, Rob Ducey, Fred McGriff and Ernie Whitt combined to hit 10 home runs in one game.

Great Moments #9

SEPTEMBER 14, 1987 • *Blue Jays 18, Orioles 3*

The Blue Jays were on a roll as the 1987 season was winding down. Fresh off a recent six-game winning streak, the Blue Jays had all but eliminated the New York Yankees from pennant contention by taking two of three games from them in a key weekend series. Saturday's game was a 13–1 rout in which the Blue Jays had slugged five home runs. But as it turned out, the team was just getting warmed up! Two days later, the Blue Jays battered Baltimore pitchers for a major-league-record 10 home runs in an 18–3 drubbing of the Orioles.

The barrage began in the second inning when Ernie Whitt slugged a solo homer off Ken Dixon. Two batters later, Rance Mulliniks went deep with Jesse Barfield on base. After two outs and a walk to Nelson Liriano, Lloyd Moseby slugged another two-run homer. Eric Bell was on the mound to start the third inning, but he fared little better than Dixon. George Bell took his namesake deep leading off and Mulliniks launched his second home run in as many innings. Whitt clubbed his second of the night in the fifth, while Bell went deep again in the sixth. He now had 45 home runs on the season and 122 RBIs.

Leading 10–2, the Blue Jays began to go to their bench in the seventh inning, but the home runs just kept on coming as Rob Ducey launched a three-run shot for the first round-tripper of his career. Ducey's blast was the Blue Jays' eighth of the night, tying the major league record. When Manny Lee and Lou Thornton followed with a pair of singles, Ernie Whitt came to the plate with a chance to break the record. Facing him was Tony Arnold, Baltimore's fifth pitcher of the night.

"There's no question I was going up there thinking home run," Whitt admitted after the game. "When the count got to 3-and-1, I was looking for a pitch [to hit] and I got it." A Monday night crowd of 27,446 roared its approval as the ball sailed over the fence. In addition to breaking the record, Whitt had become the first Blue Jays player since Otto Velez to hit three home runs in a single game. "When I get into a home run groove, I usually hit them in bunches, but not like this!"

The tenth home run of the evening came an inning later, when Fred McGriff led off the bottom of the eighth with a longball. His bat was taken to the Baseball Hall of Fame in Cooperstown. But in addition to the Blue Jays' offensive explosion, the game against the Orioles was unique for another reason. After the top of the eighth inning, with the score then 17–3, Baltimore manager Cal Ripken Sr. took his son out of the game and replaced him with utility infielder Ron Washington. Though Lou Gehrig's ironman record was still several years in the future, the move marked the first time since June 4, 1982 — a streak of 8,243 innings — that the Orioles had taken to the field without Ripken on the diamond.

Baltimore	AB	R	H	RBI	Toronto	AB	R	H	RBI
Stanicek, dh	5	0	0	0	Liriano, 2b	4	3	3	1
BRipken, 2b	3	1	1	0	Moseby, cf	4	1	1	2
Sheets, rf	4	1	2	0	Ducey, cf	2	1	1	3
Murray, 1b	4	0	3	0	Fernandez, ss	4	0	1	1
CRipken, ss	4	0	2	2	Lee, ss	2	1	1	0
Washington, ss	0	0	0	0	Bell, lf	4	2	2	2
Knight, 3b	4	0	0	0	Thornton, lf	1	1	1	0
Gonzales, 3b	0	0	0	0	Whitt, c	5	3	3	5
Kennedy, c	3	0	0	0	Barfield, rf	5	1	4	0
Nichols, c	1	0	1	0	Mulliniks, 3b	3	2	2	3
Young, lf	4	0	0	0	Gruber, 3b	2	0	0	0
Hart, cf	4	1	2	1	McGriff, dh	4	2	1	1
					Upshaw, 1b	4	1	1	0
Totals	36	3	11	3	Totals	44	18	21	18

Baltimore .... .001 001 010 – 3
Toronto .... .052 111 71x – 18

Baltimore	IP	H	R	ER	BB	SO
Dixon (L, 7-10)	1⅓	5	5	5	1	2
EBell	1⅓	2	2	2	0	1
Griffin	2	3	2	2	2	0
Kinnunen	1⅔	6	6	6	1	0
Arnold	1⅔	5	3	3	0	0
Connor	⅔	0	0	0	0	1

Toronto	IP	H	R	ER	BB	SO
Clancy (W. 13-10)	7	7	2	2	1	6
Eichhorn	1	2	1	1	0	1
Henke	1	2	0	0	0	0

GW RBI – Whitt E – None. DP – Baltimore 1, Toronto 1.
LOB – Baltimore 7, Toronto 6. 2B – Murray, CRipken, Liriano, Barfield.
HR – Whitt 3 (17), Mulliniks 2 (10), Moseby (23), Bell 2 (45), Ducey (1), McGriff (19), Hart (4). WP – Clancy.
T – 3:18. A – 27,446.

Bad Breaks, Near Misses and Disappointments #13

SEPTEMBER 24, 1987 • *Blue Jays 4, Tigers 3*

As the final days of the 1987 season approached, the Blue Jays knew their fate was in their own hands. Seven of their last 10 games were against the Detroit Tigers, starting with a four-game weekend set at Exhibition Stadium.

When the Tigers came to town on Thursday night, September 24, they had a record of 92–59. Toronto was 93–59, for a lead of only half a game. The series opener pitted Tigers ace Jack Morris against Mike Flanagan, the crafty left-hander whom the Blue Jays had acquired from the Baltimore Orioles on August 31. The Blue Jays erased Detroit's early 2–0 lead when they erupted for a quartet of runs in the third inning thanks to a two-run single from Ernie Whitt and a costly wild pitch by Jack Morris. However, the key play of the game — and the season — had come in the top of that inning.

With the game still scoreless, the Tigers had Bill Madlock on base and Kirk Gibson at the plate. Gibson bounced a ball to Nelson Liriano at second base. Liriano flipped to Tony Fernandez for the first out, but there would be no double play. After taking the feed from Liriano, Fernandez was clipped by Madlock, who clearly rolled out of the baseline in an attempt to break up the double play. Fernandez spun in the air and came down hard on the turf, dislocating his elbow.

Utility infielder Manny Lee was pressed into action and quickly paid dividends for the Jays, climbing the ladder to make a sensational catch of a screaming line drive to snuff out a Tigers rally in the sixth inning. Flanagan combined with a pair of relievers to tame the Tigers with a 4–3 win. As the team was celebrating the victory, Fernandez was having season-ending elbow surgery. He would fly back home to the Dominican Republic a few days later, before the season was even over.

(Above) Ernie Whitt scored a key run in the first game of the Toronto/Detroit showdown at Exhibition Stadium when he raced home from third following a Jack Morris wild pitch. The Tigers pitcher ended up on his back in the play at the plate. (Left) The Blue Jays' hopes for a divisional championship took a serious dive when Tony Fernandez smashed his elbow trying to avoid a hard-sliding Bill Madlock.

A Game of Inches: Manny Lee and Lloyd Moseby watch as Kirk Gibson's blooper falls between them to give the Motowners a come-from-behind 3–2 win that started the slide that cost the Jays the pennant.

Bad Breaks, Near Misses and Disappointments #14

SEPTEMBER 27, 1987 • *Tigers 3, Blue Jays 2*

With the injury to Tony Fernandez, Manny Lee was thrust into the spotlight for the first time in his career. He had made a key defensive play in the first game, and on Friday night he starred with the bat when his two-run triple off Willie Hernandez scored Jesse Barfield and Rick Leach to wipe out Detroit's 2–0 lead in the bottom of the ninth. Tigers manager Sparky Anderson then ordered Mike Henneman to load the bases with intentional walks, but the ploy backfired when Lloyd Moseby's grounder was misplayed by second baseman Lou Whitaker, allowing Lee to scurry home with the winning run.

The following afternoon, newly acquired Juan Beniquez provided the dramatics as the Blue Jays rallied for another clutch come-from-behind ninth inning miracle. With the bases loaded and Toronto trailing 9–7, Beniquez drilled a rising line drive just over the outstretched glove of Tigers shortstop Alan Trammell. The ball found the gap perfectly, rolling to the fence and allowing all three runners to scamper home. But on Sunday, it was the Tigers' turn to score an emotional victory.

Former Blue Jays pitcher Doyle Alexander had posted a perfect record of 8–0 for the Tigers after being picked up from Atlanta during the summer. Toronto fans had been angered by the way he grumbled himself out of town in 1986, and were looking forward to some revenge. Fans flashed "Foil Doyle" signs printed up by the *Toronto Sun*, but Alexander was nearly perfect that day. After surrendering a run in the bottom of the first, Alexander waged a classic pitchers' duel with Jim Clancy. The Blue Jays still clung to a 1–0 lead when Tom Henke entered the game to pitch the top of the ninth.

The first batter Henke faced was Tigers slugger Kirk Gibson. "The Terminator" had already saved a league-leading 34 games, but Gibson deposited his second offering over the right field fence.

The game was tied and 43,000 screaming fans were silenced.

When the Blue Jays failed to score in the ninth, the game headed into extra innings. After Alexander blanked the Blue Jays again in the tenth, Darrell Evans put Detroit ahead with a solo homer in the top of the 11th. The Jays scratched back to tie it on a clutch two-out single by Jesse Barfield, but in the unlucky 13th, Gibson delivered once again. This time he blooped an RBI single in front of a charging Lloyd Moseby to plate the eventual winning run.

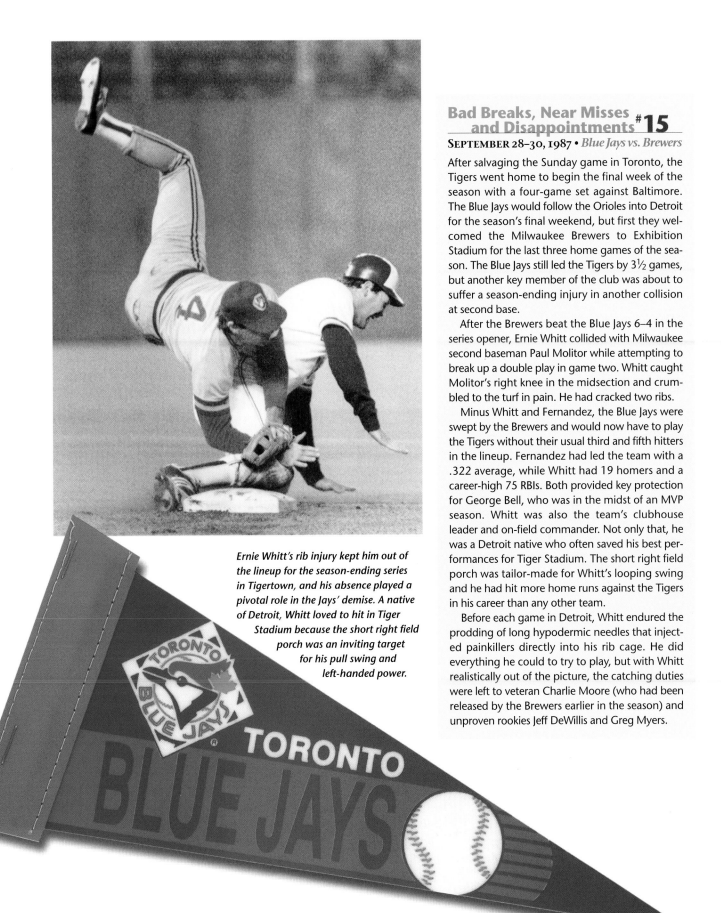

Bad Breaks, Near Misses and Disappointments #15

SEPTEMBER 28–30, 1987 • *Blue Jays vs. Brewers*

After salvaging the Sunday game in Toronto, the Tigers went home to begin the final week of the season with a four-game set against Baltimore. The Blue Jays would follow the Orioles into Detroit for the season's final weekend, but first they welcomed the Milwaukee Brewers to Exhibition Stadium for the last three home games of the season. The Blue Jays still led the Tigers by 3½ games, but another key member of the club was about to suffer a season-ending injury in another collision at second base.

After the Brewers beat the Blue Jays 6–4 in the series opener, Ernie Whitt collided with Milwaukee second baseman Paul Molitor while attempting to break up a double play in game two. Whitt caught Molitor's right knee in the midsection and crumbled to the turf in pain. He had cracked two ribs.

Minus Whitt and Fernandez, the Blue Jays were swept by the Brewers and would now have to play the Tigers without their usual third and fifth hitters in the lineup. Fernandez had led the team with a .322 average, while Whitt had 19 homers and a career-high 75 RBIs. Both provided key protection for George Bell, who was in the midst of an MVP season. Whitt was also the team's clubhouse leader and on-field commander. Not only that, he was a Detroit native who often saved his best performances for Tiger Stadium. The short right field porch was tailor-made for Whitt's looping swing and he had hit more home runs against the Tigers in his career than any other team.

Before each game in Detroit, Whitt endured the prodding of long hypodermic needles that injected painkillers directly into his rib cage. He did everything he could to try to play, but with Whitt realistically out of the picture, the catching duties were left to veteran Charlie Moore (who had been released by the Brewers earlier in the season) and unproven rookies Jeff DeWillis and Greg Myers.

Ernie Whitt's rib injury kept him out of the lineup for the season-ending series in Tigertown, and his absence played a pivotal role in the Jays' demise. A native of Detroit, Whitt loved to hit in Tiger Stadium because the short right field porch was an inviting target for his pull swing and left-handed power.

Bad Breaks, Near Misses and Disappointments #16

OCTOBER 2, 1987 • *Tigers 4, Blue Jays 3*

The Blue Jays' lead in the American League East was down to just a single game as they prepared to take on the Tigers in the Friday opener of the season's final series. The Blue Jays would need two victories to win the division outright, while a single win would set up a one-game playoff back at Exhibition Stadium. Only a sweep by the Tigers would leave Toronto without any title hopes.

Doyle Alexander was on the mound for the Tigers, but the Blue Jays got to him early when Manny Lee, of all people, belted a three-run homer in the top of the second. It was his first home run of the season. Jim Clancy then ambled back out to the mound with a 3–0 lead, but promptly gave up a big chunk of it when Scott Lusader poked a two-run home run to left field. Alan Trammell led off the third with another home run and the game was tied. The Tigers took the lead later in the inning when a double-play ball off the bat of Chet Lemon chased home Darrell Evans. Evans should never have been in position to score, as a Jesse Barfield throw from right field had him nailed at third base only moments before, but Rance Mulliniks let the ball pop out of his glove for a costly error.

Alexander made Detroit's 4–3 lead hold up through seven innings before turning the ball over to rookie reliever Mike Henneman. He got into some trouble in the eighth, but escaped when Juan Beniquez grounded into a double play. The Blue Jays got another runner on base in the ninth, but Greg Myers — who was making his first start behind the plate — hit into a game-ending double play. With two games to go, Toronto and Detroit were tied atop the division at 96–64.

Nelson Liriano stretches but fails to make this defensive play. The Blue Jays' trusted defense had more blips than beauties in their season-ending series against Detroit.

Bad Breaks, Near Misses and Disappointments #17

OCTOBER 3, 1987 • *Tigers 3, Blue Jays 2*

It was perhaps the greatest pitching performance in team history, and therefore one of the biggest disappointments. Mike Flanagan gave the Blue Jays 11 gutsy innings only to see the game slip away in the 12th on a ball that should have been a double play.

The Blue Jays took a 1–0 lead on Jack Morris in the top of the first, but the Tigers reached Flanagan for an unearned run to tie it in the third. The two teams traded runs in the fifth, and the score was deadlocked at 2–2. It remained that way for inning after inning after inning. Manager Jimy Williams had a pitcher up and ready throughout the latter stages of the game, but Flanagan never faltered. Morris jumped off after nine innings, but Flanagan was back on the mound for the tenth. Then the 11th. He had allowed just eight hits and two walks while striking out nine, but he had thrown 139 pitches. Flanagan told Williams he could still go out there to pitch the 12th, but Williams had seen enough and went to the bullpen. Tom Henke had warmed up three times during the game when it seemed that Toronto might take the lead. He was more than ready to pitch, but Williams didn't want to use him in a tie game and turned to Jeff Musselman instead.

With one out in the bottom of the 12th, Musselman allowed back-to-back singles to Lou Whitaker and Bill Madlock. He then walked Kirk Gibson to load the bases and bring Alan Trammell to the plate. Trammell was Detroit's hottest hitter and a clutch performer. Williams brought in Mark Eichhorn to face him and instructed his infielders to play in on the edge of the grass to try to cut off the run at the plate. Trammell took Eichhorn's first pitch for a strike. Then he scorched a two-hop grounder right at shortstop Manny Lee. For an instant, it looked like the double-play ball the Blue Jays needed, but as Lee bent down to play the second hop, the ball hugged the long infield grass and scooted between his legs. The game was over.

OCTOBER 4, 1987 • *Tigers 1, Blue Jays 0*

There was now only one game to go in the 1987 season and the Blue Jays needed to win it just to force a playoff. Why hadn't Jimy Williams turned to Tom Henke on Saturday with the game on the line?

"What if I used him for two innings [in a tie game] and then I have to use him for another inning [to get a save] on Sunday? I wouldn't have been able to use him on Monday."

But the Blue Jays might not have needed Monday if they'd won on Saturday. Now they desperately needed a win on Sunday and sent Jimmy Key to the mound to get it. He was opposed by Frank Tanana. Toronto's young starter actually out-performed Detroit's crafty veteran — except for one key moment in the second inning when Larry Herndon lofted a long fly ball to left.

Key thought it would be a routine out.

So did Jays outfielder George Bell.

But the ball snuck into the seats.

The Tigers had a 1–0 lead.

The Blue Jays had their best chance to get that run back in the top of the fourth inning when Cecil Fielder reached base with a one-out single. Third base coach John McLaren flashed the sign for a hit-and-run, but batter Manny Lee didn't see it. Fielder took off with Tanana's next pitch but when Lee didn't swing, Cecil was an easy out at second base. Lee then clubbed Tanana's next offering to the base of the right field wall for a triple that could have tied the game. Instead of being the hero, Lee became no more than one of eight runners the Blue Jays left on base that afternoon.

Key pitched brilliantly, but the Blue Jays had only managed six hits off Tanana and still trailed 1–0 entering the ninth. After retiring Fielder and Lee, Tanana then induced Garth Iorg to slap a weak one-hopper back to the mound for the final out.

The season was over.

The collapse was complete.

The Blue Jays had lost seven in a row.

Four losses had been by a single run.

They had hit just .130 as a team in the final week.

They were 3-for-26 with men in scoring position during the last weekend.

One bloop, one bleeder, even a Tigers error could have spelled the difference.

But it never came.

It was all over.

(Above) Acquired from Baltimore in a perfectly executed deadline deal, Mike Flanagan provided the Jays with a veteran presence in the locker room and another trusty left-handed arm on the hill. (Right) A bewildered Jimy Williams meets the troops to discuss strategy before addressing tragedy during the final weekend of the 1987 season.

Famous Firsts and Records #16

NOVEMBER 17, 1987 • *George Bell*

There could be no doubt that George Bell had enjoyed a career year in 1987. He had led the American League with 134 RBIs. His 47 home runs ranked second behind Mark McGwire, who slugged 49, and he finished among the league leaders in virtually every other offensive category. It was clear that Bell's abilities had captured the attention of baseball fans when he became the first Blue Jays player to be elected to start in the All-Star Game, but would he be recognized by the baseball media as the American League's Most Valuable Player?

Certainly Bell's numbers spoke volumes, but there was his slump in September to worry about. Whether it was the result of the beanball he took off the side of his nose in Milwaukee early in the month, or the fact that he lost his protection at the plate when Tony Fernandez and Ernie Whitt were both injured later, Bell's slump coincided with the slide that saw the Blue Jays lose seven in a row to end the season. In fact, Bell had just two hits in his last 26 at-bats, and was a non-factor during the final weekend series in Detroit when the Tigers overtook Toronto to win the East Division.

Alan Trammell, on the other hand, had come up big when his team needed him most. The Tigers shortstop had also enjoyed a brilliant season in 1987, batting .343 with 28 homers and 105 RBIs while supplying top-notch defense at the game's most difficult position. Clearly the race for the MVP would come down to a decision between Trammell and Bell. This time, the Blue Jays came out on top. When the results of the MVP voting were announced on November 17, Bell had received 16 first-place votes and 12 second-place selections from the panel of 28 members of the Baseball Writers' Association of America, giving him a total of 332 points. Trammell got 12 first-place votes, 15 seconds and one third for a total of 311. Though Carlos Delgado came close in 2000, Bell remains the only Blue Jays player to be named the American League's Most Valuable Player.

George Bell's slump down the stretch may have hurt the Jays' chances of winning the 1987 AL East title, but his overall performance during the season earned him the nod as the American League's Most Valuable Player.

1987

1988

87–75 .537 T3rd -3

The Jays had an exceptional year, leading the league in home runs (158), triples (47) and slugging percentage (.419). The pitching staff topped the AL with 17 shutouts and a 3.90 team ERA. Dave Stieb rebounded to win 16 games while Jimmy Key (12 wins, 3.29 ERA) and Mike Flanagan (13–13) were also solid. Fred McGriff (34 HR) and Kelly Gruber (81 RBI) emerged as new stars while Bell, Barfield and Moseby combined for 52 homers and 194 RBIs.

Not Again!: Dave Stieb can only look to the sky after losing yet another bid for a no-hitter with two out in the ninth inning.

Great Moments #10

APRIL 4, 1988 • *Blue Jays 5, Royals 3*

Toronto	AB	R	H	RBI	Kansas City	AB	R	H	RBI
Liriano, 2b	4	0	0	0	Wilson, cf	5	1	2	0
Moseby, lf	4	1	0	0	Seitzer, 3b	3	1	1	1
Fernandez, ss	4	0	0	0	Brett, dh	5	1	2	2
Bell, dh	4	3	3	4	Tartabull, rf	4	0	2	0
Mulliniks, 3b	4	1	1	0	White, 2b	4	0	1	0
Gruber, 3b	0	0	0	0	Balboni, 1b	3	0	0	0
Whitt, c	4	0	1	0	Madison, 1b	1	0	0	0
Barfield, rf	3	0	1	1	Jackson, lf	4	0	1	0
McGriff, 1b	4	0	2	0	Macfarlane, c	4	0	2	0
Campusano, cf	4	0	1	0	Stillwell, ss	4	0	0	0
Totals	**35**	**5**	**9**	**5**	**Totals**	**37**	**3**	**11**	**3**

Toronto	010 300 010	– 5
Kansas City	200 000 100	– 3

Toronto	IP	H	R	ER	BB	SO
Key (W. 1-0)	6	8	2	2	1	4
Wells	⅓	2	1	1	0	0
Eichhorn	⅔	1	0	0	0	0
Henke (S1)	2	0	0	0	0	1

Kansas City	IP	H	R	ER	BB	SO
Saberhagen (L. 0-1)	8	7	5	3	0	7
Quisenberry	1	2	0	0	0	0

GW RBI – Bell E – Balboni. DP – None. LOB – Toronto 5, Kansas City 9.
2B – Macfarlane 2, Tartabull 2, Mulliniks, Jackson, Campusano.
McGriff. 3B – Wilson. HR – Brett (1), Bell 3(3). SB – Seitzer (1).
S – Liriano. SF – Barfield.
T – 2:58. A – 40,648.

After the bitter disappointment of the final week of the 1987 season, changes were planned in 1988. The Blue Jays hoped to platoon promising youngsters Rob Ducey and Sil Campusano in center field. Lloyd Moseby would be moved to left. Despite being named the American League's Most Valuable Player in 1987, George Bell was ticketed to become the club's full-time designated hitter.

Manager Jimy Williams had advised Bell of the plan during the offseason, and while Bell wasted no time in voicing his displeasure over the idea, it didn't stop him from inking a three-year, $5.8 million contract. However, when he finally showed up — late — to spring training, he refused to accept the DH job. He went so far as to sit out an exhibition game against Boston on March 17, forcing Williams to pinch hit for him as he sat in the bullpen defiantly. An uneasy peace was eventually reached and when the Blue Jays opened the season in Kansas City on April 4, Campusano was in center, Moseby was in left and George Bell was the designated hitter. The experiment would last just two weeks, but the only one voicing his displeasure on opening day was Royals starting pitcher Bret Saberhagen.

After George Brett had staked Kansas City to a 2–0 lead with a two-run homer off Jimmy Key in the bottom of the first, Bell led off the Blue Jays second by taking Saberhagen deep on a first-pitch fastball. Two innings later, Bell gave the Blue Jays a 3–2 lead with a two-run homer off a Saberhagen curve. Toronto was leading 4–3 when Bell came to bat again in the eighth inning. This time, Saberhagen fell behind 2-and-1 in the count and tried to sneak another fastball past him. When Bell deposited it into the seats, he had become the first player in baseball history to slug three home runs on the opening day of the season.

Bell followed up his record-breaking display with another heroic performance in the second game of the young campaign. This time he became just the fifth player in Blue Jays history to record five hits in a game as Toronto romped to an 11–4 victory over the Royals. Pat Borders made his major league debut that evening and went 3-for-4 with a triple and five RBIs.

George Bell, whose offseason tirades and training camp antics earned him scorn from the media and the fans, silenced his critics by slugging a major-league-record three home runs during the Jays' 1988 season opener in Kansas City.

Bad Breaks, Near Misses and Disappointments #19

SEPTEMBER 24, 30, 1988 • *Dave Stieb*

After starting the 1988 season with two straight wins, the Blue Jays slipped below .500 when they fell to 4–5 on April 13. They would not reach the break-even mark again until mid-August, and it was not until September that the team finally hit its stride, motoring through the final month of the season with a franchise-best 22 wins against only seven losses. When Boston and Detroit both faltered down the stretch, the Blue Jays were even able to get into some semblance of the pennant race, but nothing better illustrates what was essentially a season of frustration and disappointment than two games in late September.

Fresh off a shutout of the Indians at home in his most recent start, Dave Stieb was back on the mound at Cleveland's Municipal Stadium on the night of September 24. Through eight innings, he had managed to shut down the Indians again but this time he had not allowed a single hit. The Blue Jays finally broke through for the game's first run in the top of the ninth, so everything was on the line when Stieb took to the mound for the final time that night.

First to face Stieb in the bottom of the ninth was Andy Allanson. He went down on strikes. Then former Blue Jay Willie Upshaw grounded out, bringing Julio Franco to the plate. Stieb started him with ball one, then fired two called strikes. He was only one strike away, but Franco fouled off the next three pitches then took another ball. With the count now 2-and-2, Stieb induced a routine grounder to second base. The Blue Jays were already beginning to race from the dugout as Manny Lee set himself to field the ball, but suddenly it took a crazy hop off a chunk of turf and bounded into center field. It was as fluky a single as anyone had ever seen.

Amazingly, in his next start against Baltimore back at Exhibition Stadium, Stieb lost another no-hit bid on a 2-and-2 count with two out in the ninth. This time the villain was Jim Traber. He took a wicked slider off the fists and muscled a little looper over the outstretched glove of first baseman Fred McGriff. Stieb became only the sixth pitcher in major league history to toss back-to-back one-hitters, but the first to miss twice in a row with two out in the ninth.

Perhaps Dave Stieb's icy demeanor on the mound came from the days when he was playing pro ball in Alaska. Regardless, it was often the opponents' bats that became frigid and cold. Stieb holds the club record by pitching 10 no-hit, one-hit or two-hit games.

DAVE STIEB
with Kevin Boland

TOMORROW I'LL BE PERFECT

Manuel Lee, who was acquired from Houston in the Rule 5 Draft in December of 1984, batted a career-high .291 in 1988.

When Pat Gillick dispatched Dale Murray to New York, he asked that a young prospect named Fred McGriff be tossed into the deal. Mile-long McGriff went on to hit 125 home runs for the Blue Jays and he continues to slug the longball for Tampa Bay.

1989

89–73 .549 1st +2

Manager Jimy Williams was replaced by Cito Gaston and the club responded by winning their second East Division crown. Newcomer Junior Felix and key midseason acquisitions Mookie Wilson and Lee Mazzilli helped carry the team to the title. George Bell drove in 104 runs and Fred McGriff hit 36 homers. Dave Stieb (17–8, 3.35 ERA), David Wells (7–4, 2.40) and Todd Stottlemyre (7–7, 3.88) combined with the bullpen tandem of Tom Henke and Duane Ward (35 saves) to create a powerful pitching staff.

Dave Stieb leads the charge out of the dugout as the Blue Jays beat Baltimore to win the East Division and cap a tremendous comeback season.

Great Moments #11

Whether it was the dismal record of 9–16, the loss of Tony Fernandez to a fractured cheekbone, or the trade of Jesse Barfield, the opening month of the 1989 season provided few highlights for Blue Jays fans. But there was one moment amid the April showers that shone above the rest. On April 16, 1989, Kelly Gruber hit for the cycle (single, double, triple, homer), victimizing four different Kansas City pitchers in a come-from-behind 15–8 victory.

The Royals had already ripped Dave Stieb for six runs in the top of the first when Kelly socked a solo homer off Royals starter Floyd Bannister in the bottom of the inning. In the second, he cracked a two-run double off Bret Saberhagen that cut Kansas City's lead to 7–6. He knocked in two more runs with a triple off Tom Gordon in the seventh and the Blue Jays went ahead 11–8. When Gruber came to the plate again in the eighth inning, he needed only a single to become the first Blue Jay to hit for the cycle. The pitcher he faced this time was Jerry Don Gleaton.

"I could hear the fans and I was anxious," said Gruber afterwards.

Gruber took the first pitch for a ball, then lofted a little looper into shallow right field. It dropped in and took a big bounce off the artificial turf. Gruber could probably have stretched the hit into a double, but considering the significance of the single — and the fact that the score was already 13–8 — no one minded when he took a wide turn but decided to hold up at first base.

"I probably wouldn't have gone even if I knew for sure I had a chance to make it," Gruber admitted. "If I'd hit a double or a triple, I might have had to pull up lame."

Kansas City	AB	R	H	RBI	Toronto	AB	R	H	RBI
Wilson, cf	3	1	1	1	Moseby, cf	3	1	0	0
Eisenreich, cf	1	0	0	0	Gruber, 2b	6	4	4	6
Seitzer, 3b	4	1	0	0	Borders, c	6	1	2	2
Brett, 1b	5	2	3	1	Bell, lf	5	2	3	2
Tartabull, rf	4	1	1	0	Ducey, lf	0	0	0	0
Buckner, dh	5	1	2	1	McGriff, 1b	4	1	2	2
Jackson, lf	3	1	1	2	Barfield, rf	5	1	2	3
Boone, c	3	0	0	1	Brenly, dh	1	0	0	0
Thurman, pr	0	0	0	0	Mulliniks, dh	3	0	1	0
Macfarlane, c	1	0	0	0	Lee, ss	5	2	2	0
Pecota, ss	2	1	1	0	Lawless, 2b	2	3	1	0
White, ph-2b	2	0	0	0					
Wellman, 2b	3	0	3	2					
Tabler, ph	1	0	0	0					
Stillwell, ss	0	0	0	0					
Totals	37	8	12	8	Totals	40	15	17	15

```
Kansas City . . . . . . . . . . . . . . . . . . . . 610 010 000 – 8
Toronto . . . . . . . . . . . . . . . . . . . . . . . 240 300 33x – 15
```

Kansas City	IP	H	R	ER	BB	SO
Bannister	1⅔	9	6	6	0	1
Saberhagen (L. 1-1)	2⅓	3	3	3	2	2
Montgomery	2	0	0	0	3	2
Gordon	1	2	3	3	3	2
Gleaton	1	3	3	3	1	0

Toronto	IP	H	R	ER	BB	SO
Stieb	⅓	4	6	6	3	0
Wells (W. 1-0)	4	6	2	2	1	3
Castillo (S1)	4⅔	2	0	0	1	2

E – None. DP – Toronto 1. LOB – Kansas City 9, Toronto 11.
2B – Jackson, Bell 2, McGriff, 2 Borders 2, Gruber, Pecota.
3B – Gruber. HR – Gruber (3), Barfield (4). SB – Pecota, Wellman, Brett, Moseby, Bell, Lawless. S – Moseby. SF – Wilson.
HBP – by Castillo (Boone). WP – Castillo
T – 3:38. A – 35,210.

When Kelly Gruber connected for the single he needed to complete the cycle, Mike Squires — the Jays first base coach — almost needed a lasso to rope the young Texan. Gruber's poke easily could have been a double, but Gruber remained anchored at first and made Blue Jays history.

Oddities and Others #15

APRIL 23, 28, 1989 • *Nelson Liriano*

How bad were things for the Blue Jays in April of 1989? Well, they set a new club record for losses in the opening month with 16. They lost 10 of 13 during one two-week stretch and were shut out three times — twice in a span of three days. They batted just .249 as a team and came within an inning of being no-hit twice in less than a week.

Nolan Ryan of the Texas Rangers seemed to be on the verge of his sixth career no-hitter when he blanked the Blue Jays through eight innings on April 23. He was forced to settle for his tenth career one-hitter and a 4–1 victory after Nelson Liriano lined a triple into right field with one out and came around to score on Kelly Gruber's grounder. Liriano was the "hero" again on April 28 after Canadian-born Kirk McCaskill held the Blue Jays hitless through eight. Pinch hitting for Tom Lawless to lead off the ninth, Liriano ripped a double into left center field but was left stranded on base as McCaskill also settled for a one-hitter and a 9–0 victory.

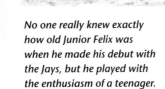

No one really knew exactly how old Junior Felix was when he made his debut with the Jays, but he played with the enthusiasm of a teenager.

Full Nelson: Nelson Liriano, a slap-hitting second baseman, broke up two no-hitters in a single week during the first month of the 1989 season.

Oddities and Others #16

MAY 4, 1989 • *Angels 3, Blue Jays 2*

Junior Felix was discovered by Blue Jays Latin American scout Epy Guerrero at a track meet when he was 18 years old. He had not played baseball since childhood, but the Blue Jays signed him and shipped him to their Medicine Hat rookie team in 1986. Felix hit .285 and stole 37 bases in 46 attempts. A year later, he was promoted to Class-A Myrtle Beach and hit .290 with 68 steals. He had 40 stolen bases at Double-A Knoxville in 1988 and was promoted to Triple-A Syracuse to begin the 1989 season. The switch-hitting Felix homered in his first at-bat with the Chiefs and had a .276 batting average with 13 steals in just 21 games when he got the call to Toronto on May 2.

The recent trade of Jesse Barfield had opened up a spot for an outfielder on the Blue Jays roster, and on May 3, 1989, Junior Felix made his major league debut as a defensive replacement in right field. The next day, Felix got his first major league start against the California Angels. He came to the plate for the first time in the third inning and, batting left against righty Kirk McCaskill, lined the first pitch he saw over the fence in right field. Felix was the 54th player in major league history to homer in his first at-bat, and just the 11th to do so on the very first pitch.

Despite the lift Junior Felix had given them, the Blue Jays were beaten 3–2 in 10 innings that night and were swept by the Angels in a three-game series. Soon, though, Felix would play a big part in the club's turnaround.

Great Moments #12

MAY 28, 1989 • *Blue Jays 7, White Sox 5*

After a three-game sweep by the Twins in Minnesota saw the Blue Jays' record fall to a dismal 12–24, Jimy Williams was fired as the club's manager on May 15. Hitting coach Cito Gaston was reluctant to accept the position as the Blue Jays' new manager, but agreed to take on the task until someone else could be found. One candidate was Bob Bailor, manager of the team's Syracuse farm club. Another was White Sox third base coach Terry Bevington. Secretly, the man Pat Gillick really wanted was Lou Piniella. Piniella had been fired by the Yankees after the 1988 season, but was still under contract. George Steinbrenner wanted more compensation than the Blue Jays GM was willing to give up, so Cito — who had put up seven wins in his first 11 games as bench boss — was still at the helm when the Blue Jays played their final game at the CNE grounds on May 28, 1989.

A crowd of 46,120 was on hand to say goodbye to baseball at Exhibition Stadium. The visitors for the last game were the same ones who had

(Above) Bell's blast. (Below) The Blue Jays bid bye-bye. The team had a record of 491–475 at Exhibition Stadium.

been there for the first — the Chicago White Sox. Doug Ault had been the hero back on a snowy day in 1977. This time it was George Bell who provided the longball excitement in the bottom of the tenth inning on a warm, sunny afternoon.

It had not looked like such heroics would be necessary as the game headed into the final innings. In the sixth, Pat Borders had put the Blue Jays ahead 3–2 with a two-run double and Lloyd Moseby followed with a two-run homer. Toronto took a 5–2 lead into the eighth inning, but Dave Stieb put the first two men on base and then Duane Ward allowed three runs to score. The White Sox had a chance to go ahead in the ninth, but Tom Henke ended the threat when he struck out Ivan Calderon on three straight pitches with a runner at third. He then pitched a scoreless tenth, allowing only an infield single.

Bobby Thigpen came on to face the Blue Jays in the bottom of the tenth and he promptly surrendered a leadoff double to Kelly Gruber. Thigpen threw a strike to George Bell, but when he tried to power an 0-and-1 fastball by him, Bell blasted it into the seats and the Blue Jays had a 7–5 victory.

"We came in here as winners and we're leaving as winners," said Cito Gaston. "It was a special feeling standing on the field before the game, but now the fans will have a better place to watch baseball."

Chicago	AB	R	H	RBI	Toronto	AB	R	H	RBI
Guillen, ss	4	0	0	0	Felix, rf	5	0	0	0
Gallagher, cf	4	1	2	0	Fernandez, ss	4	0	1	0
Baines, dh	4	1	2	0	Gruber, 3b	4	2	4	1
Calderon, rf	4	1	0	0	Bell, lf	4	2	1	2
Walker, 1b	3	1	2	0	McGriff, 1b	3	0	0	0
Manrique, 2b	2	0	1	1	Borders, dh	3	1	1	2
Lyons, 2b-3b	5	1	1	0	Mulliniks, ph	1	0	0	0
Pasqua, lf	4	0	2	3	Moseby, cf	4	1	1	2
Martinez, 3b-1b	4	0	0	0	Brenly, c	2	1	1	0
Merullo, c	4	0	1	1	Whitt, ph-c	1	0	0	0
Karkovice, c	0	0	0	0	Liriano, 2b	4	0	1	0
Totals	**38**	**5**	**11**	**5**	**Totals**	**35**	**7**	**10**	**7**

Chicago					.010	100	030	0 – 5	
Toronto					.001	004	000	2 – 7	

None out when winning run scored

Chicago	IP	H	R	ER	BB	SO
Rosenberg	5	3	3	3	5	2
Reuss	⅓	2	2	2	0	0
McCarthy	3	3	0	0	0	1
Thigpen (L. 0-1)	⅔	2	2	2	0	0

Toronto	IP	H	R	ER	BB	SO
Stieb	7	8	4	3	1	4
Ward	1⅓	2	1	1	2	0
Wells	⅓	0	0	0	0	0
Henke (W 3-3)	1⅓	1	0	0	0	3

Rosenberg pitched to two batters in sixth
Stieb pitched to two batters in eighth
Thigpen pitched to two batters in tenth

E – Gruber, Merullo. DP – Chicago 1, Toronto 1. LOB – Chicago 9, Toronto 6. 2B – Gallagher, Fernandez, Merullo, Walker, Baines, Borders, Gruber 2, Liriano. HR – Moseby (5), Bell (6). SB – McGriff, Gruber, Lyons. S – Gallagher. SF – Pasqua. HBP – by Stieb (Martinez).
T – 3:19. A – 46,120.

1989

Great Moments #13

JUNE 2–4, 1989 • *Blue Jays vs. Red Sox*

Following the finale at Exhibition Stadium, the Blue Jays left town for a six-game road trip. The first stop was Cleveland where, despite three losses to the Indians, it was officially announced that Cito Gaston had agreed to become the full-time manager. The Blue Jays responded with an emotional sweep of the Boston Red Sox in a weekend series that featured Junior Felix in the starring role.

The Blue Jays were trying to win their tenth straight game at Fenway Park as they clung to a 3–2 lead in the latter innings of the series opener on Friday night. Duane Ward had just escaped a bases-loaded jam in the bottom of the eighth, and now the Blue Jays had three runners on board in the top of the ninth. That's when Felix lofted a long drive into center field. The ball barely eluded the glove of Ellis Burks and while he chased it, Ernie Whitt, Rance Mulliniks and Nelson Liriano came in to score as Junior raced around the bases behind them. When he dove safely across home plate he became the first (and only) player in Blue Jays history to hit an inside-the-park grand slam and Toronto had a 7–2 victory. Felix drove in four more runs in a 10–2 romp on Saturday afternoon — but the best was yet to come!

In the Sunday game, the Blue Jays sent raw rookie Alex Sanchez to the mound for his third major league start, but Boston knocked him out with five runs in the first inning. The score was 10–0 for the Red Sox after six innings but, as they say, no lead is safe in Fenway Park and the Blue Jays began to chip away. They scored two runs in the top of the seventh, then four in the top of the eighth, and when Tony Fernandez led off the ninth with an infield single, Boston manager Joe Morgan called on his closer to protect what was now just a four-run lead. Lee Smith responded by walking Kelly Gruber and serving up an RBI double to George Bell. After Fred McGriff struck out, Smith walked Lloyd Moseby to load the bases for Ernie Whitt.

"I was just trying to get a hit to keep the momentum going," said the Blue Jays catcher later. "I wasn't thinking home run." But he crushed the ball into the right field seats and suddenly the Blue Jays had an 11–10 lead. The Red Sox tied it off Tom Henke in the bottom of the ninth and had a chance to win, but David Wells came on to retire Marty Barrett with two runners on and the game headed into extra innings.

Duane Ward and former Blue Jay Dennis Lamp battled through the tenth and 11th before Tom Lawless led off the top of the 12th with a single. After a sacrifice bunt from Nelson Liriano, Junior Felix belted a two-run homer to center field, giving the Blue Jays a sweep of the Red Sox and the rookie outfielder 11 RBIs in the three-game series.

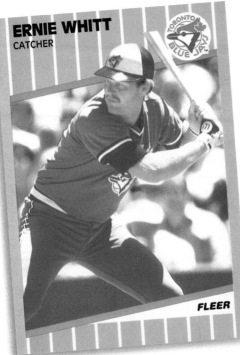

Ernie Whitt (left) and Junior Felix (right) were the heroes of the Fenway field day.

Toronto	AB	R	H	RBI	Boston	AB	R	H	RBI
Felix, rf	4	3	2	4	Reed, ss	5	0	1	0
Fernandez, ss	5	0	1	1	Barrett, 2b	4	0	1	0
Gruber, 3b	4	0	1	0	Boggs, 3b	3	1	1	0
Bell, lf	3	0	1	1	Greenwell, lf	3	0	0	1
McGriff, 1b	4	0	1	0	Evans, dh	2	0	0	0
Moseby, cf	4	0	1	0	Burks, cf	4	0	0	0
Whitt, c	3	1	1	0	Esasky, 1b	4	1	2	0
Mulliniks, dh	4	1	0	0	Kutcher, rf	2	0	1	0
Liriano, 2b	3	2	1	0	Heep, ph-rf	1	0	0	0
					Cerone, c	3	0	1	1
					Horn, ph	1	0	0	0
Totals	34	7	9	6	**Totals**	32	2	7	2

Toronto ....102 000 004 – 7
Boston ....000 011 000 – 2

Toronto	IP	H	R	ER	BB	SO
Cerutti (W. 2-3)	5⅓	5	2	2	3	1
Ward (S4)	3⅔	2	0	0	2	3

Boston	IP	H	R	ER	BB	SO
Dopson (L. 5-4)	3⅔	4	3	3	2	2
Murphy	3⅓	3	0	0	0	4
Stanley	2	2	4	0	1	1

E– Liriano, Cerone, Barrett, Reed. DP – Toronto 2, Boston 1. LOB – Toronto 4, Boston 9. 2B – Fernandez, Bell, McGriff. 3B – Boggs. HR – Felix (3). SB – Liriano. SF – Bell. HBP – by Ward (Boggs). Balk – Dopson.
T – 3:05. A – 33,548.

Toronto	AB	R	H	RBI	Boston	AB	R	H	RBI
Felix, rf	5	0	3	4	Boggs, 3b	4	0	2	1
Fernandez, ss	5	0	1	0	Barrett, 2b	4	0	0	0
Infante, ss	0	0	0	0	Heep, 1b	2	0	1	0
Gruber, 3b	4	0	0	0	Esasky, ph-1b	1	0	0	0
Bell, lf	4	1	1	0	Greenwell, lf	4	0	1	0
Ducey, lf	0	0	0	0	Evans, rf	3	1	1	0
McGriff, 1b	4	3	2	1	Burks, cf	4	1	2	0
Moseby, cf	5	3	3	1	Horn, dh	2	0	0	0
Whitt, c	3	1	1	0	Quintana, dh	2	0	1	0
Mulliniks, dh	2	1	1	1	Gedman, c	4	0	1	1
Liriano, 2b	5	1	1	1	Romero, ss	4	0	2	0
Totals	37	10	13	10	**Totals**	34	2	9	2

Toronto ....010 401 031 – 10
Boston ....020 000 000 – 2

Toronto	IP	H	R	ER	BB	SO
Stieb (W. 4-3)	5	7	2	2	2	2
Wells	3	2	0	0	0	2
Henke	1	0	0	0	0	2

Boston	IP	H	R	ER	BB	SO
Boddicker (L. 3-5)	5⅔	9	6	5	3	3
Lamp	1⅓	2	3	3	3	1
Price	1	0	0	0	0	0
Smith	1	1	1	1	0	1

Lamp pitched to four batters in eighth

E – Burks, Evans. DP – Toronto 1, Boston 1. LOB – Toronto 6, Boston 7. 2B – Mulliniks, Burks, Greenwell. HR – McGriff (12), Moseby (6). SB – Moseby, Liriano.
T – 3:05. A – 33,942.

Toronto	AB	R	H	RBI	Boston	AB	R	H	RBI
Felix, rf	7	1	3	3	Reed, ss	6	1	1	1
Fernandez, ss	7	1	2	0	Romero, 2b	6	2	1	0
Gruber, 3b	6	1	1	0	Boggs, 3b	4	2	2	0
Bell, lf	6	2	2	1	Greenwell, lf	3	2	2	1
McGriff, 1b	6	1	1	0	Heep, rf	0	0	0	0
Moseby, cf	4	1	1	0	Horn, 1b	1	0	0	0
Whitt, c	5	2	2	4	Evans, rf	3	1	2	0
Mulliniks, dh	3	1	2	1	Burks, cf	4	1	2	5
Lawless, pr-dh	1	1	1	0	Kutcher, rf	1	0	0	0
Liriano, 2b	5	0	1	1	Quintana, dh	5	1	1	0
					Esasky, 1b-lf	5	1	1	0
					Gedman, c	5	0	1	0
Totals	50	13	16	12	**Totals**	44	11	13	9

Toronto ....000 000 245 002 – 13
Boston ....511 102 001 000 – 11

Toronto	IP	H	R	ER	BB	SO
Sanchez	⅓	5	5	5	3	0
Hernandez	6⅔	8	5	2	3	2
Henke	1⅔	2	1	1	0	3
Wells	⅓	0	0	0	0	0
Ward (W. 2-6)	3	0	0	0	1	3

Boston	IP	H	R	ER	BB	SO
Smithson	6	4	2	2	3	5
Stanley	1⅔	3	5	4	1	1
Murphy	⅓	2	1	1	0	0
Smith	⅓	1	1	0	2	1
Lamp (L. 0-1)	3⅔	3	2	2	0	0

Smithson pitched to two batters in seventh
Murphy pitched to one batter in ninth

E – McGriff 3, Bell. DP – Toronto 1, Boston 1. LOB – Toronto 8, Boston 12. 2B – Felix, Mulliniks, Quintana, Burks. HR – Burks (7), Whitt (5), Felix (4). SB – Lawless. S – Kutcher, Gedman, Burks, Liriano. SF – Evans, Burks.
T – 4:36. A – 33,760.

Famous Firsts and Records #17

JUNE 5, 1989 • *Brewers 5, Blue Jays 3*

Talk of building a domed stadium in Toronto had begun about the same time the Blue Jays began playing baseball at Exhibition Stadium, but it was the rain and sleet at the 1982 Grey Cup football game between the Argos and Edmonton that finally got the ball rolling. Slowly, but surely, plans were approved, and in April of 1986, site preparation began at the foot of the CN Tower. Groundbreaking took place in October of that year. It was hoped that construction could be completed by the beginning of the 1989 season, but delays moved the date back a few months. An opening gala was held on June 3, 1989, and two days later, the SkyDome was finally ready for baseball.

With 48,378 fans on hand — the largest baseball crowd to that point in Toronto history — Jimmy Key tossed the first pitch at the SkyDome for a strike past Paul Molitor of the Milwaukee Brewers. Two pitches later, Molitor doubled to left field for the new stadium's first hit. After Robin Yount laid down a sacrifice bunt, Molitor scored the first run on a Gary Sheffield ground out.

The Blue Jays began making their own SkyDome history in the second inning when Fred McGriff slugged the first home run with George Bell aboard on a walk. McGriff would later steal the first base in the sixth inning, but by then the Brewers had taken a 5–2 lead. Bell slugged a home run in the bottom of the eighth and Bob Brenly appeared to tie the game for the Blue Jays three batters later when he lifted a long fly ball to left field with a runner on base.

"I thought it was out," admitted the Brewers' Glenn Braggs, who drifted back to make the catch.

"There were maybe five or six balls we hit that would have gone out [at Exhibition Stadium]," said manager Cito Gaston.

"I've never had any luck hitting in this park," cracked Brenly.

When the Brewers held on for a 5–3 win, the Blue Jays became the eighth consecutive major league team to open its new stadium with a loss. After Milwaukee won again the following night, the Blue Jays recorded their first Dome victory with a 4–2 win on June 7.

Dome Opener: Cambridge, Ontario's Rob Ducey warms up before the first game at the SkyDome. (Inset) Ernie Whitt and Fred McGriff pose for a publicity shot prior to the Dome's official opening.

AUGUST 4, 1989 • *Blue Jays 2, Yankees 1*

With the two near misses of 1988 still fresh in his mind, Dave Stieb finally made history against the New York Yankees . . . but not the kind of history he would have liked. Stieb became the first (and only) pitcher in baseball history to lose three no-hit bids with two out in the ninth inning. Only this time, he lost more than just a no-hitter. Stieb lost a perfect game.

"I don't care," he told reporters afterwards. "No-hitters are bonuses. It's all luck anyway. They hit balls at guys all night. I'm not making them hit it there." But later Stieb admitted that it had been very exciting. "It'll probably bother me a lot more tomorrow," he said.

Heading into the ninth inning, Stieb had retired all 24 batters to face him. The Yankees were marvelling at his devastating slider, but actually "most of the damage was done by my curve. It was really working." With a record SkyDome crowd of 48,789 roaring on every pitch, Stieb used the curve to strike out pinch hitters Hal Morris and Ken Phelps to begin the ninth, giving him a season-high 11 Ks for the game and bringing ninth hitter Roberto Kelly to the plate. Stieb had only thrown two balls to three hitters all night, but he quickly fell behind Kelly 2-and-0. On the next pitch, the Yankees center fielder slashed a double into left.

"I knew he had a perfect game," said Kelly, "and I wanted to break it up. Besides we were still in the game, only two runs down." When Steve Sax followed Kelly's double with an RBI single, the Blue Jays' lead was cut to 2–1 and suddenly Stieb might lose the game as well. With both Duane Ward and Tom Henke warmed up, Cito Gaston went to the mound but decided to leave Stieb in to face Luis Polonia. Polonia ripped a ground ball to Kelly Gruber, who snared it and threw to second for the final out.

"If I haven't got the no-hitter by now," said Stieb, "I doubt I ever will."

(Above) Dave Stieb missed out on another no-hitter in 1989, but his time was going to come. (Right) The infectious spirit and tremendous tenacity of Mookie Wilson delighted the fans. Acquired from the New York Mets, "the Mookster" stole 46 bases and was caught only eight times during his tenure with Toronto.

Great Moments #14

SEPTEMBER 29–30, 1989 • *Blue Jays vs. Orioles*

After their dismal start to the 1989 season, the Blue Jays did not pull over .500 to stay until August 15, but by September 1 they had passed the surprising Baltimore Orioles for first place in the American League East. The acquisitions of Lee Mazzilli and, especially, Mookie Wilson, had helped propel the Blue Jays to a club-record 20 wins in August and set the stage for an exciting September. The Blue Jays were in first place throughout the month, but were never more than 2½ games ahead of Baltimore. The lead was down to just a single game when the Orioles came to the SkyDome for the final series of the season.

In the lid-lifter on Friday night, Baltimore's Phil Bradley jumped on starter Todd Stottlemyre for a solo homer on the first pitch of the game. Both teams had plenty of opportunities to score, but the O's clung to a 1–0 lead until the eighth inning when the Blue Jays finally tied the game. A single, a steal, a ground out and a wild pitch by bullpen ace Gregg Olson allowed Tom Lawless to race home with the tying run. The game remained deadlocked until the 11th inning, when the Orioles elected to walk Junior Felix and pitch to Lloyd Moseby with two out. Moseby responded by drilling a Mark Williamson offering off the wall in left-center to drive home Nelson Liriano with the winning run.

The following afternoon, the Blue Jays put the finishing touches on one of their most exciting seasons with yet another come-from-behind victory. From the start it looked as though luck was conspiring against Baltimore. Scheduled starter Pete Harnisch stepped on a nail while returning to his hotel room on Friday night and had to be scratched, but spot starter Dave Johnson took his place and baffled the Blue Jays for seven innings, pitching on guts and adrenaline. The Orioles carried a 3–1 lead into the eighth inning, but when Johnson walked Nelson Liriano to lead off, manager Frank Robinson went to the bullpen. Kevin Hickey came on to walk Rob Ducey, then Mark Williamson was summoned to face Lloyd Moseby once again. This time "the Shaker" dropped down a sacrifice bunt to move the tying runs into scoring position. Mookie Wilson followed with a single to drive home one run and Fred McGriff cashed in another. George Bell then

Ernie Whitt leaps into Tom Henke's arms after "the Terminator" nailed down the final out. Kelly Gruber and Dave Stieb are ready to celebrate, while Orioles coach Cal Ripken Sr. beats a hasty retreat.

stepped up to the plate and lifted a high fly ball to right field. It easily scored Wilson, who had hustled around to third on McGriff's single, and suddenly the Blue Jays had a 4–3 lead. Tom Henke took over from there. He mowed down the Orioles in the ninth, striking out Larry Sheets for the final out as the Jays rushed onto the field to celebrate their second divisional flag.

Tom Henke cries champagne tears after saving the pennant-clinching win in 1989.

Baltimore	AB	R	H	RBI	Toronto	AB	R	H	RBI
PBradley, lf	5	1	2	1	Moseby, cf	3	0	2	1
Hulett, 2b	4	0	0	0	MWilson, lf	4	0	1	0
BRipken, 2b	1	0	0	0	McGriff, 1b	4	0	0	0
CRipken, ss	5	0	2	0	Lawless, pr	0	1	0	0
Orsulak, rf	3	0	1	0	Olerud, 1b	1	0	0	0
SFinley, rf	1	0	0	0	Bell, dh	4	0	0	0
Milligan, 1b	4	0	1	0	Gruber, 3b	5	0	1	0
Tettleton, dh	1	0	0	0	Fernandez, ss	3	0	0	0
JBell, pr	0	0	0	0	Lee, 2b	5	0	1	0
Sheets, ph	1	0	0	0	Liriano, pr	0	1	0	0
Worthington, 3b	5	0	0	0	Borders, c	3	0	2	0
Devereaux, cf	1	0	0	0	Whitt, c	2	0	0	0
Quirk, c	4	0	0	0	Hill, rf	2	0	1	0
					Mazzilli, ph	1	0	1	0
					Felix, rf	0	0	0	0
Totals	**39**	**1**	**7**	**1**	**Totals**	**37**	**2**	**9**	**1**

Baltimore						100	000	000	00 – 1
Toronto						000	000	010	01 – 2

Two out when winning run scored

Baltimore	IP	H	R	ER	BB	SO
Ballard	7⅓	6	1	1	4	3
Olson	2⅔	1	0	0	2	2
Williamson (L. 10-4)	⅔	2	1	1	1	0

Toronto	IP	H	R	ER	BB	SO
Stottlemyre	5	4	1	1	3	2
Acker	4	2	0	0	2	3
DWard	0	1	0	0	0	0
Henke (W. 8-3)	2	0	0	0	0	4

DWard pitched to one batter in tenth

E – None. DP – None. LOB – Baltimore 11, Toronto 12. 2B – CRipken, Borders, Gruber, Milligan. HR – PBradley (11). SB – Moseby (24), PBradley (20), Milligan (9), Lawless (12). S – Moseby, MWilson. HBP – by Stottlemyre (Tettleton). WP – Olson.
T – 3:57. A – 49,636.

Baltimore	AB	R	H	RBI	Toronto	AB	R	H	RBI
PBradley, lf	4	1	2	1	Moseby, cf	2	1	0	0
Jefferson, rf	4	0	1	0	MWilson, lf	4	1	1	1
SFinley, rf	0	0	0	0	McGriff, 1b	4	0	1	1
CRipken, ss	4	1	1	1	Bell, dh	3	0	1	2
Milligan, 1b	4	0	1	1	Fernandez, ss	4	0	0	0
Worthington, 3b	4	0	0	0	Whitt, c	2	0	0	0
Tettleton, dh	4	0	0	0	Gruber, 3b	3	0	1	0
Devereaux, cf	3	1	2	0	Liriano, 2b	2	1	0	0
Orsulak, ph	1	0	0	0	Felix, rf	2	0	0	0
Melvin, c	3	0	1	0	Lee, ph	0	0	0	0
Sheets, ph	1	0	0	0	Ducey, rf	0	1	0	0
Hulett, 2b	3	0	1	0					
Totals	**35**	**3**	**9**	**3**	**Totals**	**26**	**4**	**4**	**4**

Baltimore						002	100	000 – 3
Toronto						100	000	03x – 4

Baltimore	IP	H	R	ER	BB	SO
DJohnson	7	2	2	2	3	0
Hickey	0	0	1	1	1	0
Williamson (L. 10-5)	1	2	1	1	0	0

Toronto	IP	H	R	ER	BB	SO
Key	8	3	3	3	0	6
Wills (W. 3-1)	4	1	0	0	0	1
Henke (S20)	1	0	0	0	0	2

DJohnson pitched to one batter in eighth
Hickey pitched to two batters in eighth

E – None. DP – None. LOB – Baltimore 5, Toronto 4. 2B – Jefferson, Devereaux, CRipken, Melvin, Gruber, Hulett. SB – Jefferson (10).
S – Moseby. SF – Bell.
T – 2:52. A – 49,553.

Playoff Moments #6

Their lineup boasted the game's best leadoff man in Rickey Henderson, followed by sluggers like Carney Lansford, Jose Canseco and Mark McGwire. Their pitching staff had three of the American League's four winningest pitchers in Dave Stewart (21–9), Storm Davis (19–7) and Mike Moore (19–11), plus Bob Welch, who had won 17 games in 1989 and would win 27 in 1990. The Oakland A's had won 104 games in 1988, yet lost the World Series to the Los Angeles Dodgers. They won 99 games in 1989 and were looking for greater success in the postseason.

Oakland was a team that could win with power, but, led by cerebral manager Tony LaRussa (one of only five managers in major league history to hold a law degree), the A's played as much with their minds as their muscle. Yet their script for success was simple: take an early lead, protect it until the late innings, then turn the ball over to ace closer Dennis Eckersley. It was a blueprint the A's followed to near perfection against Toronto in the 1989 American League Championship Series.

The Blue Jays actually led the series opener in Oakland 3–2 after five innings until a hard slide into second by Henderson in the bottom of the sixth forced a throwing error by Nelson Liriano. Oakland scored a pair of unearned runs and went on to a 7–3 victory. Henderson, who had riled the Blue Jays by stealing second without even bothering to slide, then had two timely hits and four stolen bases in Game Two as Oakland won 6–3. Dave Parker homered for the A's in that one and further added to Toronto's frustration with his long, slow trot around the bases.

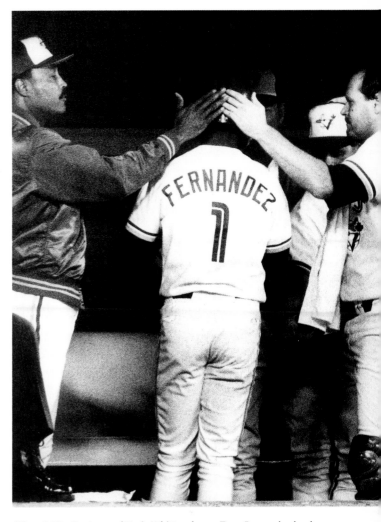

(Above) Cito Gaston and Ernie Whitt welcome Tony Fernandez back to the dugout after a key at-bat. (Left) Rickey Henderson's hustle on the basepaths harassed the Blue Jays throughout the 1989 ALCS. He stole a record-setting eight bases during the series.

After a day of travel, the American League Championship Series resumed with Game Three at the SkyDome. The Blue Jays were badly in need of a win, but it didn't look like they'd get it as Rickey Henderson scored a pair of runs and Oakland jumped out to a 2–0 lead after three. The A's scored again in the top of the fourth, but the Blue Jays scored four times in the bottom of the inning to take the lead. The key drive came from Tony Fernandez, who doubled in Mookie Wilson. When Jose Canseco misplayed the ball in right, Fred McGriff also came in to score. A bloop single from Ernie Whitt then plated Fernandez, who shouted in triumph as he crossed the plate with the go-ahead run. Toronto later put the game away with three more runs in the bottom of the seventh, highlighted by another Fernandez double.

A crowd of more than 50,000 had been much louder that night than the usual assemblage of Blue Jays fans. As they celebrated the 7–3 victory, there was a real feeling that the team was right back in the series.

Playoff Moments #7

Good as he had been in the first three games of the 1989 American League Championship Series, it was Rickey Henderson's performance in the last two that really made the difference. In the end, he would hit .400 with a .609 on-base percentage and a 1.000 slugging percentage, score eight runs and steal a postseason-record eight bases.

After two scoreless innings in Game Four, Oakland got on the board when Henderson took Mike Flanagan deep for a two-run homer. Two batters later, Jose Canseco came to the plate. He had been one of baseball's most feared sluggers since belting 33 home runs and being named the American League Rookie of

the Year in 1986. He became baseball's first 40–40 man with 42 homers and 40 steals in 1988, but in 1989 he had gone deep just 17 times after injuries forced him to miss the first 88 games of the season. Obviously, he was still a dangerous hitter, and in the third inning of Game Four, Canseco became the first player to hit a fair ball into the fifth deck at SkyDome. The heroic homer landed in the fifth row of section 540, a distance of some 480 feet from home plate.

After the Blue Jays got on the scoreboard in the bottom of the fourth, Henderson upped the lead to 5–1 when he rocketed another two-run shot into the seats in dead center field. After Toronto scored again in the sixth, Canseco pushed Oakland's lead to 6–2 with an RBI single in the top of the seventh. The Blue Jays struck back with a run in the bottom of the inning and two more in the eighth, but Dennis Eckersley put out the flames to earn his second save of the series in a 6–5 win.

In Game Five, Oakland broke out to a 1–0 lead when Henderson singled, stole second and scored on a Canseco base hit. The lead was up to 4–0 after seven, but the Blue Jays finally got on the board when Lloyd Moseby launched a solo homer in the bottom of the eighth. A George Bell homer and a sacrifice fly from Kelly Gruber brought Toronto within a run of the A's in the ninth. Tempers flared when Cito Gaston accused Eckersley of scuffing the ball, but after a few minutes of gesturing and finger-pointing, Oakland wrapped up the series with a 4–3 victory.

(Left) Canseco connects: The SkyDome would become Jose's personal launching pad, as his 17 home runs there are the most by an opposing player. He hit 25 at the Dome as a Blue Jay in 1998. (Below) Better luck next year: The Blue Jays say goodbye to the fans after their ALCS loss to the A's.

1990

86–76 .531 2nd -2

The Blue Jays finished two games behind the Boston Red Sox. Kelly Gruber had a career year (31 HR, 118 RBI) while Fred McGriff (35 HR), John Olerud (14 HR, 48 RBI) and Glenallen Hill (12 HR) all made fine contributions. The pitching staff was anchored by Dave Stieb (18–6), Jimmy Key (13–7) and David Wells (11–6). Tom Henke and Duane Ward combined for 43 saves. The highlight of the season came on September 2, when Stieb recorded the first no-hitter in Blue Jays history.

Pat Borders became the Jays' number-one catcher in 1990, hitting .286 with 15 homers and 49 RBIs.

Kelly Gruber was at home at third and at the dish in 1990, setting career highs with 31 homers and 118 RBIs, totals that ranked him fifth and second respectively in the American League. He also won a Gold Glove. Kelly played in the All-Star Game in 1990 and stole two bases, tying a record set by Willie Mays.

Bad Breaks, Near Misses and Disappointments #21

JUNE 29, 1990 • *Athletics 5, Blue Jays 0*

The Blue Jays had just been knocked out of first place by the Red Sox in a four-game series sweep at Boston when they returned to the SkyDome to begin a four-gamer against Oakland. Things didn't get any better that Friday night as Athletics ace Dave Stewart pitched the first no-hitter in Toronto since the Blue Jays had entered the American League in 1977.

Stewart walked the first two men he faced that night before retiring the next 26 batters in a row. After a two-out walk to Junior Felix in the bottom of the ninth, Stewart got Tony Fernandez on a routine fly out to complete this masterpiece.

"By far the highlight of my career," said Stewart afterwards. "I've never pitched a no-hitter. Never even came close. Not in the minors or even in Little League. This is something I'll remember always."

The only close call of the evening came when Fred McGriff led off the bottom of the eighth with a towering fly ball to center field.

"My heart stopped for a moment," admitted Stewart, "but he hit it to the deepest part of the park. I knew it would stay in. I'm just glad that [Dave Henderson] ran it down."

Later that night in Los Angeles, Dodgers pitcher Fernando Valenzuela tossed a no-hitter at the St. Louis Cardinals, marking the first time in 92 years that no-hit games had been pitched on the same day.

Dave Stewart was masterful on the evening of June 29, 1990, as he no-hit the Blue Jays for the only no-no ever tossed in Toronto.

Great Moments #15

SEPTEMBER 2, 1990 • *Blue Jays 3, Indians 0*

When he wrote his autobiography in 1986, Dave Stieb had called it *Tomorrow I'll Be Perfect*. Over the years, the title had become almost like a curse — particularly when he lost three no-hit bids with two out in the ninth inning. But on a cool September Sunday in Cleveland, Dave Stieb really was perfect — or at least close enough — as he finally became the first (and only) Blue Jays pitcher to toss a no-hitter. It was the ninth no-hit game in the major leagues in 1990. Never before had there been more than six tossed in a single season.

Stieb walked leadoff hitter Alex Cole to begin the game and later threw four balls to Carlos Baerga with two out in the second. Both baserunners were erased trying to steal, and Stieb settled into a groove when he struck out the side in the third inning. That's when he began to think about a no-hitter. "But I wasn't living and dying on every pitch," he said, "because when I've thought about no-hitters in the past it's always been too soon."

Amen!: Dave Stieb finally erased years of frustration when he pitched the first — and only — no-hitter in team history, whitewashing the Cleveland Indians 3–0.

Fred McGriff put the Blue Jays in front 1–0 with a home run in the top of the fourth and Manny Lee upped the lead to 2–0 with an RBI double in the fifth. Given some runs to work with, Stieb continued to retire the Indians in order through seven innings. He then survived his first close call of the afternoon when Ken Phelps ripped a pitch down the right field line to lead off the eighth.

It hooked a few feet foul.

Phelps eventually worked Stieb for a leadoff walk, but he recovered to retire the next three in a row. After McGriff socked

Fred McGriff, whose fourth-inning home run provided Stieb with all the offensive support he would need on no-hitter day, was a key part of the blockbuster trade that brought Joe Carter and Robbie Alomar to Toronto.

another solo homer, Stieb returned to the mound to work the bottom of the ninth.

First to face him was pinch hitter Chris James.

Stieb retired him on a fly out.

Then Candy Maldonado came off the bench.

Stieb got him swinging at strike three.

Two out.

Again.

But it turned out that the fourth time was a charm for Dave Stieb. After Alex Cole walked on four straight pitches, Jerry Browne lined a ball into right field where Junior Felix caught it for the final out.

Toronto	AB	R	H	RBI	Cleveland	AB	R	H	RBI
Wilson, dh	4	0	0	0	Cole, cf	2	0	0	0
Fernandez, ss	4	0	2	0	Browne, 2b	4	0	0	0
Gruber, 3b	3	0	0	0	DJames, lf	3	0	0	0
McGriff, 1b	4	2	2	2	Phelps, dh	2	0	0	0
Borders, c	4	0	1	0	Jacoby, 1b	3	0	0	0
Hill, lf	4	0	1	0	Baerga, 2b	2	0	0	0
Williams, cf	4	1	1	0	Snyder, rf	3	0	0	0
Lee, 2b	4	0	1	1	Brookens, 3b	2	0	0	0
Felix, rf	3	0	0	0	CJames, ph	1	0	0	0
					Skinner, c	2	0	0	0
					Maldonado, ph	1	0	0	0
Totals	34	3	8	3	Totals	25	0	0	0

Toronto				.000 110 001 – 3
Cleveland				.000 000 000 – 0

Toronto	IP	H	R	ER	BB	SO
Stieb (W. 17-5)	9	0	0	0	4	9

Cleveland	IP	H	R	ER	BB	S
Black (L. 10-9)	7	5	2	2	1	5
Orosco	1	2	1	1	0	1
Olin	1	1	0	0	0	0

Orosco pitched to one batter in ninth

E – DJames. LOB – Toronto 5, Cleveland 2. 2B – Williams, Lee. HR – McGriff 2 (31).
T – 2:27. A – 23,640.

OCTOBER 3, 1990 • *Orioles 3, Blue Jays 2*

Though they had held down first place at times throughout the season, the Blue Jays never really found their stride in 1990 — but they were never really out of contention either. They fell as far as 6½ games out of first place in late August, but a stretch of 12 wins in 14 games in early September put them back on top. The Blue Jays actually led the Red Sox by a game-and-a-half on September 24, but five losses in their next six games had them on the verge of elimination. Still, the Blue Jays had an opportunity to force a tiebreaking playoff in the AL East when the season — extended three extra days because of a lockout in spring training — reached its final game.

The Blue Jays had kept their chances alive with a 2–1 victory over the Orioles the night before, but they had needed help from the Chicago White Sox, who beat the Red Sox in 13 innings. Now the Blue Jays would have to beat Baltimore again and hope for another Chicago victory. Toronto players were watching the out-of-town scoreboard as they entered the final inning of their game in Baltimore, so they knew the White Sox were staging a furious rally at Fenway Park. Unfortunately, the Chicago comeback was snuffed out when Boston's Tom Brunansky made a miraculous sliding catch in the right field corner at Fenway Park. The Red Sox had clinched the division. Moments later, a demoralized Tom Henke served up a game-losing home run.

The disappointing end to an underachieving season prompted big changes on the Blue Jays. Pat Gillick had earned the nickname "Stand Pat" for his reluctance to make major moves in recent years, but he was about to lose that reputation for good. On December 2, 1990, Gillick sent Junior Felix and two other players to the California Angels in a deal that gave the Blue Jays Devon White. Three days later, he pulled off one of the biggest trades in baseball history, sending Fred McGriff and Tony Fernandez to the San Diego Padres for Joe Carter and Roberto Alomar.

Big Tom Henke continued to be the ace in the Blue Jays bullpen in 1990, recording 32 saves and a sparkling 2.17 ERA. The bespectacled bricklayer from Missouri struck out 644 batters in only 563 innings during his career with the Jays for an average of 10.29 Ks per nine innings pitched.

1991

91–71 .562 1st +7

Pat Gillick completely rebuilt the roster of the Toronto Blue Jays, highlighted by a blockbuster trade for Joe Carter and Roberto Alomar. The new additions helped the Jays win their third AL East title, but the club faltered in the playoffs, losing to Minnesota. The loss overshadowed the contributions of newcomer Juan Guzman (10–3), Alomar (.295, 53 steals), Carter (33 HR, 108 RBI), Tom Henke (32 saves) and Todd Stottlemyre (13–8, 3.78 ERA).

Roberto Alomar is a study in grace as he effortlessly avoids a sliding Minnesota Twins player and relays his throw to first base.

Bad Breaks, Near Misses and Disappointments #23

MAY 1, 1991 • Rangers 3, Blue Jays 0

The Blue Jays had held down first place for most of April, but May 1 found them a half-game behind the Boston Red Sox on what would become a memorable day in baseball history. In a game played earlier that afternoon, Rickey Henderson had surpassed Lou Brock with his 939th stolen base and declared himself "the greatest of all time." But that evening, Nolan Ryan knocked Henderson out of the next day's headlines.

The Texas Rangers had not been expecting much when Ryan took to the mound against the Blue Jays. He'd been complaining about pain in his back and his legs while warming up in the bullpen. Ryan did strike out Devon White to get the game under way, but after retiring Roberto Alomar, he walked Kelly Gruber and appeared to be uncomfortable. Still, he got Joe Carter to end the inning. In the second, Ryan fanned John Olerud and Glenallen Hill with sharp-breaking curveballs. In the third, he got Manny Lee on a changeup and it was apparent that he had all of his pitches working.

By the fourth inning, the fans at Arlington Stadium began to sense something special. The Rangers had given Ryan a 3–0 lead and he responded by striking out Alomar, popping up Gruber and fanning Carter. In the fifth, Olerud popped up, Mark Whiten flew out and Hill was K'd a second time. Ryan rang up his tenth strikeout victim when he fanned Greg Myers to open the sixth, but then Manny Lee got his bat on the ball and lofted a little looper into center field.

"I thought Lee's hit had a chance to fall in," admitted Ryan later, but Gary Pettis raced in to make the grab.

In the seventh, Ryan struck out Alomar again, then whiffed Gruber on three pitches. Carter worked him for a walk, but Olerud popped up and Ryan left the mound to chants of "NO-LAN, NO-LAN!" Whiten lined his first offering of the eighth into right field — but right at Ruben Sierra. Then Hill and Myers went down on strikes.

The "NO-LAN" chant was deafening when Ryan took to the mound for the ninth inning. He retired Manny Lee on a weak grounder to second, then got Devon White on another ground ball. Then Roberto Alomar came to the plate. He swung at strike one, then fouled off a pitch. After Ryan threw a ball, Robbie fouled off two in a row. Then he swung and missed. Ryan had his 16th strikeout of the night and had pitched the seventh no-hitter of his remarkable career.

The best of the American and National leagues line up along the chalk at the 1991 Midseason Classic. Devon White (insert), who was nearly out of baseball after a dismal 1990 season with the California Angels, was a ballerina in the Blue Jays outfield, making center field his stage and the fans his audience. (Below) Joe Carter delivers a sweet single during the 1991 All-Star Game in Toronto.

Famous Firsts and Records #18

JULY 9, 1991 • *All-Star Game*

In 1991, the All-Star Game was held outside the United States for just the second time in baseball history. The city of Montreal had hosted the Mid-Summer Classic at Olympic Stadium back in 1982. Now it was Toronto's turn.

Roberto Alomar, whose defensive brilliance and clutch hitting had made him an instant fan favourite, became just the second Blue Jay to be voted to the AL's starting lineup. He would be joined on the team by Joe Carter, whose American League Player of the Month performance in June (.352/11 HRs/29 RBIs) had vaulted the Blue Jays into first place. Jimmy Key, who'd gone 10–4 in the first half, was also added to the All-Star Team. Festivities at the SkyDome got underway on July 8 with the All-Star workout, oldtimers game and a home run contest. The AL foursome of Carter, Danny Tartabull, Cecil Fielder and Cal Ripken out-powered National Leaguers Chris Sabo, Paul O'Neill, Howard Johnson and former Blue Jay George Bell by a score of 20–7. The star of the show was Ripken, who slugged 12 longballs into the SkyDome seats. Ripken was the hero again the following night when his three-run homer sparked the American League to a 4–2 victory.

A crowd of 52,382 fans — including Canadian Prime Minister Brian Mulroney and U.S. President George Bush — had packed the SkyDome for the All-Star Game. Legends Joe DiMaggio and Ted Williams were honoured before the game, and Canadian Hall of Famer Fergie Jenkins tossed out the first pitch. Many had expected Jimmy Key to start the game at home, but Oakland manager Tony LaRussa gave that honour to Jack Morris. Key came on to pitch the top of the third and surrendered a double to Ryne Sandberg but got out of the inning unscathed. When Ripken went deep off Montreal's Dennis Martinez in the bottom of the third, Key's one inning of work qualified him as the winner. Joe Carter entered the game in the fifth inning and drew a walk. He singled in the seventh inning and later came around to score an insurance run on a sacrifice fly by Harold Baines. Roberto Alomar was held hitless, but had the rare distinction of playing all nine innings in an All-Star Game.

Oddities and Others #17

AUGUST 7, 1991 • *Blue Jays 5, Tigers 2*

Tom Henke had saves for the Blue Jays in each of his first two appearances of the 1991 season, but an injury suffered on April 12 gave Duane Ward his first taste of the closer's role. Ward performed brilliantly, notching 12 saves in 13 opportunities before "the Terminator" was able to return.

From the time that he rejoined the team in late May, Henke proved almost unhittable. He was nine-for-nine in save opportunities to help the Blue Jays take over first place in June, and went seven-for-seven in July when his stingy ERA of 1.80 earned him team honours as Pitcher of the Month. After closing out three more Blue Jays victories in the first six days of August, Henke had earned 24 straight saves — tying a major league record.

Henke's chance to establish a new mark came against the Detroit Tigers on August 7. Juan Guzman had worked seven innings of two-hit ball and Duane Ward had pitched a 1–2–3 eighth when Henke entered the game in the ninth inning. He closed out the Blue Jays' 5–2 victory and his record-breaking 25th consecutive save was in the books.

The following night, Henke entered a scoreless tie in the top of the 12th inning. Though he struck out six in just 2.1 innings, he suffered his first loss of the season when the Tigers reached him for four runs in the 14th. Because it was not a save situation, Henke's streak was still alive. It finally came to an end when Paul Molitor took him deep for a three-run homer in a 5–4 Milwaukee come-from-behind victory on August 13. Henke bounced back to notch six more saves in August (tying his own team record of 10 in a month) and the Blue Jays won seven straight to head into September with a 3½ game lead in the American League East.

Once again, Tom Henke had an outstanding season in 1991. This time he managed to enter the record books as well when he set a new major league mark with 25 consecutive saves.

Great Moments #16

OCTOBER 2, 1991 • *Blue Jays 6, Angels 5*

The Blue Jays had stretched their division lead to 5½ games when they beat Cleveland on September 8, but they knew they would need each and every bit of that advantage. Toronto was the so-called "swing team" in 1991, meaning that after the win against the Indians, the Blue Jays would close out the season with 23 straight games against West Division clubs — all of whom were playing at or above the .500 mark.

No swing team had ever won the East Division, but the Blue Jays were still out in front when the California Angels came to the SkyDome for the last home series of the season. After a loss in the series opener, rookie sensation Juan Guzman notched his tenth consecutive victory and the Blue Jays were on the verge of clinching. A crowd of 50,324 jammed the SkyDome for the home finale, hoping to watch history being made. In fact, the fans themselves had already made history because the crowd that night pushed attendance for the season to 4,001,526 — marking the first time a team had cracked four million. Unfortunately, the prospects of seeing the Blue Jays wrap up the division title seemed bleak when the Angels went ahead 5–4 in the top of the ninth inning and then sent Bryan Harvey — the American League saves leader — out to the mound to protect the lead.

First to face Harvey in the bottom of the

ninth was leadoff hitter Devon White. He got things started with a single, but then Roberto Alomar hit an apparent rally killing double-play ball right at second baseman Kevin Flora. However, in his haste to erase the speedy White, Flora threw the ball away. The error allowed White to race in with the tying run and moved Alomar into scoring position for the game-winner. Robbie then moved up 90 feet more by stealing third base, so all Joe Carter needed was a sacrifice fly to deliver the division title.

Hoping to keep the Blue Jays' top slugger from extending his arms, Harvey jammed Joe with a slider up and in. Carter managed to get the handle of his bat on the ball and he muscled it just over the drawn-in infield. Alomar jogged home with his arms raised in triumph and the Blue Jays were back in the playoffs.

(Above) The Jays salute the SkyDome faithful after the club set a new major league attendance mark by attracting over 4,000,000 fans during the 1991 season. (Below) The front page of the Toronto Sun says it all.

California	AB	R	H	RBI	Toronto	AB	R	H	RBI
Polonia, lf	4	0	1	0	White, cf	5	1	2	1
Venable, rf	2	0	1	1	Alomar, 2b	3	1	0	1
Gallagher, ph-cf-rf	2	0	1	1	Carter, rf	5	0	1	1
Felix, cf	2	0	0	0	Olerud, 1b	3	1	1	0
Amaro, ph-rf	2	0	1	0	Gruber, 3b	4	0	0	0
Parrish, c	0	0	0	0	Maldonado, lf	4	1	1	2
Winfield, dh	4	2	2	1	Parker, dh	2	1	1	0
Stevens, 1b	4	1	1	0	Wilson, pr-dh	1	0	0	0
Gaetti, 3b	4	0	2	2	Borders, c	3	1	1	0
Schofield, ss	4	0	1	0	DBell, pr	0	0	0	0
Orton, c	3	0	0	0	Myers, c	0	0	0	0
Abner, pr-cf	0	1	0	0	Lee, ss	2	0	1	0
Flora, 2b	2	1	0	0	Mulliniks, ph	1	0	0	0
					Tabler, ph	1	0	0	0
					Gonzales, ss	0	0	0	0
Totals	**33**	**5**	**10**	**5**	**Totals**	**33**	**6**	**8**	**5**

| California | | | | | | | 001 | 200 | 011 | — | 5 |
| Toronto | | | | | | | 000 | 022 | 002 | — | 6 |

None out when winning run scored

California	IP	H	R	ER	BB	SO
Grahe	4⅓	1	2	2	5	4
Lewis	⅔	0	0	0	0	0
Bailes	⅓	2	2	2	1	0
Eichhorn	2⅓	3	0	0	0	5
Young	⅓	0	0	0	0	0
Harvey (L. 2-4)	0	2	2	2	0	0

Toronto	IP	H	R	ER	BB	SO
Candiotti	6⅓	7	3	3	2	2
Wells	2⅓	1	2	2	2	1
Timlin (W. 11-6)	⅓	2	0	0	0	0

Harvey pitched to three batters in ninth

E – Gaetti, Flora. DP – California 1. LOB – California 7, Toronto 9. 2B – Stevens, Gaetti, Schofield, Olerud, Parker. HR – Winfield (28), Maldonado (12). SB – Felix (7), Gaetti (5), Flora (1), Alomar (53). S – Flora. SF – Venable.
T – 3:04. A – 50,324.

Playoff Moments #8

OCTOBER 8–13, 1991 • *Blue Jays vs. Twins*

An odd scheduling quirk saw the Blue Jays finish out the 1991 season where they would start the playoffs — on the road in Minnesota. Toronto took two of three games from the Twins that final weekend, giving them victories in eight of 12 head-to-

Roberto Alomar slides past Twins catcher Brian Harper. The Blue Jays split two games at the Metrodome only to be swept at home.

head matchups during the season. But the postseason was another story.

To open the 1991 American League Championship Series, the Blue Jays sent Tom Candiotti to the mound at the Metrodome to face Jack Morris. Morris had won 18 games in his first season with the Twins after 15 years in Detroit. Candiotti had won 13 games in a season split between Toronto and Cleveland. Pat Gillick had acquired him for the Blue Jays on June 27, sending highly touted prospects Glenallen Hill, Mark Whiten and Denis Boucher to the Indians for the knuckleballer and utility outfielder Turner Ward. Candiotti had been a consistent winner with generally poor Cleveland teams. He had gone just 6-7 in Toronto, but his 2.98 ERA in 19 games was the best among Blue Jays starters. His 2.65 mark overall was second best in the league and Cito Gaston turned to him in the ALCS opener.

Unlike most knuckleball pitchers, Candiotti did not rely totally on the trick pitch, yet he seemed to abandon it almost completely against the Twins, who teed off on him to the tune of five runs in just 2.2 innings. Though the Blue Jays bullpen

would shut them down for the rest of the game, the Twins didn't need to score again. Toronto scored a run in the fourth and three in the sixth on five consecutive hits off Morris, but Minnesota held on for a 5-4 victory. It was a frustrating game that set the tone for a frustrating series.

The Blue Jays drew even with a 5-2 victory in Game Two, but the momentum of the series swung back dramatically in the Twins' favour in Game Three at the SkyDome. Joe Carter's homer and an RBI double from Candy Maldonado put Toronto ahead 2-0 after one, but Minnesota evened matters with runs off Jimmy Key in the fifth and sixth. The score remained 2-2 until Mike Pagliarulo slugged a pinch-hit homer off Mike Timlin in the top of the tenth. Equally discouraging as the 3-2 loss was the fact that Joe Carter had been forced to leave the game after severely spraining his ankle attempting to make a circus catch off the right field fence in the sixth inning. Although Carter served as the designated hitter in Game Four, he was in obvious discomfort and had great difficulty turning on the ball with any authority. The Jays' main offensive threat was silenced, and from that point on the Twins took over. They romped to a 9-3 victory, then wrapped up the series with an 8-5 win in Game Five.

Joe Carter continued to play in the series after he severely sprained his ankle in Game Three, but his mobility was limited and he couldn't swing the bat with authority.

The Blue Jays rolled through the regular season in 1992, gained a measure of revenge by ousting the Oakland A's in the ALCS, then became the first team outside the United States to win a World Series title. The offensive heroes for the club were Joe Carter (34 HR, 119 RBI), Robbie Alomar (.310, 76 RBI) and Dave Winfield (.290, 108 RBI). Jack Morris (21–6), Juan Guzman (16-5), Jimmy Key (13–13) and Todd Stottlemyre (12–11) all reached double digits in wins.

1992

96–66 .593 1st +4

The Phantom Triple Play: As this picture clearly demonstrates, Kelly Gruber's glove is making contact with Atlanta's Deion Sanders, completing what should have been a triple play. Inexplicably, umpire Bob Davidson missed the call and the Jays missed a chance at history.

APRIL 6, 1992 • *Blue Jays 4, Tigers 2*

Although the 1991 version of the Blue Jays was a well-molded team, the playoff defeat at the hands of the Twins proved that something was still missing. Pat Gillick felt the team needed help in the starting rotation and at designated hitter. Two key free agent acquisitions during the winter addressed those needs and help set a new tone for the 1992 season. Jack Morris and Dave Winfield would prove their worth right from opening day.

The 1992 season began in Detroit, where former Tiger Morris made his record-breaking 13th consecutive opening day start. Before he even took to the mound, Morris had been given a 1–0 lead thanks to an RBI single from Dave Winfield. It had been questionable as to whether or not Winfield would even play that day, having missed the team's last 10 spring training games with a sore hamstring, but he wound up collecting three hits in the opener. Morris pitched shutout ball through eight innings, allowing the Tigers just three singles as the Blue Jays built up a 4–0 lead thanks to home runs by John Olerud and Pat Borders. In the ninth, Morris gave up a leadoff home run to Cecil Fielder and a two-out blast to Rob Deer. Both Tom Henke and Duane Ward were warmed up, but Morris hung on for a complete-game victory.

"I'd thrown a lot of pitches, but I still felt fine," said Morris "Complete games matter to anybody with pride," added Cito Gaston, "but we've got a great bullpen here and we're going to use it. I don't see him going 140 pitches all year."

Morris actually threw 144 pitches and had seven strikeouts. He struck out the side in the second and the fourth, ending Detroit's only real threat of the day when he fanned Milt Cuyler with two out and the bases loaded in the second inning. The Blue Jays went on to win six in a row, and nine of 10, as they opened the season with the best start in franchise history.

The Master: Jack Morris proved to be the lion the Jays needed to tame the rest of the American League and move into the World Series.

Juan Guzman continued his superb pitching in 1992, winning 16 games with a microscopic 2.64 ERA.

Great Moments #17

Late-inning heroics were a key to the Blue Jays' success in 1992. Beginning with a Pat Borders ninth-inning homer that triggered a 4–3 win over the Orioles in the home opener on April 10, the Blue Jays went on to win 17 games in their last at-bat over the course of the season. None of those victories was more dramatic than a ninth-inning explosion at the Kingdome in Seattle on May 7.

Home runs by Kevin Mitchell and Ken Griffey Jr. had the Mariners in front 6–0 through three innings, and when Junior knocked out Jack Morris with another home run in the fifth, Seattle's lead was 7–1. Pat Hentgen came on in relief and blanked the Mariners on just one hit over 3.2 innings, but the Blue Jays still trailed 7–3 as the game headed for the top of the ninth.

With one out, Greg Myers doubled off reliever Calvin Jones. When Manny Lee followed with an RBI single, the deficit was cut to three runs. Jones then issued a walk to Devon White, and Mariners manager Lou Piniella turned to relief ace Mike Schooler. Schooler retired Roberto Alomar for the inning's second out, but then walked Joe Carter to bring up Dave Winfield with the bases loaded.

"I started thinking about being up there with the bases loaded with a couple of batters to go before me," Winfield admitted after the game. "You have to have heart to want to be up there in those situations, and I wanted it."

On a two-strike pitch, Winfield drove a Schooler offering deep to left field. The whole bench erupted as the ball sailed into the seats. It was Winfield's tenth career grand slam, and it lifted his season average to .360 with six homers and 20 RBIs. When Tom Henke came on to nail down the victory in the bottom of the ninth, the Blue Jays had improved to 21–9 on the season and maintained their slim one-game lead over the Orioles in the American League East.

Toronto	AB	R	H	RBI	Seattle	AB	R	H	RBI
White, cf	4	1	2	0	Reynolds, 2b	4	1	3	0
Alomar, 2b	5	0	0	0	E.Martinez, 3b	4	1	1	0
Carter, dh	4	1	0	0	Griffey Jr, cf	4	2	2	4
Winfield, rf	5	2	2	4	Mitchell, lf	4	2	2	1
Gruber, 3b	4	0	1	0	O'Brien, dh	4	1	2	0
Olerud, 1b	4	1	1	0	Buhner, rf	3	0	1	2
Maldonado, lf	4	1	2	1	T.Martinez, 1b	4	0	0	0
Myers, c	3	1	1	1	Valle, c	4	0	0	0
Lee, ss	4	1	1	1	Schaefer, ss	4	0	0	0
Totals	**37**	**8**	**10**	**7**	**Totals**	**35**	**7**	**11**	**7**

Toronto			.000	010	205 – 8
Seattle			.204	010	000 – 7

Toronto	IP	H	R	ER	BB	SO
Morris	4⅓	9	7	7	4	0
Hentgen (W, 3-0)	3⅔	1	0	0	0	4
Henke (S4)	1	1	0	0	0	0

Seattle	IP	H	R	ER	BB	SO
Hanson	6⅔	7	3	3	0	6
Jones	1⅔	2	3	3	2	3
Schooler (L, 0-2)	⅔	1	2	2	1	0

E – Olerud, Valle, Schaefer. DP – Toronto 2. LOB – Toronto 6, Seattle 6. 2B – Maldonado, Martinez. HR – Griffey Jr 2 (5), Mitchell (2), Winfield (6). SB – Reynolds (8). SF – Myers, Griffey Jr.
WP – Morris 2.
T – 3:08. A – 13,347.

When Dave Winfield was brought aboard prior to the 1992 season, it was hoped he had enough juice left in his bat to create some timely offense. Winfield still had power to spare, and he unleashed some of that excess energy on the Seattle Mariners by belting a grand slam in the ninth inning to complete a masterful five-run comeback and propel the team towards the pennant.

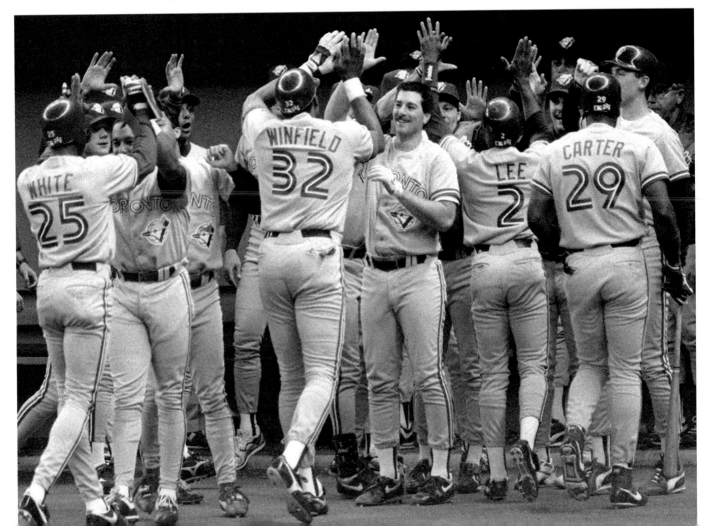

AUGUST 28, 1992 • *Brewers 22, Blue Jays 2*

As they had done in 1991, the Blue Jays played their best ball as they approached the All-Star break in 1992. They had been in first place for most of April and May, but it wasn't until late June that they finally enjoyed as much as a two-game lead atop the division. Eight consecutive wins in early July pushed the advantage to four games by the All-Star break, but the starting pitchers began to slump in August. Indeed, in 17 of 29 games from August 2 to 31, the starters failed to go even six innings and the lead atop the AL East shrank from 4½ to just 1½ games.

With Jimmy Key, David Wells and Todd Stottlemyre all struggling, and with Juan Guzman on the disabled list, Pat Gillick took action. He sent promising young infielder Jeff Kent and outfielder Ryan Thompson to the New York Mets for David Cone on August 27. Cone arrived in Toronto the following day — just in time to witness one of the worst pitching performances in franchise history. The Milwaukee Brewers set an American League record with 31 hits as they pounded the Blue Jays 22–2. No team had collected so many hits in a game since the National League's New York Giants also had 31 way back in 1901.

The onslaught started early when Paul Molitor launched a two-run homer off Key in the first inning. It was the only Brewers homer on the night — though 26 singles and four doubles did plenty of damage as Milwaukee scored in every inning but the fifth. Each of the six Blue Jays pitchers on the night (Key, Mike Timlin, Doug Linton, Bob MacDonald, Mark Eichhorn and David Wells) gave up at least three runs. Linton was the hardest hit, giving up six runs on six hits while recording just one out in the fourth inning. Scott Fletcher and Kevin Seitzer led the Brew Crew with five hits apiece, and Fletcher and Darryl Hamilton both collected five RBIs. The score could have been even worse than 22–2, but the Brewers left 16 runners on base.

"It was incredible the way the hits continued to pile up," said Molitor. "I told John Olerud one time at first [base] that you can never figure this game out. He just shook his head. They weren't too talkative out there."

David Cone's first night at SkyDome as a member of the Jays was a bit ominous. Manager Cito Gaston (left), who missed part of the 1991 season with a sore back, was probably wishing he was still in sick bay after watching his Jays cough up 31 hits to Milwaukee.

SEPTEMBER 4, 1992 • *Blue Jays 16, Twins 5*

The Blue Jays' lead atop the East Division had shrunk to just a half-game in early September and Dave Winfield had a message for Toronto fans. The team needed their support now more than ever. "It's a symbiotic relationship," the slugger explained. Players feed off the fans' enthusiasm and crowds at the SkyDome just weren't loud enough.

In other words . . . Winfield wanted noise!

And there was certainly plenty to cheer about when the team took to the field for the first time after Winfield's plea went public. The Blue Jays crushed the Twins 16–5. The telling blows came early in this one as the Jays scored eight runs in the second inning on a team-record 10 consecutive hits.

There was one away when Kelly Gruber came to the plate in the second and legged out an infield single off Twins starter Kevin Tapani. Pat Borders, Manny Lee, Devon White (double) and Roberto Alomar all followed with hits before a Joe Carter triple chased Tapani from the game. Tom Edens emerged from the Twins bullpen, and Winfield greeted him with a single that scored Carter. The slugger was tagged out trying to stretch his hit into a double, but as he headed back to the dugout he waved at the shouting, stomping fans and encouraged them to keep the noise level up.

John Olerud followed Winfield to the plate and ran the hitting streak to eight straight with a single. Candy Maldonado's triple tied a team record at nine, then Gruber's second hit of the inning (a double) gave the

Blue Jays 10 hits in a row, setting a new team record and tying the American League mark first established by the Boston Red Sox in 1901 and matched by the Tigers in 1983. The big inning put Toronto on top 8–3 and helped David Cone overcome a shaky start to record his first victory as a Blue Jay.

And what did Dave Winfield think of the fans' efforts that night?

"If their lungs are tired and they've got a smile on their faces, then they did their job," he said with a grin.

Minnesota	AB	R	H	RBI	Toronto	AB	R	H	RBI
Knoblauch, 2b	2	0	1	0	White, cf	5	2	4	2
Rebolet, 2b	1	0	0	0	Alomar, 2b	3	2	1	2
Larkin, 1b	3	1	1	1	Griffin, 2b	1	0	0	0
Bush, 1b	1	0	0	0	Carter, rf	5	2	3	4
Puckett, cf	3	0	0	0	T.Ward, rf	1	0	0	0
Bruett, cf	1	0	0	0	Winfield, dh	4	0	1	1
Hrbek, dh	4	0	1	0	Mulliniks, ph-dh	0	0	0	0
Mack, lf	3	0	0	0	Olerud, 1b	6	2	4	0
Reed, lf	2	0	0	0	Maldonado, lf	5	3	2	3
Harper, c	2	1	0	0	Gruber, 3b	4	1	2	1
Webster, c	1	0	0	0	Quinlan, ph-3b	2	0	0	0
Davis, rf	4	3	4	1	Borders, c	4	1	1	0
Munoz, pr-rf	0	0	0	0	Sprague, c	1	0	1	0
Leius, 3b-ss	4	0	0	0	Lee, ss	1	2	1	1
Gagne, ss	3	0	2	1	Zosky, ph-ss	2	1	1	0
Pagliarulo, 3b	1	0	0	0					
Totals	35	5	9	3	Totals	44	16	21	14

| Minnesota | . . . . | .120 | 101 | 000 – 5 |
| Toronto | . . . . | .083 | 102 | 20x – 16 |

Minnesota	IP	H	R	ER	BB	SO
Tapani (L. 14-10)	1⅓	7	6	6	1	1
Edens	⅔	4	2	2	0	0
West	4	6	6	5	5	2
Abbott	2	4	2	2	2	4

Toronto	IP	H	R	ER	BB	SO
Cone (W. 1-1)	6	7	5	4	3	6
Eichhorn	1	1	0	0	0	2
D.Ward	1	1	0	0	0	1
Henke	1	0	0	0	1	1

E – Rebolet, West, Maldonado. LOB – Minnesota 9, Toronto 12. 2B – Davis, Gagne, White, Olerud (2), Gruber. 3B – Carter, Maldonado. HR – Davis (9), Carter (30), Maldonado (19). SB – Knoblauch 2 (26), White (31), Alomar (39). SF – Larkin. HBP – by Cone (Harper). WP – Eichhorn. PB – Borders 2.
T – 3:23. A – 50,420.

The acquisition of David Cone late in the 1992 season gave the Jays the extra arm and the confidence they needed to take the final step towards the title.

Say What?: Dave Winfield's plea to the Toronto fans to create a "symbiotic relationship" with the team had even the most knowledgeable scholars digging for the dictionary. When all was said and done, what big Dave meant was "Winfield Wants Noise!"

Famous Firsts and Records #19

SEPTEMBER 24, 1992 • *Blue Jays 8, Orioles 2*

With a two-run home run off Baltimore's Ben McDonald in the top of the first inning, Dave Winfield became the oldest player in baseball history to drive in 100 runs in a season. Just nine days shy of his 41st birthday, Winfield's total of 101 RBIs made him the first 40-year-old to reach the century mark. Darrell Evans of Detroit had knocked in 99 at age 40 in 1987, while Tigers legend Ty Cobb had collected 102 ribbies as a 39-year-old back in 1925.

"The oldest guy," said Winfield. "That's nice, but I really can't understand why no 40-year-old has done it before. Maybe everyone else retired and was playing with their grandchildren."

Winfield upped his season total to 103 RBIs with a two-run double in a five-run second inning as the Blue Jays romped to an 8–2 victory. The win virtually eliminated the Orioles from contention in the AL East, leaving only the Milwaukee Brewers in the race.

Dave Winfield celebrates the joys of aging while Jack Morris (right) checks the weather.

Famous Firsts and Records #20

SEPTEMBER 27, 1992 • *Blue Jays 12, Yankees 2*

Jack Morris had a chance to become the Blue Jays' first 20-game winner in Baltimore on September 23, but he dropped a 4–1 decision to the Orioles. Four nights later, he was on the mound at Yankee Stadium. This time, nothing short of an act of God was going to stop him — and it almost did!

With Devon White, Roberto Alomar, Joe Carter and Dave Winfield going a combined 10-for-10 with two walks through the first three innings, the Blue Jays jumped out to an early 9–0 lead. The score was still 9–0 when the skies opened up with the Blue Jays batting in the top of the fifth. The game had to reach the bottom of the fifth to become official, so a rainout would wipe out Morris's victory. Even if the game continued, a lengthy delay might leave him too stiff to return to the mound and record the three outs he needed to qualify as the winning pitcher.

The rain delay eventually lasted more than two hours, but Morris was back on the mound to face the Yankees in the bottom of the fifth. He needed just nine pitches to retire the side, then stuck around to work a 1–2–3 sixth. After Mark Eichhorn, Duane Ward and Tom Henke worked an inning apiece to finish it out, the Blue Jays had their first 20-game winner.

"It's always a nice feeling," said Morris, who had won 20 for the Tigers in 1983 and 1986. "I'd be a fool to sit here and say it doesn't mean anything, but I'd also be a fool not to compliment my teammates. They've more than done the job offensively for me."

Great Moments #19

OCTOBER 3, 1992 • *Blue Jays 3, Tigers 1*

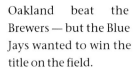

From the start of spring training, the Blue Jays had focused on three objectives: to defend their title in the AL East, to capture their first American League pennant and to win the World Series. Throughout the season, each member of the team wore undershirts with the slogan "We can, We are, We will – 3 for 3 in 1992" to emphasize their dedication to these goals. The first one was within their grasp on the final Saturday of the regular season. The Blue Jays were two games ahead of second-place Milwaukee and could clinch the division even if they lost to the Tigers — provided that

Oakland beat the Brewers — but the Blue Jays wanted to win the title on the field.

Joe Carter got things started early with a two-run homer that scored Devon White in the bottom of the first. The 50,412 fans in the stands were on their feet as Carter settled into his home run trot, circling his arm as he passed first base.

Juan Guzman had set the Tigers down in order in the top of the inning, and he went on to retire the first 12 men to face him before walking Cecil Fielder and Mickey Tettleton leading off the fifth. He settled down to get out of the inning with a ground ball and a pair of three-pitch strikeouts. Guzman punched the air and dashed to the dugout while the fans leaped to their feet again. "When he's on," said Cito Gaston after the game, "Juan has an overpowering fastball."

The score was 3–0 when the Tigers finally got to Guzman with a single in the sixth, but it was the only hit that he would give up through eight innings. Then Tom Henke came on to try to nail down the division title. "The Terminator" had tied his own team record with 34 saves, but this was destined to be a nervous ninth.

With the fans clapping their hands in anticipation, Henke retired Lou Whitaker on a pop up. But then he loaded the bases on two hits and a walk. He got Rob Deer on another pop up, but a walk to Scott Livingstone brought home a run. Then Cito signalled for Duane Ward. Ward was usually Henke's setup man, but now he was being called on to record the biggest save of his career. He needed just two pitches to induce a towering pop up from Dan Gladden. John Olerud squeezed it for the final out and the Blue Jays were headed to the postseason for the third time in four years.

Pyramid Party!: The Jays celebrate their second consecutive AL East crown with the full knowledge the job was only just beginning.

Detroit	AB	R	H	RBI	Toronto	AB	R	H	RBI
Phillips, cf	4	0	0	0	White, cf	4	1	2	0
Whitaker, 2b	4	0	0	0	Alomar, 2b	2	0	1	0
Fryman, ss	4	1	1	0	Carter, rf	3	1	1	2
Fielder, 1b	3	0	1	0	Winfield, dh	3	0	0	1
Barnes, pr	0	0	0	0	Olerud, 1b	3	0	0	0
Tettleton, c	2	0	0	0	Maldonado, lf	4	0	0	0
Deer, rf	4	0	0	0	Gruber, 3b	4	0	2	0
Livingstone, 3b	3	0	0	1	Borders, c	4	0	1	0
Gladden, lf	4	0	0	0	Lee, ss	2	1	2	0
Carreon, dh	2	0	1	0					
Totals	30	1	3	1	Totals	29	3	9	3

```
Detroit ............................. .000  000  001 – 1
Toronto ............................. .200  010  00x – 3
```

Detroit	IP	H	R	ER	BB	SO
Haas (L, 5-3)	4⅔	6	3	3	4	3
Leiter	1⅔	1	0	0	1	1
Munoz	⅔	0	0	0	1	0
Kiely	1	2	0	0	0	1

Toronto	IP	H	R	ER	BB	SO
Guzman (W, 16-5)	8	1	0	0	3	9
Henke	⅔	2	1	1	2	0
DWard	⅓	0	0	0	0	0

E – None. DP – Detroit 2. LOB – Detroit 7, Toronto 9. 2B – Borders. HR – Carter (34). SB – Alomar 2 (49).
T – 2:54. A – 50,412.

Playoff Moments #9

OCTOBER 7–10, 1992 • *Blue Jays vs. Athletics*

Oakland had reached the American League Championship Series for the fourth time in five years, while Toronto was back for the second straight season and looking to avenge not only the previous year's loss to Minnesota, but also their 1989 defeat by the A's. The two teams had been remarkably even in 1992, both posting records of 96–66 and each winning six games against the other.

Jack Morris (21-6) was on the mound at the SkyDome in Game One, but he was not at his best. Morris gave up first-inning home runs to Mark McGwire and Terry Steinbach for an early 3-0 Oakland lead. After the Blue Jays fought back to tie the game in the eighth, Harold Baines took Morris deep in the ninth and the A's had a 4–3 victory.

Needing a win to avoid heading to Oakland down two games to nothing, David Cone took to the mound in Game Two and delivered a solid performance in a tight pitchers' duel with Mike Moore. Though the Blue Jays managed only four hits, one was Kelly Gruber's two-run homer that put Toronto ahead 2-0 in the fifth. The Blue Jays upped the lead to 3-0 in the seventh when Gruber doubled and came in to score on a sacrifice fly by Manny Lee. Cone continued to keep Oakland off the scoreboard until finally surrendering a run in the top of the ninth. Tom Henke came in to end the threat, earning his first career postseason save as the Blue Jays held on for a 3–1 victory. He earned

his second save two days later when the ALCS resumed in Oakland. The Blue Jays scored a 7–5 victory in Game Three despite being outhit 13–9. Home runs from Roberto Alomar and Candy Maldonado — as well as three Oakland errors — helped the Blue Jays' cause as Toronto put together a pair of wins in the postseason for the first time since 1985.

(Above) Safe!: Robbie Alomar narrowly beats the throw to first. (Right) Candy Maldonado hit a pair of homers and drove home six in the 1992 ALCS. Here, he welcomes Kelly Gruber back to the plate.

Playoff Moments #10

OCTOBER 11, 1992 • *Blue Jays 7, Athletics 6*

Game Four was the turning point of the 1992 American League Championship Series. It may well have been the turning point in the history of the Blue Jays franchise. Toronto rallied from a 6–1 deficit after seven innings to win 7–6 in 11.

Game One starter Jack Morris was back on the mound in Game Four, but lasted just three innings. The A's batted around on Morris in the third, scoring five runs to take a 5–1 lead. (John Olerud had homered for Toronto in the top of the second.) Todd Stottlemyre allowed just one run in relief as he pitched through the seventh inning, but the Blue Jays could not score again on Oakland starter Bob Welch until they finally got to him and reliever Jeff Parrett in the eighth. With one run in and two runners on base, A's manager Tony LaRussa turned to Dennis Eckersley. Eckersley had saved Game One for Oakland and had kept the A's close in Game Three. This time, he gave up back-to-back singles on his first two pitches and suddenly the game was 6–4. Ed Sprague represented the go-ahead run when he came to the plate with runners on second and third, but Eckersley struck him out. He then glared into the Blue Jays dugout, pumping his fist and pointing his finger.

Roberto Alomar goes deep off of Dennis Eckersley.

In 1989, Eckersley's theatrics had been intimidating.

In 1992, they were fuel for the fire.

After Mike Timlin blanked Oakland in the bottom of the eighth, Eckersley returned to the mound. The A's were 81–1 in their previous 82 attempts at holding a ninth-inning lead, but Devon White got the Blue Jays in flight with a single to left field. He went all the way to third after Rickey Henderson misplayed the ball. Roberto Alomar batted second. He worked the count to 2-and–2 before slamming Eckersley's next offering deep to right field. Alomar threw his arms in the air and hollered the moment the ball left his bat. He had no doubt where it was going. When his drive sailed into the seats, the game was tied!

But there was more excitement to come.

In the bottom of the ninth, Duane Ward gave up a leadoff single to Harold Baines. Rookie Eric Fox came in to pinch run and stole second base. He then moved to third on Mark McGwire's sacrifice bunt. Terry Steinbach came to the plate needing only a fly ball to win the game, but he poked a Ward fastball on the ground to Alomar at second. Fox tried to score on the play, but Robbie's throw was on the money and Pat Borders applied the tag. In the top of the 11th, Borders came to the plate with Candy Maldonado on first and Derek Bell on third. The Blue Jays catcher delivered the fly ball his Oakland counterpart had not and Toronto had a 7–6 lead. Tom Henke came on to wrap it up, retiring Fox and McGwire after a one-out single by Ruben Sierra. The Blue Jays were within one game of the World Series for the first time since 1985.

Playoff Moments #11

As in 1985, the Blue Jays followed up a Game Four thriller with a flat effort in Game Five. This time Dave Stewart went the distance against them as a Ruben Sierra homer and some sloppy Toronto defense led to a 6–2 Oakland victory.

"We came out here with a goal of winning two out of three," said Dave Winfield, "and we did. I'd rather be in our situation than theirs. They probably feel like they dodged a bullet today . . . but we get to go back to our ballpark with 51,000 fans behind us helping make things happen."

They happened fast.

Leading off the bottom of the first in Game Six, Devon White lifted a fly ball down the left field line. Rickey Henderson, who had terrorized the Blue Jays in 1989, drifted under it . . . and dropped it! Two batters later, Joe Carter took Mike Moore deep to straight-away center and the Blue Jays had a 2–0 lead. Later, with another run already in, Candy Maldonado came to the plate in the third inning and sent a drive even deeper to left center. It was now 6–0 and the Blue Jays were cruising. Juan Guzman, who had recorded Toronto's only victory in the 1991 ALCS and had already beaten Oakland in Game Three, was in complete control. He allowed only one run in seven innings, surrendering just five hits and striking out eight. It was 7–1 Blue Jays when Duane Ward entered the game in the eighth.

After he gave up a meaningless run, Toronto pushed two more across the plate and headed for the ninth with a 9–2 lead.

Tom Henke was on the mound for the Blue Jays. He had saved all three wins in the series so far, and though this game was not a save situation it would be the biggest win Henke had ever closed out. He walked Walt Weiss, then retired the next two batters before walking Carney Lansford to prolong the drama. Finally, Henke induced a high fly ball off the bat of Ruben Sierra. The time was 6:23 p.m. when Candy Maldonado squeezed the final out in his glove.

The string of late-season failures was finally over!

The Blue Jays had won the pennant at last!

Toronto was going to the World Series!

Roberto Alomar was named the Most Valuable Player of the 1992 American League Championship Series. In addition to belting the key homer in Game Four, he had batted .423 and stolen five bases. "I'm very happy to win this award," said Alomar, "but it's a team thing. I feel really proud we won, but it's not over yet. We still have to go to the World Series and we have to win there."

As the fans spilled out of the SkyDome to celebrate Canada's first pennant and the champagne flowed in the clubhouse, Jack Morris was in the bullpen. He was preparing for his start in Game One of the 1992 World Series.

Kelly Gruber is the center of attraction in the victory scrum while Tom Henke (above) points out the obvious — the Jays are going to the World Series.

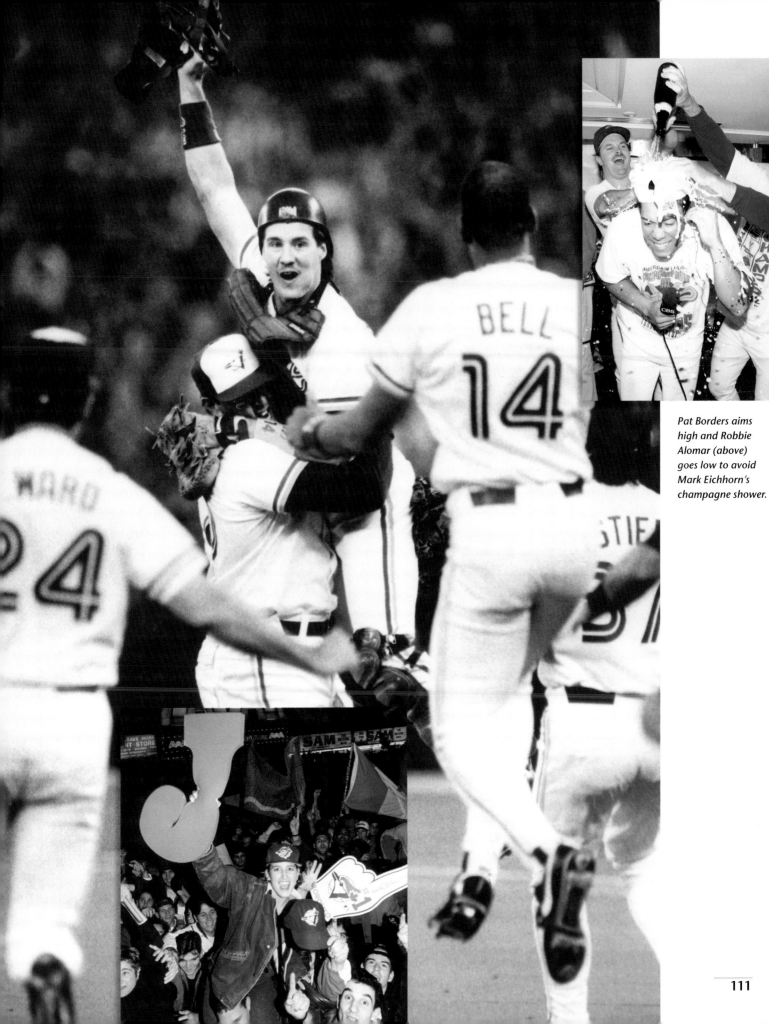

Pat Borders aims high and Robbie Alomar (above) goes low to avoid Mark Eichhorn's champagne shower.

Playoff Moments #12

For the first time in baseball history, a Canadian team would be taking part in the Fall Classic. Seven years after Jim Sundberg's wind-blown triple, Toronto had finally made it to the World Series. Facing the Blue Jays would be the Atlanta Braves and their skipper Bobby Cox, the man who had managed Toronto into the postseason for the first time back in 1985.

Opening the 89th World Series in the National League park meant some lineup changes for Game One. The designated hitter would not be used, but manager Cito Gaston wanted to keep Dave Winfield's bat in the order. Winfield had played just 26 games in the outfield during the 1992 season, but he would begin the World Series in right field. Joe Carter would move to first base, where he had played just four games during the season. John Olerud was on the bench.

On the mound (and batting ninth) for the Blue Jays in Game One was Jack Morris. Not only had the longtime Toronto nemesis become the team's first 20-game winner during the 1992 season, he was also working on a streak of 13 consecutive shutout innings against Atlanta from the 1991 World Series, including a brilliant 10-inning shutout when the Minnesota Twins had beaten the Braves 1–0 in Game Seven. Morris would run that streak to 18 innings in 1992, but he was not nearly as effective in Game One as he had been the year before in Game Seven. Though Braves batters had only reached him for two hits through five innings, Morris had also surrendered four walks — but he continued to dodge bullets until the bottom of the sixth.

The Blue Jays led the game 1–0 on Joe Carter's fourth-inning homer when Dave Justice worked Morris for a one-out walk in the sixth inning. Sid Bream followed up with a single. After Morris retired Ron Gant, Damon Berryhill came to the plate. Normally the Braves' backup catcher, Berryhill had been forced into a starting role when Greg Olson suffered a broken leg late in the season. A .228 hitter during the season, Berryhill drove a Morris forkball deep to right field and into the seats. The 3–1 lead would be all Braves starter Tom Glavine needed.

A 20-game winner for the second straight season in 1992, Glavine was in total command during Game One of the World Series. He allowed only 30 Blue Jays batters to come to the plate all night, spinning a complete-game four-hitter with no walks and six strikeouts. As for Morris: "I hung a forkball and [Berryhill] killed it, what more can I say? But Oakland beat us in the first game of the playoffs, too. Remember, it takes four games to win this."

Toronto	AB	R	H	RBI	Atlanta	AB	R	H	RBI
White, cf	4	0	0	0	Nixon, cf	3	0	1	0
Alomar, 2b	4	0	0	0	Blauser, ss	4	0	0	0
Carter, 1b	4	0	1	0	Belliard, ss	0	0	0	0
Winfield, rf	3	1	1	1	Pendleton, 3b	4	0	0	0
Maldonado, lf	3	0	0	0	Justice, rf	2	1	0	0
Gruber, 3b	3	0	0	0	Bream, 1b	3	0	1	0
Borders, c	3	0	2	0	Gant, lf	3	1	0	0
Lee, ss	3	0	0	0	Berryhill, c	4	1	1	3
Morris, p	2	0	0	0	Lemke, 2b	3	0	1	0
Tabler, ph	1	0	0	0	Glavine, p	2	0	0	0
Totals	**30**	**1**	**4**	**1**	**Totals**	**28**	**3**	**4**	**3**

Toronto				.000	100	000 — 1
Atlanta				.000	003	00x — 3

Toronto	IP	H	R	ER	BB	SO
Morris (L 0-1)	6	4	3	3	5	7
Stottlemyre	1	0	0	0	0	2
Wells	1	0	0	0	1	1

Atlanta	IP	H	R	ER	BB	SO
Glavine (W. 1-0)	9	4	1	1	0	6

E — None. DP — Atlanta 1. LOB — Toronto 2, Atlanta 7. HR — Carter (1), Berryhill (1). SB — Nixon (1), Gant (1). WP — Morris.
T – 2:37. A – 51,763.

Atlanta and Toronto await the start of the World Series, October 17, 1992.

Playoff Moments #13

OCTOBER 18, 1992 • *Blue Jays 5, Braves 4*

Ed Sprague added his name to the list of World Series heroes with a dramatic ninth-inning pinch-hit home run, but Game Two of the 1992 Fall Classic was almost as noteworthy for an event that took place before a pitch had even been thrown. A member of the U.S. Marine Color Guard marched onto the field for the pregame ceremonies with the Canadian flag hanging upside down. (Fortunately, the "flag incident" was put to rest before Game Three when the Marines requested the privilege of presenting the Canadian colours correctly.)

David Cone was the Blue Jays' starting pitcher in Game Two, but he proved more effective at the plate than on the mound. Cone became the first American League hurler to collect two

hits in a game since Mickey Lolich in 1968. Unfortunately, he surrendered five hits (and five walks) in just 4.1 innings, allowing the Braves four runs and a 4–2 lead before turning the ball over to David Wells. The score might have been closer except that plate umpire Mike Reilly had ruled Roberto Alomar out at home after he appeared to have scored on a passed ball. Alomar did later score Toronto's third run when Dave Winfield drove him home with a single in the top of the eighth. Thanks to some solid relief work by Wells, Todd Stottlemyre and Duane Ward, the score was 4–3 for the Braves as the game headed to the ninth inning.

On the hill for the Braves as the game entered its final frame was Jeff Reardon. Baseball's all-time saves leader had been traded to Atlanta from the Boston Red Sox in August. In 31 career appearances against the Blue Jays, Reardon had only been beaten once and had recorded 23 saves. He had come on to close out a Toronto rally in the eighth inning and now faced Derek Bell, pinch hitting for Manny Lee, with one out in the ninth. Named the Minor League Player of the Year in 1991, Bell had seen very limited action for the Blue Jays in 1992 and had been hitless in just two at-bats coming off the bench. Working Reardon to a full count, it appeared Bell had struck out when umpire Reilly signalled ball four. With the pitcher's spot due up next, Cito Gaston turned to another

unproven youngster when he sent Ed Sprague to the plate. Sprague had just 83 games of major league experience, including only 22 games and 47 at-bats in 1992, when he stepped in to face Reardon. The Braves closer served him a first-pitch fastball and Sprague lined it into the left field seats. A deathly silence filled Atlanta's Fulton County Coliseum as Sprague and Bell celebrated at home plate.

Sprague joined Kirk Gibson as the only players in World Series history to hit a pinch homer that lifted a trailing team into the lead. After a nervous bottom of the ninth in which Tom Henke walked one batter and hit another, Toronto had a stunning 5–4 victory. Instead of trailing in the World Series two games to nothing, the Blue Jays were all even and heading home with momentum on their side.

(Left) The flag flap. (Below) Ed Sprague punches the air after hitting the biggest home run of his life.

Toronto	AB	R	H	RBI	Atlanta	AB	R	H	RBI
White, cf	5	0	1	1	Nixon, cf	5	0	0	0
Alomar, 2b	4	1	1	0	Sanders, lf	3	1	1	0
Carter, lf	3	0	1	0	Pendleton, 3b	4	1	1	0
Winfield, rf	4	0	1	1	Justice, rf	3	1	1	1
Olerud, 1b	4	0	0	0	Bream, 1b	1	1	0	0
Gruber, 3b	4	0	0	0	Hunter, ph-1b	1	0	0	1
Borders, c	3	1	1	0	Blauser, ss	3	0	1	0
Lee, ss	3	1	1	0	Belliard, ss	0	0	0	0
DBell, ph	0	1	0	0	Berryhill, c	3	0	0	0
Griffin, ss	0	0	0	0	Lemke, 2b	4	0	1	1
Cone, p	2	0	2	1	Smoltz, p	3	0	0	0
Maldonado, ph	1	0	0	0	LSmith, ph	0	0	0	0
Sprague, ph	1	1	1	2	Gant, pr	0	0	0	0
Totals	34	5	9	5	**Totals**	30	4	5	3

```
Toronto .....................000 020 012 – 5
Atlanta .....................010 120 000 – 4
```

Toronto	IP	H	R	ER	BB	SO
Cone	4⅓	5	4	3	5	2
Wells	1⅔	0	0	0	1	2
Stottlemyre	1	0	0	0	0	0
Ward (W. 1-0)	1	0	0	0	0	2
Henke (S1)	1	0	0	0	1	0

Atlanta	IP	H	R	ER	BB	SO
Smoltz	7⅓	8	3	2	3	8
Stanton	⅓	0	0	0	0	0
Reardon (L. 0-1)	1⅓	1	2	2	1	1

E – Lee, Bream Borders. DP – Toronto 2, Atlanta 1. LOB – Toronto 6, Atlanta 6. 2B – Borders, Alomar. HR – Sprague (1). SB – Justice (1), Blauser (1), Sanders 2 (2), Gant 2 (2). SF – Hunter. HBP – by Henke (LSmith). WP – Cone, Smoltz 2.
T – 3:30. A – 51,763.

Playoff Moments #14

The third game of the 1992 Fall Classic marked the first time in history that a World Series game had been played outside the United States. While that fact itself would have made the game memorable, Blue Jays fans will always recall Game Three for "the Catch": Devon White's graceful, acrobatic grab that should have started the first World Series triple play since 1920.

"I don't know if it's my best catch ever," White would say after the game, "but it definitely came in the most important situation of my career."

Two-sport star Deion Sanders, who had angered Braves management by flying off to join his other team — the NFL's Atlanta Falcons — during the 1992 National League Championship Series, had led off the top of the fourth inning against the Blue Jays with an infield single off Juan Guzman. Sanders moved up to second on a Terry Pendleton single and, with Dave Justice coming to the plate, the Braves had a chance to blow open a scoreless ball game. Justice drilled a Guzman fastball to straightaway center field and Devon White took off in pursuit. "Devo" leaped when he reached the warning track and crashed facefirst into the wall . . . with the ball in his glove! White's catch was immediately compared to the grab made by Willie Mays in the 1954 World Series, but Devo wasn't done yet. He bounced off the wall and fired the ball to Roberto Alomar, who then relayed it to John Olerud at first base to double off Pendleton. (Pendleton, who had expected the ball to fall in for extra bases, had already been ruled out when he passed Sanders on the base path.) Sanders took off for third base, but Olerud's throw to Kelly Gruber beat him to the

bag. Gruber ran Sanders back toward second base, lunging at him and tagging his heel for what should have completed the triple play except that umpire Bob Davidson blew the call. No matter, as Juan Guzman calmly K'd Lonnie Smith on three pitches to end the inning and keep the game scoreless.

The SkyDome crowd was still buzzing in the bottom of the fourth when Joe Carter stepped to the plate and promptly deposited Steve Avery's first pitch into the media section of the left field stands. The Braves tied the game at 1–1 in the top of the sixth and went ahead 2–1 in the eighth with a run set up by a Gruber error. Kelly atoned by knotting matters with a solo homer in the bottom of the inning, breaking off a record 0-for-23 postseason slump. Guzman then turned the game over to Duane Ward and, after a key double play and a strikeout, Roberto Alomar led off the bottom of the ninth with a single. An Alomar steal, a Carter walk, Dave Winfield's sacrifice and a walk to pinch hitter Ed Sprague then loaded the bases with just one out. Candy Maldonado stepped up to the plate and Jeff Reardon came in to pitch. Reardon bent a couple of sliders over the corner of the plate, but when he tried to sneak a third slider past him, Maldonado muscled it into right field and the Blue Jays had a 3–2 victory.

Atlanta	AB	R	H	RBI	Toronto	AB	R	H	RBI
Nixon, cf	4	1	0	0	White, cf	4	0	0	0
Sanders, lf	4	1	3	0	Alomar, 2b	4	1	1	0
Pendleton, 3b	4	0	2	0	Carter, rf	3	1	1	1
Justice, rf	3	0	1	1	Winfield, dh	3	0	1	0
LSmith, dh	4	0	1	1	Olerud, 1b	3	0	0	0
Bream, 1b	4	0	2	0	Sprague, ph	0	0	0	0
Hunter, pr-1b	0	0	0	0	Maldonado, lf	4	0	1	1
Blauser, ss	4	0	0	0	Gruber, 3b	3	1	1	1
Berryhill, c	4	0	0	0	Borders, c	2	0	1	0
Lemke, 2b	3	0	0	0	Lee, ss	2	0	0	0
Totals	**34**	**2**	**9**	**2**	**Totals**	**29**	**3**	**6**	**3**

Atlanta	....	.000	001	010 — 2
Toronto	....	.000	100	011 — 3

One out when winning run scored

Atlanta	IP	H	R	ER	BB	SO
Avery (L, 0-1)	8	5	3	3	1	9
Wohlers	1/3	0	0	0	1	0
Stanton	0	0	0	0	1	0
Reardon	0	1	0	0	0	0

Toronto	IP	H	R	ER	BB	SO
Guzman	8	8	2	1	1	7
Ward (W, 2-0)	1	1	0	0	0	2

Avery pitched to one batter in ninth
Stanton pitched to one batter in ninth
Reardon pitched to one batter in ninth

E – Gruber. DP – Atlanta 1, Toronto 2. LOB – Atlanta 6, Toronto 5. 2B – Sanders. HR – Carter (2), Gruber (1). SB – Sanders (3), Gruber (1), Nixon (2), Alomar (1). S – Winfield.
T – 2:49. A – 51,813.

After celebrating his own home run (left), Gruber greets Alomar after Maldonado made Atlanta reliever Jeff Reardon "look sick." (Opposite) Devo does Willie: Devon White seems glued to the center field fence after making "the Catch."

Playoff Moments #15

OCTOBER 21, 1992 • *Blue Jays 2, Braves 1*

Jimmy Key is the winningest left-handed pitcher in Blue Jays history, but he was not at his best in 1992. With a record of just 13–13, he had been relegated to number-four starter behind Jack Morris, David Cone and Juan Guzman. That meant that when Cito Gaston elected to go with a three-man rotation for the

John Olerud slaps a swipe tag on Otis Nixon after the speedy Atlanta outfielder failed to negotiate a safe return to first base.

American League Championship Series, Key was sent to the bullpen. Since making his last start of the season on September 29, he had pitched just once: a three-inning stint in a Game Five loss to Oakland. Now, nine days later, he was being called on to start Game Four of the World Series.

The first batter Jimmy Key faced was Otis Nixon, who led off the game with a ringing single. The Braves had been running wild on the bases so far in the series with nine steals in three games, but Key had an exceptional pickoff move. He threw over to first and nailed Nixon. He then settled in for a classic pitchers' duel with Tom Glavine, shutting out the Braves into the eighth inning and retiring 16 batters in a row during one stretch. Key's

catcher Pat Borders had put the Blue Jays on the scoreboard with a solo homer in the third, extending a streak that would see him collect at least one base hit in every postseason game that year and help him be named the Most Valuable Player in the World Series. After the Borders homer, Glavine held the Blue Jays in check until a Devon White single in the bottom of the seventh cashed in Kelly Gruber. Gruber dove across the plate head first, bashing his chin on the dirt and nearly knocking himself unconscious. Still dazed in the top of the eighth, Kelly made a brilliant barehanded play on a ground ball and threw to first for a game-saving putout. A run did score on the play, cutting the Blue Jays' lead to 2–1 and spelling the end of the line for Jimmy Key. He had pitched 7.2 innings, allowing just five hits, walking none and striking out six. He left the field to a standing ovation.

"It popped into my mind as I was walking off that this might be my last game here," said Key, who was about to become a free agent. "That's why I tipped my hat. I don't usually do that but this was a special moment. I'll never forget it."

Duane Ward came on in relief of Key and faced Jeff Blauser with two runners on base. Bobby Cox had left-handed hitters Deion Sanders and Sid Bream on his bench, but elected to stay with his shortstop. Blauser smashed a ground ball down the first base line but John Olerud dove to make the play. The inning was over.

"Why Olerud was playing right there I'll never know," Cox grumbled.

The Braves had one last chance in the top of the ninth, but Tom Henke shut the door with a 1–2–3 inning and his second save of the World Series. The Blue Jays won the game 2–1 and were now just one win away from becoming champions.

In his swan song appearance in Toronto, Jimmy Key was masterful, shutting down the Braves through seven innings in a 2–1 Blue Jays victory.

Atlanta	AB	R	H	RBI	Toronto	AB	R	H	RBI
Nixon, cf	4	0	2	0	White, cf	4	0	3	1
Blauser, ss	4	0	1	0	Alomar, 2b	3	0	0	0
Pendleton, 3b	4	0	0	0	Carter, rf	3	0	0	0
LSmith, dh	4	0	0	0	Winfield, dh	3	0	0	0
Justice, rf	4	0	0	0	Olerud, 1b	3	0	2	0
Gant, lf	3	1	1	0	Maldonado, lf	3	0	0	0
Hunter, 1b	3	0	1	0	Gruber, 3b	2	1	0	0
Berryhill, c	3	0	0	0	Borders, c	3	1	1	1
Lemke, 2b	3	0	0	1	Lee, ss	3	0	0	0
Totals	32	1	5	1	Totals	27	2	6	2

Atlanta ....000 000 010 – 1
Toronto ....001 000 10x – 2

Atlanta	IP	H	R	ER	BB	SO
Glavine (L. 1-1)	8	6	2	2	4	2

Toronto	IP	H	R	ER	BB	SO
Key (W. 1-0)	7⅔	5	1	1	0	6
Ward	⅓	0	0	0	0	1
Henke (S2)	1	0	0	0	0	1

E – None. DP – Atlanta 2. LOB – Atlanta 4, Toronto 5. 2B – White., Gant.
HR – Borders (1). SB – Blauser (2), Alomar (2), Nixon (3). WP – Ward.
T – 2:21. A – 52,090.

(ticket stub)
GATE 5 • AISLE 120 • ROW 27 • SEAT 10
1992 FALL CLASSIC
SKYDOME
ESPLANADE
NET $61.54
GST 4.31
PST 6.15
TOTAL ..... $72.00 CDN
TORONTO BLUE JAYS
VS.
NATIONAL LEAGUE CHAMPIONS
1992
World Series
RAIN CHECK subject to the conditions set forth on back hereof.
DO NOT DETACH THIS COUPON
FRANCIS T. VINCENT, JR.
Commissioner of Baseball
4

Morris retired the first two batters.

Then Otis Nixon reached him for a single.

Four batters later, the Braves had a run in and Lonnie Smith at the plate. Smith lofted a high fly ball into right field. Joe Carter drifted back with it, then watched helplessly as the ball landed in the Atlanta bullpen. Smith's grand slam gave the Braves a 7–2 lead.

Unlike his start in Game Two, this time John Smoltz would not allow the Blue Jays to strike back. He got through the sixth inning, then turned over the ball to Mike Stanton. The stocky left-hander with the high leg kick allowed the Blue Jays just a single hit over the final three innings. The lone bright spot in the latter stages of the game came when Devon White threw out Mark Lemke at the plate in the top of the ninth, but all that really did was ensure that the final score would remain 7–2. There would be no celebrations in Toronto this night. If the Blue Jays were going to win the World Series now they were going to have to do it in enemy territory in front of the tomahawk-chopping fans of Atlanta.

Jack Morris looks back in anger after surrendering a decisive grand slam homer to Lonnie Smith in Game Five of the World Series.

Playoff Moments #16

OCTOBER 22, 1992 • *Braves 7, Blue Jays 2*

A crowd of 52,268 — the largest attendance ever for a baseball game in Toronto — jammed the SkyDome for Game Five. The fans were in the mood for a celebration. They began flocking to the ballpark some two hours before game time, filling the Dome with a party atmosphere. Everyone wanted to see the Blue Jays win their first World Series championship on home turf. "Tonight's the Night," the newspapers had boasted. Radio stations broadcasted the parade route throughout the day. But there was still the matter of winning one more game.

Jack Morris was back on the mound for the Blue Jays. The 20-game winner had struggled so far in the postseason, but he was a big-game pitcher and this was the scenario club management had envisioned when they signed him to a contract for $15 million over three years. Facing Morris would be John Smoltz, the same opponent he had duelled with so brilliantly in Game Seven in 1991. There would be no shutout this night, however, as the Braves got to Morris for a run in the top of the first inning. The Blue Jays got that one back when Pat Borders drove in John Olerud in the second. Atlanta went ahead again in the top of the fourth, but Borders evened matters for a second time when he singled in Olerud again in the bottom of the inning.

Then came the fifth.

It started innocently enough.

Atlanta	AB	R	H	RBI	Toronto	AB	R	H	RBI
Nixon, cf	5	2	3	0	White, cf	4	0	0	0
Sanders, lf	5	1	2	1	Alomar, 2b	3	0	0	0
Pendleton, 3b	5	1	2	1	Carter, rf	4	0	1	0
Justice, rf	3	2	1	1	Winfield, dh	4	0	1	0
LSmith, dh	4	1	1	4	Olerud, 1b	3	2	2	0
Bream, 1b	4	0	0	0	Sprague, ph-1b	1	0	0	0
Blauser, ss	4	0	1	0	Maldonado, lf	2	0	0	0
Belliard, ss	0	0	0	0	Gruber, 3b	4	0	0	0
Berryhill, c	4	0	1	0	Borders, c	4	0	2	2
Lemke, 2b	4	0	2	0	Lee, ss	3	0	0	0
Totals	**38**	**7**	**13**	**7**	**Totals**	**32**	**2**	**6**	**2**

```
Atlanta . . . . . . . . . . . . . . . . . .100  150  000 – 7
Toronto . . . . . . . . . . . . . . . . . .010  100  000 – 2
```

Atlanta	IP	H	R	ER	BB	SO
Smoltz (W, 1-0) 6		5	2	2	4	4
Stanton (S1) 3		1	0	0	0	1

Toronto	IP	H	R	ER	BB	SO
Morris (L, 0-2) 4⅔		9	7	7	1	5
Wells 1⅓		1	0	0	0	0
Timlin 1		0	0	0	0	0
Eichhorn 1		0	0	0	0	1
Stottlemyre 1		3	0	0	0	1

Smoltz pitched to one batter in seventh

E – None. DP – Atlanta 1, Toronto 1. LOB Atlanta 5, Toronto 7.
2B – Nixon, Pendleton 2, Borders. HR – Justice (1), LSmith (1).
SB – Nixon 2 (5).
T – 3:05. A – 52,268.

OCTOBER 24, 1992 • *Blue Jays 4, Braves 3*

"For the first time in history," said CBS announcer Sean McDonough, "the world championship banner will fly north of the border. The Toronto Blue Jays are baseball's best in 1992 . . . Oh Canada, what a series!"

What a finish!

For eight innings it had been a tense, well-played ball game. For the final three, it was a gut-wrenching thriller.

The Braves might have had momentum on their side entering Game Six, but the Blue Jays had not lost back-to-back games since the last weekend in August and they got off to a quick start against Atlanta. Devon White led off the game with a single off Braves starter Steve Avery. After a stolen base, a Roberto Alomar grounder moved White to third. He then scored on Joe Carter's sacrifice fly. David Cone, working with a full four days rest, was much sharper than he'd been in Game Two, and he shut the door on the Braves after allowing them to tie the score in the bottom of the third. Candy Maldonado restored Toronto's lead with a home run in the fourth, and Cone plus three Blue Jays relievers made the 2–1 score hold up until Tom Henke took over in the bottom of the ninth. No Toronto pitcher had blown a save since July 24, and with the ever-reliable "Terminator" on the mound, the World Series seemed as good as over.

But Jeff Blauser got aboard to lead off the ninth and, after a Damon Berryhill sacrifice, former Blue Jays farmhand Francisco Cabrera (the hero of Atlanta's pennant playoff with Pittsburgh) nearly forced Game Seven with a shot that was pulled in by Maldonado in left field. After the nerve-racking second out, the Blue Jays moved within one strike of victory when Henke fired two pitches past Otis Nixon . . . but then Nixon bounced a ball through the left side. Blauser scored and the game was tied! Ron Gant had a chance to win it for the Braves, but Henke retired him on a fly ball to center and the game headed for extra innings.

Game Four starter Jimmy Key was summoned from the bullpen to bail out Henke in the bottom of the tenth, and he stayed in the game to bat for himself leading off the 11th. Key worked fellow lefty Charlie Leibrandt to a 2-and-2 count before popping out foul behind first base. Leibrandt then nicked White with a pitch. Alomar followed with a base hit. When Carter popped out to shallow center, Dave Winfield came to the plate with two on and two out.

After fouling off several tough sliders from Leibrandt and running the count full, Winfield ripped a double down the left field line! White scored easily and waved in a hard-charging Alomar behind him. Toronto now had a 4–2 lead and looked ready to wrap up the series, but nothing ever came easily for the Blue Jays.

Jeff Blauser led off the bottom of the 11th by whacking the first pitch into left field. Jimmy Key then induced a ground ball off the bat of Berryhill, but the routine three-hopper that should have been an easy double play took a wild bounce and skipped off the glove of shortstop Alfredo Griffin.

Now Atlanta had runners at the corners and nobody out.

Foam tomahawks chopped and Braves fans chanted crazily.

A sacrifice bunt moved runners to second and third. Then a grounder cut Toronto's lead to 4–3 and brought ninth-inning hero Otis Nixon back to the plate.

Nixon was hitting .343 against lefties in the series, but only .263 against right-handers. Mark Eichhorn and Mike Timlin were both warming up in the Blue Jays bullpen. Cito Gaston went to the mound and signalled for the little-used Timlin. Then he warned him to watch for a bunt. Nixon bunted the second pitch to the right side of the mound.

Timlin pounced on it.

He fired the ball to Carter at first.

It arrived a half-step before the fleet-footed Nixon.

The Toronto Blue Jays were World Series Champions!

Toronto	AB	R	H	RBI	Atlanta	AB	R	H	RBI
White, cf	5	2	2	0	Nixon, cf	6	0	2	1
Alomar, 2b	6	1	3	0	Sanders, lf	3	1	2	0
Carter, 1b	5	0	2	1	Gant, ph-lf	2	0	0	0
Winfield, rf	5	0	1	2	Pendleton, 3b	4	0	1	1
Maldonado, lf	6	1	2	1	Justice, rf	4	0	0	0
Gruber, 3b	4	0	1	0	Bream, 1b	3	0	0	0
Borders, c	4	0	2	0	Blauser, ss	5	2	3	0
Lee, ss	4	0	1	0	Berryhill, c	4	0	0	0
Tabler, ph	1	0	0	0	Smoltz, pr	0	0	0	0
Griffin, ss	0	0	0	0	Lemke, 2b	2	0	0	0
Cone, p	2	0	0	0	LSmith, ph	0	0	0	0
DBell, ph	1	0	0	0	Belliard, ph	0	0	0	0
Key, p	1	0	0	0	Avery, p	1	0	0	0
					PSmith, ph	1	0	0	0
					Treadway, ph	1	0	0	0
					Cabrera, ph	1	0	0	0
					Hunter, ph	1	0	0	1
Totals	**44**	**4**	**14**	**4**	**Totals**	**38**	**3**	**8**	**3**

Toronto			100	100	000	02	–	4		
Atlanta			001	000	001	01	–	3		

Toronto	IP	H	R	ER	BB	SO
Cone	6	4	1	1	3	6
Stottlemyre	⅔	1	0	0	0	1
Wells	⅓	0	0	0	0	0
Ward	1	0	0	0	1	1
Henke	1⅓	2	1	1	1	0
Key (W. 2-0)	1⅓	1	1	0	0	0
Timlin (S1)	⅓	0	0	0	0	0

Atlanta	IP	H	R	ER	BB	SO
Avery	4	6	2	2	2	2
PSmith	3	3	0	0	0	0
Stanton	1⅔	2	0	0	1	0
Wohlers	⅓	0	0	0	0	0
Leibrandt (L 0-1)	2	3	2	2	0	0

E – Justice, Griffin. DP – Atlanta 1. LOB – Toronto 13, Atlanta 10. 2B – Sanders, Borders, Carter 2, Winfield. HR – Maldonado (1). SB – White (1), Alomar (3), Sanders 2 (5). S – Gruber, Berryhill, Belliard. SF – Carter, Pendleton. HBP – by Leibrandt (White). T – 4:07. A – 51, 763.

Dave Winfield stings a line drive down the third base line to plate both Alomar and White and set the stage for the Blue Jays' first World Series celebration.

(Above) Joe Carter has Mike Timlin's relay of Otis Nixon's failed bunt attempt safely in hand to clinch the 1992 World Series title. (Below) Carter does the Blue Jay bounce. (Right) A beaming Carter, an exuberant Jimmy Key and a relieved Jack Morris are among the faces in the Blue Jays victory scrum following the final out of the 1992 World Series.

(Above) Pat Borders with his World Series MVP trophy.
(Right) Robbie Alomar pours on the charm, and the champagne.
(Below) The fans in Toronto party hearty. Boisterous but ultimately polite, Blue Jays fanatics raced through the downtown streets of Toronto until dawn and beyond.

(Top, left) Joe Carter's beaming smile was constantly on display during the World Series parade. (Top, right) Proud Canadians everywhere gave the Jays the "We're #1" salute. (Above) Fans with their World Series T's. (Right) Jimmy Key's final salute to the fans that loved, respected and would soon miss him.

The Toronto Blue Jays and Philadelphia Phillies await the start of the 1993 World Series.

1993

95–67 .586 1st +7

Toronto won its second straight World Series title in 1993, downing the Philadelphia Phillies in six games. John Olerud (.363), Paul Molitor (.332) and Robbie Alomar (.326) were the top three hitters in the League. Every member of the team's starting lineup drove in at least 50 runs. Joe Carter (33 HR, 121 RBI) Pat Hentgen (19–9), Juan Guzman (14–3) and Duane Ward (45 saves) were the other main components that helped drive the Jays to victory.

Great Moments #20

Joe Carter joined Otto Velez, Ernie Whitt and George Bell in the Blue Jays record book when he slugged three home runs in a game at the SkyDome on August 23, 1993. But Carter did more than just write his name into Blue Jays history that day. His home run hat trick against Cleveland marked the fifth time he had hit three round-trippers in a single game, breaking the American League record of four he had previously shared with Lou Gehrig. Carter's four previous three-home-run games had all come while he was a member of the Indians. He accomplished the feat twice as a visitor at Fenway Park (in 1986 and 1987), then later did it at Texas and Minnesota in a span of three weeks in the summer of 1989.

Carter's first home run in the record-breaking game came in his first at-bat when he took Indians starter Albie Lopez deep with Roberto Alomar on board to tie the game 2–2. His second homer came as part of back-to-back blasts with John Olerud in the fifth and helped the Blue Jays take a 7–5 lead. The Indians had gone in front 9–7 by the time Carter took reliever Jeremy Hernandez deep in the eighth, but unfortunately 9–8 would be as close to Cleveland as the Blue Jays would get.

"I showed a little emotion going around first," said Carter after the game. "To be in the company of Lou Gehrig is something I'll always be proud of. It's a great record, but we needed the win."

Indeed, the loss to the Indians dropped Toronto out of sole possession of first place in the American League East. However, Carter's three-run homer in the first inning the following night (his fifth homer in three games) sparked the Blue Jays to an 8–6 victory that put them alone in front again.

Joe Carter watches the flight of the longball as his third home run of the day clears the outfield wall. (Left) Devon White, who snagged his third consecutive Gold Glove award in 1993, led off five games with a home run during the 1993 season.

Cleveland	AB	R	H	RBI	Toronto	AB	R	H	RBI
Lofton, cf	4	2	3	0	White, cf	3	0	0	0
Kirby, rf	4	0	1	0	Alomar, 2b	3	1	1	0
Maldonado, ph-rf	2	0	1	1	Molitor, dh	4	0	0	0
Baerga, 2b	6	1	2	2	Carter, rf	4	3	3	4
Belle, lf	6	1	3	3	Olerud, 1b	3	1	1	1
Sorrento, 1b	2	0	0	0	Fernandez, ss	4	1	1	0
Milligan, ph-1b	2	1	1	0	Coles, lf	3	2	2	1
Jefferson, dh	6	0	0	0	Canate, lf	1	0	0	0
Thome, 3b	2	2	1	0	Sprague, 3b	4	0	2	1
Espinoza, 3b	0	0	0	0	Borders	4	0	1	1
Fermin, ss	4	1	2	1					
Alomar Jr, c	5	1	3	2					
Totals	**43**	**9**	**17**	**9**	**Totals**	**33**	**8**	**11**	**8**

```
Cleveland . . . . . . . . . . . . . . . . . . . . . .201 111  120 – 9
Toronto . . . . . . . . . . . . . . . . . . . . . . . .210 220  010 – 8
```

Cleveland	IP	H	R	ER	BB	SO
Lopez	4⅔	9	6	6	2	0
Mutis	2	1	1	1	1	0
Hernandez (W. 4-2)	1⅓	1	1	1	1	0
Dipoto (S4)	1	0	0	0	1	2

Toronto	IP	H	R	ER	BB	SO
Morris	4⅓	8	5	5	3	3
Leiter	2	5	2	2	1	3
Williams	⅓	1	0	0	0	0
Castillo	⅓	1	0	0	0	0
Eichhorn (L. 2-1)	2	2	2	0	4	2

E – Sprague. DP – Cleveland 5, Toronto 2. LOB – Cleveland 15, Toronto 3. 2B – Belle, Thome, Coles. HR – Baerga (19), Belle (33), Carter 3 (27), Olerud (23). SB – Lofton (50), Sorrento (2).
T – 3:18. A – 50,518.

Great Moments #21

SEPTEMBER 27, 1993 • *Blue Jays 2, Brewers 0*

In the offseason that had followed their 1992 world championship, four of the team's key players — Tom Henke, Jimmy Key, David Cone and Dave Winfield — signed elsewhere as free agents. By the time the 1993 season started, 11 members of the 1992 team were no longer with the club. Some replacements came from within — such as Ed Sprague, who took over from Kelly Gruber at third base, and Duane Ward, who was promoted from setup man to stopper. Others came from outside the organization — including four-time 20-game winner Dave Stewart and perennial .300 hitter Paul Molitor. Later, the Blue Jays brought back Tony Fernandez, but no team in baseball history had ever overcome such a major facelift to repeat as World Series champions, and the 1993 season started slowly.

After treading water around the .500 mark for most of April and May, the Blue Jays put together a streak of 13 wins in 16 games late in June and had finally climbed into first place by the end of the month. Then a streak of 10 losses in 11 games heading into the All-Star break saw their lead become tenuous by the end of July. Pat Gillick tried to swing a deal with Seattle for Randy Johnson, but when that fell through he grabbed Rickey Henderson from Oakland at the trade deadline on July 31.

For the remainder of the campaign, the Blue Jays bent but they never broke. Although they were tied for first place on 20 separate occasions, they never relinquished top spot. After the Orioles pulled into a tie for first on September 9, Toronto won nine in a row and 12 of 14. Heading into Milwaukee on September 27, the Blue Jays had a chance to clinch the American League East division title for the third year in a row and the fourth time in five seasons.

Former Brewer Paul Molitor got the Blue Jays started early with a solo homer in the top of the second. Toronto went up 2–0 when Devon White singled in Ed Sprague in the third, and Pat Hentgen made the lead stand up through 6.2 rain-soaked innings before turning it over to the bullpen. Tony Castillo and Mike Timlin protected the lead into the ninth, where Duane Ward nailed it down, ending the game by inducing Kevin Reimer to hit into a double play.

"This is what it's all about," said Molitor, who had not celebrated a division title since winning with Milwaukee back in 1982. "It's such a great feeling."

"This is great," agreed Juan Guzman, "but it's only one step. There's two more ahead of us — making the World Series, then winning it."

On a chilly night in Milwaukee, the Jays clinched their third straight AL East flag with a tidy 2–0 win over the Brew Crew.

Toronto	AB	R	H	RBI	Milwaukee	AB	R	H	RBI
Henderson, lf	4	0	0	0	Hamilton, rf	4	0	1	0
White, cf	3	0	0	1	Yount, cf	4	0	1	0
Alomar, 2b	3	0	1	0	Surhoff, 3b	4	0	2	0
Carter, rf	3	0	0	0	Vaughn, dh	4	0	1	0
Olerud, 1b	4	0	0	0	Jaha, 1b	3	0	0	0
Molitor, dh	4	1	1	1	Nilsson, c	4	0	0	0
Fernandez, ss	4	0	2	0	Bell, 2b	3	0	0	0
Sprague, 3b	3	1	1	0	Lampkin, ph	1	0	0	0
Borders, c	3	0	2	0	O'Leary lf	3	0	1	0
					Valentin, ss	2	0	1	0
					Reimer, ph	1	0	0	0
Totals	**31**	**2**	**7**	**2**	**Totals**	**33**	**0**	**7**	**0**

| Toronto | | | | | | | 011 | 000 | 000 — 2 |
| Milwaukee | | | | | | | 000 | 000 | 000 — 0 |

Toronto	IP	H	R	ER	BB	SO
Hentgen (W. 19-8)	6⅔	7	0	0	2	7
Castillo	⅓	0	0	0	0	0
Timlin	1	0	0	0	0	0
D.Ward (S43)	1	0	0	0	1	0

Milwaukee	IP	H	R	ER	BB	SO
Eldred (L. 16-16)	9	7	2	2	2	7

E – None. DP – Toronto 1. LOB – Toronto 5, Milwaukee 9.
2B – Fernandez, Borders. HR – Molitor (22). SF – White.
WP – Hentgen
T – 2:53. A–14,931.

Great Moments #22

OCTOBER 3, 1993 • Blue Jays 11, Orioles 6

No set of teammates had finished 1–2–3 in a baseball batting race for 100 years, but heading into the final day of the 1993 season three Blue Jays had a chance to duplicate a feat last accomplished by Hall of Famers Billy Hamilton, Sam Thompson and Ed Delahanty of the Philadelphia Phillies in 1893.

John Olerud had long since wrapped up the American League batting title. After flirting with the .400 mark as late as August 2, he finished the year with a .363 average, which remains the best single-season total in franchise history. While Olerud's average dipped a bit in the final months, Paul Molitor's just kept getting better. He hit .361 after the All-Star break to finish the season second in the league at .332. His 211 hits on the year were the most in the major leagues, while his 22 homers and 111 RBIs established personal highs.

Like Molitor, Roberto Alomar enjoyed a great second half. Alomar batted .360 in August and .357 in September/October, but still had to finish with a flourish in order to pass Cleveland's Kenny Lofton for third place in the batting race. Alomar knew he needed some hits on the last day of the season, and with Lofton collecting two for the Indians, Robbie had three in four at-bats for the Blue Jays. He finished the year with a .326 average. Lofton was fourth at .325. Alomar also drove in five runs to power the Blue Jays to an 11–6 victory over the Orioles.

"He knew he needed a couple of hits and he got three," said an excited Joe Carter after the game. "To have three guys in our lineup [lead the league] is really unbelievable. This is a very offensive-minded ballclub."

Indeed it was. Carter himself had clubbed two home runs in a single inning (the eight-run second) in the season finale to finish the year with 33 homers and 121 RBIs. He was one of three Blue Jays, along with Molitor and Olerud, to drive in more than 100 runs. Four players — Molitor, Olerud, Alomar and Devon White — scored more than 100 runs, and the list reached five when Rickey Henderson was counted. He'd scored 37 of his 114 runs on the season after being acquired by the Blue Jays.

"A lot of great things happened this year," said manager Cito Gaston. "It's been some kind of season for these guys."

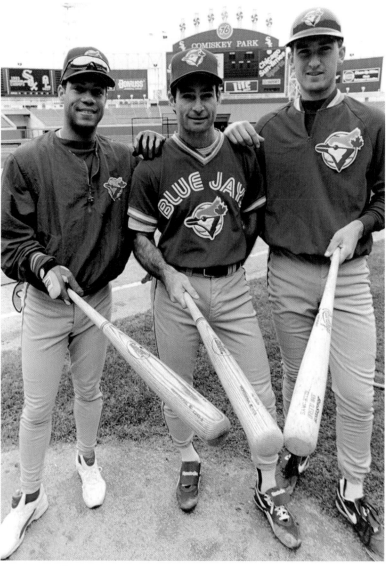

Toronto	AB	R	H	RBI	Baltimore	AB	R	H	RBI
Henderson, lf	1	1	0	0	Anderson, cf	5	0	0	0
Butler, lf	1	2	0	0	McLemore, rf	3	1	0	0
White, cf	3	2	1	0	CRipken, ss	4	2	1	0
Canate, cf	1	0	0	0	Baines, dh	4	0	1	1
Alomar, 2b	4	1	3	5	Hoiles, c	3	2	2	3
Cedeno, pr-2b	1	0	0	0	Pagliarulo, 3b	3	1	2	1
Carter, rf	2	2	2	3	Voigt, lf	4	0	0	0
Green, rf	2	0	0	0	Segui, 1b	3	0	1	1
Olerud, 1b	0	1	0	0	Reynolds, 2b	4	0	0	0
DMartinez, ph-1b	3	0	1	0					
TWard, ph-1b	1	0	1	0					
Molitor, dh	4	1	1	0					
Delgado, ph-dh	1	0	0	0					
Fernandez, ss	1	1	1	1					
Griffin, ph-ss	4	0	1	0					
Sprague, 3b	4	0	0	0					
Coles, 3b	1	0	0	0					
Borders, c	4	0	0	0					
Totals	**38**	**11**	**11**	**9**	**Totals**	**33**	**6**	**7**	**6**

Toronto					.080 102 000 — 11	
Baltimore					.202 000 020 — 6	

Toronto	IP	H	R	ER	BB	SO
Brow (W. 1-1)	6	4	4	4	2	3
Flener	2	3	2	2	2	0
Timlin	1	0	0	0	0	1

Baltimore	IP	H	R	ER	BB	SO
McDonald (L.13-14)	1⅔	5	8	8	3	2
O'Donoghue	2	1	1	1	2	2
Oquist	2⅓	4	2	2	1	1
Cook	2	1	0	0	1	2
Frohwirth	1	0	0	0	0	1

E – Pagliarulo, Segui. DP – Baltimore 1. LOB – Toronto 7, Baltimore 6. 2B – Alomar, Molitor, Pagliarulo. HR – Hoiles (29), Carter 2 (33). SB – Butler (2), Alomar (55), Molitor (22), Fernandez (15), Anderson (24). SF – Hoiles. HBP – by Brow (Ripken). WP – Flener. T – 3:04. A – 45,913.

The Triumphant Trio: John Olerud, Paul Molitor and Robbie Alomar finished 1–2–3 in the AL batting race, the first time this had been accomplished in the 20th century.

1993

single before turning the ball over to closer Duane Ward. Ward promptly walked the first two White Sox batters to give Chicago some hope. He then struck out the side to end the game.

One day later, the Blue Jays sent Dave Stewart to the mound in Game Two. Stewart had never lost a game in the ALCS, running up a record of 6-0 during his years with the Oakland A's. He pitched six solid innings, allowing just one run on four hits as the Blue Jays scored a 3–1 victory to take a 2–0 lead in the series. The key moment came during Stewart's final inning when he loaded the bases with nobody out, then escaped the jam without surrendering a run. Stewart recorded the final out himself, inducing a ground ball back to the mound and then racing over to first base to make the play unassisted. Al Leiter took over to pitch the seventh and eighth, before Ward came in to save the game in the ninth.

Juan Guzman extended his magical stretch of playoff success in 1993, winning his fourth consecutive postseason game with a 7–3 victory in Game One of the ALCS. (Below) Dandy Duane Ward appeared in four of the six games in the ALCS, earning a pair of saves, including one in the pennant-clinching victory.

Playoff Moments #18
OCTOBER 5–6, 1993 • *Blue Jays vs. White Sox*

The postseason road to a second straight World Series title began in Chicago in 1993. Game One of the American League Championship Series pitted the league's winningest pitcher (Cy Young Award winner Jack McDowell, 22–10) against the pitcher with the league's best winning percentage (Juan Guzman, 14–3, .824). Neither man would be very effective as the Blue Jays emerged with a 7–3 victory over the White Sox at the new Comiskey Park.

Toronto got on the scoreboard first when Ed Sprague tripled to right field with John Olerud and Paul Molitor on board in the top of the fourth. Chicago then used its half of the inning to produce three runs on just two hits as a wild Guzman allowed nine batters to come to the plate. Guzman did manage to hold the White Sox in check despite giving up eight walks in six innings. He allowed only five hits and left the game with a 5–3 lead. Olerud's two-run double had highlighted a three-run fifth that put Toronto back on top. McDowell lasted 6.2 innings, surrendering 13 hits and all seven Blue Jays runs, including a Paul Molitor homer. A trio of White Sox relievers came on to shut down Toronto for the rest of the game. Danny Cox worked a shutout seventh and eighth, allowing only an Ozzie Guillen

Playoff Moments #19

OCTOBER 12, 1993 • *Blue Jays 6, White Sox 3*

The trend of road teams winning in the 1993 American League Championship Series continued in Toronto when the White Sox arrived at the SkyDome and evened the series with a pair of wins. Wilson Alvarez went the distance as he outpitched Pat Hentgen for a 6–1 victory in Game Three. Tim Belcher was the hero in relief of Jason Bere as Chicago beat Toronto 7–4 in Game Four. Roberto Alomar guided the Blue Jays to victory in Game Five, reaching base in all five plate appearances (three hits, two walks) as Toronto moved to within a single win of the AL pennant with a 5–3 victory. The Blue Jays had to survive a nervous ninth inning that saw Duane Ward surrender a two-run homer to Robin Ventura before striking out Bo Jackson to end the game.

A confident group of Blue Jays took to the field back at Comiskey Park in Game Six, but it would be White Sox errors as much as anything that brought Chicago's season to an end. With the score tied 2–2 in the fourth inning, a Ventura error on a ground ball to third put Paul Molitor on base. He later came around to score the go-ahead run when second baseman Joey Cora threw the ball into the first base dugout. Still leading 3–2 in the ninth, the Blue Jays exploded for three more runs with another error providing the key. After a Devon White solo homer, White Sox reliever Scott Radinsky threw away what should have been the final out and opened the door for Paul Molitor to triple in a pair of insurance runs. Ward allowed a Warren Newson homer in the bottom of the ninth, but the White Sox got no closer and Toronto returned to the World Series with a 6–3 victory.

Dave Stewart pitched 7.1 innings to pick up the win in Game Six, allowing the White Sox two runs on just four hits. Stewart won both his starts against Chicago to run his ALCS record to a perfect 8–0. He had given up just three runs and eight hits in 13.1 innings for a 2.03 earned run average and was named the Most Valuable Player of the 1993 American League Championship Series.

Dave Stewart improved his ALCS record to an amazing 8–0 when he pitched the Blue Jays to victory in Game Six. (Below) Robbie Alomar continued his outstanding defensive play at second base for the Blue Jays.

Playoff Moments #20

OCTOBER 16, 1993 • *Blue Jays 8, Phillies 5*

Cito Gaston and Jim Fregosi were on-field foes in the 1970s before becoming managerial opponents in the 1993 Fall Classic. Seven years later, they would be bench partners with the Blue Jays.

For the first time in major league history, the World Series began on Canadian soil as the Blue Jays were back to defend their championship in 1993. Many expected the 90th Fall Classic to be a repeat of the previous year's matchup after the Atlanta Braves won 104 times and outduelled the San Francisco Giants by a single game in a thrilling race in the National League West. Statistically, the Braves dominated the National League Championship Series, but still they were beaten by the Philadelphia Phillies, who had gone from "worst to first" in the NL East.

On the mound to face the Blue Jays in Game One of the World Series was National League Championship Series MVP Curt Schilling. Juan Guzman started for Toronto. He was 14–3 during the season and had beaten the White Sox twice in the ALCS, but Guzman looked shaky in the opener. He walked Lenny Dykstra to lead off the game, then allowed him to steal second base. Dykstra came around to score on a John Kruk single. Darren Daulton then drove in Kruk and Philadelphia led 2–0. After holding the Phillies in check in the top of the second, the Blue Jays rallied with four singles and a fielder's choice to tie the game 2–2 after two. The teams exchanged runs in the third, but the Phillies took the lead again with another run in the fifth. The damage could have been worse had it not been for a brilliant fielding play by Roberto Alomar. The Blue Jays second baseman dove headlong to snare Dykstra's looping liner behind first base. The play definitely saved a run when

Mariano Duncan followed Dykstra with a triple. In the bottom of the fifth, Toronto tied the game again when Devon White took Schilling deep.

Al Leiter came on in relief of Guzman in the sixth inning and promptly found himself in a bases-loaded jam. He escaped unharmed by striking out Kruk on a 3-and-2 pitch to retire the side. Moments later, John Olerud put the Blue Jays in front for the first time all night with a one-out solo homer to right. In the bottom of the seventh, four consecutive hits by Pat Borders, former postseason nemesis Rickey Henderson, White and Alomar plated three more runs and upped Toronto's lead to 8–4.

Leiter, who would prove to be the winning pitcher, worked into the eighth inning before turning the ball over to closer Duane Ward. Ward got the final out of that inning, then mopped up in the ninth, allowing an unearned run on two hits and an error. The Blue Jays had an 8–5 victory.

Philadelphia	AB	R	H	RBI	Toronto	AB	R	H	RBI
Dykstra, cf	4	1	1	0	Henderson, lf	3	1	1	0
Duncan, 2b	5	2	3	0	White, cf	4	3	2	2
Kruk, 1b	4	2	3	2	Alomar, 2b	4	0	1	2
Hollins, 3b	4	0	0	0	Carter, rf	3	1	1	1
Daulton, c	4	0	1	1	Olerud, 1b	3	2	2	1
Eisenreich, rf	5	0	1	1	Molitor, dh	4	0	1	1
Jordan, dh	5	0	1	0	Fernandez, ss	3	0	0	1
Thompson, lf	3	0	0	0	Sprague, 3b	4	0	1	0
Incaviglia, ph-lf	1	0	0	0	Borders, c	4	1	1	0
Stocker, ss	3	0	1	0					
Totals	38	5	11	4	Totals	32	8	10	8

```
Philadelphia . . . . . . . . . . . . . . . . . . . . . . . .201  010  001 – 5
Toronto . . . . . . . . . . . . . . . . . . . . . . . . . . .021  011  30x – 8
```

Philadelphia	IP	H	R	ER	BB	SO
Schilling (L, 0-1)	6⅓	8	7	6	2	3
West	⅓	2	1	1	0	0
Anderson	⅔	0	0	0	1	1
Mason	1	0	0	0	0	0

Toronto	IP	H	R	ER	BB	SO
Guzman	5	5	4	4	4	6
Leiter (W, 1-0)	2⅔	4	0	0	1	2
Ward (S1)	1⅓	2	1	0	0	3

West pitched to two batters in seventh

E – Thompson, Alomar, Sprague, Carter. DP – Philadelphia 1, Toronto 1. LOB – Philadelphia 11, Toronto 4. 2B – White, Alomar. 3B – Duncan. HR – White (1), Olerud (1). SB – Dykstra (1), Duncan (1), Alomar (1). SF – Carter. WP – Guzman. PB – Daulton.
T – 3:27. A – 52,011.

Playoff Moments #21

Game Two of the 1993 World Series featured a matchup of veteran pitchers: Blue Jays right-hander Dave Stewart against Philadelphia lefty Terry Mulholland. Still, the game, like the entire series, would not be much of a pitchers' duel.

Stewart and Mulholland both put up a pair of goose eggs to begin the game, but then Stewart walked two batters to begin the third. By the time the inning was over he had surrendered five runs. The big blow came from Jim Eisenreich. A .318 hitter during the regular season, Eisenreich had hit just seven home runs but he took Stewart deep for a three-run blast that capped the Phillies uprising. Stewart would survive three more innings, keeping Philadelphia off the scoreboard while the Blue Jays pecked away at the deficit. Joe Carter connected in the fourth inning for his first of two World Series homers, cutting the Phillies' lead to 5–2. Two innings later, the Blue Jays bats knocked Mulholland out of the game, but Roger Mason came on to limit the damage to a single run and Toronto still trailed 5–3 after six.

Tony Castillo entered the game for the Blue Jays in the seventh inning, but he surrendered a leadoff homer to Lenny Dykstra. "Nails," as he was known, had led the National League with 194

hits and 143 runs in 1993. He would be a thorn in the side of the Blue Jays throughout the World Series, batting .348 with four homers and eight RBIs. He also provided stellar defense in center field. In Game Two alone he made two glitter catches, crashing into the wall on both occasions.

Dykstra's homer had given the Phillies some breathing room, but the Blue Jays were not about to give up. Paul Molitor led off the eighth with a double and after Joe Carter moved him to third, Phillies manager Jim Fregosi called on his closer, Mitch Williams, to face John Olerud.

A hard-throwing left-hander, Williams had saved 43 games in 1993, but with 44 walks in just 62 innings he was not known as "the Wild Thing" for nothing. He allowed Olerud to drive in Molitor with a sacrifice fly, then walked Roberto Alomar. With Tony Fernandez at the plate, Alomar stole second base to move himself into scoring position. Then he tried to move up another 90 feet. Unfortunately, he had not gotten a proper read on the Williams delivery. "The Wild Thing" nailed him at third base. The inning was over.

Tony Fernandez was still at the plate when the Blue Jays began the bottom of the ninth. He worked Williams for a walk, which brought up the tying run in the person of Ed Sprague. But Sprague could do no better than a fielder's choice. Williams then retired Pat Borders and Rickey Henderson to save Philadelphia's 6–4 victory. The World Series was tied at one win apiece.

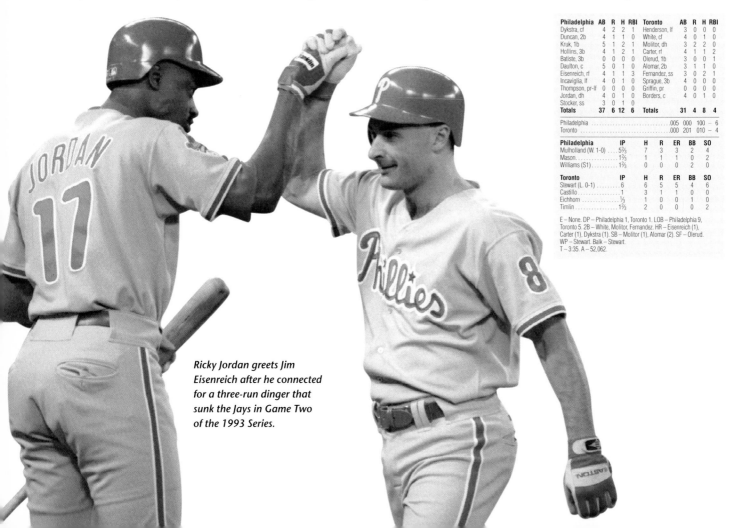

Ricky Jordan greets Jim Eisenreich after he connected for a three-run dinger that sunk the Jays in Game Two of the 1993 Series.

Philadelphia	AB	R	H	RBI	Toronto	AB	R	H	RBI
Dykstra, cf	4	2	2	1	Henderson, lf	3	0	0	0
Duncan, 2b	4	1	1	0	White, cf	4	0	1	0
Kruk, 1b	5	1	2	1	Molitor, dh	3	2	2	0
Hollins, 3b	4	1	2	1	Carter, rf	4	1	1	2
Batiste, 3b	0	0	0	0	Olerud, 1b	3	0	0	1
Daulton, c	5	0	1	0	Alomar, 2b	3	1	1	0
Eisenreich, rf	4	1	1	3	Fernandez, ss	3	0	2	1
Incaviglia, lf	4	0	1	0	Sprague, 3b	4	0	0	0
Thompson, pr-lf	0	0	0	0	Griffin, pr	0	0	0	0
Jordan, dh	4	0	1	0	Borders, c	4	0	1	0
Stocker, ss	3	0	1	0					
Totals	**37**	**6**	**12**	**6**	**Totals**	**31**	**4**	**8**	**4**

Philadelphia . . . . .005 000 100 — 6
Toronto . . . . .000 201 010 — 4

Philadelphia	IP	H	R	ER	BB	SO
Mulholland (W, 1-0)	5⅔	7	3	3	2	4
Mason	1⅔	1	1	1	0	2
Williams (S1)	1⅔	0	0	0	2	0

Toronto	IP	H	R	ER	BB	SO
Stewart (L, 0-1)	6	6	5	5	4	6
Castillo	1	3	1	1	0	0
Eichhorn	⅓	1	0	0	1	0
Timlin	1⅔	2	0	0	0	2

E – None. DP – Philadelphia 1, Toronto 1. LOB – Philadelphia 9, Toronto 5. 2B – White, Molitor, Fernandez. HR – Eisenreich (1), Carter (1), Dykstra (1). SB – Molitor (1), Alomar (2). SF – Olerud. WP – Stewart. Balk – Stewart.
T – 3:35. A – 52,062.

Playoff Moments #22

As the scene of the 1993 World Series shifted to Veterans Stadium in Philadelphia, Blue Jays manager Cito Gaston had a tough choice to make. The designated hitter would not be used in the National League park, but Gaston wanted to get Paul Molitor's bat into the lineup. Realistically, first base (where he had played 23 games during the season) was the only position that Molitor could play, but to do that Gaston would have to bench batting champion John Olerud. Third base was another option, but Molitor had not played that position regularly since 1989. Gaston's decision was to sit Olerud and play Molitor at first base against the left-handed Danny Jackson in Game Three. Molitor would then play third in place of Ed Sprague against right-handers in Games Four and Five.

Though rain delayed the start of Game Three by 72 minutes,

Molitor wasted little time in rewarding his manager's strategy. With Rickey Henderson and Devon White on base to begin the game, Molitor socked a two-run triple. He then came in to score on Joe Carter's sacrifice fly. In the third, Molitor belted a solo homer to up Toronto's lead to 4–0. The Blue Jays added another run in the sixth when Roberto Alomar singled, stole second and third, then came in to score on a sacrifice fly from Tony Fernandez.

The beneficiary of all these runs — as he had been for much of the season — was Pat Hentgen. In his first full season with the Blue Jays, Hentgen had posted a 19–9 record (including a 12–2 mark on the road) and had been supported with a team-best 6.1 runs per game. After surviving a bases-loaded jam in the bottom of the first, Hentgen continued his mastery on the road by working an effective six innings before turning the game over to the bullpen with a 5–1 lead. The lead became 8–1 in the top of the seventh as the Blue Jays beat up on Phillies reliever Ben Rivera. Two more runs in the top of the ninth pushed the advantage to 10–2. Duane Ward came on for an inning of work in the bottom of the ninth. He allowed a solo homer to Milt Thompson and, in the end, Toronto scored a convincing 10–3 victory.

Paul Molitor finished the night with three hits, three RBIs and three runs scored. Roberto Alomar was 4-for-5 with two runs scored and two RBIs, while Rickey Henderson and Tony Fernandez both contributed a pair of singles to Toronto's 13-hit attack. But the offensive onslaught in Game Three was nothing compared to what would be seen the following evening.

After nearly two decades of postseason frustration, Paul Molitor (left) was given the opportunity to deliver and he didn't waste it — batting .500, popping a pair of homers and driving in eight runs to win the World Series and the MVP Award. (Above) Pat Hentgen was the forgotten ace of the Blue Jays staff in 1993. The Michigan native won 19 games in the regular season before recording a key win in Game Three of the World Series.

Toronto	AB	R	H	RBI	Philadelphia	AB	R	H	RBI
Henderson, lf	4	2	2	0	Dykstra, cf	5	0	1	0
White, cf	4	2	1	1	Duncan, 2b	5	0	2	1
Molitor, 1b	4	3	3	3	Kruk, 1b	3	1	2	0
Carter, rf	4	1	1	1	Hollins, 3b	3	0	0	0
Alomar, 2b	5	2	4	2	Daulton, c	3	0	0	0
Fernandez, ss	3	0	2	2	Eisenreich, rf	4	0	1	1
Sprague, 3b	4	0	0	1	Incaviglia, lf	3	0	0	0
Borders, c	4	0	0	0	Thigpen, p	0	0	0	0
Hentgen, p	3	0	0	0	Morandini, ph	1	0	0	0
Cox, p	1	0	0	0	Anderson, p	0	0	0	0
Ward, p	0	0	0	0	Stocker, ss	4	0	1	0
					Jackson, p	1	0	0	0
					Chamberlain, ph	1	0	0	0
					Rivera, p	0	0	0	0
					Thompson, lf	2	2	2	1
Totals	**36**	**10**	**13**	**10**	**Totals**	**34**	**3**	**9**	**3**

Toronto						.301	001	302	—	10
Philadelphia						.000	001	101	—	3

Toronto	IP	H	R	ER	BB	SO
Hentgen (W. 1-0)	6	5	1	1	3	6
Cox	2	3	1	1	2	2
Ward	1	1	1	1	0	2

Philadelphia	IP	H	R	ER	BB	SO
Jackson (L. 0-1)	5	6	4	4	1	1
Rivera	1⅓	4	4	4	2	3
Thigpen	1⅔	0	0	0	1	2
Andersen	1	3	2	2	0	0

E – Carter. DP – Toronto 2. LOB – Toronto 7, Philadelphia 9.
2B – Henderson, Kruk. 3B – White, Molitor, Alomar. HR – Molitor (1), Thompson (1). SB – Alomar 2 (4). SF – Carter, Fernandez. HBP – by Thigpen (Henderson).
T – 3:16. A – 62,689.

Playoff Moments #23

OCTOBER 20, 1993 • *Blue Jays 15, Phillies 14*

Game Four of the 1993 World Series was the wildest in the history of the Fall Classic. At four hours and 14 minutes, it was also the longest. When it was all over, Toronto had rallied from a pair of five-run deficits (12–7 and 14–9) to pull out a thrilling 15–14 victory. The two teams had combined for a World Series–record 29 runs and 32 hits. Eleven other records were tied or broken. Remarkably, considering the cold and rain in which the game had been played, no errors were made.

The tone of the evening was set in the very first frame when the Blue Jays scored three runs after two were out, yet came out of the inning trailing. That was because Todd Stottlemyre promptly walked four Phillies before giving up a Milt Thompson triple that made the score 4–3. Phillies starter Tommy Greene had issued two free passes of his own in the first, then walked Stottlemyre in the second. He managed to escape the inning without any further damage when Todd was gunned down trying to go from first to third on a Roberto Alomar single. Stottlemyre banged himself up with a head-first dive and took to the mound in the bottom of the second with blood glistened on his wounded chin. He promptly allowed Greene to touch him for a single, then surrendered a two-run bomb by Lenny Dykstra. The second inning ended 6–3 for the Phillies and Stottlemyre was done. He was taken off the hook when the Blue Jays batted around in a four-run third to take a 7–6 lead.

Al Leiter came on to replace Stottlemyre, and though he blanked the Phillies in the bottom of the third he would prove to be more effective with the bat than he was with the ball. After allowing the Phillies to tie the game in the fourth, Leiter managed to hit a double in his first plate appearance since high school. Unfortunately, he then surrendered five runs in the bottom of the fifth — including two-run homers by Dykstra and Darren Daulton — and was lifted for Tony Castillo. The Blue Jays responded with a pair of runs in their next at-bat, but the Phillies got those back when they reached Castillo for single tallies in the bottom of the sixth and the bottom of the seventh. The seventh-inning run crossed the plate when Castillo hit Daulton with the bases loaded.

The score was now 14–9 for the Phillies as Larry Andersen returned to the mound in the eighth. He retired Roberto Alomar on a ground ball to third baseman Dave Hollins, but after a double by Joe Carter, a walk to John Olerud and another two-bagger by Paul Molitor, Jim Fregosi called on Mitch Williams to put out the fire.

He didn't.

"The Wild Thing" surrendered a run-scoring single to Fernandez, then a walk to Pat Borders. After striking out pinch hitter Ed Sprague, Williams gave up a two-run single to Rickey Henderson. Suddenly, the Phillies' five-run lead had been cut to 14–13 and the go-ahead runs were still on base. When Devon White lifted a triple into right field, Borders and Henderson came in to score and the Blue Jays had taken the lead.

Mike Timlin came on to start the bottom of the eighth and retired two batters before Lenny Dykstra came to the plate. Duane Ward was brought in to face him. Dykstra was already 3-for-4 on the night. He had slugged two home runs and just missed a third, but Ward struck him out! Then, in the bottom of the ninth, the Blue Jays stopper retired the Phillies in order. Toronto had an improbable victory and was just one win away from its second straight World Series championship.

Toronto	AB	R	H	RBI		Philadelphia	AB	R	H	RBI
Henderson, lf	5	2	2	2		Dykstra, cf	5	4	3	4
White, cf	5	2	3	4		Duncan, 2b	6	1	3	1
Alomar, 2b	6	1	2	1		Kruk, 1b	5	0	0	0
Carter, rf	6	2	3	0		Hollins, 3b	4	3	2	0
Olerud, 1b	4	2	1	0		Daulton, c	3	2	1	3
Molitor, 3b	4	2	2	2		Eisenreich, rf	4	2	1	1
Griffin, 3b	0	0	0	0		Thompson, lf	5	1	3	5
Fernandez, ss	6	2	3	5		Stocker, ss	4	0	0	0
Borders, c	4	1	1	1		Greene, p	1	1	1	0
Stottlemyre, p	0	0	0	0		Mason, p	1	0	0	0
Butler, ph	1	1	0	0		Jordan, ph	1	0	0	0
Leiter, p	1	0	1	0		West, p	0	0	0	0
Castillo, p	1	0	0	0		Chamberlain, ph	1	0	0	0
Sprague, ph	1	0	0	0		Andersen, p	0	0	0	0
Timlin, p	0	0	0	0		Williams, p	0	0	0	0
Ward, p	0	0	0	0		Morandini, ph	1	0	0	0
						Thigpen, p	0	0	0	0
Totals	44	15	18	15		Totals	41	14	14	14

| Toronto | | | | | | | 304 | 002 | 060 | – 15 |
| Philadelphia | | | | | | | 420 | 151 | 100 | – 14 |

Toronto	IP	H	R	ER	BB	SO
Stottlemyre	2	3	6	6	4	1
Leiter	2⅔	8	6	6	0	1
Castillo (W. 1-0)	2⅓	3	2	2	3	1
Timlin	⅔	0	0	0	0	2
Ward (S2)	1⅓	0	0	0	0	2

Philadelphia	IP	H	R	ER	BB	SO
Greene	2⅓	7	7	7	4	1
Mason	2⅔	2	0	0	1	2
West	1	3	2	2	0	0
Andersen	1⅓	2	3	3	1	2
Williams (L. 0-1)	⅔	3	3	3	1	1
Thigpen	1	1	0	0	0	0

E – None. DP – None. LOB – Toronto 10, Philadelphia 8.
2B – Henderson, White, Carter, Leiter, Dykstra, Hollins, Thompson, Molitor. 3B – White, Thompson. HR – Dykstra 2 (3), Daulton (1). SB – Henderson (1), White (1), Dykstra (2).
HBP – by Castillo (Daulton), by West (Molitor)
T – 4:14. A – 62,731.

Playoff Moments #24

As in 1992, the Blue Jays entered Game Five of the 1993 World Series with a chance to win it all. In 1992, they were beaten by the bat of Lonnie Smith. In 1993, it would be the arm of Curt Schilling that did them in.

Game Five was a rematch of Game One's starting pitchers, as the Blue Jays' Juan Guzman faced Schilling. By this time, the Phillies bullpen was worn out. WILL PITCH MIDDLE RELIEF FOR FOOD said a sign in the stands at Veterans Stadium. The team needed a big performance from their ace starter, and they got it. Guzman, on the other hand, looked shaky at the outset.

He walked leadoff hitter Lenny Dykstra, then allowed him to steal second before he came around to score on a John Kruk groundout. Guzman settled down after allowing another run on a pair of doubles in the second, but Schilling already had all the support he needed. One night after watching the Blue Jays score 15 runs on 18 hits, Schilling shut them down with a five-hitter, walking three but striking out six. The only time he got into trouble was in the top of the eighth inning.

Pat Borders led off the eighth with a single, and was then lifted for pinch runner Willie Canate. This was the first, and only, appearance the rookie outfielder would make in the postseason. As a player obtained through the Rule 5 Draft, the Blue Jays had had to keep Canate on their roster all season, but he had played in just 38 games and had come to bat just 47 times. A pinch-hit single by Rob Butler sent Canate around to third with nobody out, but his inexperience on the base paths showed when Rickey Henderson followed with a ground ball back to the pitcher. Schilling trapped Canate between third base and home, throwing to catcher Darren Daulton, who ran him back towards Dave Hollins, who applied the tag. The Blue Jays still had two runners on, but Schilling struck out Devon White and induced another ground ball from Roberto Alomar to end the threat. The Blue Jays went quickly and quietly in the ninth and the Phillies had a 2–0 victory.

Schilling's heroic mound masterpiece sent the series back to Toronto and ensured that the World Series title would be captured on foreign soil for the first time in history.

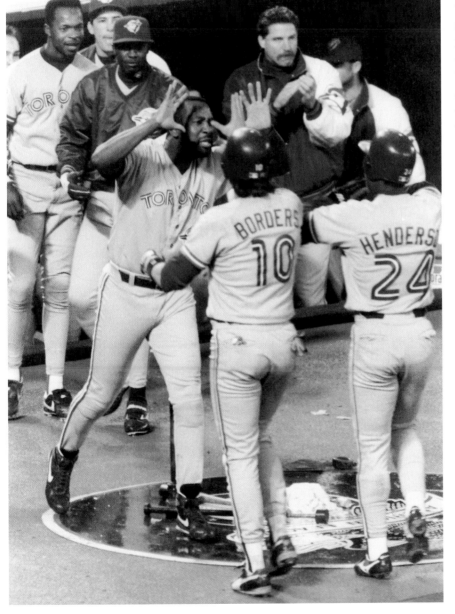

Joe Carter greets Pat Borders and Rickey Henderson after they both crossed the plate to give the Jays a Game Four lead they would never surrender.

Toronto	AB	R	H	RBI	Philadelphia	AB	R	H	RBI
Henderson, lf	3	0	0	0	Dykstra, cf	2	1	0	0
White, cf	3	0	0	0	Duncan, 2b	4	0	0	0
Alomar, 2b	3	0	1	0	Kruk, 1b	3	0	1	1
Carter, lf	4	0	0	0	Hollins, 3b	3	0	1	0
Olerud, 1b	4	0	0	0	Batiste, 3b	0	0	0	0
Molitor, 3b	4	0	1	0	Daulton, c	4	1	1	0
Fernandez, ss	3	0	0	0	Eisenreich, rf	4	0	0	0
Borders, c	3	0	2	0	Thompson, lf	3	0	0	0
Canate, pr	0	0	0	0	Stocker, ss	2	0	1	1
Knorr, c	0	0	0	0	Schilling, p	2	0	1	0
Guzman, p	2	0	0	0					
Butler, ph	1	0	1	0					
Cox, p	0	0	0	0					
Totals	**30**	**0**	**5**	**0**	**Totals**	**27**	**2**	**5**	**2**

```
Toronto . . . . . . . . . . . . . . . . . . . . . . . . . .000  000  000 – 0
Philadelphia . . . . . . . . . . . . . . . . . . . . . .110  000  00x – 2
```

Toronto	IP	H	R	ER	BB	SO
Guzman (L, 0-1)	7	5	2	1	4	6
Cox	1	0	0	0	2	3

Philadelphia	IP	H	R	ER	BB	SO
Schilling (W, 1-0)	9	5	0	0	3	6

E – Borders, Duncan. DP – Toronto 1, Philadelphia 3.
LOB – Toronto 6, Philadelphia 8. 2B – Daulton, Stocker.
SB – Dykstra (3). S – Schilling.
T – 2:53. A – 62,706.

Playoff Moments #25

OCTOBER 23, 1993 • *Blue Jays 8, Phillies 5*

"Touch 'em all Joe!" shouted Tom Cheek on the radio. "You'll never hit a bigger home run in your life!"

He was right. Only once before in World Series history had a team won it all on a home run. Never had a team come from behind to win it on one swing of the bat. When Game Six of the 1993 World Series started, it didn't look like such dramatics would be necessary, but when it was over Joe Carter had added his name to the list of World Series legends and the Blue Jays were champions once again.

Game Six had begun three hours and 27 minutes earlier when Dave Stewart struck out Phillies leadoff hitter Lenny Dykstra. The Blue Jays appeared to take command of the game in the bottom of the first when Paul Molitor tripled in one run and scored another to highlight a three-run outburst. Molitor got to Terry Mulholland again in the fourth when a solo homer restored the three-run lead after the Phillies had touched Stewart for a run in the top of the inning. In the fifth, errors by Roberto Alomar and Ed Sprague loaded the bases, but Stewart escaped the jam unscathed. The Blue Jays pushed across another run in the bottom of the fifth and seemed to have the game well in hand as they took a 5–1 lead into the seventh inning. That's when things took a turn for the dramatic.

Kevin Stocker led off the top of the seventh with a walk. Mickey Morandini followed with a single. Next up was Dykstra, who continued his red-hot hitting by launching a shot into the left field seats. The Phillies were back in the game, and they weren't done yet. They continued to hammer Danny Cox, who came on from the Blue Jays bullpen. The Phillies tied the game when Mariano Duncan singled, stole second and came in to score on a Dave Hollins single. After a walk and a single loaded the bases, pinch hitter Pete Incaviglia hit a sacrifice fly off Al Leiter and Philadelphia had its first lead of the night. There were still runners on first and third, but Leiter prevented any further damage by striking out Stocker to finally put an end to the uprising.

Toronto had a great opportunity to battle back in the eighth, but, with the bases loaded, Larry Andersen enticed a pop up from Pat Borders and the score remained 6–5 Philadelphia

heading into the ninth. Duane Ward was brought in to keep the game close, and after he breezed through the top of the inning, Mitch Williams was summoned to pitch the bottom of the ninth.

True to his nickname, "the Wild Thing" walked leadoff hitter Rickey Henderson on four straight pitches. Devon White lifted a fly ball to left for the first out, but Paul Molitor slashed a single to center and brought Joe Carter to the plate.

Carter took the first two pitches for balls.

Williams's third offering was taken for a strike.

The fourth pitch was low, but Joe swung through it.

Then, with a count of 2-and-2, Williams tried to sneak another slider by him.

But Carter connected, hooking the ball deep down the left field line. A crowd of 52,195 — plus millions more tuning in on television — watched the flight of the ball. When it cleared the left field wall 15 feet to the right of the foul pole, there was an explosion of emotion. Carter danced and hopped around the bases as his teammates gathered at the plate. As soon as he touched home, Carter was lifted onto their shoulders.

Paul Molitor, who had actually scored the winning run, wept openly.

He had waited 16 years to win the World Series.

Now he was the Most Valuable Player.

Molitor had collected 12 hits in 24 at-bats for a .500 average. He had two doubles, two triples and two home runs. He had driven in eight runs and scored a record-tying 10 times.

"Hey, this is for you," Carter told him.

"It was everything I imagined," Molitor said.

(Opposite) The Carter Clout: Back-to-back World Series champions with one swing of the bat. (Right) An emotional Paul Molitor wears his heart, and his tears, on his sleeve after finally achieving his greatest goal — a World Series championship.

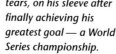

Philadelphia	AB	R	H	RBI	Toronto	AB	R	H	RBI
Dykstra, cf	3	1	1	3	Henderson, lf	4	1	0	0
Duncan, dh	5	1	1	0	White, cf	4	1	0	0
Kruk, 1b	3	0	0	0	Molitor, dh	5	3	3	2
Hollins, 3b	5	1	1	1	Carter, rf	4	1	1	4
Batiste, 3b	0	0	0	0	Olerud, 1b	3	1	1	0
Daulton, c	4	1	1	0	Griffin, pr-3b	0	0	0	0
Eisenreich, rf	5	0	2	1	Alomar, 2b	4	1	3	1
Thompson, lf	3	0	0	0	Fernandez, ss	3	0	0	0
Incaviglia, ph-lf	0	0	0	1	Sprague, 3b-1b	2	0	0	1
Stocker, ss	3	1	0	0	Borders, c	4	0	2	0
Morandini, 2b	4	1	1	0					
Totals	35	6	7	6	Totals	33	8	10	8

```
Philadelphia .............................000  100  500 – 6
Toronto ...................................300  110  003 – 8
One out when winning run scored
```

Philadelphia	IP	H	R	ER	BB	SO
Mulholland	5	7	5	5	1	1
Mason	2⅓	1	0	0	0	2
West	0	0	0	0	1	0
Andersen	⅔	0	0	0	0	1
Williams (L, 0-2)	⅓	2	3	3	1	0

Toronto	IP	H	R	ER	BB	SO
Stewart	6	4	4	4	4	2
Cox	⅓	3	2	2	1	1
Leiter	1⅔	0	0	0	1	2
Ward (W, 1-0)	1	0	0	0	0	0

Stewart pitched to three batters in seventh
West pitched to one batter in eighth

```
E – Alomar, Sprague. DP – None. LOB – Philadelphia 9, Toronto 7.
2B – Daulton, Olerud, Alomar. 3B – Molitor (2),
Dykstra (4), Carter (2). SB – Duncan (3), Dykstra (4).
SF – Carter, Sprague, Incaviglia. HBP – by Andersen (Fernandez).
T – 3:27. A – 52,195.
```

(Left) The Hero. (Below, left) The mob scene at the plate when the hero finally returned home. (Below, right) Fans fanatically finding and feeling the fun.

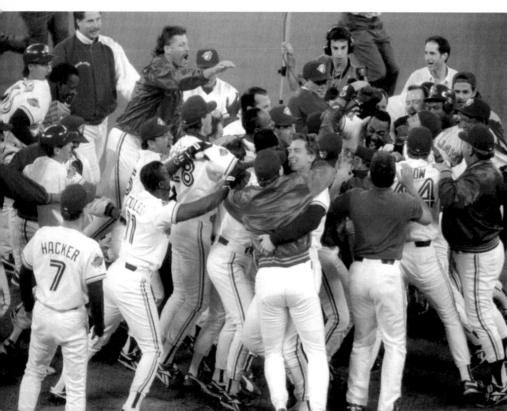

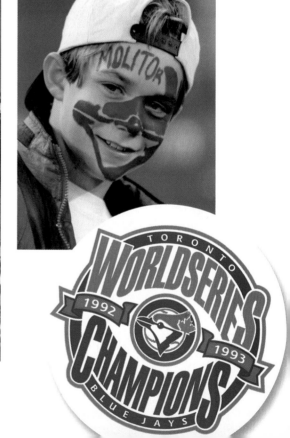

(Top) Unveil the Banner! (Above) Cito Gaston makes an emotional address to the celebratory throng at SkyDome following the World Series parade. (Right) The Thief and the Hero: Rickey Henderson and Joe Carter give the SkyDome faithful a glimpse of the World Series trophy.

The Parade, the Fans and the Pride: Hired gunslingers like Rickey Henderson (above) always love a parade. Joe Carter (left) shows and savours his true colours.

1994

55–60 .478 3rd -16

The Blue Jays finished under .500 for the first time since 1982. Carlos Delgado was an April sensation, tying a major league-rookie record with eight homers. Joe Carter was also at his best, establishing a record with 31 RBIs in the first month of the campaign. Paul Molitor hit .341 and Pat Hentgen had a team-leading 13 wins and ERA of 3.40. The surprise of the season was the emergence of Darren Hall who recorded 17 saves.

It would be a season of discontent for Paul Molitor, the Blue Jays and all of baseball in 1994.

Carlos Delgado's moon shots brought April showers as the Jays rookie launched eight home runs into the stratosphere in the opening month of the 1994 season. Joe Carter congratulates him after his first.

With Duane Ward on the shelf, career minor leaguer Darren Hall stepped into the fire and became the Jays' top bullpen flame thrower. He established a team rookie record with 17 saves.

Pat Hentgen was once again the ace of the Blue Jays rotation, winning 13 games in the strike-shortened 1994 season.

1995

56–88 .389 5th -30

Joe Carter (25 HR) led the club in round-trippers for the fifth straight season while right fielder Shawn Green set a club rookie record with 50 extra base hits. Southpaw Al Leiter (11 wins, 3.64 ERA, 153 strikeouts) finally showed his true potential. Domingo Cedeno and Tomas Perez solidified the defense and Ed Sprague (18 HR, 74 RBI) emerged as a team leader. Tony Castillo (3.22 ERA in 55 games) and split-finger specialist Tim Crabtree (3.09 ERA) were the top pitchers.

Although he was first acquired in 1989, Al Leiter didn't blossom as a starting pitcher until the 1995 season when he led the staff with 11 victories and a 3.64 ERA.

Oddities and Others [#]**19**

APRIL 26, 1995 • *Blue Jays 13, Athletics 1*

Chances of a Blue Jays "three-peat" had looked good early in 1994. The team opened the season with six wins in the first eight games and was a respectable 14–10 at the end of April. Rookie Carlos Delgado had slugged eight home runs and Joe Carter collected 31 RBIs. But without ace closer Duane Ward, who was gone for the season with an injury, that was as good as it got for the Blue Jays. When a players strike ended the 1994 season on August 12, the Blue Jays had a record of 55–60 and their first losing season since 1982.

The strike would eventually wipe out the 1994 World Series and threaten the 1995 season as well. Teams actually went to spring training with replacement players before legal action finally ended the dispute. The start of the new season was pushed back three weeks — but at least the strike was over. Because there had been no World Series, the Blue Jays were still considered defending champions. Most of the 1993 team was still intact and hopes that the slump of 1994 could be overcome received a major boost when new general manager Gord Ash re-acquired David Cone from Kansas City. Cone was coming off a 16–5 season and had won the Cy Young Award.

Cone was on the mound at the SkyDome when baseball resumed on April 26. Opposing him was former Blue Jay Dave Stewart. Stewart had recently re-signed with Oakland and was given a rude return to Toronto when the Blue Jays exploded for 11 runs in the bottom of the second. Sixteen men came to the plate as all nine batters reached base at least once via a hit or a walk. Devon White led the attack with a two-run double and a two-run single. John Olerud and Ed Sprague both scored a pair of runs. The line for the inning read 11 runs on eight hits, one error, four walks and two left on base.

Unfortunately, opening day and a pair of clutch home runs by Roberto Alomar against the White Sox a week later would prove to be the high point of the 1995 season. Without a dependable bullpen, the team began to fall apart and, as the losses mounted, players lost confidence in each other and themselves. The end result was a dismal 56–88 record for the abbreviated 144-game season and the club's first last-place finish since 1981.

Even John Olerud's sweet swing lost some of its pop in 1995, though he did bat a respectable .291 for the season.

Roberto Alomar was the only member of the Jays to hit .300 in 1995.

1996

74–88 .457 4th -18

The Blue Jays' 20th Anniversary season was highlighted by Pat Hentgen (20–10, 10 complete games and 265.2 innings) who became the first Blue Jay to win the Cy Young Award. Third baseman Ed Sprague posted career-best numbers (36 HR, 101 RBI) and Joe Carter topped the 30 homer/100 RBI plateau for the ninth time in his career. Juan Guzman led the AL with a 2.93 ERA. Youngsters like Carlos Delgado, Shawn Green, and Alex Gonzalez showed both potential and improvement.

The highlight of the Jays' 20th season was the 20-win performance of "the Human Horse," Pat Hentgen. The Michigan native led the league in complete games (10) and innings (265.2) and became the first Jays hurler to win the Cy Young Award as the league's best pitcher.

Oddities and Others #20

APR. 9, 1996 • *Level of Excellence*

As part of the celebrations of the club's 20th season in 1996, the Blue Jays created the "Level of Excellence" to recognize the tremendous achievements of past players. It is the highest award bestowed by the team, and although the players' uniform numbers are not officially retired, the name and number of the men so honoured are on permanent display inside the SkyDome.

The first players to be honoured in the Level of Excellence were George Bell and Dave Stieb. Both were on hand for the ceremony prior to the club's 1996 home opener. At the time, Bell was the Blue Jays franchise leader in home runs, RBIs, total bases, extra base hits and sacrifice flies. Stieb was the team's winningest pitcher, as well as the leader in starts, innings pitched, strikeouts, shutouts and complete games. In 1999, Stieb and Bell were joined on the Level of Excellence by Cito Gaston and Joe Carter. Carter had surpassed Bell as the Blue Jays' all-time home run hitter and, of course, hit the World Series-winning home run in 1993. Gaston led the team to two world championships, two American League pennants, four division titles and a franchise-record 681 wins in his nine seasons as manager.

Famous Firsts and Records #21

NOV. 12, 1996 • *Pat Hentgen*

Despite his brilliance in a 20–10 season that saw him lead the major leagues in shutouts (three) and innings pitched (265.2), Pat Hentgen was no shoo-in to win the Cy Young Award in 1996. Indeed, Hentgen admitted that in the weeks leading up to the announcement of the winner,

"I really felt that I was the underdog and I prepared myself to come in second." That was because Andy Pettitte had posted a 21–8 record for a New York Yankees team that had won the American League East Division and went on to win the World Series.

Head to head, Hentgen had the better individual statistics but he had pitched in relative obscurity while Pettitte had faced the pressure of a pennant race. In the end, it was very close but the voters gave the edge to Hentgen. He received 16 first-place votes, nine seconds and three thirds for a total of 110 points. Pettitte got 11 firsts, 16 seconds and one third for 104.

Hentgen was the first Blue Jays pitcher to win the Cy Young Award. None before had ever really come close. Jimmy Key had finished second in the voting back in 1987, but his total of 64 points was well behind the 124 garnered by Roger Clemens. Dave Stieb had been the first Blue Jays pitcher to receive consideration. He finished fourth in balloting back in 1982 and had three more top-10 finishes through 1990. Doyle Alexander (1985), Mark Eichhorn (1986), Duane Ward (1991, 1993), Jack Morris (1992), Juan Guzman (1993) and David Cone (1995) were the only other Blue Jays to receive votes for the Cy Young Award. Hentgen had previously received one second-place vote back in 1993.

George Bell (left) and Dave Stieb (right) join Paul Beeston as the two former stars become the inaugural members of the Blue Jays' "Level of Excellence."

1997

76–86 .469 5th -22

Free agent acquisition Roger Clemens captured his fourth Cy Young Award (21 wins, 292 Ks, 2.05 ERA) becoming the first Jays hurler to win the "Triple Crown" of pitching. Joe Carter passed George Bell as the club's all-time home run leader and Carlos Delgado (30 HR, 91 RBI) and Shawn Green (16 HR, 53 RBI) both emerged as offensive weapons. Pat Hentgen (15 wins) had another solid season.

Youth, home-grown talent (such as shortstop Alex Gonzalez, seen here firing a feed past a sliding David Segui) and the greatest pitcher in modern American League history were the key components of the 1997 Blue Jays squad.

Oddities and Others #21

JUNE 30 TO JULY 2, 1997 • *Blue Jays vs. Expos*

The Blue Jays and Expos had not met in midseason since the Pearson Cup game was scrapped in 1987. The annual exhibition game had been held from 1978 until 1986 (with the exception of the strike-shortened 1981 campaign), but the teams never met in meaningful competition until baseball introduced interleague play in 1997. The first three-game series between the Blue Jays and Expos was played at the SkyDome around the Canada Day holiday and provided fans with some of the season's best baseball.

The opening game between the Expos and Blue Jays pitted defending American League Cy Young Award winner Pat Hentgen against future National League Cy Young champ Pedro Martinez. Both pitchers went the distance with Hentgen allowing just two runs on six hits, but Martinez surrendered just a single run on three hits to improve his record to 10–3 with a 2–1 victory. Pedro had retired the first 12 men he faced before walking Carlos Delgado in the fifth inning. The right-hander, who struck out 10, lost his no-hitter on a leadoff single by Alex Gonzalez in the sixth. Delgado ended Martinez's shutout bid with a homer in the seventh. Vladimir Guerrero had homered for the Expos back in the second inning.

The largest crowd since opening day in 1995 (50,436) jammed the SkyDome to witness game two of the series on Canada Day. The Blue Jays sported red jerseys and red caps for the occasion, but it was Expos starter Jeff Juden who was red hot. Pitching against boyhood idol Roger Clemens, Juden held the Blue Jays hitless until Shawn Green led off the eighth inning with a home run. Juden wound up allowing just two hits over 8.1 innings and had 14 strikeouts. When Ugueth Urbina nailed down the final two outs in the ninth, the Expos had another 2–1 victory.

The Blue Jays finally found their bats in the series finale. Joe Carter, who had been 0-for-8 with six straight strikeouts in the first two games, launched a three-run homer in the fifth inning to give the team a 5–4 lead. He later plated the game-winning run with a bloop single, as the Blue Jays won a thriller 7–6 in 13 innings.

After stints in the outfield and a period behind the plate, super slugger Carlos Delgado finally found a home at first base.

Great Moments #23

JULY 12, 1997 • *Blue Jays 3, Red Sox 1*

The Rocket: After four years of mediocrity, Roger Clemens returned to health and to the spotlight, winning his fourth Cy Young Award by leading the AL in wins (21), strikeouts (292) and ERA (2.05). Clemens saved the finest performance of the season for his first return to Boston on July 12, 1997. "The Rocket" whiffed 16 Bosox batters and delivered a defiant stare towards the Red Sox executive offices before hitting the showers.

After 13 seasons with the Boston Red Sox, Roger Clemens signed with the Blue Jays in 1997. Injuries and inconsistency had plagued Clemens since 1993, but he seemed to regain his status as a dominant pitcher from his very first appearance in Toronto. Clemens pitched a complete-game six-hitter against the White Sox for a 6–1 victory at the SkyDome on April 2 and went on to set a club record for starting pitchers by winning 11 games in a row through June 6. His record was 13–3 when the Blue Jays visited Boston in July.

Clemens made his first start as a visiting player at Fenway Park on a hot and humid Saturday. Red Sox fans didn't know whether to cheer him or boo him — and they did plenty of both throughout the afternoon. Clemens heard jeers in the first inning when Nomar Garciaparra singled on his second pitch and John Valentin did the same off his fourth. Then Clemens hit Mo Vaughn with his sixth pitch of the inning and suddenly found the bases loaded with nobody out. He got out of the jam with just one run against him thanks to a ground ball and two strikeouts.

"My adrenaline was high," explained Clemens later, "but it wasn't jitters. I had to buckle down pretty quickly though." When he struck out the side in the second, he seemed to win over the Fenway faithful.

Clemens continued to rack up the Ks as he mowed down the Red Sox inning after inning, but the one run against him was looming large. The Blue Jays finally got on the scoreboard when Shawn Green launched a mammoth 440-foot home run with Ed Sprague on base in the seventh inning.

"It felt great," said Green, "knowing how important this game was to Roger. We kept talking about how we had to get him something; how we couldn't let the game slip away when he'd given such a great performance."

After the Blue Jays upped their lead to 3–1 in the top of the eighth, Clemens returned to the mound in the bottom of the inning and needed just 10 pitches to strike out the side again. The three Ks gave him 16 for the game, breaking the previous Blue Jays record of 14 set by Pat Hentgen in 1994. He had allowed just four hits and no walks, but the long, emotion-filled day in the hot sun had taken its toll and Cito Gaston decided to go to the bullpen. It took four relief pitchers to get through the nervous ninth but when they did, Clemens had his victory.

"It was a great day," said Rocket Roger. "A great deal of fun."

Toronto	AB	R	H	RBI	Boston	AB	R	H	RBI
Nixon, cf	4	1	1	0	Garciaparra, ss	4	1	1	0
Merced, rf	3	0	1	0	Valentin, 3b	4	0	2	0
Carter, lf	2	0	1	0	Vaughn, 1b	3	0	0	0
Brumfield, lf	2	0	1	1	Cordero, lf	3	0	0	0
Delgado, 1b	4	0	0	0	Jefferson, dh	3	0	0	1
Sprague, 3b	3	1	0	0	Mack ph	0	0	0	0
Green, dh	4	1	1	2	O'Leary, rf	3	0	0	0
O'Brien, c	4	0	0	0	Stanley, ph	1	0	0	0
Brito, 2b	4	0	1	0	Hatteberg, c	3	0	0	0
Gonzalez, ss	4	0	0	0	Tavarez, pr	0	0	0	0
					Bragg, cf	4	0	0	0
					Frye, 2b	3	0	1	0
Totals	34	3	6	3	Totals	31	1	4	1

Toronto .... .000 000 210 – 3
Boston .... .100 000 000 – 1

Toronto	IP	H	R	ER	BB	SO
Clemens (W. 14-3)	8	4	1	1	0	16
Escobar	⅓	0	0	0	0	0
Plesac	0	0	0	0	1	0
Quantrill	⅓	0	0	0	0	0
Spoljaric (S3)	⅓	0	0	0	1	0

Boston	IP	H	R	ER	BB	SO
Sele (L. 10-7)	7	5	3	3	0	11
Henry	2	1	0	0	1	2

Sele pitched to one batter in eighth
Plesac pitched to one batter in ninth

E – Delgado, Valentin (2), Hatteberg. DP – Boston 1. LOB – Toronto 6, Boston 7. 2B – Carter, Valentin. HR – Green (8). SB – Brito (1), Frye (8). T – 3:02. A – 33, 106.

Famous Firsts and Records #22

NOV. 10, 1997 • *Roger Clemens*

Roger Clemens was far and away the Blue Jays' biggest story in 1997. He tied a club record with 21 wins and set a new one (as well as establishing a personal high) with 292 strikeouts. Combined with his 2.05 ERA, Clemens became the first pitcher since Hal Newhouser in 1945 to win the unofficial American League pitcher's Triple Crown by leading the league in wins, strikeouts and ERA. When it came time to hand out the Cy Young Award, Clemens easily outdistanced runner-up Randy Johnson with 25 first-place votes and three seconds for 134 points. Johnson had two first-place votes, 21 seconds and four thirds for 77 points. The other first-place vote when to Orioles reliever Randy Myers, who had led the majors with 45 saves.

"Maybe this brings me a step closer to the Hall of Fame," said Clemens, who joined Greg Maddux and Steve Carlton as the only pitchers to win the Cy Young Award four times. Clemens said this award was for his 18-month-old son Kody — having already given his three previous plaques to sons Koby, Kory and Kacy. Of course, Clemens would earn one more to keep for himself in 1998 when he became the first pitcher to win the Cy Young Award five times.

After two seasons as a utility player, Ed Sprague (below) became the everyday third baseman in 1993 and manned the hot corner for six seasons. He earned Player-of-the-Year honours in 1996 with a 36 homers and 101 RBIs, but was never the same after an injury-plagued 1997 season.

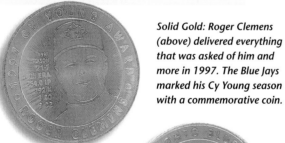

Solid Gold: Roger Clemens (above) delivered everything that was asked of him and more in 1997. The Blue Jays marked his Cy Young season with a commemorative coin.

1998

88–74 .543 3rd -26

The team struggled before exploding into wild-card contention in August. Free agent Jose Canseco returned to form, slamming 46 homers and swiping 29 bases. The infield defense was solidified with the addition of Tony Fernandez, who led the team with a career-best .321 batting average. Shawn Green joined the exclusive 30–30 club with 35 homers and 35 steals. Carlos Delgado led the Jays with 115 RBIs, while Roger Clemens (20–6) earned his fifth Cy Young Award.

Potential and promise finally became production for Shawn Green in 1998. The sweet-swinging lefty drove in 100 runs and became the first Blue Jays player to steal at least 30 bases and hit at least 30 home runs in the same season.

JUNE 18, 1998 • *Dave Stieb*

When the Blue Jays invited Dave Stieb to spring training in 1998, they had no idea that they were about to ignite a comeback bid that would mirror Stieb's meteoric rise to the majors as a rookie back in 1979.

Stieb attended spring training as a guest coach and received favourable reviews about the quality of his pitches after throwing off a mound. "He's in great shape," said Pat Hentgen. "He looks 30, not 40, and he's had a wicked slider his whole life." When he realized the sore elbow that had ended his career in 1993 was no longer bothering him, Stieb decided to approach Gord Ash about the possibility of pitching again. Ash agreed to give him a chance, and Stieb was assigned to Dunedin of the Florida State League. He was promoted to Triple-A Syracuse after going 2–0. Stieb then made nine starts with the SkyChiefs and though his record was only 5–4, his 2.73 ERA was third in the league and he had allowed only 44 hits in 66 innings.

When the Texas Rangers offered Stieb a major league contract in June, Toronto had 48 hours to promote him or lose him. The Blue Jays purchased his contract from Syracuse on June 17 and the next day, Stieb joined the team in Baltimore — the site of his major league debut almost exactly 19 years before. "He's the same competitor," said Ash. "He still wants to win."

Manager Tim Johnson wasted little time putting Stieb to use, bringing him out of the bullpen in the ninth inning of a game the Blue Jays led 13–6. Despite allowing three hits (including a blooper to center and an infield single), Stieb got out of the jam without allowing a run. He went on to pitch in 19 games for the Blue Jays, including three as a starter. After five years away from the game, Dave Stieb posted a respectable record of 1–2 with a pair of saves and a 4.83 ERA.

After five years away from the game, Dave Stieb (left) came out of retirement in 1998 and proved he still had the mettle to compete. He appeared in 19 games, saving a pair of victories and compiling a decent 4.83 ERA.

Promoted from Syracuse midway through the 1997 season and used as a closer, Kelvim Escobar (right) became a key member of the Jays' starting rotation in 1998, compiling a 7–3 record with a 3.73 ERA.

Famous Firsts and Records #23

JULY 4, 1998 • *Tony Fernandez*

When Tony Fernandez returned to Toronto again in 1998, he became the first (and only) player with three tours of duty as a Blue Jay. He would go on to reach two major milestones that year. The first occurred on July 4 when Fernandez became the Blue Jays' all-time hit leader. His first-inning single in an 8–0 win over Tampa Bay at the SkyDome gave Fernandez 1,320 hits in a Blue Jays uniform — one more than Lloyd Moseby.

"The record means a lot," said Tony, "because a lot of good ball players have come through here."

With a total of 1,994 hits in his career overall, Fernandez found himself just six hits shy of joining Julio Franco, Felipe Alou and Cesar Cedeno as the only players from the Dominican Republic to collect 2,000 hits. He reached that milestone in Baltimore on July 13.

Fernandez hit .346 for the second half of the 1998 season and, at the age of 35, finished the season batting .321 for his highest total since hitting .322 back in 1987. After flirting with the .400 mark through June of 1999, he would eventually establish a career high with a batting average of .328 that season. Fernandez also surpassed Julio Franco as the Dominican Republic's all-time hit leader with his 2,178th on June 20, 1999.

Tony Fernandez acknowledges the cheers after becoming the all-time hits leader in Blue Jays history.

Jose Cruz Jr. slugged 11 homers and plated 42 runners in 1998.

Once again, Roger Clemens was the AL's top pitcher, leading all junior circuit hurlers in wins (20), strikeouts (271) and ERA (2.65), numbers that brought Clemens his major-league-record fifth Cy Young Award.

Alex Gonzalez (below) batted only .239 in 1998, though he did hit 13 homers and flashed a quick glove at shortstop.

With the exception of Nolan Ryan, no power pitcher in baseball history has been as dominant for as long as Roger Clemens. In his first full major league season back in 1986, Clemens had set a record with 20 strikeouts in a single game. Ten years later, he matched it. In his first season with the Blue Jays in 1997, a 35-year-old Clemens established a career high in strikeouts with 292. On July 5, 1998, Clemens fanned Randy Winn of the Tampa Bay Devil Rays to become just the 11th pitcher in history to reach 3,000 career strikeouts. On August 25, Clemens topped 200 strikeouts in a season for the tenth time. He also set a Blue Jays single-game record that day when he recorded 18 strikeouts. As in both of his 20-strikeout performances, Clemens did not walk a single batter during the game.

Clemens, who had struck out 15 just 10 days before, put his first K on the board when he fired a called third strike past Kansas City's Jose Offerman in the first inning. He struck out the side in the second and did not allow the Royals to get their first hit until the fourth. He did not allow another hit until the top of the seventh. The Blue Jays had only a 1–0 lead at the time, but Clemens got a bit more breathing room when the team scored two more in the bottom of the inning. He then continued to pour it on, striking out two in the eighth to tie his own team record of 16. Two more strikeouts in the ninth put the finishing touches on a brilliant three-hit shutout.

Clemens had now tied his own club record with 11 straight wins and had also thrown two shutouts in a row. He became the first pitcher in Blue Jays history to throw three consecutive shutouts when he blanked Minnesota 6–0 for his 12th straight win. Clemens went on to run his winning streak to 15 games.

Shannon Stewart (left) provided the club with speed, tight defense and surprising power. He stole 51 bases and clubbed 12 home runs.

Great Moments #24

SEPTEMBER 4, 1998 • *Blue Jays 12, Red Sox 1*

With three hits already, Shawn Green had done most of his damage while the game with Boston was still close. He had also made a fine running catch with a runner on base in the top of the seventh to help preserve what was then just a 4–1 lead. But Green's biggest moment of the evening came after the Blue Jays broke the game open with a seven-run bottom of the seventh. Batting for the final time in the eighth inning, Green drove a first-pitch changeup from Red Sox reliever Carlos Reyes deep to right field for his 30th home run of the season. Having stolen his 30th base in a 4–3 victory the night before, Green became the first player in Blue Jays history to enter the 30-30 Club.

"It's an honour to be the first to do it," Green said. "There are not many times you go up there definitely thinking home run, but that was one of them. Jose [Canseco] pushed me all year. He's probably going to get there tomorrow or the next day."

Canseco had 38 homers and 28 steals at the time, and though he would go on to club 46 round-trippers, a leg injury would leave him with just 29 stolen bases. Still, it was Canseco — the first player to have a 40-40 season when he was with Oakland in 1988 — that had begun talking to Green about his 30-30 potential back in spring training.

"I'm extremely happy for Shawn," Canseco said. "I consider him one of the coming superstars of the game."

The 12–1 romp over the Red Sox that night gave the Blue Jays eight wins in a row. They went on to push their streak to 11 straight as they made a late surge to get back into the playoff picture. Toronto was 12½ games behind Boston for the wild-card spot when the streak began but had pulled to within five games when it ended. Though they would eventually fall four games short, the Blue Jays' won/loss record of 34-18 in August and September pushed them to a mark of 88-74 for the season — the best win total since the World Series years.

Few opponents could run down Shawn Green in 1998, as he swiped 35 bags during the season. He also hit 35 home runs.

Boston	AB	R	H	RBI	Toronto	AB	R	H	RBI
DLewis, cf	4	0	1	0	Stewart, lf	4	2	1	1
Mitchell, rf	0	0	0	0	Green, rf	4	3	4	2
Valentin, 3b	3	0	1	0	Canseco, dh	4	2	1	3
Vaughn, 1b	3	0	1	0	Crespo, ph-dh	1	0	0	0
Garciaparra, ss	4	0	0	0	Delgado, 1b	3	1	1	1
Snopek, 2b	0	0	0	0	Cruz, cf	4	1	1	0
O'Leary, lf	4	0	1	0	Fernandez, 3b	4	1	1	2
Stanley, dh	4	1	1	1	Dalesandro, 3b	0	0	0	0
Bragg rf-cf	3	0	0	0	Fletcher, c	4	1	2	2
Hatteberg, c	1	0	1	0	Santiago, c	0	0	0	0
Vantek, ph-c	1	0	0	0	Grebeck, 2b	3	1	1	0
Benjamin, 2b	2	0	0	0	Gonzalez, ss	4	0	0	0
Romero, ph	1	0	0	0					
Sadler, 2b-ss	0	0	0	0					
Totals	30	1	6	1	Totals	35	12	12	11

```
Boston .....................010 000 000 – 1
Toronto ....................211 000 71x – 12
```

Boston	IP	H	R	ER	BB	SO
Wakefield (L. 15-7)	6⅓	8	8	6	2	5
West	0	1	2	2	1	0
Reyes	1⅔	3	2	2	1	1

Toronto	IP	H	R	ER	BB	SO
Hentgen (W. 12-10)	6⅓	4	1	1	4	2
Sinclair	⅓	0	0	0	1	0
Stieb (S2)	2⅓	2	0	0	0	1

West pitched to two batters in seventh

E – Garciaparra, Hatteberg. DP – Boston 1, Toronto 2. LOB – Boston 6, Toronto 5. 2B – Hatteberg, Green, Fernandez, Grebeck. HR – Green (30), Canseco (38), Fletcher (8), Stanley (28). SB – Stewart (44), Green (32). SF – Delgado. HBP – by Wakefield (Stewart). PB – Hatteberg. T – 2:30. A – 29,166.

SEPTEMBER 27, 1998 • *Blue Jays 2, Tigers 1*

Roy Halladay was a September call-up who had made just one previous start in his major league career when he nearly pitched himself into the Blue Jays record book. In the final game of the 1998 season, Halladay came within one out of pitching a no-hitter.

Halladay was brilliant throughout the game against the Tigers, retiring the first 12 men to face him before second baseman Felipe Crespo erred on a Tony Clark grounder leading off the fifth inning. Halladay, who went to two balls on just five batters and never had the count go to three balls on anyone, allowed no other Detroit batters to reach base until the ninth inning.

With a crowd of 38,036 roaring its approval, Halladay retired Deivi Cruz for the first out. Then he got Paul Bako to bring pinch hitter Bobby Higginson to the plate with two away.

"I told [Tigers manager] Larry Parrish that I wanted to have a chance to break it up," said Higginson.

The Blue Jays' scouting report on the Tigers regular right fielder was to feed him fastballs away, but when Halladay tried that, Higginson drove his first pitch some 379 feet into the Blue Jays bullpen. The ball was caught there by Dave Stieb.

"It reminded me of my three near misses," said the only man in Blue Jays history to pitch a no-hitter. "The last out is always the toughest."

Halladay bounced back from the Higginson homer to retire Frank Catalanotto for a complete-game 2–1 victory. He had thrown just 94 pitches, 73 of them for strikes.

"I told myself around the sixth or seventh inning that if [a hit] happened I wasn't going to be disappointed. But when it did, it was a little disappointing."

On the final day of the 1998 regular season, and with Dave Stieb watching from the bullpen, Roy Halladay lost his bid for a no-hitter with two outs in the ninth inning when pinch hitter Bobby Higginson took the first pitch he saw from "Doc" and deposited it over the wall. Who caught the ball? Dave Stieb, of course.

Pepperpot Craig Grebeck was a fan favourite with his enthusiastic play and his diminutive size.

1999

84–78 .519 3rd -20

The Jays established franchise records with a .280 team batting average and 883 runs scored. Shawn Green, who had a league-high 28-game hitting streak, crushed 42 homers. Carlos Delgado had 44 homers and 134 RBIs and Tony Fernandez, Homer Bush and Shannon Stewart all hit above .300. Fireballing freshman Billy Koch set a new American League rookie record with 31 saves. Kelvim Escobar (14–11), Pat Hentgen (11–12) and David Wells (17–10) all reached double-digits in victories.

Obtained from Arizona as shortstop insurance after Alex Gonzalez was injured, Tony Batista showed he belonged in the starting lineup by slugging 26 homers in only 398 at-bats.

Famous Firsts and Records #25

JUNE 29 TO JULY 31, 1999 • *Shawn Green*

After racing out of the gate with 12 wins in their first 16 games in 1999, the Blue Jays suffered a three-game sweep at the hands of the Yankees in late April and then slumped through most of May and June. They finally pulled themselves back into the postseason picture by posting a record of 19–7 in July. Leading the Blue Jays on their mid-summer charge was Shawn Green, who collected at least one hit in every game from June 29 to July 31, establishing a new team record with a 28-game hitting streak. He batted .366 (41-for-112) during the stretch, with 12 homers and 26 RBIs.

On July 30, Green surpassed John Olerud's previous team record of hitting in 26 consecutive games. He launched his 30th home run of the season in the first inning that evening, leading the Blue Jays to an 8–2 win over the Tigers. The following day, he ran his hitting streak to 28 games — halfway to Joe DiMaggio's record of 56 — with a single and another home run in a 7–6 victory. The streak finally came to an end when Green was held hitless in a thrilling 8–5 win over Detroit on August 1. He did play a key part in that game, however, driving in the go-ahead run with a sacrifice fly in the seven-run seventh inning. He also drove a ball to the warning track in the first inning, lifted a soft liner that nearly got through the infield in the third, and sent Gabe Kapler to the center field wall for an excellent catch in the eighth.

"That was a great play," said Green.

And as for the hitting streak: "It was a lot of fun. It was good for the fans and I had a great time with it. I was happy that it ended in a good win for us. If it had been broken in a game we lost 3–2, it would have been a lot more frustrating."

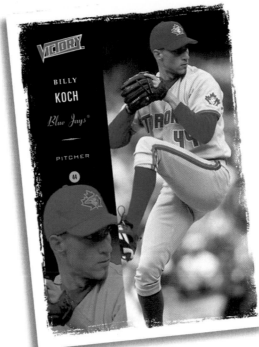

Though he had never been used as a reliever in his entire career, Billy Koch's 100-miles-per-hour fastball and equally dominant slider made him a natural closer. He established a new AL rookie save record by putting out the flames in 31 Blue Jays victories.

This Bird Has Flown: After a season of career highs in 1999, Shawn Green shocked the Toronto baseball establishment by demanding to be traded.

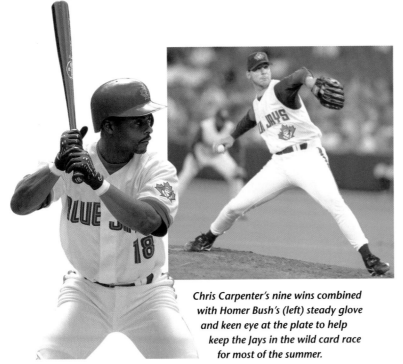

Chris Carpenter's nine wins combined with Homer Bush's (left) steady glove and keen eye at the plate to help keep the Jays in the wild card race for most of the summer.

Oddities and Others #24

AUGUST 6–11, 1999 • *Carlos Delgado*

On August 6, 1999, Carlos Delgado launched three solo homers to lead the Blue Jays to a 5–4 win over the Texas Rangers. The home run hat trick came almost a year to the day (August 4, 1998) after Delgado had hit three home runs against Texas the season before. He is the only player in Blue Jays history to enjoy more than one three-homer game.

The Blue Jays were shut out the following night, but then Delgado regained his home run stroke and launched a 411-foot bomb to left center on August 8. It helped the team score an 8–7 victory and gave Carlos 12 home runs at The Ballpark in Arlington, tying him with Jose Canseco for the most homers hit there by a Rangers opponent. Delgado broke the tie with another home run the very next game. His three-run blast in the first inning sparked the Blue Jays to a 19–4 blowout of the Rangers as the team pounded out a club-record 25 hits.

The Blue Jays moved on to Minnesota and Delgado continued his hot hitting when he clubbed two more roundtrippers in a 10–6 victory. He then ran his home run streak to four straight games with another longball in a 6–3 win. He had hit eight home runs in his last six games, including five during the last four. It was just the sixth time in franchise history that a Blue Jay had homered in four consecutive games — and Delgado was the first to do it twice.

Carlos Delgado propelled himself into a vaunted circle of pure power hitters in 1999, blasting 44 homers and tying a club record with 134 RBIs.

Bad Breaks, Near Misses and Disappointments #25

AUGUST 13–15, 1999 • *Blue Jays vs. Athletics*

In the middle of August, the Blue Jays found themselves holding down the wild-card spot in the American League playoff race. Though they had made late runs for the postseason in both 1997 and 1998, this was the first time since the World Series years that the team could control its own destiny. But the race was a tight one. Toronto was only a half-game ahead of Boston and just 2½ in front of Oakland when the A's came to the SkyDome to begin an important three-game series. Unfortunately, the standings would look a lot different at the end of the weekend.

The series got off to an ominous beginning on Friday night when scheduled starter David Wells was scratched with a stiff back. Roy Halladay got the ball instead, but he coughed up two Blue Jays leads in the first three innings. The score was tied 3–3 in the fifth when Halladay loaded the bases with two outs. Left-handed slugger Matt Stairs was at the plate, so manager Jim Fregosi went to the bullpen for lefty Paul Spoljaric. He came on to serve up a grand slam and suddenly the A's had a 7–3 lead. Though the Blue Jays chipped away, Oakland went on to a 9–8 victory.

The A's continued to swing hot bats on Saturday when Joey Hamilton — who had battled injuries and inconsistency all season — couldn't even survive the first inning. He surrendered eight runs on four hits, two walks, an error and a hit batsman. The big blow was another grand slam, this one by A.J. Hinch, and the A's cruised to a 13–5 victory. A 9–5 win on Sunday completed a three-game sweep that saw Oakland score 31 runs on 42 hits — including nine home runs. Boston now held the wild-card spot. The A's were a game out and the Blue Jays trailed by a game-and-a-half. There were still six weeks to go in the season, but the Blue Jays never really threatened again, losing 11 straight at home.

"I'm sure it was as frustrating to watch as it was to be a part of," said Shawn Green of the lost weekend. "Oakland was just hitting the ball hard everywhere. They kept putting it on us non-stop."

Medic!: Manager Jim Fregosi gives "Doc" Halladay a fatherly tap on the shoulder before taking the ball from his rookie right-hander. The Blue Jays' 1999 wild card aspirations were swept away when the club was smoked by the Oakland A's, losing all three games and allowing 31 runs on 42 hits.

2000

83–79 .512 3rd -4.5

The Blue Jays led the American League in home runs (244) and extra-base hits (593). Seven different Jays hit at least 20 homers as Carlos Delgado (41), Tony Batista (41), Jose Cruz (31) and Brad Fulmer (32) all reached the 30-homer plateau. Delgado had career highs in average (.344), doubles (57) and RBIs (137). David Wells was the staff ace, notching 20 wins and nine complete games. Frank Castillo won 10 games with an ERA of 3.59.

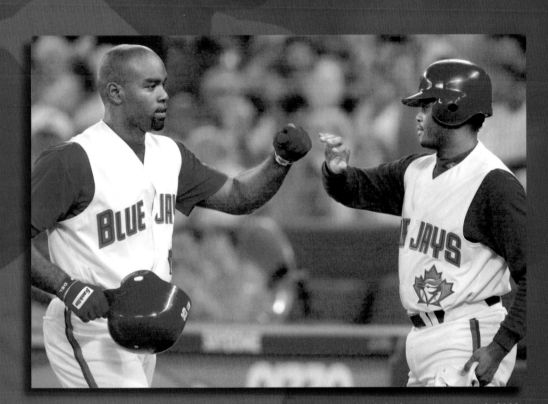

Carlos Delgado had a monster season in 2000. His .344 average was the second best in franchise history and his 137 RBIs set a new club record. Tony Batista now holds the team's single-season mark for most home runs by a shortstop and a third baseman.

JUNE 25, 2000 • *Blue Jays 6, Red Sox 5*

The Blue Jays had been struggling to win consistently through the first two months of the 2000 season. As late as May 30, the team was just 27–26, but they were about to go on a tear. From May 31 to June 25, the Blue Jays hit home runs in 23 consecutive games, shattering the previous team record of 14 straight and vaulting themselves into contention in the American League East.

The Blue Jays trailed Boston by just a half-game for top spot in the division when the Red Sox arrived at the SkyDome on June 23 to open a weekend series. They pulled into first place with a 5–4 win in the opener, then scored a 6–4 victory on Saturday. But they would have to face Pedro Martinez in the series finale. The Sunday game had the feel of a pennant race, and why not? The last time the Blue Jays had been in first place this late in the season was 1993.

Martinez was 9–3 on the year with a 1.18 ERA. He had already beaten the Blue Jays 8–0 earlier in the season, and though Toronto had eked out a 3–2 win against him on May 23, the prospects of beating the best pitcher in baseball for a second time did not look good when Chris Carpenter allowed the Red Sox to take a 2–0 lead in the top of the first. Shannon Stewart got one run back when he homered off Martinez leading off the bottom of the inning, but Boston scored two more in the third to take a 4–1 lead. The Red Sox led 5–2 until Tony Batista socked a solo homer in the fifth, but Martinez had not allowed more than three earned runs in a game all season.

Boston was still leading 5–3 in the seventh inning when Martinez faced Carlos Delgado with two out and a runner on. Pedro had not given up a home run with a man on base since

September of 1998, but when he fell behind in the count, Delgado hoped for a pitch he could drive.

"It was 3-and-2. I'm a fastball hitter and I was looking for a fastball. I got it."

The crowd of 31,022 fans went crazy as Delgado's mammoth drive headed for the seats. They kept standing and cheering until Carlos finally came out of the dugout to acknowledge their ovation.

"It was a great feeling," he explained, "but it was only a tie game. We hadn't won anything and we still had a lot of work to do."

It would take until the 13th to complete the job, but after 10 scoreless innings of work by the bullpen, Tony Batista singled in Chris Woodward for the game-winning run in a thrilling 6–5 victory.

Boston	AB	R	H	RBI		Toronto	AB	R	H	RBI
Offerman, 1b	5	1	2	0		Stewart, lf	6	2	1	1
Frye, 2b	6	0	1	1		Woodward, ss	7	2	1	0
Everett, cf	5	1	2	0		Batista, 3b	7	1	3	2
Garciaparra, ss	7	0	1	2		Delgado, 1b	5	1	1	2
Daubach, dh	5	1	1	0		Fullmer, dh	6	0	3	1
Alcantara, rf	6	1	1	0		Cruz, cf	4	0	0	0
Hatteberg, c	6	0	3	2		Cordova, rf	5	0	1	0
Veras, 3b	5	0	1	0		Castillo, c	4	0	0	0
Varitek, ph	1	0	0	0		Bush, 2b	6	0	0	0
Alexander, 3b	0	0	0	0						
Pride, lf	6	1	3	0						
Totals	**52**	**5**	**15**	**5**		**Totals**	**50**	**6**	**10**	**6**

```
Boston . . . . . . . . . . . . . . . . 202 100 000 0 – 5
Toronto . . . . . . . . . . . . . . . 101 010 200 1 – 6
          Two out when winning run scored
```

Boston	IP	H	R	ER	BB	SO
PMartinez	6⅔	6	5	4	1	10
Garces	1⅓	0	0	0	1	0
Lowe	2	2	0	0	2	2
Beck	⅔	0	0	0	0	0
Cormier	1⅓	1	0	0	0	1
Florie (L. 0-2)	⅔	1	1	0	0	0

Toronto	IP	H	R	ER	BB	SO
Carpenter	3⅓	7	5	5	3	1
Painter	1⅔	1	0	0	0	1
Frascatore	2	1	0	0	0	1
Borbon	1	0	0	0	0	2
Koch	1	1	0	0	1	0
Quantrill	3	4	0	0	0	2
Dewitt (W. 1-0)	1	0	0	1	1	1

```
E – Garciaparra, Veras, Offerman, Everett. DP – Boston 1, Toronto 1.
LOB – Boston 14, Toronto 12. 2B – Garciaparra, Hatteberg, Pride,
Daubach, Veras, Fullmer, Batista. HR – Stewart (10), Batista (19),
Delgado (27). S – Castillo. WP – Painter. HBP – by PMartinez 2
(Stewart, Cordova).
T – 4:25. A – 31,022
```

(Left) Carlos Delgado is greeted by teammates after taking Pedro Martinez downtown. (Below) Designated hitter Brad Fullmer flexed his mighty muscles to jack 32 balls out of the yard and drive home 104 runners, establishing a pair of team records in the process.

Portly David Wells became the first portside pitcher to reach the 20-win plateau for the Blue Jays.

Oddities and Others #25

SEPTEMBER 17, 2000 • *Blue Jays 14, White Sox 1*

The Blue Jays established all sorts of home run records during the 2000 season en route to slugging an American League-leading 244 roundtrippers — the fourth-highest total in baseball history. But an awesome offense could only take the team so far.

Carlos Delgado, Raul Mondesi, Tony Batista and Jose Cruz Jr. combined to set a major league record when all four of them hit 20 home runs before the All-Star break. When Brad Fullmer, Shannon Stewart and Darrin Fletcher topped 20 in the second half, it marked just the second time in history that seven teammates had hit 20 home runs in one season. Delgado, Batista, Fullmer and Cruz also combined to tie the record for most teammates with 30 home runs. Another Blue Jays home run record that fell during the 2000 season was the club mark for grand slams. With Darrin Fletcher leading the way with three, the Blue Jays surpassed their previous single-season high of eight (set in 1989) when Carlos Delgado slugged the team's ninth grand slam on September 17. Delgado's big blast led the Blue Jays to a 14–1 win over the White Sox.

In addition to setting a new team record, Delgado's grand slam made him the first Blue Jays slugger to hit 40 home runs two years in a row. It also helped propel the Blue Jays on a late-season run for the division title, as they came home from Chicago to sweep the Yankees in a three-game series at the SkyDome. Having fallen as far as 10 games off the pace just a week before, the Blue Jays had drawn within 4½ games of top spot and fuelled hopes of a miracle finish. Unfortunately, this was as close as the Blue Jays would get.

Shannon Stewart proved he was one of the top leadoff men in baseball with a .319 average and five game-starting homers.

Tony Batista (above) tied Carlos Delgado for the team lead with 41 home runs, while crafty reliever Paul Quantrill (below) allowed only 25 walks in 83.2 innings during the 2000 campaign.

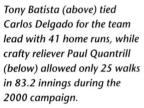

(Top, right) Darrin Fletcher batted a career-high .320 with 20 homers over the course of the 2000 season. (Right) Jose Cruz Jr. emerged as a legitimate power threat by clouting 31 homers during the 2000 season. He also demonstrated improved defense in center field.

2001

The Blue Jays' 25th season marked the beginning of a new era, as a new local owner (Ted Rogers) and a new club president (Paul Godfrey) committed the organization to building a competitive club. General manager Gord Ash hired former catcher and broadcaster Buck Martinez as the field manager, and he filled the team with a new confidence beginning with an opening day win in Puerto Rico.

Raul Mondesi and teammates celebrate after beating the Yankees. Mondesi's steal of home was a key play in the victory. With his quick bat, strong throwing arm and speed on the basepaths, Mondesi is a powerful presence in the lineup.

(Left) Club president Paul Godfrey and owner Ted Rogers officially took control of the Blue Jays in September of 2000. (Below) General manager Gord Ash chose Buck Martinez as the Blue Jays' new field boss.

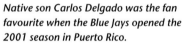

Native son Carlos Delgado was the fan favourite when the Blue Jays opened the 2001 season in Puerto Rico.

An eight-year minor-league journeyman with just three major league games to his credit, 30-year-old Chris Michalak earned a spot in the starting rotation with an impressive performance at spring training.

The Early Jays

ALISON GORDON

On opening day each year, the ballparks are full of ghosts, on the field and in the stands, representing the tradition that is the lifeblood of the sport we all love. They are our memories, of players on other opening days, and of our companions of years gone by: the friends we have lost touch with, or the favourite relative who is gone from our lives. They are our link with our baseball past.

Of course, there are ghosts, and there are ghosts. Venerable cathedrals like Yankee Stadium or Fenway Park are haunted by the men whose likenesses grace the Hall of Fame. In comparison, Blue Jays tradition has been pretty thin on the ground.

But now the Jays are 25 years old, and we have lots of our own memories piling up in SkyDome's corners. The five-year-old who sat on his mother's knee on Opening Day, 1977, may have a five-year-old of his own to introduce to the wonders of the game. And our Boys of Summer who stood in the snowstorm along the third base line while Anne Murray sang the anthem on that Opening Day, while not celebrated within Cooperstown's hallowed halls, have provided us with baseball memories that we cherish to this day.

The history of the team is in the scorebooks, in the lists of transactions, in the opening day rosters, year by year, but this information is not the stuff of most fans' memories. They tend to be, or mine tend to be, anyway, like photos in an album, moments frozen in time, to be recalled at odd moments. Some are shared by thousands, like Joe Carter's World Series-winning home run. Others, more quirky, are shared by only a few. But each of us has our own album, or maybe a personal highlight reel. Here are some of mine:

1977: W 54, L 107
Opening Day lineup: John Scott LF, Hector Torres SS, Doug Ault 1B, Otto Velez DH, Gary Woods CF, Steve Bowling RF, Pedro Garcia 2B, Dave McKay 3B, Rick Cerone C, Bill Singer P.
My own opening day wasn't in the snow that season. In 1977, my first Blue Jays game was, fittingly, in the place I had watched my first baseball game as a girl: Yankee Stadium. It was a Monday afternoon game two weeks into the inaugural season. I went to the game with a Canadian who lived and worked in New York, and one of his friends, a dedicated Yankee hater. Since New Yorkers were not flocking in droves to see the Blue

> *The five-year-old who sat on his mother's knee on Opening Day, 1977, may have a five-year-old of his own to introduce to the wonders of the game.*

Jays play, we were able to get great seats a few rows above the visiting dugout. Decked out in Blue Jays hats and tee shirts we root-root-rooted for the visiting team. Even then, the Blue Jays played the big teams tough, and the Jays won that game, to the accompaniment of our cheers. I can't remember who was pitching — Dave Lemanczyk, perhaps — but I do remember that Otto Velez hit a home run and Reggie Jackson struck out four times, much to our glee. The Blue Jays seemed quite astonished at finding a rooting section in this unlikely place. They looked at us a bit nervously as they came off the field between innings, until one of them, Jim Mason, I think, tipped his hat. You see what I mean? How many personal highlight reels do you think feature Jim Mason? But how could that game not stand out in my mind? It brought me back to the sport I had loved as a girl, and, as it turned out, changed my life.

1978: W 59, L 102
Opening Day lineup: Rick Bosetti CF, Alvis Woods LF, Roy Howell 3B, Rico Carty DH, John Mayberry 1B, Tommy Hutton RF, Dave McKay 2B, Luis Gomez SS, Alan Ashby C, Dave Lemanczyk P.
John Mayberry is remembered fondly by Blue Jay fans to this day, as we see every old-timers day. His lumbering home-run trot is etched in many a brain. But how many remember the game one afternoon in August against the Minnesota Twins when Hosken Powell (later to become a Blue Jay) beat out an infield single in the first inning? The fans were still straggling into Exhibition Stadium when Mayberry asked Powell to step off the bag so he could clean it. Powell obliged, and Mayberry tagged him out with the ball he had faked throwing back to Jim Clancy on the mound. The old hidden ball trick — how often do we get to see it in the big leagues? It was the first time for me. And the last.

1979: W 53, L 109
Opening Day lineup: Alfredo Griffin SS, Bob Bailor RF, Roy Howell 3B, Rico Carty DH, John Mayberry 1B, Rick Bosetti CF, Bobby Brown LF, Dave McKay 2B, Rick Cerone C, Tom Underwood P.
My perspective on the game shifted in 1979, when I moved from the stands to the press box, and many of my memories of that season focus on the difficulties I encountered as the first woman

on the baseball beat in the major leagues. Perhaps that's why it's a couple of rookies that stand out in my memories of 1979. The first was the irrepressible Alfredo Griffin, who impressed enough people around the league to share Rookie-of-the-Year honours. The other rookie was, of course, Dave Stieb, who had sped through the minor league system like a runaway train to make it to the majors in less than a year. He would plague me with his arrogance for the next five years, but I remember well his debut, in Baltimore. He lost the game, but struck out five and impressed both teams with his stuff. Afterwards, all he wanted to talk about were the back-to-back home runs he had given up in the sixth inning. They were, amazingly, the first home runs of his career.

1980: W 67, L 95
Opening Day lineup: Alfredo Griffin SS, Bob Bailor RF, John Mayberry 1B, Otto Velez DH, Roy Howell 3B, Barry Bonnell LF, Rick Bosetti CF, Damaso Garcia 2B, Ernie Whitt C, Dave Lemanczyk P.

At the end of the previous season, the Jays jettisoned their first manager, the hapless Roy Hartsfield, and turned over the team to Bobby Mattick, their scouting director. He was a classic old-style baseball guy with a colourful way of talking but dubious management skills. I remember one game in particular when Alfredo Griffin stole third base in a completely inappropriate situation, with two outs in the inning in a game the Jays were losing. Asked about it afterwards, Mattick confessed that he had forgotten that the signal for a steal was for him to cross his arms in the dugout, and he had done it without realizing. But he was a refreshing change from Hartsfield, for the players and reporters alike. He treated his players like big leaguers, and they responded with their best season yet. It was also the first season that there were more prospects than suspects on the roster. Damaso Garcia came over from the Yankees to team up with Griffin to form the keystone combination that would delight the fans for the next five years, and Lloyd Moseby was called up from Syracuse in midseason. The crawl towards respectability had begun.

Garth Iorg makes the play while Dave Stieb ducks out of his way. Ernie Whitt watches intently. Survivors of the lean years, all three were key figures in the rise to respectability.

1981: W 37, L 69
Opening Day lineup: Alfredo Griffin SS, Lloyd Moseby CF, Otto Velez DH, John Mayberry 1B, Willie Upshaw LF, Damaso Garcia 2B, Barry Bonnell RF, Danny Ainge 3B, Ernie Whitt C, Jim Clancy P.

The 1981 season was split by a players strike and resembled something out of *Dr. Jekyll and Mr. Hyde*. All the hopes raised by the team's improved showing in the previous season were crushed by an appalling 16–42 start, but they came back after the strike to go 21–27, and were even, briefly, in contention for the second half playoffs.

The season also saw the debut of many of the players who would go on to define the Jays for the rest of the decade: Jesse Barfield came up from the Jays farm system, which was developing into a powerful talent pool, and George Bell, left unprotected by the Phillies, was snapped up by Pat Gillick, the attentive general manager. Willie Upshaw had been snatched from the Yankees in similar fashion back in 1978, and was soon to emerge as a regular. These young players brought with them confidence and energy, and a hunger for respectability that changed the chemistry of the team. It was a building period, and Mattick and his coaches worked tirelessly to give them the tools to win.

But most of all, they were having fun. They were the guys on their way up; replacing the more marginal players the Jays had been fielding for too long. If it wasn't for that basketball player at the hot corner, they could pass for a major league team, in certain lights. Mercifully, Danny (Two-Sport) Ainge would soon choose the NBA over the American League, putting an end to what was at best an embarrassing experiment.

First teamed together in 1981, then again in 1983, George Bell (left), Jesse Barfield (right) and Lloyd Moseby (center) became known as the best outfield in baseball.

1982: W 78, L 84
Opening Day lineup: Alfredo Griffin SS, Alvis Woods LF, Lloyd Moseby CF, Willie Upshaw 1B, John Mayberry DH, Jesse Barfield RF, Ernie Whitt C, Damaso Garcia 2B, Rance Mulliniks 3B, Mark Bomback P.

> *As the other players did their best to ignore him, Lemongello hauled off and slugged himself in the face, repeatedly.*

Mark Bomback? If anything symbolized the futility of the Blue Jays pitching staff in their first five years, it was Mark (Boom-Boom) Bomback as the Next Great Hope. He was one of a series of flawed pitchers with potential that the Jays dragged in to shore up their shaky staff. One of my personal favourites was another Mark: Lemongello, who once beat himself up — literally — during a bad start in Cleveland. He was sitting in the dugout while the Jays were at bat, head bowed, hands clenched in front of him. As the other players did their best to ignore him, Lemongello hauled off and slugged himself in the face, repeatedly.

Bomback, on the other hand, was merely the latest in a series of wrong answers to the pitching question. But under the leadership of their new manager Bobby Cox, the team was able to climb out of the cellar for the first time in 1982, even if climbing out of the cellar meant that they tied with Cleveland

for sixth place. And along the way, three Blue Jays starters, Dave Stieb, Jim Clancy and the baffling Luis Leal, reached double-digit win totals.

It was also the year of the platoon, with Garth Iorg/Rance Mulliniks at third and Buck Martinez sharing the catching with Ernie Whitt. The expansion era was over.

1983: W 89, L 73
Opening Day lineup: Damaso Garcia 2B, Dave Collins LF, Willie Upshaw 1B, Cliff Johnson DH, Jesse Barfield RF, Ernie Whitt C, Lloyd Moseby CF, Rance Mulliniks 3B, Alfredo Griffin SS, Dave Stieb P.
Blue Jays Fever struck for the first time in 1983, with the team posting its first winning record after leading the AL East at the All-Star break. The bandwagon began to fill with new believers. Unfortunately, the bandwagon's wheels started to loosen during the dog days of August, the tough part of the schedule when winning teams know how to dig deeper, and they fell off during the last week of that month during a tough visit to Baltimore. The Orioles, who would go on to win the World Series that year, showed the Blue Jays what champions do: they switched into overdrive, a gear the Blue Jays seemingly lacked. The game that symbolized the futility and frustration of that season is the one in which relief pitcher Tippy Martinez let the first three Blue Jays on base, and then picked them off, one by one. They never recovered, and finished the season in fourth place.

But they had made their move, and announced to the league, and their fans, that they were nobody's patsies any more.

My snapshot of that season was supplied by Dave Collins, the speedy left fielder who had come from New York in a trade for Dale Murray. He was in a major batting slump at one point, hitting just .210 when, before a game, he confided to me that he liked day games better than night games.

"Why, do you see the ball better in the daytime?"

"No," he said, deadpan. "It's just that during a day game, when someone sees my batting average on the scoreboard, he might think it's the time."

1984: W 89, L 73
Opening Day lineup: Damaso Garcia 2B, Rance Mulliniks 3B, Lloyd Moseby CF, Willie Upshaw 1B, Cliff Johnson DH, George Bell LF, Jesse Barfield RF, Ernie Whitt C, Alfredo Griffin SS, Jim Clancy P.
I had turned in my scorebook at the end of the 1983 season, and was back in the stands for Opening Day 1984. My timing felt right. I had followed the team from oblivion to contention, and it was time for me to move on. I don't remember much about the home opener, which Luis Leal lost to the Texas Rangers, but I remember distinctly my relief that I didn't have to go to the clubhouse to collect quotes when it was over. For five years, baseball had been my job, and I was happy to welcome it back as a pastime and a pleasure.

From my new perspective, I was able simply to enjoy the emergence of Tony Fernandez as an astonishing shortstop, diving to catch ground balls, and flipping them sidearm to first, making impossible plays look simple. This was before he began to carry the weight of the world on his sloping shoulders, when he was still having fun.

The surprising ace of that year's staff was Doyle Alexander, with his 17 wins. It had been difficult to cover him the previous season since he had refused to speak to me after taking umbrage at something I had written. Watching him from the stands wasn't much more fun, admittedly, because of his tendency to use every corner of the field and fill every available base with runners before getting the final out of the inning. He was a gloomy sort of fellow, and his games were always torture, but he, undeniably, did the job.

1985: W 99, L 62
Opening Day lineup: Damaso Garcia 2B, Lloyd Moseby CF, George Bell LF, Jesse Barfield RF, Jeff Burroughs DH, Willie Upshaw 1B, Buck Martinez C, Garth Iorg 3B, Tony Fernandez SS, Dave Stieb P.
The last snapshot of the Blue Jays' first era is a gimme — the same one is shared by thousands of fans across the country: George Bell, on his knees, with his hands raised, clutching the last out in the pennant clinching game.

The Blue Jays had, as Jerry Howarth would say, taken flight.

This was all very long ago, I guess, but it lives within the minds, and hearts, of all the fans who were around to watch the early Jays. I can still feel the chill in my bones from those days early and late in the season. I can remember the interminable rain delays and taste those awful Exhibition Stadium hot dogs. Sure the team was pretty lame, and of course they found a new way to lose every night, but still, there were moments of grace and joy to savour. After all, they were still playing the glorious game we all love. And you know what? Unless my memory is terribly flawed, we all had a lot of fun.

George Bell celebrates his pennant-clinch catch with Tony Fernandez. The early days were over.

In the Press Box

BOB ELLIOTT

After six seasons covering the Montreal Expos, it was a shocking experience to walk into Exhibition Stadium for the first time in August of 1985.

There was a postgame routine to covering the Expos. After the final out, the media would head downstairs and enter the manager's office, whether it was Dick Williams, Jim Fanning or Buck Rodgers. Then, it would be on to the clubhouse — or the excuse room, as Scott Young once described it — to hear the players' version of the happenings.

The first time we went downstairs at Exhibition Stadium after a game — the Toronto Blue Jays had dropped a nail-biting, gut-wrencher in extra innings — we walked into manager Bobby Cox's office to find only an empty desk. Cox was eventually found in the clubhouse sucking on a beverage, sitting with his coaches. He was so angry he was spitting out words between sips: "No . . . for me . . . he pitched good . . . he pitched . . . just super."

The press box at Exhibition Stadium was different too. In

> *Plenty of booted ground balls, a ton of home runs hit into the football stands at the Ex and a few home runs off the windows of the Hard Rock Cafe inside SkyDome.*

Montreal the majority of the inhabitants spoke French. In Toronto everyone spoke English. Except for Allan Ryan of the *Toronto Star*. He spoke something known as "Bear-ese."

And now here we are in 2001.

The 25th anniversary season.

There has been a lot of water under the bridge. Plenty of booted ground balls, a ton of home runs hit into the football stands at the Ex and a few home runs off the windows of the Hard Rock Cafe inside SkyDome.

What's stayed the same since 1985?

Let's take a quick look.

• Baseball is still a wonderful game; it's the business part that has changed so drastically. Whether it was Lloyd Moseby, Devon White or now Shannon Stewart legging out a triple to beat two perfect relays with a fade-a-way slide to avoid the tag on a bang-bang play, it's still a thing of beauty.

• Cito Gaston is still here. He was the hitting coach in 1985, managed the Jays from 1989 to 1997 — guiding them to back-to-back World Series titles in 1992 and 1993 — and returned for his second stint as the batting instructor in 2000.

With speed, skill and baseball smarts, Roberto Alomar is arguably the greatest player in Blue Jays history.

• Back then first baseman Willie Upshaw was a home run force. He passed the baton to Fred McGriff, who begat John Olerud, who was succeeded by Carlos Delgado. Prior to Upshaw were Doug Ault and John Mayberry. Now, like always, first base is the power supply and the deepest talent pool in the organization's 25-year history.

• In days of old, the Jays were led in the outfield by a larger-than-life player from the Dominican Republic named George Bell. Now, Dominican Raul Mondesi plays hard in right field.

• Allan Ryan wrote the best game stories in 1985 and it's still the case today.

When the Jays opened among the snow-drifts on April 7, 1977, sportswriting legends like Milt Dunnell, Jim Proudfoot, Neil MacCarl, Trent Frayne, George Gross and Jim Hunt were there. There was a constant noise coming from the press box at the Ex and we don't mean Ol' Hunt. It was the clackity-clack of the Underwood typewriters as writers pounded out their stories.

Then, writers would give their stories to CanFax operators who would electronically file the stories to the newspaper offices. But things began to change. Newspaper technology took off in 1980 and writers took to carrying telegram portable computers.

We were told that they were "lightweight."

One brand weighed 40 pounds.

Eventually, laptops surfaced in the mid-1980s, and they became smaller and lighter. They have reached the stage now where they weigh less than two pounds, even if some are ridiculous colours. Today, writers carry cell phones and palm pilots and are able to watch out-of-town games pitch-by-pitch on Internet sites. Nowadays, instead of a typewriter, the loudest noise coming from the press box — aside from Ol' Hunt's weekly visits — is the bong and the beep from the laptops powering up.

Has the volume of coverage changed over the years? The answer is a resounding yes — especially when it comes to statistics. To compare, we looked at coverage from the second game of the 162-game season at five-year intervals. (Game two coverage is fairly routine after the overkill of Opening Day.)

In 1977 the *Toronto Sun* ran a game story, two columns, two side bars and a boxscore. (Box scores from other games around the majors were not a major staple in any Toronto paper during the Jays' first few years of existence.) In 1982, there was a game story, a column and a box score. The coverage in 1987 included a game story, a column, two side bars, a notebook and a box score. In 1992, there was a game story, a column, two side bars, a notebook and a boxscore. By 1997 there was a game

story, two columns, a side bar, a notebook, a chart, a boxscore and a stats package.

But some things never change. Baseball writers often play a game over a Diet Coke after deadlines. They ask each other who was the best player you ever covered? Or which player did you have the best and worst relationship with?

Early in the 1980s my answer to the question of best player was Andre Dawson of the Expos. Later it switched to George Bell, and a few years ago it was adjusted to second baseman Robbie Alomar.

We remember the Jays' first trip into Kansas City in 1991. Alomar was on first base when Joe Carter flew to the warning track in center. We remember writing down an F-8 in our book and hearing a noise. Alomar had not gone half way as most runners do. In his first trip into Royals Stadium, he'd been alert enough to tag and we looked up to see him sliding in ahead of the throw.

Often we remember the Jays playing the infield back with a man on third, conceding a run. A hard ground ball would be hit to Alomar, the runner would break for home and Alomar would still throw him out at the plate. He had a defensive series to remember against the Yankees in 1993. Twice, he took relay throws on balls in the gap. Most would throw home, but both times Alomar looked, threw behind the runner rounding third and nailed him to record the final out of the inning. In the same

There was a constant noise coming from the press box at the Ex and we don't mean Ol' Hunt. It was the clackity-clack of the Underwood typewriters as writers pounded out their stories.

Blue Jays broadcasters Early Wynn (left) and Tom Cheek call the play on radio during a spring training game against the Phillies in Clearwater, Florida, in 1980. Cheek has never missed a Jays game!

series, we saw a similar throw to Alomar take a bad bounce and skip 15 feet away. It didn't matter. The Yankees third base coach, burned before, had already held the runner.

And how about those slow dribblers into no-man's land off first base where he would dive and use only his glove to flip the ball to the first baseman for the out?

Or diving back of second and flipping behind his back to the shortstop for the force?

The player we had the worst relationship with is the same player we had the best relationship with: George Bell.

Early in 1987, Bell threw a tantrum because he was pencilled in as the DH with Rick Leach starting in left field. Bell became angry, had a closed-door meeting with manager Jimy Williams, and the lineup was re-written.

We wrote that it was Bell's job to drive in runs and not make up the lineup, and that Leach's starts were as important to Leach as Bell's were to Bell.

The cone of silence descended.

Bell refused to speak to me, which is his right, but it was difficult covering a guy on his way to the American League Most Valuable Player award who wouldn't speak to me, especially on the road.

One series in Baltimore was especially difficult as Bell had the game-winning hit in three straight wins against Orioles starters Mike Flanagan, Mike Boddicker and Scott McGregor — each in the seventh inning or later.

We had learned a long time before that in order to write a story you didn't need to talk to one person. So the first night we talked to Flanagan about Bell's MVP-like season. The second night we talked to hitting coach Gaston. The third night, after being blown off by Bell again, a clubhouse attendant in the visitors room asked what the problem was. I said, "Well, we have a nodding relationship right now . . . he says 'nodding' to me, I say 'nodding' to him."

So, he told me that each night Bell had been on a postgame radio or TV show and he'd been given an appearance gift, he'd come into the clubhouse and given his watch to "that clubhouse kid" over there picking up uniforms, a free dinner for two to "that clubby" over there cleaning shoes and a gift certificate to "that clubhouse attendant" cleaning up the postgame spread.

Then he told me that the two best tippers in the American League were George Brett and Bell.

Two months later, we turned a corner in the bowels of the Oakland-Alameda County Coliseum the day before the 1987 All-Star Game and bumped into Bell.

"What the hell are you doing here?" Bell demanded.

"I came here to cover you," I answered.

"Oh," he said.

After that things were fine, and in 1990 I helped Bell write a book. Tom Henke calls Bell "the best teammate I ever had."

Sometimes his competitive spirit got the best of him, but George Bell was the team's best player — as well as the heart and soul of the Blue Jays.

We knew it was against the rules but we did develop a few favourites over the years. People like Jim Acker, who claimed he was the finest outlaw hunter in the state of Texas; Mike Flanagan, the funniest ball player we've ever met; Mookie Wilson, who once said "Mookie is not a name, it's a personality"; Al Leiter, who signed so many autographs he had blisters; Devon White, who never forgot his roots, sponsoring the American Legion team he played for as a high schooler in Harlem; Todd Stottlemyre, who wore his emotions on his sleeve, or his chin, in Philadelphia during the 1993 World Series and Ed Sprague because of his answers.

Of course we'd be re-miss if we didn't mention Paul Molitor, for the way he played the game — alertly, with even more base-running smarts than Alomar — and for his insight.

As a colleague once wrote: "Not only does Paul Molitor always have time to talk, he takes notes during the game and saves them for the writers."

The Jays were born with a five-year plan, then had 11 straight winning seasons and won back-to-back World Series titles.

Some say we were spoiled watching those teams of 1992 and 1993, but I say baseball remains as it was in 1977 — a great game to watch.

Flakes and Funnymen

ALLAN RYAN

A funny thing happened on the way to the Blue Jays' 25th anniversary season. Probably more than a couple, you'd have to think. We mean, 379 players over the years . . . 25 at a time . . . how could you miss?

So, yes, these Blue Jays had characters. All kinds of 'em. Jerks, clowns, stylers, malingerers, salts of the earth, stand-up guys, flakes. The wise beyond their years, the great beyond their talents, the humble, the God-fearing, the carousers. The laid-back country boys and not-always-so-laid-back Latins, the proud and the paranoid, the devout and the delusional, the cocksure and the cock-ups.

Just like the rest of the world.

George Bell, for instance. Now, there was a human.

It was July 5, 1989, a long, somber hour after Bell had misplayed a couple more balls in left, prompting another mess of boos. The greatest lightning rod for public opinion that ever put on a Blue Jays suit, George had been having a bad week.

There were three guys left in a long-emptied clubhouse . . . your friendly correspondent; Bell, still stinging from the rain of razz; and, in a distant corner, but listening ever intently, Dave Stieb.

Eventually, Bell got around to: "You tell those (bleeping) Canadian fans they can kiss my (bleeping) purple ass."

Funny huh?

Well, now it is. Back then, though, Stieb groaned; we probably winced. Despite all the times he had threatened, playfully, to "keeeel" us, Bell was worth caring about. We appreciated his heart, admired the way he bulldozed through whatever clubhouse cliques wanted to exist. Pitchers, hitters. Bell didn't care. Every day guys, rookies, spare parts. Bell didn't care. Whites, blacks, Latins . . . shut up and deal the cards.

So, we're sure we sort of tried to give Bell an out that night . . . a second to reconsider.

"This goes in the paper, George, you'll never hear the end of it."

"You write it!" Bell insisted.

And we did.

Next afternoon, Bell was in the clubhouse, four, five hours before game time, as per usual. He corralled a clubhouse guy, asked him to bring him the paper. Bell didn't know which one,

asked for them all. He started flipping, found what he was looking for, then, according to our initially wary witness, simply began cackling with glee.

Bell's probably still cackling, but no flake he — our definition of "flake" being a guy who just *might* be putting you on but one whose general or even occasional behavior and/or thought and/or speech processes clearly strayed mightily into . . . well, eccentricity. Bell was just, ah, real. Often a riot. He played the game right — meaning hard and with joy — and was also able to display a charming and disarming grasp of his own . . . well, defensive deficiencies.

We think back, for instance, to the second-last night of the 1990 regular season as the Jays, already winners in Baltimore, packed around the clubhouse TV, desperately in need of a Chicago win in Fenway. A White Sox hit that bounced in front of, then past, a sprawling Mike Greenwell, the Red Sox left fielder, would help a bit.

"Wow!" Bell hooted. "He played that like me."

This prompted some much-welcomed comic relief (ultimately, the Beaners would prevail) as well as John Candelaria's last crack as a Blue Jay.

"Yeah, George," he said. "That's why we're having to watch this game."

Probably true.

And speaking of "last cracks," the following might have been the funniest thing ever uttered by Roger Clemens dur-

> "When I see Randy in camp, I know the country's safe," noted Clemens, deadpan. "If he went missing, I'd turn on CNN because I'd know we were going after Saddam."

ing his entire two-year stay. Except maybe (heh, heh) for that bit about him wanting to leave in order to pitch closer to his home in Houston. Like the south Bronx. In any case, the occasion was new closer Randy Myers finally turning up for spring training in 1998.

"When I see Randy in camp, I know the country's safe," noted Clemens, deadpan. "If he went missing, I'd turn on CNN because I'd know we were going after Saddam."

Okay, so maybe Roger wasn't so funny. He does, in this instance, serve to introduce Myers, who, with his camouflage outfits, stun gun, daily kielbasa rituals and strange locker contents that one dare not look at too intently, was what you might want to call the Blue Jays' last true "flake." Hard to imagine Myers putting this all on, but we do recall one otherwise quiet postgame clubhouse that erupted with Myers exploding on some startled young radio guy. Something about "What kind of stupid question is that?" . . . a staple for some ballplayers these days. Myers ranted a minute or two until achieving the desired effect, then picked up and huffed out of the room. But not before stopping at another reporter with a wink and a whispered "What was the question?"

True flakes, of course, are hard to come by. Mark Fidrych would've been one. Same for Bill Lee. Rick Bosetti? Well, just because his stated intent was to "sign" every outfield he played in, we don't think so. Just don't eat the yellow Astroturf.

Mark Lemongello? Well, okay, probably. This was a journeyman pitcher who touched down here in 1979, going 1–9 then clinching his release by firing an ashtray past the ear of then-president Peter Bavasi. Along the way, he'd bitten himself on the shoulder, smashed hair dryers, torn uniforms to shreds, punched himself in the jaw and barricaded himself at his locker behind a wall of cardboard boxes. Tough interview.

Couple of years later, Lemongello got charged with armed robbery and kidnapping down in Largo, Florida. Seems he'd had a little trouble with a couple of his cousins, whom he felt had stiffed him on some roofing job. Beat that rap, he did, but we have no idea of the outcome not too many years ago when he agreed to assemble a team of men to play a "friendly" with the all-woman Colorado Silver Bullets. Game sort of disintegrated when Lemongello had his pitchers throw at the girls.

Speaking of lockers, we remember Tony Fernandez once sitting at his, quietly munching at a plate of postgame victuals. Perfectly normal but for the fact that this was during the bubbly-soaked, immediate aftermath of a division-clinching celebration. For these deals, clubhouse guys would cover the lockers, floor to ceiling, with protective plastic. Took a while to find Tony that night, but there he was, fully inside his cubicle (a concept for which these lockers were not designed), behind the plastic.

Ah, Tony, Tony. Maybe the most complex character ever to grace these parts, a status he solidified with each of his three separate comings. Talented? Supremely. Moody? No question. He was the abbot of the clubhouse, also known as Mr. Gadget for the myriad self-devised training aids he employed (ropes and balls and traffic cones, French doors, cacti, small rodents, you name it). They also called him Old Man for his stooped, head-down walk and for the aches and pains and weight of the world he so often seemed to be carrying on his shoulders. But there was an awful lot of little kid in this guy and, of course, he'd always lead the team in trying to stretch singles into . . . well, triples.

But funny?

Tony Fernandez?

Yes, very. Only subtly.

Fernandez cost a game in Cleveland once when he lost a pop-up in the sun, then took a pile of grief for having neglected to wear his sunglasses. Many hours later, well past midnight, he boarded the team bus, pointedly wearing shades.

Regularly, for reasons known only to him, Fernandez would not be talking to this reporter or that . . . and this reporter many times. At one postgame locker, apparently, it was because of something we'd written. This time, this was particularly puzzling since we couldn't remember recently writing anything about Fernandez at all, never mind something he'd possibly perceive as offensive. Besides, Fernandez claimed to never read the papers. Someone, he said, had sent him a clipping.

"But, Tony, what was it about?"

"You know what you wrote," he said.

Well, yeah, we did (most times) . . . and then a whole new approach suggested itself . . .

"Tony, are you sure you know what paper I [enough with that royal "we" business] even write for? Do you even know what my name is?"

"You're the Bear."

"Well, okay, but that's not my name. That's not what my paper puts at the top of my stories. Tony, who am I?"

Fernandez was stumped for, like, about three seconds, then ended this goofy little dialogue with, "You know who you are."

Tony Fernandez was supremely talented, winning four straight Gold Gloves from 1986 to 1989. He was also moody, but he had his funny side too.

Injuries: Jays had a few.

- Glenallen Hill scored a one-of-a-kind entry on the disabled list in 1990 when he barged out of a nightmare he was having about spiders and suffered multiple scrapes and bruises on his feet, knees and elbows. A month later, he gave the movie *Arachnophobia* two-and-a-half stars.

"Out of five," said Hill. "I mean, I love scary movies but this wasn't scary at all. *The Exorcist*, now that was scary . . . but this was just another insect movie, a creature feature Saturday special. And, look, I'm uneasy with spiders but I don't think it's spiders that caused that nightmare. It might've been diet, might've been stress . . . more of a sleeping disorder. Spiders just happened to be what I dreamt about that night. It could have been about a car that kept running over me. It could've been about . . . you know, caterpillars."

- In 1993, the Jays rented Rickey Henderson for the stretch but lost him for a couple of days because of . . . freezer-burn on his foot. The trainer left a chemical ice-pack on too long.
- And Todd Stottlemyre, one spring, put a fishhook through a finger as he tried to wriggle the hook out of a mistakenly (we're assuming) snared . . . alligator.
- The Jays came this close to another beauty one night in Milwaukee in 1993 when a skunk wandered into the outfield, directly past the one and only Willie Canate, then patrolling in right. Canate was delighted, clearly thinking it was a cat and, at the urging of center fielder Turner Ward, was actually giving it chase until Alfredo Griffin, frantically waving as he ran out from shortstop, got him to back off. "We don't have those in the Dominican," said Griffin. Willie might've really learned something.

A year before, in 1992, September call-up Mike Maksudian pocketed $800 for his own unique wildlife experience. His teammates anted up the money to watch him chomp down on a vivid-green, two-inch long locust that Devon White had stumbled across in a Kansas City outfield. (Did we mention it was still alive?)

"I started out in the bullpen with a small grasshopper, then a bigger one," said Maksudian. "I got $1.50 for that. You have to pretend it's a strawberry or something — and get it fast so it doesn't wriggle around so much. I've got a limited role on this club and I just do it to keep 'em loose. It's nothing I didn't do in the minors."

In 1990 and 1991, it was Kenny Williams (yes, *that* Kenny Williams, the guy who shipped the Jays Mike Sirotka this spring) running over third base coach John McLaren. Later, Williams figured he had the capper to an ongoing debate over Robbie Alomar's sliding head-first into first base. We mean, was this a faster way of getting there or not?

Our argument, with which even Alomar was ready to agree, was that if, indeed, it was faster to leave one's feet, why didn't we see more 100-metre sprinters diving across finish lines? (And, hey, they could put a pit of sand out there.)

"Oh yeah," said Williams. "Well, if it's not faster, how come we always slide when we're stealing second?"

Oh, we don't know, Ken. Maybe something to do with having to stop?

So much funny, so little space.

- Rubber-faced, non-stop trash-talking Derek Bell, rendered virtually speechless atop the dugout steps one Fan Appreciation Day as Joe Carter, grinning, waving, drove in from the outfield in the giveaway Jeep. It was Bell's vehicle.
- Reliever Dale Murray staggering into a Sunday morning clubhouse in Anaheim after an obviously long, hard California night. "Just coming from church?" someone asked. "Ah'd gladly go to church every Sunday morning," he drawled, "if'n it wasn't so close to Saturday night."
- Kelly Gruber, in that homespun way of his, standing up to a couple of back-to-back throwing errors that cost a game: "I'm sure you don't eat all the time without spilling something."

Hey, no need to get personal there, Kelly.

- And for the benefit of all those wary of flying, Rance Mulliniks, on every landing: "This is it! We're going downnnnnnnn!"

Mike Flanagan, Tom Henke, Lloyd Moseby, Jim Acker, Manny Lee, Garth Iorg, Jose Nunez, Pat Borders, Paul Molitor, Mark Eichhorn, Dennis Lamp, David Wells, Duane Ward, John Olerud, Damaso Garcia, Dave Stieb, Jim Clancy, Luis Leal, Frank Wills, Tom Lawless, Dan Plesac . . .

So little space.

But maybe just enough for one final line from the master, George Bell. No paranoid he.

"Hey you. Stop talking about me behind my neck."

> *In 1993, the Jays rented Rickey Henderson for the stretch but lost him for a couple of days because of . . . freezer-burn on his foot.*

Epy's Academy

STEPHEN BRUNT

Everyone has a unique memory of when the Toronto Blue Jays first came fully into fashion. For some, it was Day One with Doug Ault in the snowstorm; for others it was the first pennant in 1985, for others, hard cases, it might even have been the World Series years.

But for some of us who lived and died through the first awful expansion seasons, the great epiphany came one night in 1983 when *Monday Night Baseball* (yes, kids, there was such a thing) first came to town. Howard Cosell and company arrived at the makeshift confines of Exhibition Stadium to take a token look at a team that had, for years, been roundly ignored south of the border. That night, Alfredo Griffin enjoyed the defensive game of his life, making a series of apparently impossible plays, and Cosell couldn't stop with the superlatives. Since what others thought, especially Americans, was always so important in

Rico Carty hailed from San Pedro de Macoris, the tiny town in the Dominican Republic that would become known as "the Shortstop Factory." Carty and John Mayberry (right) were the Blue Jays' first swing-for-the-fences power hitters.

Toronto, that game — as much as the fact that the Blue Jays were in contention for the first time — was an affirmation that good times were in the offing.

Alfredo Griffin was the first young Blue Jay to make a name for himself in the wider world when he shared honours as Rookie of the Year back in 1979. To be entirely accurate, though, Griffin was not a product of the Blue Jays system. He had arrived via a trade from Cleveland for reliever Victor Cruz (who was very briefly sensational in Toronto, then got fat and lost it all at once after he left). But the fact that he was Latino, from a baseball crazy town in the Dominican Republic, was very much a measure of the franchise.

No history of the Toronto Blue Jays could be written without a nod to the Latin American players who starred for the team: Griffin; Rico Carty; Damaso Garcia; Nelson Liriano; Luis Leal; Toronto's first most valuable player, George Bell; the best player ever developed entirely within the organization, Tony Fernandez; the best player ever to wear the uniform, Roberto Alomar; and two current stars, Carlos Delgado and Kelvim Escobar.

Especially in the 1980s, when the team went from laughing stock to model franchise, the Jays were known for their deep connections in the Caribbean. Those links were part of a strategy born of necessity, a way to fast-track an expansion franchise in the general direction of the World Series. As it turned out, it worked better than anyone could possibly have imagined.

Peter Bavasi, the first president of the Toronto Blue Jays, had been raised steeped in the traditions of the Brooklyn and Los Angeles Dodgers, where his father, Buzzy, learned the business of baseball. One of the pillars of the "Dodger Way," the organization's method for staying one step ahead of the competition, was to invest heavily in Latin America. Professional baseball players had been coming from the Caribbean for many years by the time the Jays came into existence, yet few franchises really concentrated their recruiting there.

Plus, by the late 1970s, the islands were one of the last vestiges of the old, free market for baseball talent. American-born players were no longer available to be signed as 16-year-olds — they went into a draft, which meant that every team had a 1-in-26 chance to select them, and that there were fewer triumphs of the old, bird-dog scouting methods. But in Latin America it was still open season, with every gifted kid in a dirt-poor town just waiting to be discovered and signed. For an expansion team that hoped to move forward fast and that had a minor league system to populate from scratch, it made sense to focus where a huge number of players could be recruited in a hurry.

"There were a number of ways to build a club," former Jays general manager Pat Gillick said. "There was the Amateur Draft, the Rule 5 Draft, trades, and signing Latin Americans. If you were going to accelerate the process, Latin America was the place. You could sign players there at a younger age and develop them yourself."

That notion originally came from Bavasi. From Gillick, who had learned his trade in the Houston and New York Yankee organizations, came the key to the enterprise, Epifanio "Epy" Guerrero.

Guerrero had been a minor league player, an outfield prospect who left the Dominican Republic for the United States with countryman Rico Carty. Unlike "the Beeg Mon," he never made it to the big leagues, and returned to the island to work in his father's wholesale grocery business. But he kept a hand in baseball; he kept an eye on the local kids, and one day he seized the chance to return to the game in a new role.

"I've got a player I want to show you," he said to Gillick, then a scout for the Astros visiting the Dominican. The player turned out to be future star Cesar Cedeno, and a life long business and personal relationship was born. When Gillick moved to the Yankees, Guerrero went along with him. When Gillick was hired by the Blue Jays, Guerrero wasn't far behind, becoming Toronto's director of scouting in the region.

"He just kept growing in the job," Gillick said.

And with Guerrero came a grand idea, the plan to go beyond mere scouting, to build an entire complex in the Dominican Republic that would house and train and acclimatize young ballplayers. They would be schooled in the fundamentals of the game. They would be given English lessons, to help them prepare for the day when they'd head for the minor leagues. They would be given three square meals a day, many of them for the first time in their lives.

"Epy really is the guy who had this vision," Gillick said — and so naturally it was dubbed Epy's Academy.

The treatment of young Latin ballplayers worked in concert with the unusually humane approach to the business of baseball espoused by Blue Jays chairman Peter Hardy, and carried out by those who worked for him (it included meal plans for minor leaguers, extra time off for minor league coaches and managers, and other perks unknown outside the organization). In the Dominican, Gillick said, it wasn't just the right thing to do, but it also paid dividends. Latin ballplayers had long felt they were treated like second-class citizens, even after they became stars in the major leagues (and they generally lacked the political clout seized by African American players in the wake of

> *And with Guerrero came a grand idea, the plan to go beyond mere scouting, to build an entire complex in the Dominican Republic that would house and train and acclimatize young ballplayers.*

pioneers like Jackie Robinson and, as a manager, Frank Robinson). The Blue Jays did everything they could to send out the message that they were one organization that respected its Latin American talent.

"I found Latin Americans to be very loyal," Gillick said. "If they got some place where they felt comfortable, and they felt like they were being treated equal to everyone else, they weren't as ready to run away the first time they got the chance."

It wasn't just that they weren't so inclined to run away as free agents, but that when they went home in the offseason to play winter ball, they spread the word that Toronto was a very good place to play baseball.

"They were really our best missionaries," Gillick said, "because they were going back home." At the peak of the Jays' Dominican operations, when Bell, an icon on the island, was one of the best players in the game, it was normal to see kids in the streets wearing not Dodger blue or Yankee pinstripes, but Toronto Blue Jays caps.

Two of the most important signings in the history of the Toronto franchise, the best player of the 1980s, and the best of the moment, can be traced directly to the Guerrero-Gillick

Epy Guerrero followed Pat Gillick to Toronto in 1979. A former outfield prospect who never made it to the majors, Guerrero headed up Latin American scouting for the Blue Jays through the 1995 season.

(Left to right) Otto Velez of Puerto Rico, Panama's Juan Berenguer, Tony Fernandez of the Dominican Republic and Venezuela's Luis Leal relax during spring training in 1982.

connection. In 1980, Guerrero was passing by the stadium in San Pedro de Macoris, the Dominican baseball hotbed, where he saw a young outfielder taking batting practice. He noted the swing, noted the power, and noted the name: George Bell. Bell was a minor league property of the Philadelphia Phillies then, but was listed as disabled. Guerrero phoned Gillick, who sent one of his scouting directors, Al LaMacchia, to confirm what Guerrero had seen. The Jays followed by selecting Bell in the Rule 5 Draft, paying the Phillies the grand sum of $25,000.

"That might have been the draft of the century," Guerrero said — and he may be right, given what Bell would accomplish for Toronto.

Eight years later, the baseball environment had changed considerably. Puerto Rico was on the verge of being included in the territory for the Amateur Draft. Guerrero had been alerted by one of his local scouts about a 16-year-old power-hitting catching prospect named Carlos Delgado. Gillick went and watched him work out. Understanding that time was of the essence, understanding that the Texas Rangers were also in hot pursuit, he offered what was then huge bonus money: $96,000. Delgado, instead of waiting for the draft, was persuaded to sign.

Of course, the Jays didn't always get their man. The Rangers,

who also concentrated heavily on the Caribbean, beat them out for Ruben Sierra and Juan Gonzalez. Pudge Rodriguez they flat out missed. And not all of Guerrero's sure things were sure things in the end: remember Sil Campusano, the star of the future who never was? Guerrero had a tendency towards self-promotion, and perhaps that's part of the reason why, not long after Gillick stepped aside as the Jays' general manager, his favourite scout was given his walking papers. Toronto, the front office announced, would be going in a new direction in the Caribbean, concentrating not on quantity, but on quality.

As of now, the franchise's line of homegrown Latin super-stars ends with Delgado and Escobar, a Venezuelan who was also signed when Guerrero was still with the team. The academy is now supported by the Milwaukee Brewers, who hired Guerrero as their director of international scouting. And the Seattle Mariners, under the presidency of Pat Gillick, have their own Guerrero on staff — Patrick, son of Epy, named after his boss.

Said Gillick: "I think he's going to do all right."

Home Away From Home

STEVE WULF

Above my desk is a framed lineup card from Game Four of the 1993 World Series. It still has creases in it, because it was the Phillies' lineup card, and their manager, Jim Fregosi, crumpled it up after the 15–14 Blue Jays victory and threw it on the floor of the dugout. A *Sports Illustrated* photographer picked it up and gave it to me, thinking I might want it.

To this day, I smile when I look at it. Some of my amusement comes from the remembrance of that wild game. But my pleasure goes deeper than that. With each Blue Jay name — Henderson, White, Alomar, Carter . . . Borders, Sprague, Knorr, Butler — I'm reminded of how the franchise was built, and in each crease, I'm reminded of my own history with the club.

My life with the Blue Jays began in the spring of 1980, when, as a young writer for *Sports Illustrated*, I was dispatched to Toronto to do an early-season story on the surprising Blue Jays and Athletics, who were both in first place in their divisions. I was given two days to turn in the story. In return, I got 20 years of friendships and a hundred stories.

After the first game of that series, a Jesse Jefferson two-hitter as I recall, I sat in with the Jays beat writers, then introduced myself to Bobby Mattick, the 64-year-old manager at the time. "Wanna beer?" he said, producing a Labatt's Blue out of his freezer. I said sure. A Blue Jays employee, whom I did not know, walked in, introduced himself to me, helped himself to a beer and took a seat in an office chair against the wall. For the next hour, Bobby Mattick, Paul Beeston and I talked baseball.

The experience was both eye-opening and mind-expanding. I had been covering baseball for a few years, and while people had been friendly to me before, never had they actually welcomed me into their world. And there was no artifice to this invitation, no sense that they were currying favour with an out-of-town writer from a national magazine. They were just being themselves. They were just being nice.

Being a non-Canadian, I'm not sure whether Canadians consider being called nice a stereotype or a compliment. So please don't be offended by what I just said. Besides, nice is such an inadequate word. What I experienced was more than nicety or courtesy. It was real consideration, real connection.

And on that first trip to the Ex, I connected with so many people: Howard Starkman, the finest public relations man in the game; Pat Gillick, the general manager whose encyclopedic

> *Being a non-Canadian, I'm not sure whether Canadians consider being called nice a stereotype or a compliment.*

memory was matched by his heart; executive-at-large Michael Firestone, a mensch's mensch; utility infielder Garth Iorg, whom I had once covered when he was with the Fort Lauderdale Yankees and I was with the *Fort Lauderdale News*; any number of writers who went out of their way to help me.

I wasn't fooled by that particular Blue Jays team: Rick Bosetti was not going to lead them to the promised land. But I also sensed that what was going on in Toronto was very special, that while Bob Bailor, Roy Howell and J.J. Cannon were not the building blocks for the future, patience, intelligence and a uniquely Canadian warmth were.

Over the next few years, I jumped at or volunteered for every assignment involving the Blue Jays: a short piece on Damo Garcia, a look at crossover pioneer Danny Ainge, stories about other teams that involved trips to the Ex. I always enjoyed talking baseball with Gillick and Bobby Cox, Willie Upshaw and Buck Martinez, catching up with Beeston and Mattick and Firestone and operations chief George Holm. Journalists are not supposed to play favourites, but I found myself rooting for the Blue Jays even after their inevitable eliminations from contention.

In 1983 I was sent north to do a cover story heralding the Blue Jays and Expos together. I still cringe when I think back to my lead on that one, done in both *Canajun* and *Franglais*. I now look back on the piece as a betrayal of friendship: It's one thing for Dave Thomas and Rick Moranis to parody Canadians, but it's quite another when a smart-ass New York writer does it. But I also remember one smart thing I did in that story, namely using this quote from Pat Gillick: "The best analogy I can think of for the way we built this team is that childhood game, Mother May I? Instead of trying to take giant steps, we decided to take little bitty baby steps."

After their flirtation with first in 1983, they finished the season fourth. Then second. Then first, only to lose to the Kansas City Royals in seven games in the 1985 ALCS. They were not ready for the World Series, or maybe it was the other way around. Had the Jays made it to the stateside showcase, I'm afraid the Great White North jokes would have drowned out a true appreciation for the franchise.

In the meantime, I kept in touch. One winter in the Dominican, I hooked up with Beeston, Starkman, Firestone and board member Herb Solway at Casa de Campo, the resort outside of San Pedro de Macoris. They were there for George Bell's golf tournament. I was there to try to round up all the Dominican starting shortstops in the major leagues for a photo: Mariano Duncan, Julio Franco, Jose Uribe, Rafael Santana, Rafael Belliard and, of course, Tony Fernandez. We got them all in a horse-driven cart on the central square in San Pedro. The driver in the photo was the not-very-Dominican looking but *muy loco* Firestone.

Later, inside a restaurant called El Piano, I witnessed the greatest play ever made by a shortstop. All the players were seated around a long, rectangular table, with *Cabeza* — Fernandez — at one end, and Duncan at the other. A box of balls was produced, and they signed while eating. At one point, Duncan fired his ball the length of the table at Fernandez, who had his head down. Tony, without looking up, caught the ball with his left hand and continued to eat with his right.

In June of 1989, SkyDome was about to open, and the *SI* writer initially assigned to the story couldn't do it. So I filled in. My instructions were clear: A retractable roof stadium is inherently ridiculous, so have fun with it. In other words, they were looking for a rip job. When, upon arrival, I saw the concrete turtle-like shell, and later, when I got absolutely no cooperation from the stadium authority, I was inclined to do just that. But then I called Beeston, the newly named president of the Blue Jays, and asked him if there was any way I could get inside the Dome before opening night. "Where are you staying?" he said. "L'Hotel," I said. "Be out in front in five minutes," he said. Five minutes later, Beeston, sockless as always, pulled up in his red convertible — actually driving on the sidewalk — opened the passenger door and said, "Get in."

In the same way he had opened my eyes to the warmth of Canada nine years before, Beeston opened my eyes to the inherent beauty of SkyDome. Later, after talking with the architect, Roderick Robbie, and the engineer who designed the roof, Michael Allen, I came to realize that this was not just a novelty, but a work of art and more . . .

"Sphere and obelisk," said Robbie, speaking of the relationship of SkyDome to the CN Tower. "I wanted something soft, organic and mysterious to contrast with the hardness of the tower. Vagina and penis." My editors at *SI* didn't let me go that far, but they did buy into my overwhelmingly positive review of the facility and the vision behind it.

A year later, I was back in Blue Jay land, only it was Medicine Hat, Alberta, where the Jays had a Pioneer League team. I had pitched a story on a first-year manager for a minor-league package in *SI*, and I just happened to pick Garth Iorg. It turned out to be a great assignment because it reminded both of us of our days in Fort Lauderdale, when we were both starting out in our respective careers. I was struck by how beautifully he handled these kids, firmly but gently. On the bus ride back from a tough loss to Great Falls (featuring Pedro Martinez and Raul Mondesi),

Iorg gave a little talk that literally lifted their heads up. He also told them they were about to meet a great man. Bobby Mattick was coming to town to teach them about playing the infield.

(Gillick later told me about a repercussion of my Medicine Hat story. Turns out I had painted such an unflattering, albeit accurate portrait of life in the Pioneer League that the Jays' first draft pick that year insisted on going to Class A St. Catharines instead of Medicine Hat. That draft pick? Future Heisman Trophy winner Chris Weinke.)

Meanwhile, back in the big leagues, SkyDome became an immediate success, only adding to the allure of Toronto. I couldn't wait to take my wife there, and after one visit, she couldn't wait to go back. And thanks to the success of the ballclub on the field, there were plenty of reasons to do so. The disappointing five-game losses in the 1989 and 1991 ALCS were leavened by the certainty that the Blue Jays would also be back.

And in 1992, they were. With their hard-fought ALCS payback triumph over Oakland, the Jays became the first Canadian team in the World Series. But after a 3–1 loss to Atlanta in the first game, prospects of an actual non-American champion seemed unlikely. Enter "the Trenches," that silly little group of reserves who tried to ignite rallies from the dugout steps. This may have already been lost to memory, but Derek Bell would pull out a bat belonging to the next man up and pass it off to Ed Sprague, who would fire off an imaginary volley at the opposing pitcher. If they needed a big rally, they would turn the bat around and make it a bazooka. And if one of "the Trenches" happened to get in the game, his place would be taken by their commander-in-chief, Dave Winfield. As it happened, Sprague

Two helpful Blue Jays fans remind the Americans which way is up after the Marines flew the Canadian flag upside down in Game Two of the 1992 World Series.

hit a two-run homer in the top of the ninth of Game Two to turn a 4–3 deficit into a 5–4 win.

As history well knows, the Blue Jays won the next two games — the first Series games outside of the United States — and ultimately the World Series. In retrospect, I'm struck by three things. After putting the Jays ahead for good with his homer in Game Four, Pat Borders told the media he really owed his career to the Blue Jays scout who converted him from infielder to catcher: Bobby Mattick. Except that Borders forgot his name. "Bobby Maddox" he called him. Knowing Mattick, he wouldn't have minded his "I owe my career to whatshisname" status. After all, he moved Borders for the good of the club, and winning the World Series was all that mattered.

The second thing was the shout in the visitors' clubhouse after the Jays edged the Braves 4–3 in Game Six. As you recall, Mike Timlin had fielded Otis Nixon's bunt for the final out. Well, the shout in the clubhouse was "PFP, PFP . . ." PFP — Pitchers Fielding Practice. One of the most disliked, unappreciated drills in spring training is PFP, but lo and behold, the World Series was won on a play practiced ad nauseam in March. It seemed like a fitting tribute not only to the importance of preparation, but also to doing things the right way.

Then there was the post-victory celebration in an Atlanta hotel after Game Six. It was more of a confirmation or bar

Seventh inning sweat: Blue Jays fans look tense after the Phillies scored five runs in the top of the seventh to take the lead in Game Six. Joe Carter would take care of that.

mitzvah party than a raucous bacchanal. The Blue Jays had finally come of age, and they had done it with the same corps of people who started the whole thing. There was even a real sense of sympathy for old friend Bobby Cox, the Braves manager who had played an integral part in the club's development.

Athletes often say after a big victory that "it hasn't sunk in yet." But watching old friends toast and hug one another that night, I realized that the importance of their victory had already sunk in. Yes, they had completed a long, hard task, and yes, they had brought the Commissioner's Trophy north of the border for the first time. But most importantly, they had done it together.

A year later, they celebrated again, this time on Canadian soil, thanks to that wild 15–14 game and Joe Carter's walkoff homer — just below where I was sitting in the left field auxiliary press box. The image I'm left with from that postgame celebration is the champagne-soaked, cigar-smoking Beeston putting his arm around everyone he could, laughing the laugh I first heard 13 years before.

As with all good things, the Blue Jays "dynasty" came to an end. Ownership changed hands, Gillick left, Beeston was called to New York, empty seats began to appear, managers came and went. Winning was no longer a habit, and in fact seemed to happen about as often as it did when Rick Bosetti was a god. But still I followed the Jays as if they were my hometown team. And now that they're off to a nice start in 2001 under an old friend, Buck Martinez (whose first base coach is Garth Iorg!), I'm certain they're headed in the right direction.

A few years ago, I returned to Toronto to do a story on Shawn Green for *ESPN The Magazine*. The manager, ironically enough, was Jim Fregosi, and while no Bobby Mattick, he was friendly enough when I visited him in his office. I told him I actually had his lineup card from Game Four of the '93 Series and asked him if he wanted it back.

"Nah, I never want to see the damn thing again," he said. "You keep it."

I will.

To the victor goes the spoils: Cito Gaston poses with back-to-back World Series trophies.

Gillick & Beeston

WAYNE PARRISH

On the day he met the man who would become his mentor, Paul Beeston wore no socks or tie. His hair was unaccountantly long. He had a cigar clenched between his teeth, and was flipping through a copy of *The Racing Form*. He had absolutely no clue who it was that had just popped in to shake hands and introduce himself.

"Who's Peter Hardy?" he asked when the fellow left the room.

"He's the vice-chairman," came the answer.

And so it began, the construction of the three-legged management stool that would, in time, come to support baseball's model franchise — not to mention a pair of World Series champions. Along the way, two of the three men would become celebrated as the most successful sports management team their city had known, though neither would ever forget

The Odd Couple: A career baseball man with a mind like a computer (Pat Gillick) and an outgoing accountant who never wore socks (Paul Beeston) made the Blue Jays the best team in baseball.

or fail to acknowledge the quiet leadership of the third.

"Peter Hardy kind of set the tone, not only for us but for the other guys at Labatts, for the staff, for everybody," an old pickoff artist named Pat Gillick is saying on the third day of his 42nd season in professional baseball, a bright, sunny morning in downtown Seattle, a city still obsessing over the recent rude departures of major dotcom fortunes, as well as Junior and A-Rod.

A quarter-century earlier, the Mariners were not Gillick's employer but rather the enemy of sharpest focus, the other expansion team ushered into the American League alongside his own Toronto Blue Jays. The Toronto club had made a 29-year-old cigar-masticating accountant from Welland, Ontario, named Beeston their first employee, and had subsequently hired to run the show a pedigreed baseball man, Peter Bavasi, who proved smart enough to know what he didn't know about baseball and thereby entice Gillick north from the Steinbrenner Zoo in the Bronx. In the 18 seasons that followed, as the Hardy/Beeston/Gillick ensemble played its first tentative notes and then crescendoed into a Gillick/Beeston duet that left an indelible mark on a city and perhaps even the game, the Blue Jays would win 191 more games than the Mariners. Not to mention those five division titles and two World Series. By comparison, Seattle had just two (barely) winning seasons — one was by two games, the other by one — over the same span.

Mind you, it didn't seem to be shaping up that way in the early days. Seattle won 10 more games than Toronto back in 1977, 14 more in 1979 and seven more in strike-shortened 1981. That fall, though, two significant things occurred. Beeston quit, or at least threatened to, and Hardy was given to understand that Gillick would likely not be far behind. The issue was Bavasi, whose relentless, micro-managing style had nudged both to the brink. Hardy made the only move he could make, taking the presidential reins himself and giving Beeston and Gillick their head to run the business and baseball operations as they each — and both together — saw fit. Gillick was 42, and had apprenticed a lifetime for the opportunity. Beeston was 35, and a little worried that he had bitten off more of a Havana Special than he could reasonably chew. Not that he would have conceded that at the time.

The contributions of Norman Edgar (Peter) Hardy to the success of the Blue Jays are not widely known, but both Pat Gillick and Paul Beeston credit him as the key to the smooth relationship between management and ownership.

"Beast," as Gillick loved to call him, is savouring some of that long-ago trepidation on a spring morning 20 years later. This from a seat at his favourite breakfast table at New York's Regency Hotel, a few blocks along Park Avenue from the headquarters of Major League Baseball, of which Beeston has been chief operating officer for nearly four years.

"I remember our first item was to go see Steve Comte, who was [outfielder] Barry Bonnell's agent," he says. "Steve leaves the room for a minute and Pat turns to me and says, 'OK, tell him our offer.' I go 'B-b-b-b . . . but . . . but . . . I'm so nervous I don't know if I can get the words out . . . .'"

As Beeston chuckles softly, either at the memory or how far and well he has come, an older gentleman stops by the table to emit a genuinely delighted "Mr. Beeston . . . so nice to see you."

The visitor, it develops, is Bob Tisch, who, among other things, is co-owner of football's New York Giants, owner and co-chairman of Loews Corporation and erstwhile Postmaster General of the United States. The noted New York philanthropist is also owner of the swank Regency, home-away-from-home for the boy from Welland during the five days a week he oversees America's national pastime. Tisch gently chastises Beeston for not making the Yankees' home opener — he passes on the helpful warning that "George" commented on his absence — but Beeston replies that he was in San Juan, watching the Blue Jays play A-Rod's Rangers in baseball's fourth consecutive opener staged on foreign — or, in Puerto Rico's case, quasi-foreign — soil.

"You can't be everywhere at once," he says, laughing. Tisch concurs and suggests they get together socially soon.

A certain kinship between the two is apparent and, once you learn a bit more about Tisch, that's not surprising. Tisch is renowned as a mogul with a common touch. *Manhattan Inc.* magazine once noted that everyone who knows him has a story along these lines: "I was with Bob in New York/on the Riviera/in California and we walked into a hotel/restaurant/factory. He not only greeted a bellman/chef/foreman by his first name, he asked about the person's child/parent/spouse." In his years with the Blue Jays, and now in his major league role, such words could double as Beeston's calling card. He has always seemed perpetually gregarious, forever smiling, laughing and backslapping, seemingly at ease in any situation. But the demeanor of a very good used car salesman disguises a CEO's fertile brain. With the Blue Jays, the combination stood him in excellent stead with the players and agents, and, when crossed with Gillick's very different but equally devastating mix of people and brain skills, the result was a wide swath cut through the best free agents and trade targets in the game. Toronto became the place to be, the place to go, surly customs officials be damned.

"Pat and I would fly all over the country, meeting players, agents, everybody," Beeston recalls. "Pat was amazing, he would set up all the travel by himself. He could remember everything — names, phone numbers, all of it in his head. It [the relationship between them] never had to be defined. We were very, very, very close. There were no jealousies, no problems. I had a relationship with the players and agents. The baseball was his. He was the author, he was the architect. We were all along for the ride."

Well, not entirely. As Gillick recalls it, "We'd sit around and kind of bounce around the players with him, more so than he'd do with me with the financial stuff. When it came down to the ultimate decision, he left it up to the baseball guys." That meant Bob Mattick and Bob Engle and Al LaMacchia and Wayne Morgan and Bobby Prentice and Gord Lakey and, most of all of course, the sheriff's son from the world's almond capital, Chico, California.

Gillick's parents — his father had pitched in the Pacific Coast League, his mother had been a child actress in silent movies with Buster Keaton and later appeared in "talkies" with the Marx brothers — had divorced when he was three months old. He grew up mostly with his grandmother, attending military academy, graduating from high school at 16, attending community college for a year then heading north, to Vulcan, Alberta, of all places, in the summer of 1956 to bale hay and dig postholes by day and play ball four nights a week. His amateur team, the Granum White Sox, played mostly tournaments, and among the opposition was a raft of NHL players — the Bentleys, Max and Doug, Earl Ingarfield, Bert Olmstead. And so began the young lefty pitcher's life-long love affair with hockey, and Canada. He had an okay fastball, a decent breaking ball and a pickoff move his old pal Davey Johnson, veteran major league manager, once called the best he'd ever seen. Gillick toiled two summers in Alberta while going to USC, where he earned a business degree, helped pitch the team to the national championship in 1958 and earned the nickname Segap Wolley — Yellow Pages backwards — for his prodigious memory.

Signed by the Orioles, Gillick pitched a year in Vancouver and five seasons in all, but couldn't crack the Orioles staff in 1962. With his shoulder gone slightly wonky, he decided to pack it in.

"I was going to give it five years," he recalls. "I had some arm problems but everybody had a problem with their arm in those days. The difference was, you didn't talk about it then. Today, they put guys on the DL for 15 days for something you didn't even talk about."

Gillick was 25 and had decided he wanted to be an FBI agent. Then Eddie Robinson, who had scouted for the Orioles before taking over as farm director of the expansion Houston Colt 45s, called. J. Edgar Hoover went on hold. The kid progressed rapidly, blessed with a feel for the game and a feel for people, especially the old scouts. He learned most from the legendary Paul Richards, and this most of all: "To trust your own initial judgment, the more you think on whether you like a player, you can talk yourself out of it." The memory came in handy, too. And the phone. A scout once said Gillick was the only guy he ever met to wield a phone as a weapon. He doesn't have a phone book. He didn't have a computer in his office in Toronto. Names, numbers, faces, moments, it doesn't matter — he just remembers.

And there was the other thing, too. The emotional side. He has been known to cry upon learning that a kid he scouted has just gotten his first major league hit. He broke down when telling his Yankee scouts he had taken the job in Toronto, when he told Bob Bailor he'd been traded to the Mets, when Dave Parker got a standing O for his first pinch-hit double as a Blue Jay at SkyDome in 1991, when he sold Willie Upshaw to Cleveland, when he told John McLaren he wouldn't be back as a Blue Jays coach. On that last one, he flew into Dallas and met McLaren at the American Airlines Admirals Club. The firing was over in 20 minutes. But Gillick cancelled his flight and the next one. The two of them talked for three hours.

A guy once asked McLaren what they talked about: "A kid shortstop at Myrtle Beach," he said. "We told stories about Medicine Hat and the bus breaking down. We wondered about these kids and what they were doing now that they got on with their lives. We laughed. We cried. It went on for hours." Today, McLaren is the bench coach in Seattle.

When it came to the decisions, about who would stay and who would go, . . . Gillick would always make the tough call.

Oh yes, and then there was the postseason of 1992. The next spring, Gillick hit four cities in 48 hours to present their World Series rings in person to Tom Henke (Dallas), Dave Winfield and Derek Bell (Chicago), Manny Lee (Fort Myers, Fla.) and Rob Ducey (Oklahoma City). With, of course, misty eyes at every stop.

But when it came to the decisions, about who would stay and who would go, about acting on the instincts that Richards had taught him to trust, Gillick would always make the tough call.

"Pat had to be the dispassionate one," says Beeston. "And that was hard on him. I've never seen a guy who was so emotional. Still, he had to make the tough decisions. I had the good fortune; I could be their friend. There were so many great guys, like Alvis Woods. And when I saw Otto Velez last week, it was like we'd been brothers. I'm still friends with Dave [Stieb], Robbie [Alomar], George Bell. We were good friends. That's why it was the best job in the world. You don't work, not really. The people you meet are so great. The best part for me was going to spring training and sitting around with all the guys at the end of the day. Mattick, LaMacchia, Ellis Clary . . . these were guys who loved the game. It was a fantastic environment to learn."

As time went on, Beeston gained the respect of the baseball people in his own organization. He earned it over many beers during many long afternoons and nights. But somewhere in there, it was Gillick who ruled that world, who had afforded him the opportunity. Both were strong and persuasive negotiators,

A champagne-soaked Pat Gillick celebrates in the clubhouse with George Bell after the Blue Jays clinched the 1989 American League East Division title.

the difference being that where Gillick couldn't afford to get too close, Beeston could. In part, it may have been because he didn't have to make the call — the baseball call — but had only to execute on what Gillick and the baseball people decided was right. In part, it may have been nature. Whatever it was, it worked beautifully. Beeston was closer to George Bell, especially after Gillick and Bell's agent, Randy Hendricks, got into a brouhaha over who was better, Bell or Jesse Barfield. Gillick was tighter with John Olerud. As a 1–2 combo recruiting punch, they were deadly. Other things being equal or close to it, whom else would any intelligent star want to play for?

And always, in the background, there was Hardy, along with Howard Webster and the other senior Labatt executives. But mostly, it was Hardy.

"We were left remarkably free to do what we had to do to put a winning club on the field," says Gillick. "We weren't hassled by an owner trying to interfere. That's something that's pretty special in sports. Owners today are so hands-on and they get so involved they mess up the situation. In Toronto, they were supportive of us. They wanted the management team to be the best. If ownership wants management to be the best, it filters right down. You make the people working for you the very best, you give them some latitude, some responsibility. You give them your confidence. We were always very prepared in our presentations to the board, both on the baseball and the financial side. We would provide one-, three- and five-year game plans. They knew where we were headed and how long it would take to get there. We told them at the start that it would take 10 years to get this club competitive. I can't remember their ever wavering. Peter [Bavasi] probably got more uptight about not winning games than anyone in ownership. You always had the feeling you could do what you thought was proper. They were very, very supportive. That kind of bonding between ownership and management doesn't happen very often. We were both on the same side. When you're working for an individual, they can change direction almost every day. It leads to chaos."

Echoes Beeston, "Ownership never gets enough credit. They always get the blame when things go wrong. You're going to blame George Steinbrenner or (NHL St. Louis Blues owner) Harry Ornest. When things go right, you don't hear about them. We had Howard Webster, the Imperial Bank of Commerce and Labatts. Peter Hardy was everybody's teacher. He taught loyalty to the Blue Jays. He could never really pull it off with the baseball guys — it's hard to get them thinking that way when they're on one-year contracts — but he did with the business people. He taught openness, honesty, integrity, the ability to laugh at yourself. Don't take yourself too seriously.

> *"We were left remarkably free to do what we had to do to put a winning club on the field," says Gillick. "We weren't hassled by an owner trying to interfere."*

And to support your people. It's amazing what you can achieve if you don't care who gets the credit."

As time passed, there was enough of that to go around. The second significant occurrence back in that offseason of 1981–82 was the hiring of Bobby Cox as manager, replacing Mattick, whose two-year nurturing of the bevy of talented youngsters was deemed complete. Asked to choose a handful of defining moments of those Blue Jays glory years, Gillick and Beeston both alight on that one.

"Number one would be Mattick bringing players like Stieb and Moseby and Barfield and Bell along and then turning that group over to Cox. Passing the baton that way, that set us up for 1985," says Gillick.

"If Bobby Mattick hadn't come to Toronto, it would have been a whole different story," opines Beeston.

Gillick has three other defining moments, Beeston two.

Gillick's: "Number two would be after Jimy Williams, when I had suggested we go in another direction. We interviewed [Lou] Piniella and [Terry] Bevington, that was the direction I was headed in. But the other guys wanted Cito and he turned out to be the right guy at the right time. [Number 3 was] the [Robbie] Alomar/[Joe] Carter and [Devon] White deals. [Number 4 was] getting Jack [Morris] and [Dave] Winfield."

Beeston's: "Number two would be the new stadium [SkyDome, in 1989]. We would never have had the success we had; it would have been impossible to field the team that won it. Number three would be the decision we made at the end of 1990. We had a meeting and we said, 'Look, we've been building a team to win the AL East. But that's not good enough any more. Now, we need to build a team that can win the World Series.' Peter Hardy said to go ahead. We made the trade [Fred McGriff and Tony Fernandez for Alomar and Carter]."

Not that that one went over very well in the Gillick household. McGriff was Doris Gillick's favourite player. She phoned her husband in Chicago and, in her thick German accent, screamed, "Patrick, get the [bleep] home before you screw up the whole team!" Maybe that's why, a lifetime later, Gillick, asked to pick his favourite three players from all those years, replies, "McGriff, Oly [John Olerud] and, you know, I think maybe Tony [Fernandez]. It's funny how age mellows you."

But the McGriff/Fernandez/Alomar/Carter blockbuster didn't put the Jays over the top. They lost to Minnesota in the ALCS in 1991, then went back to the well for Morris and Winfield that offseason and finally, in the summer of 1992, made one more phone call, this to Sid Oland, who, with Hardy having stepped down a couple of years earlier, was the chap up the ladder

Gord Ash, seen here with Cito Gaston, took over from Pat Gillick as the club's general manager after the strike-shortened 1994 season. Ash would soon be required to make tough decisions of his own, replacing Gaston as manager late in the 1997 campaign.

at Labatts. "'Sid,'" I said, recalls Beeston, "'We're over budget but Pat says we need David Cone.' Sid says, 'Who's David Cone?' I say 'I don't really know much about him, except he leads the National League in strikeouts.' He says 'Okay, how much over?' I say '$1.5 million.' He says 'OK, you've got our support.' That was it."

That fall, they took the A's and Braves, both in six games. A year later, ditto the White Sox and Phillies.

There were mistakes along the way, of course. Gillick reckons his biggest was one afternoon when he took scouts Morgan and LaMacchia to Texas to watch a big high school kid throw.

"I liked [Roger] Clemens, but we took another guy instead," he says. His name was Matt Stark. He was a catcher and the Jays needed catching help. *Total Baseball* records Stark's major league tour of duty at 13 games, five with the Jays, eight with the White Sox. From then on, the Jays made it policy to pick the best player available, regardless of position.

"We did things wrong on a daily basis," laughs Beeston, "but hopefully we didn't make the same mistake twice. If we had weaknesses, they were human weaknesses. We tried to calculate everything."

And then, one day, it was over.

"Nineteen ninety-four was cataclysmic," says Beeston. There was the brutal start, then the strike. At season's end, Gillick agreed to become a consultant and Gord Ash was elevated to general manager.

"They were very big on succession," he says. "Gordie should have a shot."

Then Gerry Schwartz came banging on Labatt's corporate door one day in 1995. A small Belgian brewery came riding in on its white horse and nothing was quite the same after that.

Beeston hung in through mid-1997, when it got a little messy with him working with one potential ownership group and Interbrew looking like it might sell the team to another. That June, he hightailed it to his new post on Park Avenue. Five months later, on November 22, Peter Hardy, who had been out of the day-to-day operation since 1990, died of heart failure at the age of 80. The page had truly been turned.

"Mattick once said, 'We could screw this thing up by winning,'" says Beeston. "The chase was the thing. I think that's what happened. After we won, it wasn't quite the same. It became time to move on."

Fifty-odd years ago, Conn Smythe as general manager and Hap Day as coach won five Stanley Cup championships in eight years for the Maple Leafs. But the world was a smaller place then. The Leafs' feat was less shocking and, on reflection, probably less remarkable than a Canadian team winning back-to-back World Series titles in the 1990s. It says here, then, that Segap and Beast are the number-one sports management combo ol' T.O. has seen.

And so the one spends weekends in Toronto and Sunday to Thursday at the Regency Hotel. Beeston hob-nobs with the Tisches and the Steinbrenners and seeks, in his deceivingly jocular style, to make nice with Don Fehr, head of the players' association and the man who may shut the game down again next year. He keeps the revenue flowing from licensing and TV and the rest, and observes, ever so wistfully, "My goal would have been to remain a Blue Jay until age 85."

A continent away, his old running mate seeks to rekindle the old magic one more time. Gillick took a year off after the Jays, telling himself he might learn to fly a plane and play some serious golf, but then his old pal Davey Johnson called and he went to the Orioles for three years. Then, after a year running the U.S. Pan American team that qualified for the Olympics, he joined the Mariners to help nurse them through the franchise-wrenching back-to-back losses of Ken Griffey Jr. and Alex Rodriguez.

"It's bizarre, the compensation levels we're at," he says. "Many of the teams can't make it work, but we're doing fine here. You've just gotta work through it."

Gillick still owns three homes in Toronto. His wife Doris still runs her gallery on Spadina. Having lived and worked in Canada more than half his adult life, Gillick says, "I'm probably more Canadian than American. I feel more Canadian." The difference between us, he ventures, is "I think Canadians work to live. They really enjoy life. Down here, people live to work. They think about work all the time."

Once upon a time, of course, his own work really wasn't work at all.

"Yep," concludes Beeston. "We had some fun."

The Business of the Blue Jays

LARRY MILLSON

The first owners of the Toronto Blue Jays paid $7 million to land the team. The ownership group was a diverse and even curious mixture. There was a brewery, a Montreal financier with sporting interests and a bank. It was a partnership that was created almost casually as the pursuit of a major league baseball team for Toronto heated up late in 1975, a partnership among owners whose interests dovetailed and helped provide Toronto with some of its best sporting moments.

Labatt Breweries and R. Howard Webster's Imperial Trust, Ltd., were in for 45 percent each, while the Canadian Imperial Bank of Commerce picked up the other 10 percent. This group was able to produce what was considered for years a model expansion franchise, overcoming an inadequate facility (Exhibition Stadium) where there were too few good seats available and too few luxury boxes or suites. The novelty of a new team helped, of course. But the franchise remained strong beyond the honeymoon because the owners insisted that it be run under sound business principles.

Having a bank as a partner in a major league team seemed curious at the time, but the CIBC had done business with both Webster and Labatt and actually set up the first meeting between the two parties. When the partnership was formed late in 1975, the CIBC could be a bridge between two unfamiliar

American League chairman Joe Cronin (left) presents the Blue Jays' charter to R. Howard Webster and Peter Bavasi.

partners. It also could act as a tiebreaker on the board — but never needed to be. The involvement of the bank also added some prestige to the partnership's bid for a franchise, providing, as a CIBC representative said, the "substantial financial responsibility" needed to obtain the franchise.

The partnership worked well because each had different reasons for owning the team. There were no conflicts in that regard. Labatt saw it as a chance to promote its products. Beer and baseball and summer are an obvious triple play. Labatt wanted a tie-in with an important sports franchise to enhance its corporate visibility in Ontario. It was believed that even the attempt to bring a team to Toronto would enhance the brewery's image. Labatt president Don McDougall, one of the players in obtaining the franchise, wrote in the 1977 Labatt Corporate Newsletter: "Owing to the fact that a Toronto baseball franchise was a sound business proposition in its own right, when you add the synergistic effect to the beer business it becomes a major breakthrough."

On the other hand, Webster looked at the team as more of a sporting and business interest. Although he was from Montreal, he had considerable business interests in Toronto. He had owned *The Globe and Mail*, was involved in the Lord Simcoe Hotel and had invested in the Eaton Centre, among other things.

The CIBC was limited to its 10 percent by law. It looked upon its involvement in ownership as good public relations, playing a part in a good news story. It could also use the baseball tickets or visits to spring training as rewards for employees. The CIBC became "the Bank of the Blue Jays" and would have players visit branches for autograph sessions. Most of the people attending were already customers. It was, according to a bank representative, "a community thing, not tied to sales . . . the bank manager meeting customers he otherwise wouldn't meet . . . a special event for the staff."

The unusual alliance of brewer, banker and businessman was formed partly out of fear that too many Toronto groups acting independently might dilute the effort. Labatt and Webster both had tried previously to buy major league teams to bring to Toronto. The brewery had gone after the Cleveland Indians and then the Baltimore Orioles. Webster, who always had an interest in sports and was twice an intercollegiate golf champion, had tried to buy the San Diego Padres so they could be moved to Toronto. Other groups also were exploring the possibility of bringing major league baseball to Toronto, which had lost its once successful Triple-A franchise after the 1967 season. The Labatt partnership was originally formed to purchase the San

Francisco Giants and they announced that a deal had been struck on January 9, 1976. The price was $13.5 million, with $8 million for the franchise and the rest to buy out the 19 years left on the lease at Candlestick Park.

It is hard to quantify the value of a major sports franchise to a city. Numerous studies have been done, but some of the numbers can be questioned. But there is a value beyond the economics. There is prestige and civic pride. Just as Toronto — led by Metro Chairman Paul Godfrey — had worked hard to acquire a franchise, new San Francisco mayor George Moscone thought it was worthwhile to try to keep his city's team. He obtained a temporary injunction to prevent the National League from voting on the transfer of the Giants to Toronto so that a local owner could be found. Moscone succeeded. He helped put together a group to keep the team in San Francisco just before the March 1 deadline.

But other things were happening in baseball. The City of Seattle had filed a $14 million lawsuit over the loss of its one-year expansion team, the Seattle Pilots. (A week before the 1970 season had begun, the team had moved to Milwaukee where they became the Brewers. The cost was $10.8 million, which was paid by a group led by Bud Selig, now baseball's commissioner.)

The Labatt partnership had been seeking a National League franchise because they felt the rivalry with the Montreal Expos would be good for marketing purposes. But they began to change their sights when the American League, to avert the lawsuit, awarded Seattle an expansion team in February of 1976. That left the AL with 13 teams. They would need to add another team to balance the schedule — unless the National League agreed to add a new team and play an interleague schedule for the first time.

When the National League didn't get the unanimous vote needed to approve expansion, the American League moved to award Toronto a franchise. (Baseball commissioner Bowie Kuhn actually favoured Washington as an expansion site, but he could not find any backers there.) Now the only question about baseball in Toronto was whether the team would be awarded to the Labatt group or another led by Phil Granovsky. The Labatt group won, impressing the other American League owners with its financial clout.

Building the Blue Jays: (Standing, left to right) Pat Gillick, Howard Starkman, Bobby Mattick, Bob Miller, Al LaMacchia, Elliott Wahle, (seated, left to right) Peter Bavasi, Herb Solway, R. Howard Webster and Roy Hartsfield prior to the 1976 Expansion Draft.

When Toronto gained its franchise in 1976, baseball and all of professional sports were working in a different financial district than they are today.

In retrospect, the ownership group felt it was lucky to have gone with the American League instead of the National. They landed in the American League East with storied franchises like the New York Yankees, the Boston Red Sox, the Baltimore Orioles and the Detroit Tigers (who have since moved to the AL Central). Good rivalries all. Good for attendance.

When Toronto gained its franchise in 1976, baseball and all of professional sports were working in a different financial district than they are today. Not only did an expansion fee of $7 million provide for a team, it also included 30 players each for Seattle and Toronto — players to be selected in an expansion draft from the existing major league teams.

The expansion draft was conducted on November 5, 1976, but another important draft had taken place the day before. These were historic times in sport. The entry of the Toronto and Seattle teams coincided with a new era: the free agent era. The new teams were not allowed to take part in the draft in which the existing major league clubs selected bargaining rights to free agent players. While this draft has since been scrapped, free agency, of course, continues.

The combination of free agency and salary arbitration — plus increased revenues from national media rights and from licensed products — would lead to a salary explosion. The Blue Jays' entire player budget in 1977, their first season, was $850,000. Now backup infielders can earn that much. By 1986, the Blue Jays' payroll was $13.3-million. In 2001, it was projected to be above $70 million. The payrolls of the New York Yankees, the Boston Red Sox and the Los Angeles Dodgers will exceed $100 million. These figures, all in U.S. dollars, do not

Labatt President Don McDougall was the key to the beer company's involvement with the Blue Jays. He served as a director of the baseball team for its first three years.

include the cost of running a minor league and scouting system, nor a travel budget.

From the beginning, the Blue Jays board decided to let the baseball people run the team. Back then, not all baseball owners ran their teams that way. The Blue Jays ownership followed a basic business principle: hire people who know their stuff, let them work and make them accountable. Once the board approved the operating plan, management had the authority to freely carry out the defined areas of responsibility. Peter Hardy, who became the CEO of John Labatt Ltd. and chairman of the Blue Jays, called it participatory-type management.

"You try to put the decision-making down as low as possible," he said. "Define the job functions and job responsibilities and authorities so people know what they can do and what is expected of them."

Peter Bavasi, who became the club's first president during his four-season tenure, was really into making business plans. They were considered works of art. There were one-year and three-year objectives. The plans were broken down into different areas: public relations, operations, finances, tickets and player development. He also made sure that Blue Jays caps — and anything else with the club logo on it — were out in the public.

Paul Beeston, the first executive hired by the club and later its president and CEO, knew the plans didn't mean anything if the production on the field wasn't there. A sports franchise is different from other businesses.

"Managing a successful business basically is managing inventory and receivables," Beeston once said. "We don't have

that. We're dealing with people and personalities. So it can be very, very complex."

When the Labatt partnership was formed, the Canadian and U.S. dollars were at about the same in value. But over the years the Canadian dollar dropped and this resulted in a problem. Most of the club's expenses — mainly player salaries — were paid in U.S. dollars and most of its income was in Canadian dollars. As a result, the club was forced to try to find ways to deal with the discrepancy by such means as buying U.S. dollars forward. The financial fortunes of the club improved in June of 1989 when SkyDome opened with more and better seats, private boxes and an increase in revenue from attendance. These were the years of four million in attendance and tidy profits.

Labatt became 90 percent owner of the Blue Jays after the first four-million season in 1991. Back in 1976, the entire franchise had been purchased for $7 million. When Labatt bought out the Webster estate's 45 percent on October 31, 1991, it paid $67.5 million. No doubt the partnership had been successful. Labatt went on to enjoy two World Series championships and two more seasons of four million in attendance. But the 1994 player's strike that wiped out baseball's postseason began a downturn. Today, new challenges exist for the Blue Jays. Entertainment options have increased. The Toronto Raptors have joined the sports scene. The novelty of the SkyDome has long past.

The CIBC retained its 10 percent share of the club until September of 2000 when Rogers Communications bought 80 percent of the team for $112 million (U.S.). The Belgian Brewer Interbrew SA retained 20 percent. Interbrew had purchased Labatt in 1995 and the Blue Jays came with the purchase of the beer company. The Belgians, who came in during a period when the Blue Jays' performance on the field and at the box office lagged, had always intended to sell the team to concentrate on the brewery business.

The ownership of Rogers reflects a change in the sports business. The Rogers vision includes a sports-entertainment-communications empire. Rogers is eyeing other sports franchises, possibly an NFL team. In the meantime, the Blue Jays can contribute to the other Rogers businesses, which include cable service, wireless phones, television and radio stations, video rentals, web sites and magazines. Rogers sends cable TV to 2.2 million homes, and it wants baseball as one of the options. The Blue Jays provide content. In a few years, for example, games could be available on cell phones. Blue Jays tickets could be sold along with other Rogers products using one bill. Tickets could also be used as a promotional device.

Media conglomerates appear to be the future of sports ownership. The proof is there among other baseball owners. Rupert Murdoch owns the Los Angeles Dodgers and the Fox Network; Time Warner Inc. and its vice-chairman Ted Turner own the Atlanta Braves.

It's a whole new ballgame.

TORONTO BLUE JAYS

Statistics and Player Register

Toronto Blue Jays • Top 25 Impact Players

Roberto Alomar
Second to None

"A play on defense where I throw myself headfirst into the grass to trap the ball and get the out, a play that annoys the hitter. The biggest part of my game is fielding."
ROBERTO ALOMAR

Although his tenure with the team was sometimes tempestuous, there has never been a better second baseman in the history of the organization than Roberto Alomar. Skilled at all aspects of the game, Alomar had a potent bat, speed and smarts on the bases, amazing range in the field, a rocket for an arm and incredible instincts. Traded with Joe Carter to the Toronto Blue Jays in December of 1990, he became the general of the Jays' infield defense, winning a Gold Glove in each of his five seasons with the club. In his first campaign with the team, he stole 53 bases and established an ALCS record with nine singles in a five-game series. In 1992, he batted .310 during the regular season and shone once again in the postseason, winning the ALCS MVP Award with a .423 average. He also carried an 11-game hitting streak into the World Series. Alomar had his best season as a Jay in 1993, reaching career highs in average (.326), runs scored (109) and RBIs (93). On June 17, 1995, Alomar set a new AL record by going 90 games without an error, a streak that would eventually reach 104 games. He led all major league second sackers with just four errors in 643 total chances.

Bob Bailor
Mr. Versatility

"He can play every position, and do you know what, he probably will."
BOBBY MATTICK, APRIL, 1977

Bob Bailor was the Blue Jays' first selection in the 1976 Expansion Draft, and was one of the most popular players during the formative years of the team. As a freshman, he hit .310, which at the time was a record for a player on a first-year expansion franchise. Bailor was a hustling, versatile fielder who delighted the fans with his all-out effort. Blessed with quick hands and a strong accurate arm, he was comfortable wherever he played on the field. Bailor played every position except catcher and first base for the Jays, even taking a turn on the mound during the 1980 season. A patient hitter with an excellent eye at the plate, Bailor had a 15-game hitting streak, stroked 21 doubles and five triples, and clouted five home runs as a rookie. He also proved he had above-average speed by swiping 15 bases during the 1977 campaign. A product of the Baltimore Orioles' system, Bailor saw only limited action with the Birds before joining the Jays and went on to have an amazing 621 at-bats with Toronto in 1978. Bailor spent four seasons with the Jays before being dispatched to the New York Mets in 1981.

Jesse Barfield
Armed With a Cannon

"I've always tried to do my best on the ball field. I can't do any more than that. I always try to give one hundred percent; and if my team loses, I come back and give one hundred percent the next day."
JESSE BARFIELD, 1986

Of all the outfielders who have danced their way across the turf at Exhibition Stadium and the SkyDome, no one had a more powerful cannon for an arm than Jesse Barfield. Fans would gather early at the old Ex just to watch Barfield' s nightly warmup routine as he worked his way around the outfield, tossing ball after ball to Lloyd Moseby until he was throwing laser beams all the way across the field, from corner to corner. Blessed with a gun for an arm, and a powerful uppercut swing, he led all AL outfielders in assists from 1985 to 1987 and won a Gold Glove in both 1986 and 1987. He also excelled at the plate, topping the 20-home-run mark six times, including a major league-leading 40 big blasts in 1986. He was also the first Blue Jay to hit a pinch grand slam, and to hit 20 homers and steal 20 bases in the same season. Traded to the New York Yankees in 1989, he retired after the 1992 season.

George Bell
The Dominican Dynamo

"He's a gamer. He's a great competitor. He had a lot of ability and he had a great heart, in the respect that he'd go out there and give a good day's work."
BOBBY MATTICK, 1988

One of the American League's most dominant and feared sluggers through much of the 1980s, George Bell was drafted by Toronto from the Philadelphia Phillies' organization in 1980. A tremendous hitter and an above-average outfielder, Bell rose to prominence during the 1984 season when he slugged 26 homers, drove in 87 runs and set a new team record with 69 extra-base hits. Bell also had a healthy temper and surly attitude that ignited a few problems with the media, fans and even his own teammates. During a weekend series in August of 1985 against the White Sox, Bell demonstrated his incredible power as a slugger when he clubbed homers in four consecutive games, two of which cleared the roof of Chicago's Comiskey Park. In 1987, Bell became the only Blue Jay player to win the MVP Award after establishing new team marks with 47 home runs, 134 RBIs, 16 game-winning RBIs, 83 extra-base hits, 369 total bases and a .605 slugging percentage. Bell still holds the Jays' all-time records for extra-base hits (471) and RBIs (740).

Pat Borders
The Pivot

"It was a few games during the year when I got hot at the right time. I enjoyed it and I appreciated the reward they gave me, but it's really not that big of a deal."
PAT BORDERS ON WINNING THE WORLD SERIES MVP AWARD, OCTOBER, 1992.

The contributions of Pat Borders to the Blue Jays' two World Series titles rarely gets the attention it should. Borders was an efficient pivot behind the plate, never flashy but always consistent. He called a good game for his pitchers, gave sound advice, had a strong, accurate arm and always supplied the club with timely offense. Borders made his debut with the club in 1989, and by 1991, he had established himself as the number-one man behind the plate. In the 1992 World Series, Borders was the Jays' most productive and consistent player, hitting safely in every postseason game, leading all Jays batters with a .450 average in the World Series and earning himself the MVP Award for the Series. He went on to help the Jays win another championship banner in 1993 before departing the club as a free agent prior to the 1995 season. He returned to Toronto briefly in 1999.

Joe Carter
Touch 'em All, Joe

"People will get a chance to see what a first-class country Canada is and what a first-class city Toronto is. These are great fans here in Toronto. The best way we can repay them is to bring home the World Series."
JOE CARTER, OCTOBER, 1992.

Even if he hadn't collected the most important hit in the history of the Toronto Blue Jays, Joe Carter would still be remembered as one of the best to ever play the game. A complete player both offensively and in the field, Carter didn't receive the acclaim he deserved through much of career. Joltin' Joe drove in at least 100 runs 10 times during his career, including six of the seven seasons he played in Toronto. *The Sporting News's* 1981 College Player of the Year at Wichita State, Carter came to the Jays in a blockbuster trade prior to the 1991 season and helped lead the club to three consecutive AL East titles and a pair of World Series championships. In 1994, Carter became just the tenth player in major league history to hit 300 home runs and steal 200 bases. He had deceptive speed for a power hitter, reaching double digits in stolen bases 10 times in his career. In 1997, his final year with the club, he surpassed George Bell as the team's all-time leader in home runs with 203.

Jim Clancy
The Stallion

"Clancy was a horse. No one ever mentioned him in the same breath with Roger Clemens, but Clancy was also a big man and he had that same stubborn stoicism on the mound."
TRUNORTH BASEBALL, OCTOBER 29, 1998.

The only player to suit up for the Blue Jays in each of their first 11 seasons, Clancy was the club's all-time leader in both wins and losses when he left the organization prior to the 1989 season. Selected from Texas in the 1976 Expansion Draft, the right-hander was a keystone in the Jays' starting rotation throughout his career. A consistent, controlled hurler who was well-regarded as a valuable inning eater, Clancy reached double digits in victories in eight of his 11 years with the club, including a career-best 16–14 mark in 1982. In the same semester, Clancy started a team-record 40 games and registered a more-than-respectable ERA of 3.71, remarkable numbers considering the Jays were still a last-place (albeit tied for last) ball club. The highlight of Clancy's career as a Jay came on September 28, 1982 when he came within three outs of tossing a perfect game against Minnesota before surrendering a broken-bat single to Randy Bush and settling for a one-hit shutout.

Roger Clemens
The Intimidator

"I am intense, no question about it. Every time I toe the rubber, it's no different for me than it was in the World Series. That might be somebody's only chance to see me pitch. They might have driven four hours to get there. I'm going to be out there if I can help it."
ROGER CLEMENS

During his two seasons with the Blue Jays, Roger Clemens was the most dominating pitcher in baseball. He is the only Jays pitcher to reach the 20-win plateau twice and win back-to-back Cy Young Awards. Signed as a free agent prior to the 1997 season, Clemens had suffered through four injury-plagued seasons, winning only 40 games between 1993 and 1996. However, after the Red Sox failed to sign him, Clemens vowed to himself that he would return to the form that had made him the best right-hander in the American League. The key to his success has always been a resilient arm and a lower body that supplies much of his power. Clemens devoted himself to a rigorous offseason training program and added a devastating forkball to his repertoire. In both 1997 and 1998, Clemens won the "triple crown" of pitching, leading the AL in wins, ERA and strikeouts and capturing the fourth and fifth Cy Young Awards of his career.

Carlos Delgado
The Future

"To me, Carlos Delgado could be one of the next big stars in this game. His personality is so riveting. He is just somebody who cares about the game. He puts out one of the best images for this game. He smiles and lights up the whole room." DETROIT TIGERS G.M. RANDY SMITH, NOVEMBER 7, 2000

One of the finest young talents to emerge from the Blue Jays system, Carlos Delgado has already established himself as one the club's greatest stars. Signed as a 16-year-old in 1988, Delgado's debut with the big club in 1994 was a spectacle for the ages. In his first month in the majors, Delgado hit an American League-rookie-record eight home runs, many of them of the tape measure variety. Although he was later sent back to the minors, he had proved to fans and management that he had the talent to be a dominating performer. Although he was used in the outfield and behind the plate early in his major league career, Delgado has developed into a fine first baseman and he is one of the best in the league at scooping up errant throws around the bag. Delgado, who has driven home at least 100 runners in each of the past three seasons, had his finest year as a professional in 2000, establishing career highs in average (.344), hits (196) and a new team-record 137 RBIs.

Tony Fernandez
Smooth and Stylish

"I don't like to talk about myself. I feel uncomfortable. I just go out there and try to put the ball in play. For me, every at-bat is an adventure. It could be my last one, so I take it very seriously."
TONY FERNANDEZ IN HIS THIRD GO-ROUND WITH THE TEAM, 1999.

The Blue Jays' all-time career leader in games, at-bats, hits, doubles and triples, Tony Fernandez was the cornerstone of the organization in three different and distinct periods of the team's history. During the team's first glory days in the 1980s, Fernandez was regarded as one of the top shortstops and leadoff batters in the entire major leagues. When he returned to Toronto in 1993 to replace the injured Dick Schofield, he jump-started a team that needed a boost to defend their World Series title. And although he was no longer the defensive marvel he had been in his prime when he again rejoined the club for a third go-round in 1998, he tempered that fault by developing into a consummate professional hitter. Fernandez constantly adjusted his batting style to adapt to different pitchers. When he became the club's starting shortstop midway through the 1984 season, he showed great range, soft hands and a unique sidearm slinging throwing style. In 1986, he led all AL shortstops in putouts and fielding percentage and became the first Blue Jays player to record 200 hits in a single season. In fact, his 213 hits that season were the most ever by a major league shortstop. He also displayed some unexpected resolute toughness by playing in 403 consecutive games. In June of 1999, Fernandez passed Julio Franco as the Dominican Republic's all-time major league hits leader.

Damaso Garcia
The Igniter

"If I can't steal and run, it'll be over. I'll go back home to the Dominican and beg for money."
DAMASO GARCIA, 1986

Although at times he appeared to be a surly and moody individual, second baseman Damaso Garcia was one of the team's top players during the club's first ascent up the AL East ladder. In 1982, the Dominican native became the first Blue Jay to steal 50 bases in a season, and in 1986 he added another milestone to his resume when he became the first player to collect 1,000 hits in a Blue Jays uniform. Garcia spent seven seasons with the club, and during that time he was the team's all-time leader in at-bats, hits and stolen bases. In 1983 he compiled a 21-game hitting streak and on June 27, 1986, he tied a major league record by hustling out four doubles in a game against the Yankees. Garcia had joined the Blue Jays in 1980 after playing just 29 games in two seasons for the Yankees. He was traded to Atlanta before the 1987 season, then was released after hitting only .117 in 21 games in 1988. He caught on with the Expos in 1989 and in one of the last at-bats of his career, slugged a grand slam home run against St. Louis to cap a six-run ninth inning comeback.

Alfredo Griffin
The Human Hoover

"When you played alongside Alfredo, you didn't dare go out there and just go through the motions, or ask to be taken out of the lineup ... any more than you'd consider stepping out of a moving automobile."
JOHN ROBERTSON IN THE
TORONTO STAR, MARCH 5, 1988

Alfredo Griffin was the first Toronto Blue Jays player to earn a major award when he was named co-winner of the American League Rookie-of-the-Year Award in 1979. Although he missed reaping the rewards of the team's success in the 1980s, he did return in time to play on a pair of World Series-winning teams in the 1990s. Acquired in a trade with Cleveland in 1978, Griffin started his rookie season slowly, then reeled off a 19-game hitting streak to help him win his freshman kudos. While he was pretty sharp with the bat, it was his slick footing, quick glove and razor-sharp arm that earned him the most praise. A steady and more often than not spectacular shortstop, he spent six years with the Blue Jays and played in 392 consecutive games. Traded to Oakland in 1984, Griffin returned to Toronto in 1992 and was a key contributor to the Jays' back-to-back World Series titles.

Kelly Gruber
At Home at Third

"We really do understand that we're Canada's team. We realize this is something very important in this country."
KELLY GRUBER, OCTOBER 15, 1992

The landing wasn't always smooth and the departure was bumpy, but when Kelly Gruber was in full flight, he was one of the most exciting players to watch. Grabbed from the Cleveland Indians in the Rule 5 Draft in December of 1983, Gruber was used exclusively as a role player in a variety of positions until opening day of the 1986 season. Called upon to replace an injured Rance Mulliniks early in the game against the New York Yankees, Gruber went 4-for-6 and clouted two home runs plus an RBI double. That cemented his spot in the lineup, and he went on to hit .278 with 16 home runs and 81 RBIs. By the 1989 season, Gruber was being regarded as one of the coolest players at the hot corner in the American League. After earning a berth in the 1989 All-Star Game, Gruber raised his play to another level in 1990, blasting 31 homers, 36 doubles and driving home 118 runners. That was to be the highlight of his career with the Blue Jays. Injuries hampered him for the rest of his career, although he did hit a key home run in the World Series against Atlanta in 1992.

Tom Henke
The Terminator

"Tom Henke is the salt-of-the-earth kind of ballplayer. He's good people. He doesn't need a garage full of Mercedes to be happy."
DAVE PERKINS, OCTOBER 1, 1992

Throughout much of their early existence, the most glowing deficiency in the Jays' organization was the lack of a dominating late-inning closer. In 1985, when the team was poised to make its first postseason appearance, the problem had still not been solved. That's when a slow-talking Missouri native named Tom Henke appeared on the scene. Acquired from Texas as compensation for the Rangers' free agent signing of Cliff Johnson, Henke started the season in Triple-A Syracuse, where he was simply overpowering. Called up to the majors on July 28, 1985, Henke recorded eight saves in his first month and went on to convert 13 of his 15 save opportunities. In 1986, Henke set a new Blue Jays standard by collecting 27 saves, a mark he would shatter the following season when he closed out 34 Jays victories, allowing fewer hits (5.9) and recording more strikeouts (12.3) per nine innings than any other AL pitcher. Henke was the Jays' main closer through 1992 and he held his opponents to a .213 batting average or less in each of his of eight seasons with the club.

Jimmy Key
The Classy Lefty

"Jimmy Key was a product of the Jays' own system, he was the first and only great lefty the system had produced and a solid citizen in the clubhouse."
STEPHEN BRUNT, 1996

When Jimmy Key began his career with the Blue Jays in 1984, the club had not had a win by a left-handed starting pitcher since 1980, a span that would grow to a total of 614 games. Key would eventually bring that slide to a halt, but in his freshman campaign with the team, he was used exclusively in the bullpen. As a rookie, Key set a club record for saves by a freshman (10), as well as a new team mark for appearances with 63. The following season, Key joined the starting rotation and cruised to a 14–6 record with a tidy 3.00 ERA. In 1987, Key was the AL ERA leader (2.76) while tying a Blue Jays record with 17 wins. He is the Blue Jays' career leader in ERA (tied with Dave Stieb) and ranks third in wins and shutouts and fifth in strikeouts. The secret to Key's success was his command, effectively moving the ball in and out, spotting his curveball and using a deadly deceptive change of pace to keep the hitters off balance.

Fred McGriff
Flash that Smile and Hit it a Mile

"Consistency is Fred McGriff in a nutshell. Quiet and consistent. He has quietly been one of the best and most underrated players in the game."
BASEBALL WITH CHUCK BEDNAR

When Pat Gillick insisted that Fred McGriff be an added throw-in as part of a 1982 trade between the Blue Jays and Yankees, it was one of the more astute moves he made during his era with the team. A ferocious slugger whose mammoth home runs were awe-inspiring, Fred McGriff first gained acclaim when he broke Jesse Barfield's team record for home runs by a rookie in 1987 when he hit 20 longballs. McGriff had phenomenal power, an excellent eye at the plate and enough patience to draw an important base-on-balls. In 1988, his first season as an everyday performer, McGriff finished second in the league in both homers (34) and slugging percentage (.552). Big Fred led the entire league the following season by punching out 36 homers with a respectable .269 batting average and 92 RBIs. In his final three seasons as a starter at first base, McGriff hit at least 34 homers each year. Although he wasn't the smoothest fielder, he was more than effective, staying within the limits of his ability and rarely making foolish errors. In December of 1991, he was part of the trade that brought Joe Carter and Robbie Alomar—and a pair of World Series flags—to Toronto.

Paul Molitor
The Professional

"I think the majority of the fans weren't real familiar with the kind of game that I play. They didn't know what to expect. It took a while for them to get a feel for the way I play."
PAUL MOLITOR, OCTOBER, 1993

One of the classiest and most professional ball players to wear a Blue Jays uniform, Paul Molitor's dedication to the games, the fans and the city made him one of the most popular Blue Jays of all time. Blessed with quick hands and an eagle eye at the plate, Molitor was able to sit back and wait that extra split second before swinging the bat. With that approach, he was able to spray the ball all over the park. Signed at the age of 37 as a free agent prior to the 1993 season, Molitor became the oldest player in major league history to record his first 100-RBI season. That same year, he also became the oldest player to collect 20 homers and 20 stolen bases in the same season. He saved some of his finest moments for the postseason, batting .500 in the World Series and capturing the championship round's MVP trophy. Molitor went on to hit .341 in the strike-shortened 1994 campaign and a respectable .270 in 1995, his final season with the club.

Jack Morris
The Mercenary

"Go ahead and call me a mercenary. I don't care. I'm a paid athlete in a short career. I will do the very best I can for whomever is paying me."
JACK MORRIS, 1992

The first 20-game winner in Blue Jays history, Jack Morris was the key to the World Series puzzle for the Blue Jays. Signed as a free agent only weeks after leading Minnesota to a World Series championship in 1991, Morris's win-at-all-costs attitude and veteran posture set a perfect example for the inexperienced players to follow and try to emulate. One of Morris's enduring qualities was his on-mound demeanor and the fact that he never cared for personal statistics. His only bottom line was the performance of the team. Morris was one of the first hurlers to perfect the split-finger pitch, a nasty, sharp-breaking ball that helped him compile two 20-win seasons and toss a no-hitter on April 7, 1984. In 1992, his first season in Toronto, Morris won a team-record 21 games to help propel the club into the playoffs. Although injuries hampered his effectiveness in 1993, his influence still dominated the pitching staff. After spending one season with the Cleveland Indians, Morris retired in 1994 with three World Series rings and a trophy shelf stocked with awards.

Lloyd Moseby
The Shaker

"As a player, I used to think that if I can't come to the ballpark happy, I should quit. My real reward is giving back to the organization."
LLOYD MOSEBY

The Blue Jays' all-time leader in runs scored, walks and stolen bases, Lloyd Moseby ranks among the top five in an incredible 19 other all-time offensive categories. The second player selected overall in the 1978 free agent draft, Moseby was a talented, smooth-fielding and speedy center fielder who rose quickly through the Jays' minor league system. With his infectious smile and base-running instincts, Moseby was a fan favourite throughout his tenure with the club. In 1983, "the Shaker" became the first Blue Jay to score 100 runs in a season, the same year he also compiled a league-leading 21-game hitting streak. Moseby's greatest asset was his speed, and he was the key cog that was instrumental in creating numerous Blue Jays rallies. Although he wasn't blessed with exceptional power, he did manage to pop 26 homers in 1987 while driving home a career-best 96 runs. In 1990, after two sub-par seasons, Moseby signed with the Detroit Tigers; he toiled with the Tigers for two years before spending a pair of seasons with the Yomiuri Giants in Japan.

John Olerud
The Sweet Swing was the Thing

"John's swing is as fundamentally sound as you'll ever see. He's a line-drive hitter who sprays the ball all over the park. He has an excellent understanding of the strike zone, and above all, he is a fine young man."
RANCE MULLINIKS, 1989

Not too many major league clubs were willing to take a chance on John Olerud. Despite the fact that he had the sweetest left-handed swing since Ted Williams and was even better as a college pitcher, John had nearly died from a brain aneurysm in his senior year at Washington State University. Luckily for Blue Jays fans, Pat Gillick kept tabs on Olerud's recovery and selected him in the third round of the 1989 free agent draft. Olerud went on to become only the 16th player to make his major league debut without playing a single game in the minors. Blessed with the ability to hit the ball with power and precision to all parts of the field, Olerud was both disciplined and patient at the plate. He is the only Blue Jays player to win a batting title, hitting .363 in 1993, and shares the AL single-season record for most intentional bases on balls (33).

Dave Stieb
Never Perfect, but Always Close

"So the way I look at it, somebody's gotta be the best on the Toronto Blue Jays; somebody's gotta be the best in our league; somebody's gotta be the best in major league baseball. Why not Dave Stieb?"
DAVE STIEB, 1985

The finest pitcher to ever climb the mound for the Toronto Blue Jays, Dave Stieb was one of the most intense, focused and confident athletes to wear a Toronto uniform. Originally signed as an outfielder, Stieb was superb defensively and had set numerous batting marks at Southern Illinois State University. Switched from the field to the mound as a rookie pro, Stieb made rapid progress through the Blue Jays system. He reached the majors midway through the 1979 season, and still managed to win eight ball games. The first starting pitcher to have a winning record for the Jays (11–10 in 1981), Stieb was always among league leaders in innings pitched, complete games and ERA. Though he was always outspoken and often misunderstood, there was never any doubt about his desire to win and his dedication to his craft. Stieb, who had three no-hitters broken up with two outs in the ninth inning, finally tossed his gem when he held the Cleveland Indians hitless in a 3–0 victory on September 2, 1990.

Duane Ward
The Fireman

"Everyone is so worried that somebody is going to take your job. Hey, everybody gets old. The young guy who comes up and takes my job? He's going to get old, too. It's just the evolution of baseball."
DUANE WARD, 1994

Toronto fans had the opportunity to watch Duane Ward grow, mature, learn, and then finally excel as a member of the Blue Jays. When he arrived in town, Ward was a seemingly untamable stallion with tons of potential and a wild streak more than a mile wide. When he left the team in 1994 after his arm finally collapsed from the stress of years of coping with his devastating slider, Ward was established as one of the most dominating bullpen aces the league had ever seen. Acquired in 1986 from Atlanta, Ward was tutored and trained in the Blue Jays bullpen by Tom Henke. Together, the tandem would prove that baseball is a seven-inning game because if Toronto had taken the lead by then it was like money in the bank with Ward pitching the eighth and Henke the ninth. After Henke left as a free agent prior to the 1993 season, Ward became the primary closer and went on to set a new club record with a league-leading 45 saves. While preparing to join the club for spring training in 1994, Ward felt a twinge in his shoulder and the resulting injury was so severe that Ward could never truly resume his career.

Devon White
The Gazelle

"I'm pretty much confident that I can take my eye off the ball and still know where it's gonna go."
DEVON WHITE, COMMENTING ON "THE CATCH" IN GAME THREE OF THE 1992 WORLD SERIES.

Watching Devon White glide effortlessly through the SkyDome outfield and stop to catch the ball in a casual manner in the center of his chest was as impressive as seeing a prima ballerina at the prime of her career. White was a gazelle who could track down virtually any ball that was hit in his vicinity. Not too many Blue Jays fans were aware of White's ability when he arrived from California prior to the 1991 season. During 1990, he had been relegated to the minors and many pundits felt his career was over. But Blue Jays skipper Cito Gaston promised White the chance to not only play everyday, but also to bat in the leadoff spot in the lineup. That decision revived White's love of the game and for the next five seasons, Jays fans were treated to an awesome display of pure fielding, timely hitting and breathtaking base running. Although he was not a typical leadoff batter, White staked his own claim to Blue Jays fame by hitting a club-record 21 leadoff home runs.

Ernie Whitt
The General

"I'm sick and tired of getting our butts kicked. We have too good a team to be getting our butts kicked. We just got our butts kicked tonight and some of you don't care."
ERNIE WHITT, MAY 12, 1986

A tough taskmaster and an outspoken leader on and off the field, Ernie Whitt was one of the most popular players in the history of the Blue Jays. His tenacity and inspirational work ethic propelled him from being a marginal talent into a top-notch catcher and handler of a major league pitching staff. Of all the players who have ever been selected in a baseball Expansion Draft (Whitt was picked by the Blue Jays in 1976), only Jim Fregosi played more games with the team that selected him (the Angels) than Ernie Whitt did in Toronto. A dead pull hitter with power, Whitt stroked numerous key home runs during his career with the Jays, including three of the Jays' record-setting 10 home runs in a game against Baltimore on September 14, 1987. Although Whitt was platooned for much of his career, he still managed to appear in at least 120 games for the Jays for seven consecutive years. During that stretch, he was amazingly consistent, hitting between 15 and 19 homers over each of his six busiest seasons. Whitt also had deceiving speed for a catcher, stealing as many as five bases in a single season, and swiping a total of 22 bases in his career.

Dave Winfield
The Hero

"We're keenly aware that we don't represent just a city. We represent an entire country."
DAVE WINFIELD, OCTOBER 15, 1992

His stay with the Jays was brief, only one season, but Dave Winfield will always be remembered as the player who delivered leadership, confidence and an overwhelming need to win to a team that had come so close, so many times. After signing as a free agent in 1992, Winfield demonstrated that he could still hit, field, and carry a team to the top of the ladder by hitting .290 with 26 home runs and 108 RBIs. Those numbers helped lead the Jays to their second consecutive AL East title and eventually their first World Series championship. Along the way, Winfield claimed some sweet vindication for himself. Long labeled as a player who could not perform in the postseason, Winfield silenced his critics by hitting a pair of homers against the Oakland A's in the ALCS and stroking the eventual World Series-winning hit in Game Six of the championship round against Atlanta.

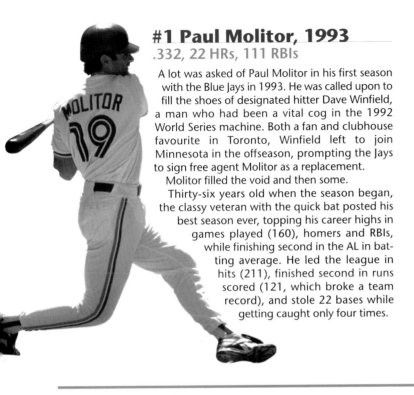

#1 Paul Molitor, 1993
.332, 22 HRs, 111 RBIs

A lot was asked of Paul Molitor in his first season with the Blue Jays in 1993. He was called upon to fill the shoes of designated hitter Dave Winfield, a man who had been a vital cog in the 1992 World Series machine. Both a fan and clubhouse favourite in Toronto, Winfield left to join Minnesota in the offseason, prompting the Jays to sign free agent Molitor as a replacement.

Molitor filled the void and then some.

Thirty-six years old when the season began, the classy veteran with the quick bat posted his best season ever, topping his career highs in games played (160), homers and RBIs, while finishing second in the AL in batting average. He led the league in hits (211), finished second in runs scored (121, which broke a team record), and stole 22 bases while getting caught only four times.

"Molly" was named AL Player of the Month in May when he batted .374 with five home runs, 22 RBIs and 25 runs scored. His run-scoring prowess was highlighted by three four-run games and a stretch of nine straight games in late July in which he scored at least one run. His 121st run came on the last day of the regular season, when he stole home, becoming the first Jay to accomplish the feat in over six years.

The splendid numbers aside, it really was the consistency with which Molitor performed throughout the whole year that gives this season its number-one ranking. Never batting below .284 for a single month (June), Molitor was hitting at a .307 clip with 55 RBIs heading into the All-Star break, and batted .361 in the second half, driving in 56.

Molitor's outstanding regular season was integral to the Blue Jays' third straight division title, but he didn't stop there. An impressive batting average of .391 with a homer, five RBIs and seven runs scored in the ALCS actually pale in comparison to a World Series MVP performance that saw him hit .500 with two homers, eight RBIs and 10 runs scored. Add in scoring the World Series-winning run and it was a near-perfect season.

#2 Carlos Delgado, 2000
.344, 41 HRs, 137 RBIs

After reaching the major leagues to stay in 1996, Carlos Delgado's power numbers increased steadily, but he had never been able to hit for a higher average than his .292 clip in 1998. In 2000, it all came together for the likeable 27-year-old as Delgado developed from rising star into one of the most dangerous hitters in baseball. He played in all 162 games and mounted a serious challenge to try to become baseball's first "triple crown" winner in 33 years.

Key to Delgado's improvement in 2000 was a new-found maturity at the plate. Coming off a career-high 86 walks in 1999, Delgado broke the team record by drawing 123 bases on balls to help propel his on-base percentage to a whopping .470. (Both marks were second in the league.) His walks outnumbered his strikeouts for the first time in his career, and his batting average of .344 was 77 points higher than his career mark. Even more remarkable was his .384 clip with runners in scoring position (second in the AL), a number that was an astonishing 122 points higher than his career pace prior to 2000.

Enjoying several hot streaks throughout the season, Delgado socked eight home runs during a13-game stretch in April. He was named AL Player of the Week once that month and again in June, the latter a result of a .556, four home run, 13 RBI stretch. His .411 month of June included a career-high 22-game hitting streak, and by the time he attended his first All-Star Game in July he had 28 homers and an eye-popping 80 RBIs. By the end of July, he was hitting at a lofty .363 clip, then produced a .368 month of August with 31 RBIs.

Delgado finished the 2000 season with Blue Jays records for RBIs, doubles (57, first in the AL), total bases (378, first), and slugging percentage (.664, second). One more extra-base hit would have made him only the tenth player in major league history to reach 100 (putting him in a group with the likes of Babe Ruth and Lou Gehrig), though the 99 he belted out were still good enough for a team record and the AL lead.

Touted as an MVP candidate all season long, Delgado finished a disappointing fourth in the voting, but was named the Major League Baseball Player of the Year by *The Sporting News*. Only a significant drop-off in the season's final month (.245, 2 HRs, 13 RBIs) keeps this year from ranking number one.

#3 George Bell, 1987
.308, 47 HRs, 134 RBIs

Thirteen years before Carlos Delgado embarked on his monster 2000 season (see #2), George Bell had staked out a career path that looks strikingly similar. Like Delgado in 2000, Bell was 27 years old in 1987. He had four seasons under his belt as an established major leaguer; he was well-known around the league as a budding superstar with tremendous ability; his power numbers had been increasing steadily and his previous season (see #23) had been excellent. Then, in his fifth season, Bell simply exploded into one of the most dominant hitters in the game.

Like Delgado, Bell was the undisputed leader of a fearsome offense, hitting cleanup and putting up numbers that would break many club records. Bell's season was punctuated by some serious hot streaks and numerous outstanding games: a 17-game hitting streak when he batted .439; a month of May that saw him hit .352 while setting franchise records with 11 homers and 31 RBIs; 11 homers again in June; nine two-home-run games; a pair of four- and five-RBI games; one six-RBI game; and one seven-RBI effort. Bell was twice named the American League Player of the Week, including one seven-game tear that saw him bat .407 with five homers and 15 RBIs.

In July, Bell became the first Toronto player to be voted onto the All-Star team, starting in left field with 29 homers and 76 RBIs. His 47 home runs (second in the AL) by season's end are still a club record and came at a time when home run totals greater than 40 were a rarity. Bell also set team records for runs (111, second in the AL), total bases (369, first), slugging percentage (.605, second), extra-base hits (83, first), and RBIs (first), while striking out just 75 times.

Unfortunately, like Delgado in 2000, Bell's numbers fell off slightly down the stretch, and the team's hopes of a playoff berth went down with them. Still, the slump did nothing to hurt Bell's season in the eyes of sportswriters, and the postseason accolades rolled in: AL MVP, *The Sporting News* Player of the Year, and *Baseball America's* AL Player of the Year among them.

#4 Roger Clemens, 1997
21–7, 2.05 ERA

On December 13, 1996, the Blue Jays made their most significant free agent move in the club's 20-year history. There had been big names signed before, but inking a three-time Cy Young Award winner with two 20-win seasons and numerous ERA and strikeouts titles was surely the biggest.

Roger Clemens had been expected to re-sign with the Red Sox, or perhaps reach a deal with the Yankees, who were in aggressive pursuit, but the fact that he was lured to Toronto was seen as a major coup on the organization's part. On the other hand, Clemens hadn't won more than 11 games in four years and at 34 years of age, many felt that the fiery Texan's best days were behind him. But Clemens burst out of the gate, silencing his critics en route to his best season yet.

Winning his Blue Jays debut with a 6–1 complete game, Clemens went on to post 11 straight victories to open the season, smashing the team record for starters by five. His six wins in six May starts garnered AL Pitcher-of the-Month honours, though his 1.96 ERA that month was his *highest* for the first half of the season. July's ERA was a minuscule 0.89, and a 4–0 August was good for another Pitcher-of-the-Month nod.

After recording his 21st victory, Clemens still had four starts left, but the Blue Jays failed to score more than three runs in any of them. Still, by the time the season was over, Rocket Roger had tied a team mark for wins, set a new one for ERA, and his strikeout total of 292 eclipsed the old record by nearly 100. In the process, Clemens became the first AL pitcher in 52 years to lead the league in all three categories, and he captured his fourth Cy Young Award. Unfortunately, the success enjoyed by Roger Clemens did not rub off on his teammates, and the Jays finished dead last in the AL East.

#5 John Olerud, 1993
.363, 24 HRs, 107 RBIs

John Olerud came to spring training in 1993 ready to show why, in 1989, the Blue Jays had made him just their second player to debut professionally in the major leagues. The quiet first baseman with the perfect stroke hit .433 that spring, demonstrating that perhaps he was ready to improve on his career batting average of .269.

The 1992 season had been Olerud's best year to date but, surrounded by a World Championship roster, he'd barely been noticed. Everyone took note of John Olerud in 1993. An April batting average of .450 was good for Player-of-the-Month honours, and proved to be 1993's best monthly mark for anyone in the game. His 26-game hitting streak and .427 clip (with 30 RBIs) in June made Olerud the first Blue Jay to win two Player-of-the-Month awards in one year.

By midseason, Olerud's chase of the .400 mark was the talk of the majors. Eleven times his average had dipped slightly below the magical mark, yet 10 times he managed to bring it back, rolling along at .400 as late as August 2. But sudden stardom did not sit comfortably with the private Olerud, and he was unable to maintain his pace. Still, in 1993, Johnny O became the first Blue Jay to win the batting title, knocking out 200 hits, including 54 doubles (the highest major league total since 1950). Olerud also scored 108 runs and drew 114 walks, all while striking out just 65 times. He wound up third in MVP voting behind Frank Thomas and teammate Paul Molitor.

All of Olerud's offensive numbers represented major leaps forward in 1993, but his .386 clip with runners in scoring position really showed what kind of hitter he had become. That number had been just .217 one year earlier. This new-found ability to hit in the clutch led to Olerud being intentionally walked an incredible 33 times, tying an AL record held by Ted Williams—the last man to hit over .400.

#6 Duane Ward, 1993
2–3, 2.13 ERA, 45 Saves

The Blue Jays roster changed dramatically from 1992 to 1993. Never before had a team made so many significant changes following a World Series title. The departure of Tom Henke and his 34 saves to Texas left the pressure-packed job of closer to Duane Ward and the tall right-hander responded by shutting the door on 45 wins, becoming the first Blue Jay to lead the league in saves and smashing Henke's team record in the process. When entering the game in the ninth inning, he didn't blow a save the entire season.

"Wardo" began 1993 by going eight-for-eight in save situations in April, earning honours as the AL Relief Pitcher of the Month and setting the tone for a year that would be marked by tremendous consistency. In 71 appearances, Ward struck out the side 10 times, and he failed to finish a game only once. Another perfect month in August (10-for-10 in save situations) garnered a second nod as Relief Pitcher of the Month, and his 10 saves tied a team record. Ward never earned fewer than six saves in a month in 1993 and he never had fewer strikeouts than innings pitched. Practically untouchable, Ward struck out a staggering 97 batters in 71.2 innings, while opponents could manage just a meagre .193 average against him.

Relied upon all year, Ward saved the division clincher and the ALCS pennant winner before recording the victory in the World Series finale. His 9.1 innings of postseason work saw Ward add another four saves and 15 strikeouts to his already magnificent season.

#7 Roberto Alomar, 1993
.326, 17 HRs, 93 RBIs

After the 1990 season, the Blue Jays' brain trust decided to break up their core group of homegrown talent and try a new approach. At the winter meetings that year, Pat Gillick swung the biggest trade in club history, shipping Fred McGriff and Tony Fernandez to San Diego for Joe Carter and Roberto Alomar. Both newcomers were a key part of the success that followed, and Alomar dazzled Toronto fans with a combination of good hitting, great speed and extraordinary defense.

Already a three-time All-Star and a postseason hero in 1992, Alomar kicked his game into high gear in 1993. Career bests in steals (53, tied for second in the AL), average (third), hits (192, fourth) and runs scored (109) demonstrated solid increases, but with his new-found power, Alomar was becoming a five-tool player. Dispelling the notion that he was just a singles hitter, Robbie got 25 starts in the number-three spot in the lineup in 1993, and hit for a .420 average there. On a club that had no shortage of clutch performers, Alomar was perhaps the best of the bunch, having a particular flair for the dramatic. An average of .320 with runners in scoring position, .322 with two outs, and .600 with the bases loaded begin to illustrate the point, but it was his uncanny ability to deliver when he had to that was most impressive. Time and time again, Alomar came through with late-inning hits that either tied games or put the Jays out in front. It seemed that whenever Robbie needed to hit, he did. In fourth place in the batting race on the last day of the season, he went 3-for-4 (with five RBIs no less) to move himself into third and the 1993 Blue Jays into the record books as a result (see page 126).

Down the stretch, Alomar hit .360 and .357 in the final two months, driving home 20 runners in each. As for his defense, his brilliant play at second base all season long garnered him a third straight Gold Glove. Robbie's average of .296 in the ALCS was bettered by a .480 World Series mark. He scored eight postseason runs, drove in 10 and swiped eight bases.

#8 Roger Clemens, 1998
20–6, 2.65 ERA

It was hard to imagine that Roger Clemens could duplicate his masterful performance of 1997 (see #4), but in 1998 he essentially did. Again he reached the 20-win plateau; again he led the league in wins, ERA and strikeouts; again he won the Cy Young Award (this time unanimously); and again he broke several significant team records. The only difference from 1997 was that it took Clemens a little longer to get warmed up in 1998.

On May 29, the Cleveland Indians beat "the Rocket" 7–3, dropping his record to 5–6 and increasing his ERA to 3.50. That game would be his last defeat of the season, as he proceeded to reel off 15 consecutive victories. Along the way, Toronto fans were treated to some of the finest pitching they had ever seen. Within a period of 22 starts were three consecutive complete-game shutouts in late August during which Clemens allowed just eight hits while striking out 31 and walking only eight in 27 innings of work. On August 25, Clemens fanned 18 Kansas City Royals, breaking his own team mark of 16 set one year earlier. He finished August with a monthly mark of 4–0 and a tiny 0.90 ERA. The scoreless-innings streak would stretch into September, winding up at a franchise record 33 frames. His 15 straight wins were also a team record, as was his mark of 11–0 and ERA of 1.71 after the All-Star break. During the season, Clemens struck out at least 10 batters 11 different times and he allowed either one or no earned runs in no fewer than 16 starts.

Along with his second consecutive "triple crown" of pitching, Clemens led the American League in a dizzying number of other categories: strikeouts per game (10.39), opponents' batting average (.198), lefties' batting average (.197), righties' batting average (.198), fewest hits per game (6.48), fewest home runs per game (0.42), slugging percentage allowed (.296), road ERA (2.44), opponents' average with runners in scoring position (.176), and pitches per game (115.36).

The Blue Jays improved as a team in 1998, but apparently not enough to satisfy Clemens. Claiming that he had expected to be pitching for a winner when he signed with Toronto, Clemens requested a trade and was granted his wish prior to the 1999 season.

#9 Shawn Green, 1999
.309, 42 HRs, 123 RBIs

With the exception of Lloyd Moseby in 1978, the Blue Jays did not have much luck with their first-round selections in the annual June Free Agent Draft until 1991. That year, they made a tall, skinny high schooler out of California the 16th pick overall. Within a few years, Shawn Green would be a star.

The breakthrough for Green came in 1998 when rookie manager Tim Johnson decided to make him the regular right fielder and the number-two hitter in the batting order. He responded with 35 homers, 35 steals and 100 RBIs. Green's smooth stroke reminded many of John Olerud, and like Olerud, he followed his best season to date with an outstanding one, blossoming into an All-Star.

Hitting in front of Carlos Delgado (see #10) in 1999, Green scored a phenomenal 134 runs to lead the league and set a new club record. But he didn't have to rely completely on his buddy and cleanup hitter. Green burst out of the gate with nine home runs in April (one of them into SkyDome's fifth deck) to tie a team record. He went on to establish career highs in batting average, home runs, RBIs and doubles (45, first in the AL), leading the league in total bases (361) and stealing 20.

Invited to his first All-Star Game, Green went into the break hitting at a .327 clip with 25 homers and 70 RBIs. He was also riding a 13-game hitting streak. The streak would go on to last 28 games, breaking Olerud's team record of 26. While Green struggled somewhat after the streak, he never went three games without getting a hit all season.

Green's outstanding offensive season saw him named to *The Sporting News* Silver Slugger team, but he also could do the job defensively. Making just one error in 347 total chances, Green led AL right fielders with a .997 fielding percentage and was awarded a Gold Glove.

#10 Carlos Delgado, 1999
.272, 44 HRs, 134 RBIs

Like his buddy Shawn Green (see #9), Carlos Delgado was tearing up the league in 1999. Although he was still one year away from adding a high batting average to his arsenal, Delgado's home run and RBI ability was already top notch. He drove in the most runs of his career (to that time), tying George Bell's single-season record, while also posting career highs in home runs, extra-base hits (83), total bases (327), runs (113), and hits (156).

Proving to be extremely durable, Delgado played every inning of every game until a fractured tibia sidelined him for the final 10 games of the year, thus spoiling his bid for club records in homers and ribbies. Along the way, he had six multi-home-run games, and appeared absolutely Ruthian during one particular stretch. From August 6 through 11, Delgado homered eight times in six games, driving in 13 runs. By month's end, he had smashed 12 roundtrippers, breaking the team record for home runs in a month, and tying another with 32 runs driven in.

The All-Star break saw Delgado sitting at 77 RBIs, but a low .244 average probably cost him an All-Star appearance. After the break, Carlos showed signs of things to come by hitting .314 and continuing his magnificent RBI pace by batting home 57 runs in 62 games. Curiously, for the first time in his career, he hit much better against left-handers than right-handers (.309 to .259), but that would set the stage for 2000 where he would have little trouble hitting anyone.

#11 Jack Morris, 1992
21–6, 4.04 ERA

As the Blue Jays and Detroit Tigers became heated rivals during the 1980s, a debate raged over which team's pitching ace was superior—Detroit's Jack Morris or Toronto's Dave Stieb. Morris smugly declared himself the better, telling reporters that all one had to do was look at his win totals and it was a no-brainer. He also went on to call Stieb "a quitter," suggesting that, unlike him, the Jays' ace rarely stuck around to finish what he started anymore. In 1992, when free-agent Morris became a Blue Jay, the two former adversaries became teammates.

While Stieb usually had a better ERA over the course of their careers, it's true that Morris almost always had more wins. And win he continued to do, becoming the first Blue Jays pitcher to reach the elusive 20-win plateau. Practicing what he preached, Morris set the tone for his season on opening day, throwing a mind-boggling 144 pitches for a complete-game victory. An eight-game winning streak from the end of May to the end of July helped the Jays cruise into first place to stay, and a 5–1 August marked the first time a Blue Jays pitcher had won five games in a month since, ironically enough, Dave Stieb in 1988.

Big Jack's ERA may seem a little high for the baseball of the early 1990s but, as had always been the case throughout his career, he would buckle down and pitch as well as he needed to. In nine of his 21 wins the Jays scored four runs or fewer, and in three of his less-than-great outings, the team was scoring totals of 16, 15 and eight runs, all resulting in Jack Morris victories. Moreover, a big-name matchup against Red Sox ace Roger Clemens in June resulted in a Morris complete-game, four-hit shutout.

Down the stretch, Morris allowed just two home runs in his last 14 starts. But though he lost only six times all year, he struggled in the postseason, going a combined 0–3. However, it is fair to say that without his 21 wins and his winning presence, the Blue Jays may never have made it to the 1992 World Series.

#12 Dave Stieb, 1985
14–13, 2.48 ERA

Dave Stieb was plagued by bad luck throughout his entire career. For whatever the reasons, he regularly suffered from poor run support. In at least seven seasons he pitched well enough to have won 20 games, but only once managed even 18. From 1982 to 1985, Stieb was absolutely dominant. He baffled batters with a wicked slider, and started two All-Star games in a row, but his won/lost record never reflected his performance. Stieb rarely got into trouble, but when he did, he would routinely pitch out of it, often leaving runners on second and third as he retired the next three hitters.

A case could be made for any one of Stieb's early 1980s seasons to be chosen for this list, and upon first glance it seems a wonder that a 14–13 record would warrant selection. However, in this instance, you had to be there. Anyone who watched Stieb work in 1985 would agree that it was a superb season.

First of all, his ERA led the league. His monthly earned run averages were as follows: 2.93, 1.69, 1.51, 2.03, 3.80 and 3.04. Opponents hit for just a .213 average against him, and yet the bad luck started right from Day One when he lost the season opener in Kansas City by a score of 2–1. Of his eight complete games in 1985, Stieb was the loser in four of them, with scores of 2–0, 2–1, 2–1 and 4–2.

But it wasn't all bad luck for Dave. He won May's AL Pitcher-of-the-Month Award with a 4–1 mark and 1.69 ERA. The loss? A 3–2 defeat. The month of May also saw Stieb string together 26 consecutive innings without yielding an earned run. He did not allow more than two runs to score in 15 of his first 17 starts.

Heading into the team's first postseason appearance, Stieb's record against the opposing Kansas City Royals was 0–3 despite a 2.70 ERA. As expected, he performed brilliantly. He pitched eight shutout innings in Game One, never allowing a single Royals baserunner past second base in a 6–1 victory. Stieb left Game Four in the seventh inning trailing 1–0, and in Game 7… Well, we all know what happened in Game Seven.

Bad luck indeed.

#13 Mark Eichhorn, 1986
14–6, 1.72 ERA, 10 Saves

When Mark Eichhorn came in from the bullpen on Opening Day, 1986, many Blue Jays fans had no idea that he was even on the team. He had last been seen in Toronto in 1982, going 0–3 with a 5.45 ERA in seven starts. Since then, he had been toiling in the minor leagues, compiling a record of 18–32 and 4.73 ERA. He had attended the Jays' 1986 spring training as a non-roster invitee, and little was expected of him.

A strained muscle in his right shoulder three years earlier had forced Eichhorn to experiment with a submarine-style delivery. By the spring of 1986, he had perfected it. He made the team and American League hitters couldn't figure him out all year.

Making his first major league appearance in four years, Eichhorn struggled a bit in that season opener. However, in his next seven appearances he allowed no earned runs in 15 innings, finishing April with an unbelievable 0.48 ERA. He continued to perform so flawlessly in middle relief that he often stayed in to finish the game. In fact, from May 11 through 24, he had four saves in six appearances.

Another stretch in August provided another 24.1 consecutive scoreless innings.

Eichhorn's ERA stayed under 2.00 almost any way you break the season down: 1.94 at home, 1.50 on the road; 1.61 vs. division rivals, 1.79 vs. the West; 1.79 prior to the All-Star break, 1.65 after; 1.13 in day games, 1.98 at night. The only blemish on an otherwise perfect season was July's ERA of 3.69, which followed a stint on the 15-day disabled list. Other monthly ERAs were: 0.48, 1.37, 1.32, 1.13, and 1.67 to finish the year.

Nearing the end of the season, Eichhorn's ERA was sure to lead the AL by a country mile if he pitched five more innings to qualify. But the selfless sidearmer felt that it would be inappropriate for a relief pitcher to win the title so, with the team already out of the race, he asked manager Jimy Williams not to find him the innings. As it stood, Mark Eichhorn in 1986 had the rare pitching distinction of giving up fewer hits and walks combined (150) than innings pitched (157).

#14 Dave Winfield, 1992
.290, 26 HRs, 108 RBIs

The Blue Jays of 1991 had been a new-look outfit but, for the third time in seven years, the division champions fell short in the ALCS. So it was then decided to try yet another angle in 1992—big-name free agents. Enter Jack Morris (see #11) and Dave Winfield.

Morris arrived in Toronto with two World Series rings to his credit, and though Winfield had never won the big one, it was felt that at 40 years of age, his experience and maturity would provide the necessary ingredient that had been missing in the past. The new plan worked perfectly.

Winfield went on to have a marvellous season, easily his best in four years. The numbers are very good to be sure, as he finished the season among the AL's top 10 in HRs, RBIs, slugging percentage (.491), extra-base hits (62) and total bases (286). But Winfield brought more than just his formidable talents on the field to the 1992 team. From the moment he arrived at spring training, he was embraced by everyone as a team leader. As baseball's active leader in home runs and RBIs, and also a one-time teammate of manager Cito Gaston, he was greatly respected by rookies, veterans, and coaches alike. Aware of his responsibility, Winfield began to convince everyone on the team that they should win the World Series. "We can, we are, we will" became the team's slogan for the season.

But Winfield wasn't just a cheerleader. The classy veteran also planned to participate in this World Championship run, and he led by example. He started fast, hitting .375 in April and riding a hitting streak that would last 17 games. In May, Winfield's dramatic ninth-inning, game-winning grand slam in Seattle pushed the team to a towering .700 winning percentage, and gave them a confidence that would last the entire year.

Winfield really caught fire in August, embarking on a 13-game hitting streak and driving in a team-record 32 runs. He would go on to break franchise records for homers and RBIs by a designated hitter, and on September 24 he became the oldest player in history to top 100 RBIs in a season.

But Big Dave wasn't content to just lead the team. Feeling that Toronto crowds were too quiet, he called upon the fans to help the club by getting louder. The "Winfield Wants Noise" campaign resulted in deafening decibel levels at the SkyDome, and the Jays played at a .733 clip at home to close out the regular season. Fittingly, it was Winfield, whose 11th-inning double in Game Six of the Fall Classic clinched the title for the Blue Jays, who unveiled the World Series banner at SkyDome two days later.

#15 Joe Carter, 1993
.253, 33 HRs, 121 RBIs

Much like the seasons of Dave Stieb (see #12 and #22) and Tom Henke (see #17), Joe Carter's years in Toronto were so consistently solid that just about any one of his Blue Jays seasons deserves strong consideration for this list. Only once in seven years did he fail to reach the century mark in RBIs (and that was lockout-shortened 1995), and never did he hit fewer than 20 home runs. Some seasons saw higher batting averages, but for the smilin' slugger, 1993 was truly a magical season right up until the very last pitch.

With the popular Dave Winfield gone, Joe comfortably assumed the role of the team's spiritual leader. Eager to lead the team to its second straight World Series title, he burst out of the gate, breaking a team record for April RBIs with 25. As the cleanup hitter in the so-called WAMCO group (White, Alomar, Molitor, Carter and Olerud), Carter was the cornerstone of the most feared lineup in baseball, leading the team in home runs and RBIs. Fourteen of his home runs either tied a game or put the Blue Jays out in front. While Cito Gaston spent much of the 1993 season auditioning outfielders to play along with Carter and Devon White, Joe played 55 games in left field and 96 in right with equal proficiency. Blessed with a strong and accurate arm, Carter led the club with seven outfield assists.

Always known as a streaky hitter, Carter performed with notable consistency in 1993. An output of 18 home runs and 65 RBIs prior to the All-Star break was followed by a 15-homer, 56-RBI second half. Only once all season did he go as many as six games without driving in a run. And of course, there were the hot patches: an 11-game hitting streak; home runs in back-to-back games six times; four homers in two games; the fifth three-home-run game of his career (to break Lou Gehrig's AL record); three four-RBI games; and two home runs in one inning (making him the first Blue Jay to perform that feat).

Having equalled his career high for RBIs during the 1993 campaign, Carter went on to drive in 10 more in the postseason, the final three courtesy of the most significant swing of the bat in Blue Jays history.

#16 Paul Molitor, 1994
.341, 14 HRs, 75 RBIs

The 1994 season was a terrible one for any baseball fan. A players strike shut down the schedule in mid-August and, for the first time in 90 years, there was no World Series. But for Blue Jays fans, it was doubly disappointing. Hoping for the first back-to-back-to-back World Series titles in 20 years, the Jays were a sub-.500 team—for the first time since 1982—when the lights went down on the 1994 season.

One of the few bright spots for the Blue Jays was the play of the ageless Paul Molitor. Committed to the pursuit of the three-peat, "Molly" picked up right were he left off in 1993 (see #1). Though the team stumbled through a 38–48 first half, he hit .342 with 54 RBIs. In July, he broke a team record by scoring 28 runs in one month. Included in that month was a Player-of-the-Week selection for batting .500 with four homers, 10 RBIs and 10 runs scored.

Playing as if he were in his early twenties, Molitor took part in every game of the season. A game in April in which he hit two home runs included an inside-the-park effort. Even more remarkable than his 20 stolen bases was the fact that he was never caught stealing once.

As in 1993, consistency and opportunism were the keys to Molitor's game in 1994. His lowest average for any month was .306 in August, and his post All-Star break average was .339. He hit at a .382 clip with runners on base, but put those runners in scoring position and he actually improved to .411. If it were not for the strike, Molitor was on pace to drive in 106 runs. He was riding a 10-game hitting streak when the season was shut down. Too bad he had to stop.

#17 Tom Henke, 1989
8–3, 1.92 ERA, 20 Saves

From the time the Blue Jays first moved into contention in the American League East in 1983 until the middle of 1985, they lacked one thing every winning team needs—a reliable closer. The moment that Tom Henke threw his first pitch in a Toronto uniform, the Jays knew they had found their man. Soon, "the Terminator" became arguably the best closer in all of baseball.

For seven more seasons, the tall bricklayer from Missouri was a tower of strength out of the Blue Jays bullpen, nailing down an average of 29 saves per season. His career was marked by such consistency that it is difficult to call one season better than the next, but the year 1989 was one that was particularly outstanding.

Henke's fortunes closely resembled the team's that year. Coming into 1989 with high expectations, the Blue Jays were a disappointing 20-31 at the end of May, and Henke had just two saves. But then Henke caught fire and went on to post 18 saves the rest of the way, coupled with an astounding 1.02 ERA. For their part, the team played .623 ball from June on and captured their second division title.

During one stretch, Henke allowed just a single earned run in 19 appearances, totaling 27.1 innings. Another stretch saw 13 consecutive scoreless appearances, where he racked up seven saves, striking out 37 in 25 innings. As the pennant race heated up, so too did Henke. The Jays headed into September in a tie for first place. That month, Henke won two games, saved six, struck out 25 in 18.2 innings, and posted a 0.96 ERA. Clinging to a one-game lead in the standings, "the Terminator" collected one win and three saves, including the division clincher, in the final week of the season.

Even with the slow start, Henke ended the year with 116 strikeouts in 89 innings, while allowing just 66 hits for a .205 opponents' batting average. Though the Blue Jays were overmatched by Oakland in the ALCS and Henke had no save opportunities, he gave up no hits, no walks, and struck out three in his three postseason appearances.

#18 Tony Fernandez, 1986
.310, 10 HRs, 65 RBIs

Even as Alfredo Griffin was in the midst of his 392-game ironman streak, it was already a well-known fact that there was a young player waiting in the wings. Tony Fernandez was reputed to be a magician at shortstop and also to have a potent bat. He arrived in Toronto in late 1983, and was beginning to take Griffin's job away from him in 1984, starting his own ironman streak in the process. When Alfredo was traded in the offseason prior to 1985, the shortstop position belonged to Tony.

By 1986, players like Fernandez and Baltimore's Cal Ripken Jr. were changing the traditional reputation of the shortstop. No longer was it thought of as just a defensive position—these guys could hit! In smashing the franchise record, Fernandez not only became the first Blue Jay to collect 200 hits in a season, but his 213 safeties were the most by a shortstop in the history of the game.

Batting mostly out of the leadoff spot, Tony's home run and RBI totals were as impressive as they were surprising, and his 294 total bases placed him seventh in the league. He was also seventh in batting average, though he led the AL in at-bats (687) and singles (161), while finishing third in triples (nine) and hits.

Both dependable and durable, Fernandez played in every one of the club's 163 games in 1986 (one was a tie in which the statistics were counted), running his consecutive-game string to 327. Throughout the season he managed three separate hitting streaks of 14, 12 and 11 games, and was invited to the All-Star Game for the first time.

Then, of course, there was his defense. Routinely going deep in the hole to corral would-be hits, Fernandez amazed fans with the accuracy of his uniquely styled underhand flip throws. Leading the league in both total chances and fielding percentage, Fernandez was rewarded with his first Gold Glove. More 1986 postseason accolades came when he was named the American League's All-Star shortstop by *The Sporting News*, UPI and the Associated Press.

#19 Pat Hentgen, 1996
20–10, 3.22 ERA

Pat Hentgen's rise to prominence in the major leagues was a rapid one. In his first season as a big-league starter in 1993, he went 19–9 with an ERA of 3.87 to help the Blue Jays to their second straight World Series title. Hentgen's win total fell with the team's in 1994, yet he bettered his ERA to 3.40. Then a relatively disastrous 1995 left fans wondering what to expect come 1996. So all the amiable right-hander did was pitch one of the best seasons in team history, becoming the first Blue Jays hurler to take home a major postseason award.

Hentgen gained momentum as the 1996 season progressed, compiling a post-All-Star break record of 12–4 with a 2.58 ERA. His first half had also been impressive, going 8–6 with a 3.86 ERA. Two of those wins had been shutouts, and one was a 1–0 victory with help from the bullpen. But it was during Hentgen's second half where the Cy Young talk began to heat up. Following the break he won five straight starts, including another shutout. By August 28, he was 9–1 in his last 10 starts, having completed five in a row. He then became the first pitcher in seven years to win back-to-back Pitcher-of-the-Month awards, taking the honour for both July and August.

Needing to win his last three starts to become the second Jays hurler to reach 20 victories, Hentgen won them all, giving up just one run in each game. By season's end, he had gone at least six innings in an amazing 34 of 35 starts. His 10 complete games and 265.2 innings pitched were good for the major league lead, and his three shutouts tied for baseball's best. Yet were it not for some bad luck along the way, Hentgen might easily have broken the team record for wins. Twice he left games with the lead only to be let down by the bullpen, and included in his 10 losses were scores of 2–1 and 3–1. In fact, in no fewer than six of his losses, the Blue Jays failed to score more than three runs. Still, Hentgen edged out Andy Pettitte of the Yankees to become the Blue Jays' first Cy Young Award winner.

#20 Jimmy Key, 1987
17–8, 2.76 ERA

The arrival of Jimmy Key into the Blue Jays' starting rotation in 1985 heralded the end of a drought that had plagued the team for nearly five years. On May 1 that year, Key became the first Blue Jays lefty to win a start since Paul Mirabella back in 1980. As it turned out, both 1985 and 1986 would be formidable seasons for the unassuming southpaw. Key won 14 games each year with ERAs of 3.00 and 3.57 respectively.

Declared the team's ace for the 1987 campaign, Key was handed the opening day assignment and went on to establish himself as the league's top left-hander. He led the league in ERA and finished runner-up to Roger Clemens in Cy Young voting. Key began the year by cruising through April, going 4–1 with a 3.03 ERA. But then, as had been the team's pattern throughout the 1980s, run support dwindled for the ace of the staff. Key won only two games in each of the next two months, yet in June his ERA was 1.55 and he allowed an amazingly low 23 hits in 40.2 innings. Things got better in July as Key posted another 4–1 month and, after a 3–0 August, he rode an eight-game winning streak into late September.

Unfortunately, never was Key's poor run support more apparent than in the last game of the 1987 season. With the Jays needing a win to force a one-game playoff with the Tigers, Key was up to the challenge. He pitched his heart out, but incredibly, a complete-game three-hitter wasn't good enough. The Blue Jays lost 1–0, and their 96-win season came up short of a playoff berth.

Key's 17 wins tied a club record, but as usual there should have been far more. In 30 of his 36 starts, Jimmy gave up three earned runs or fewer, and in his eight losses, the team supported him with a grand total of just 13 runs. If it was any consolation, *The Sporting News* didn't agree with the Baseball Writers' choice for the Cy Young Award and named Key the American League Pitcher of the Year.

#21 Willie Upshaw, 1983
.306, 27 HRs, 104 RBIs

By the end of 1983, Willie Upshaw's career very closely resembled the history of the Blue Jays. Joining the team in 1978, Upshaw had just a .215 average over parts of four seasons through 1981. The team had never finished out of the cellar, and Upshaw had never produced more than two home runs or 17 RBIs.

In early May of 1982, the Blue Jays traded Big John Mayberry to the Yankees and declared Upshaw the every day first baseman. The team finished that year with 78 wins and a sixth-place tie in the standings. Upshaw had socked 21 homers and driven in 75. Then came 1983, when Upshaw's bat asserted him as a star in the league. The Blue Jays held down first place as late as July 25 and finished fourth. The rapid rise in the standings began in June when Upshaw hit .374 and scored 26 runs. The Blue Jays were sitting atop the American League East, and baseball began to notice this young team, especially its first baseman. When the Jays went into the All-Star break still in first place, Upshaw had 15 home runs, 52 runs, 48 RBIs and a .298 average.

Upshaw began the second half by embarking on a nine-game hitting streak, during which time the Jays went 8–1 to stretch their lead in the East to a season-high three games. He hit .323 in July with 16 RBIs, and the month ended with the Blue Jays still very much in the thick of the race. But August turned out to be very disappointing. Upshaw hit just .268 with two home runs and the Jays were all but eliminated from contention—mostly due to some very shoddy bullpen work.

But Upshaw was unwilling to admit defeat. In the season's final month, he hit .353 with seven home runs and 28 RBIs, enjoying a pair of nine-game hitting streaks. He also drove in runs in eight consecutive games en route to becoming the first Blue Jays batter to collect 100 RBIs. When the year ended, Upshaw had missed only two games. He'd set new club highs in RBIs, total bases (298), extra-base hits (60) and slugging percentage (.515), and had helped to usher in a new era for the Toronto Blue Jays.

#22 Dave Stieb, 1990
18–6, 2.93 ERA

In the five years that separate his two entries in this ranking (see #12), Dave Stieb had endured an awful lot. First there was a miserable off year in 1986 where he yielded 29 first-inning runs, was banished to the bullpen, and finished at 7–12 with a 4.74 ERA. The following season ended with another high ERA (4.09), a little more bullpen duty, and zero wins in his last seven starts. Stieb bounced back in 1988, but frustration ensued with three one-hitters, two of which were consecutive no-hit bids spoiled with two out and two strikes in the ninth inning. Stieb tossed two more one-hitters in 1989, but there was still more heartache. This time it was a perfect game spoiled with two outs in the ninth.

In 1990, the complex right-hander had his best season in five years. Stieb's stunning slider was back and he held righties to a .205 average. He was nearly perfect on the road, going 9–1 with an ERA of 2.73. He broke his own team record of 17 wins (a mark he had

shared with Doyle Alexander and Jimmy Key) and his ERA ranked in the league's top five. Stieb's win total at the All-Star break (11) was the highest of his career to that point, and he finished July 3–0 with a 0.94 ERA. In 28.2 innings that month, he allowed just 16 hits.

Stieb eliminated some frustrating patterns of past years in 1990. Never before having posted a won/lost record that his great pitching warranted, his winning percentage of .750 was a welcome change, and good for another team record. In no single month was his percentage less than .600, and in early August his record stood at 14–3. The 14th win had come at Baltimore's Memorial Stadium where, prior to that, he had failed to gain a single victory in his 11 seasons. And then on September 2 in Cleveland, it finally happened. When Junior Felix squeezed Jerry Browne's liner to right in the bottom of the ninth, Sir David had finally completed the first and only no-hitter in franchise history.

#23 George Bell, 1986
.309, 31 HRs, 108 RBIs

As the 1986 baseball season approached, the so-called "best outfield in baseball" prepared to play their third full season together. The division-winning season of 1985 had seen the trio of George Bell, Jesse Barfield and Lloyd Moseby combine to smack 73 home runs, drive in 249 runners, score 273 times and steal 80 bases. A year later, the threesome's numbers had soared to totals of 92 roundtrippers and 302 ribbies, while scoring a combined 297 runs. Even though a franchise-record 40 of those home runs belonged to Barfield, it was George Bell who had emerged as the best of the three by the end of the season.

Bell had finished 1985 on a high, batting .321 in the ALCS. He began the 1986 season hot as well, hitting .361 through April with four home runs and 18 driven in. In May, his .310 mark included six consecutive two-hit games to close out the month. Eventually, this became a 15-game hitting streak, during which Bell batted .431 with five homers and 14 runs driven in.

A true clutch hitter, Bell hit .325 with runners in scoring position for the entire year. He also tied for the league lead with 15 game-winning RBIs (now a defunct statistic). Four of his 21 June RBIs came on one

swing of the bat, a ninth-inning grand slam that erased an 8–4 deficit against the Yankees. But in what was all too typical of the team's disappointing season, the Blue Jays dropped that June 20 game in the tenth. Undeterred, Bell roared through July hitting .317 with nine home runs and 23 RBIs. In one three-game stint beginning July 19, he hit four home runs. Nine days later, he went on to smash another four in six games.

The man whose defensive abilities would come to drive Toronto fans crazy in subsequent seasons actually had 17 outfield assists in 1986, including an amazing stretch of five in six games. Jesse Barfield picked up his first Gold Glove honour that year, while Bell was named a Silver Slugger for the second straight season. (Barfield also wound up a 1986 Silver Slugger.)

Bell, who would win the AL MVP the following season (see #3), finished fourth in the 1986 voting, the highest any Toronto player had finished to that point. He fell just two hits shy of 200, but scored 101 runs and became the first Blue Jay to enjoy a .300, 30 homer, 100 RBI season.

#24 Joe Carter, 1991
.273, 33 HRs, 108 RBIs

As a member of the Cleveland Indians from 1984 through 1989, Joe Carter was often rumoured to be heading to Toronto. In fact, when the Indians decided to part with the star outfielder, the Blue Jays were bitterly disappointed they were unable to land him. So when they were able to swing a deal for the perennial run producer a year later, the Jays were thrilled. For his part, Carter was too. As a visitor, he had always enjoyed the city and its fans, but more importantly, he had never played on a contending team in his big-league career, and the prospect of playing on a winner excited him.

Having driven in over 100 runs in four of his last five seasons (the one year he didn't, he missed by two), Carter was expected to "bring 'em on home" for the Jays in 1991. That's precisely what he did. Buoyed by his new surroundings, Carter went deep on Opening Day and went on to hit .337 for April with three homers, eight doubles and 15 RBIs. A 12-game hitting streak in May was followed by AL Player-of-the-Month honours in June. That month Carter simply exploded:

a .352 average, 11 homers (to tie a team record for home runs in a month), 29 RBIs and a club-record 82 total bases. On June 20, he began a Blue Jays record-tying four-game home run streak, and ended that week with a .409 average, five homers, 26 total bases, and the nod as AL Player of the Week. July brought Carter his first trip to the All-Star Game.

After the break, the RBIs kept coming, and the month of August was good for another 20. Though Joe was never a tremendous hitter for average, he hit when it counted, and with runners in scoring position and two out, he batted .308 for the year.

Unusually durable, Carter played in all 162 games for the third year in a row, all for different teams. Playing both left and right field with equal aplomb, he led the team with 13 outfield assists. And when the Blue Jays clinched their third division title on October 2, it was Joe who delivered the game-winning hit.

#25 Dennis Lamp, 1985
11–0, 3.32 ERA, 2 Saves

In January of 1984, Dennis Lamp became the second free agent signing in the history of the Blue Jays franchise. The team's chance for the postseason in 1983 had been squandered by a series of late-inning losses in August, and it was felt that by adding a quality closer they could make a run at the division title. Lamp failed miserably.

After blowing a save in the very first game of the 1984 season, Lamp went on to allow 38 walks and 97 hits in 85 innings. He lost eight games, saved only nine, and finished with a 4.55 ERA. By mid-season, manager Bobby Cox had lost faith in Lamp, and when 1984 came to a close, two other Blue Jays pitchers had more saves than their "savior." By 1985 the Blue Jays had Bill Caudill in place (another failure as it turned out) and Lamp was now in the more comfortable role of middle reliever. He went on to have a terrific season.

Things were different right from the start this year. Following a second-half ERA of 5.72 the season before, Lamp was in fine form in April, going 2–0 with a 1.42 ERA. After surrendering nine home runs in 1984, he didn't allow a single tater through his first 31.1 innings. Throughout the season, Lamp would do it all: long relief, middle relief, a few games in short relief, and even one starting assignment. At the All-Star break he was 5–0 with one save and a 3.19 ERA.

When asked about his remarkable turnaround, Lamp attributed his success to a self-hypnosis program. Whatever the reason, his fellow

Blue Jays hurlers loved him. He did not allow a single inherited runner to score over an incredible 43 appearances, from the beginning of the season through September 8, spanning 91.2 innings! On September 21, Lamp picked up a 2–1 victory over Milwaukee to run his record to 10–0, breaking the franchise record for consecutive wins.

Following one more win, Lamp was named Blue Jays Pitcher of the Year on a staff that included AL ERA leader Dave Stieb (see #12) and 17-game winner Doyle Alexander. Lamp continued to roll along in the ALCS, pitching brilliantly. In three appearances, he yielded just two hits, one walk, no runs, and struck out 10 in 9.1 innings. What a difference a year makes!

25 Honourable Mentions:

Doyle Alexander, 1984	Kelly Gruber, 1990
Roberto Alomar, 1992	Juan Guzman, 1992
Jesse Barfield, 1986	Tom Henke, 1987
Tony Batista, 2000	Tom Henke, 1990
George Bell, 1989	Tom Henke, 1991
Joe Carter, 1992	Lloyd Moseby, 1987
Joe Carter, 1994	Shannon Stewart, 2000
Joe Carter, 1996	Dave Stieb, 1982
Carlos Delgado, 1998	Dave Stieb, 1983
Tony Fernandez, 1987	Dave Stieb, 1984
Tony Fernandez, 1999	Dave Stieb, 1988
Shawn Green, 1998	Dave Stieb, 1989
	David Wells, 2000

Bobby Cox | **Jim Fregosi** | **Cito Gaston** | **Roy Hartsfield** | **Tim Johnson** | **Buck Martinez**

	D.O.B	Place of Birth	HT.	WT.	W–L	Pct.	Yrs. With Jays		D.O.B	Place of Birth	HT.	WT.	W–L	Pct.	Yrs. With Jays
Cox, Bobby	5/21/41	Tulsa, OK	6-0	185	335–292	.549	'82–'85	Hartsfield, Roy	10/25/25	Atlanta, GA	5-9	170	163–309	.345	'77–'79
Fregosi, Jim	4/4/42	San Francisco, CA	6-2	210	167–157	.515	'99–2000	Johnson, Tim	07/22/49	Grand Forks, ND	6-3	185	88–74	.543	'98
Gaston, Cito	3/17/44	San Antonio, TX	6-4	220	681–635	.517	'89–'97	Martinez, Buck	11/7/48	Redding, CA	5-10	190	–	–	2001-

Bobby Mattick | **Mel Queen** | **Gene Tenace** | **Harry Warner** | **Jimy Williams**

	D.O.B	Place of Birth	HT.	WT.	W–L	Pct.	Yrs. With Jays		D.O.B	Place of Birth	HT.	WT.	W–L	Pct.	Yrs. With Jays
Mattick, Bobby	12/5/51	Sioux City, IO	5-11	190	104–164	.388	'80–'81	Warner, Harry	12/1/28	Reeders, PA	6-2	200	3–9	.250	'78
Queen, Mel	3/26/42	Johnson City, NJ	6-1	190	4–1	.800	'97	Williams, Jimy	10/4/43	Arroyo Grande, CA	5-11	170	281–241	.538	'86–'89
Tenace, Gene	10/10/46	Russellton, PA	6-0	195	21–15	.583	'91, '94								

Bob Bailor | **Terry Bevington** | **Sal Butera** | **Galen Cisco** | **Mark Connor** | **Roly de Armas** | **Bobby Doerr** | **Lee Elia**

	D.O.B	Place of Birth	Bats/Throws	HT.	WT.	Yrs. With Jays		D.O.B	Place of Birth	Bats/Throws	HT.	WT.	Yrs. With Jays
Bailor, Bob	7/10/51	Connellsville, PA	BR/TR	5-10	165	'92–'95	Connor, Mark	5/27/49	Brooklyn, NY	BR/TR	6-2	205	2001-
Bevington, Terry	7/27/56	Akron, OH	BR/TR	6-2	205	'99–	de Armas, Roly	12/29/51	New York, NY	BR/TR	6-1	190	2000
Butera, Sal	9/25/52	Richmond Hill, NY	BR/TR	6-0	190	'98	Doerr, Bobby	4/7/18	Los Angeles, CA	BR/TR	5-11	185	'77–'81
Cisco, Galen	3/7/37	St. Mary's. OH	BR/TR	5-11	205	'88, '90–'95	Elia, Lee	7/16/37	Philadelphia, PA	BR/TR	5-11	200	2000

John Felske | **Cito Gaston** | **Alfredo Griffin** | **Epy Guerrero** | **Rich Hacker** | **Larry Hisle** | **Dennis Holmberg** | **Jack Hubbard**

	D.O.B	Place of Birth	Bats/Throws	HT.	WT.	Yrs. With Jays		D.O.B	Place of Birth	Bats/Throws	HT.	WT.	Yrs. With Jays
Felske, John	5/30/42	Chicago, IL	BR/TR	6-4	220	'80–'81	Hacker, Rich	10/6/47	Belleville, IL	BB/TR	6-0	185	'91–'94
Gaston, Cito	3/17/44	San Antonio, TX	BR/TR	6-4	220	'82–'89, 2000–	Hisle, Larry	5/5/47	Portsmouth, OH	BR/TL	6-2	205	'92–'95
Griffin, Alfredo	3/6/57	Santo Domingo, DR	BB/TR	5-11	180	'96–'97	Holmberg, Dennis	8/2/51	Fremond, NE	BL/TR	6-0	200	'94–'95
Guerrero, Epy	1/3/42	Dominican Republic	BR/TR	5-11	200	'81	Hubbard, Jack	10/4/50	Rock Hall, MD	BR/TR	5-11	185	'98

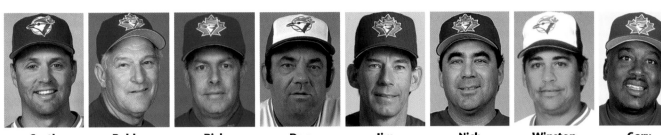

| **Garth Iorg** | **Bobby Knoop** | **Rick Langford** | **Don Leppert** | **Jim Lett** | **Nick Leyva** | **Winston Llenas** | **Gary Matthews** |

	D.O.B	Place of Birth	Bats/Throws	HT.	WT.	Yrs. With Jays
Iorg, Garth	10/12/54	Arcata, CA	BR/TR	5-11	165	'96, 2001-
Knoop, Bobby	10/18/38	Sioux City, IO	BR/TR	6-1	170	2000
Langford, Rick	3/20/52	Farmville, VA	BR/TR	6-0	185	2000
Leppert, Don	10/19/31	Indianapolis, IN	BL/TR	6-2	215	'77-'79

	D.O.B	Place of Birth	Bats/Throws	HT.	WT.	Yrs. With Jays
Lett, Jim	1/3/51	Charleston, WV	BR/TR	6-0	190	'97-'99
Leyva, Nick	8/16/53	Ontario, CA	BR/TR	5-10	190	'93-'97
Llenas, Winston	9/23/43	Santiago, D.R.	BR/TR	5-10	170	'88
Matthews, Gary	7/5/50	San Fernando, CA	BR/TR	6-3	215	'98-'99

| **John McLaren** | **Denis Menke** | **Bob Miller** | **Jackie Moore** | **Lloyd Moseby** | **Gil Patterson** | **Marty Pevey** | **Mel Queen** |

	D.O.B	Place of Birth	Bats/Throws	HT.	WT.	Yrs. With Jays
McLaren, John	9/29/51	Galveston, TX	BR/TR	6-0	200	'86-'90
Menke, Denis	7/21/40	Algoma, IO	BR/TR	6-0	200	'80-'81
Miller, Bob	2/18/39	St. Louis, MO	BR/TR	6-1	195	'77-'79
Moore, Jackie	2/19/39	Jay, FL	BR/TR	6-0	180	'77-'79

	D.O.B	Place of Birth	Bats/Throws	HT.	WT.	Yrs. With Jays
Moseby, Lloyd	11/5/59	Portland, AK	BL/TR	6-3	200	'99
Patterson, Gil	9/5/55	Philadelphia, PA	BR/TR	6-1	185	2001-
Pevey, Marty	9/18/61	Statesboro, GA	BL/TR	6-1	185	'99
Queen, Mel	3/26/42	Johnson City, NJ	BL/TR	6-1	190	'96-'99

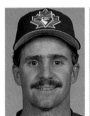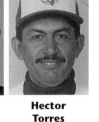

| **Eddie Rodriguez** | **Cookie Rojas** | **Billy Smith** | **Mike Squires** | **Dave Stewart** | **John Sullivan** | **Gene Tenace** | **Hector Torres** |

	D.O.B	Place of Birth	Bats/Throws	HT.	WT.	Yrs. With Jays
Rodriguez, Eddie	3/11/59	Havana, Cuba	BR/TR	5-8	170	'98
Rojas, Cookie	3/6/39	Havana, Cuba	BR/TR	5-10	165	2001-
Smith, Billy	1/14/30	High Point, NC	BL/TL	5-9	160	'84-'88
Squires, Mike	3/5/51	Kalamazoo, MI	BL/TL	5-10	191	'89-'91

	D.O.B	Place of Birth	Bats/Throws	HT.	WT.	Yrs. With Jays
Stewart, Dave	2/19/57	Oakland, CA	BR/TR	6-2	200	2000
Sullivan, John	1/3/41	Somerville, NJ	BL/TR	6-0	210	'82-'93
Tenace, Gene	10/10/46	Russellton, PA	BR/TR	6-0	195	'90-'97
Torres, Hector	9/16/45	Monterrey, Mexico	BR/TR	6-0	180	'90-'91

| **Willie Upshaw** | **Harry Warner** | **Al Widmar** | **Jimy Williams** |

	D.O.B	Place of Birth	Bats/Throws	HT.	WT.	Yrs. With Jays
Upshaw, Willie	4/27/57	Blanco, TX	BL/TL	6-0	195	'96-'97
Warner, Harry	12/1/28	Reeders, PA	BL/TR	6-2	200	'77-'80
Widmar, Al	3/20/25	Cleveland, OH	BR/TR	6-4	195	'80-'89
Williams, Jimy	10/4/43	Arroyo Grande, CA	BR/TR	5-11	170	'80-'85

Glenn Adams | Willie Aikens | Dan Ainge | Butch Alberts | Gary Allenson | Roberto Alomar | Alan Ashby | Doug Ault | Bob Bailor | Dave Baker

	Position	Birthdate	Birthplace	Bats/Throws	HT.	WT.	Yrs. With Jays	AVG	G	AB	R	H	2B	3B	HR	RBI	SH–SF	HP	BB	SO	SB–CS
Adams, Glenn	DH	10/4/47	Northbridge, MA	BL/TR	6-0	185	'82	.258	30	66	2	17	4	0	1	11	0–3	0	4	5	0–0
Aikens, Willie	DH	10/14/54	Seneca, SC	BL/TR	6-3	220	'84-85	.205	105	254	23	52	8	0	12	31	0–1	2	32	62	0–0
Ainge, Dan	2B-3B-CF	3/17/59	Eugene, OR	BR/TR	6-4	175	'79-81	.220	211	665	57	146	19	4	2	37	12–3	4	37	128	12–5
Alberts, Butch	DH	5/4/50	Williamsport, PA	BR/TR	6-2	205	'78	.278	6	18	1	5	1	0	0	0	0–0	0	0	2	0–0
Allenson, Gary	C	2/4/55	Culver City, CA	BR/TR	5-11	185	'85	.118	14	34	2	4	1	0	0	3	0–0	0	0	10	0–0
Alomar, Roberto	2B	2/5/68	Ponce, P.R.	BB/TR	6-0	185	'91-95	.307	703	2706	451	832	152	36	55	342	39–22	16	322	291	206–46
Ashby, Alan	C	7/8/51	Long Beach, CA	BR/TR	6-2	190	'77-78	.230	205	660	52	152	31	3	11	58	14–2	3	78	82	1–3
Ault, Doug	1B-DH-LF	3/9/50	Beaumont, TX	BR/TL	6-3	200	'77-78, '80	.234	247	693	66	162	28	5	17	86	5–4	7	70	105	4–5
Bailor, Bob	OF-SS-3B	7/10/51	Connellsville, PA	BR/TR	5-11	170	'77-80	.264	523	1878	230	495	75	19	8	138	21–11	15	127	107	46–28
Baker, Dave	3B	11/25/57	Lacona, IA	BL/TR	6-0	185	'82	.250	9	20	3	5	1	0	0	2	1–0	2	3	3	0–0

Jesse Barfield | Tony Batista | Kevin Batiste | Howard Battle | Charlie Beamon | Derek Bell | George Bell | Juan Beniquez | Geronimo Berroa | Casey Blake

	Position	Birthdate	Birthplace	Bats/Throws	HT.	WT.	Yrs. With Jays	AVG	G	AB	R	H	2B	3B	HR	RBI	SH–SF	HP	BB	SO	SB–CS
Barfield, Jesse	RF	10/29/59	Joliet, IL	BR/TR	6-1	205	'81-89	.265	1032	3463	530	919	162	27	179	527	13–24	27	342	855	55–40
Batista, Tony	3B-SS	12/9/73	Puerto Plata, D.R.	BR/TR	6-0	180	'99-	.271	252	995	157	270	57	3	67	193	3–8	10	57	200	7–4
Batiste, Kevin	RF-LF	10/21/66	Galveston, TX	BR/TR	6-2	175	'89	.250	6	8	1	2	0	0	0	0	0–0	0	0	5	0–0
Battle, Howard	3B-DH	3/25/72	Biloxi, MI	BR/TR	6-0	210	'95	.200	9	15	3	3	0	0	0	0	0–0	0	4	8	1–0
Beamon, Charlie	DH-3B	12/4/53	Oakland, CA	BL/TL	6-1	183	'81	.200	8	15	1	3	1	0	0	0	0–0	0	2	2	0–0
Bell, Derek	LF-CF-RF	12/11/68	Tampa, FL	BR/TR	6-2	215	'91-92	.228	79	189	28	43	6	3	2	16	2–1	6	21	39	10–4
Bell, George	LF	10/21/59	San Pedro de Macoris, D.R.	BR/TR	6-1	190	'81, '83-90	.286	1181	4528	641	1294	237	32	202	740	0–59	35	255	563	59–27
Beniquez, Juan	DH-LF-RF	5/13/50	San Sebastian, P.R.	BR/TR	5-11	165	'87-88	.284	39	81	6	23	5	1	5	21	0–1	1	5	13	0–0
Berroa, Geronimo	DH-LF	3/18/65	Santo Domingo, D.R.	BR/TR	6-0	195	'99	.194	22	62	11	12	3	0	1	6	0–0	2	9	15	0–0
Blake, Casey	3B	8/23/73	Des Moines, IA	BR/TR	6-2	195	'99	.256	14	39	6	10	2	0	1	1	0–0	0	2	7	0–0

Barry Bonnell | Pat Borders | Rick Bosetti | Steve Bowling | Steve Braun | Bob Brenly | Tilson Brito | Bobby Brown | Kevin Brown | Jacob Brumfield

	Position	Birthdate	Birthplace	Bats/Throws	HT.	WT.	Yrs. With Jays	AVG	G	AB	R	H	2B	3B	HR	RBI	SH–SF	HP	BB	SO	SB–CS
Bonnell, Barry	LF-RF-CF	10/27/53	Clermont County, OH	BR/TR	6-3	200	'80-83	.281	457	1504	184	422	76	14	33	187	10–13	6	114	187	31–16
Borders, Pat	C	5/14/63	Columbus, OH	BR/TR	6-2	200	'88-94, '99	.256	747	2309	205	590	127	9	54	272	19–17	6	112	364	6–6
Bosetti, Rick	CF	8/5/53	Redding, CA	BR/TR	5-11	185	'78-81	.252	376	1422	149	359	69	8	17	129	13–10	8	69	170	23–30
Bowling, Steve	RF-CF-LF	6/26/52	Tulsa, OK	BR/TR	6-0	185	'77	.206	89	194	19	40	9	1	1	13	3–2	0	37	41	2–3
Braun, Steve	DH	5/8/48	Trenton, NJ	BL/TR	5-10	180	'80	.273	37	55	4	15	2	0	1	9	0–0	0	8	5	0–0
Brenly, Bob	DH-C-1B	2/25/54	Coshocton, OH	BR/TR	6-2	210	'89	.170	48	88	9	15	3	1	1	6	1–0	0	10	17	1–0
Brito, Tilson	2B-3B-SS	5/28/72	Santo Domingo, D.R.	BR/TR	6-0	175	'96-97	.228	75	206	19	47	10	0	1	15	2–2	5	19	46	2–1
Brown, Bobby	LF-RF	5/24/54	Norfolk, VA	BB/TR	6-1	205	'79	.000	4	10	1	0	0	0	0	0	0–0	0	2	1	0–0
Brown, Kevin	C	4/21/73	Valparaiso, IN	BR/TR	6-2	200	'98-99	.277	54	119	18	33	9	1	2	16	3–4	2	9	34	0–0
Brumfield, Jacob	CF-RF-LF	5/27/65	Bogalusa, LA	BR/TR	6-0	185	'96-97, '99	.238	210	652	99	155	32	6	16	91	5–7	5	57	128	17–9

Jeff Burroughs | Homer Bush | Sal Butera | Rich Butler | Rob Butler | Francisco Cabrera | Miguel Cairo | Sil Campusano | Willie Canate | J.J. Cannon

	Position	Birthdate	Birthplace	Bats/Throws	HT.	WT.	Yrs. With Jays	AVG	G	AB	R	H	2B	3B	HR	RBI	SH–SF	HP	BB	SO	SB–CS
Burroughs, Jeff	DH	3/7/51	Long Beach, CA	BR/TR	6-1	200	'85	.257	86	191	19	49	9	3	6	28	0–2	0	34	36	0–1
Bush, Homer	2B-SS	11/12/72	East St. Louis, IL	BR/TR	5-11	180	'99-	.289	204	782	107	219	34	4	6	73	12–4	11	39	142	41–12
Butera, Sal	C	9/25/52	Richmond Hill, NY	BR/TR	6-0	190	'88	.233	23	60	3	14	2	1	1	6	1–0	0	1	9	0–0
Butler, Rich	LF-DH	5/1/73	Toronto, ON	BL/TR	6-1	180	'97	.286	7	14	3	4	1	0	0	2	0–0	0	2	3	0–1
Butler, Rob	LF-CF	4/10/70	East York, ON	BL/TL	5-11	185	'93-94, '99	.209	66	129	22	27	4	1	0	8	4–2	3	14	20	2–3
Cabrera, Francisco	DH	10/10/66	Santo Domingo, D.R.	BR/TR	6-4	193	'89	.167	3	12	1	2	1	0	0	0	0–0	0	1	3	0–0
Cairo, Miguel	2B	5/4/74	Anaco, Venezuela	BR/TR	6-0	160	'96	.222	9	27	5	6	2	0	0	1	0–0	1	2	9	0–0
Campusano, Sil	CF-RF-LF	12/31/65	Santo Domingo, D.R.	BR/TR	6-0	175	'88	.218	73	142	14	31	10	2	2	12	2–1	4	9	33	0–0
Canate, Willie	LF-RF-CF	12/11/71	Maracaibo, Venezuela	BR/TR	6-0	170	'93	.213	38	47	12	10	0	0	1	3	2–1	1	6	15	1–1
Cannon, J.J.	RF-LF-CF	7/13/53	Camp Lejeune, NC	BL/TR	6-3	193	'79	.177	131	192	30	34	1	1	1	9	3–0	1	1	48	14–4

Jose Canseco

Joe Carter

Rico Carty

Alberto Castillo

Domingo Cedeno

Rick Cerone

Darnell Coles

Dave Collins

Marty Cordova

Ted Cox

	Position	Birthdate	Birthplace	Bats/Throws	HT.	WT.	Yrs. With Jays	AVG	G	AB	R	H	2B	3B	HR	RBI	SH-SF	HP	BB	SO	SB-CS
Canseco, Jose	DH-LF-RF	7/2/64	Havana, Cuba	BR/TR	6-4	240	'98	.237	151	583	98	138	26	0	46	107	0–4	6	65	159	29–17
Carter, Joe	OF-DH-1B	3/7/60	Oklahoma City, OK	BR/TR	6-3	215	'91-97	.257	1039	4093	578	1051	218	28	203	736	1–65	49	286	696	78–26
Carty, Rico	DH	9/1/39	San Pedro de Macoris, D.R.	BR/TR	6-3	200	'78-79	.269	236	848	99	228	42	0	32	123	1–0	1	82	86	4–2
Castillo, Alberto	C	2/10/70	S.Juan de la Maguana, D.R.	BR/TR	6-0	185	2000-	.211	66	185	14	39	7	0	1	16	2–3	0	21	36	0–0
Cedeno, Domingo	2B-SS-3B	11/4/68	LaRomana, D.R.	BB/TR	6-1	170	'93-96	.246	190	586	81	144	18	5	6	48	13–6	4	36	56	7–6
Cerone, Rick	C	5/19/54	Newark, NJ	BR/TR	5-11	192	'77-79	.229	255	851	79	195	39	6	11	91	8–4	2	66	84	1–7
Coles, Darnell	LF-3B-1B	6/2/62	San Bernardino, CA	BR/TR	6-1	185	'93-94	.234	112	337	41	79	15	2	8	41	1–4	5	26	54	1–1
Collins, Dave	LF	10/20/52	Rapid City, SD	BB/TL	5-11	175	'83-84	.291	246	843	114	245	36	19	3	78	8–5	11	76	108	91–21
Cordova, Marty	LF-RF-DH	7/10/69	Las Vegas, NV	BR/TR	6-0	200	2000	.245	62	200	23	49	7	0	4	18	0–0	3	18	35	3–2
Cox, Ted	3B	1/24/55	Oklahoma City, OK	BR/TR	6-3	195	'81	.300	16	50	6	15	4	0	2	9	0–0	0	5	10	0–1

Felipe Crespo

Jose Cruz

Mark Dalesandro

Bob Davis

Dick Davis

Carlos Delgado

Jeff DeWillis

Carlos Diaz

Rob Ducey

Mariano Duncan

	Position	Birthdate	Birthplace	Bats/Throws	HT.	WT.	Yrs. With Jays	AVG	G	AB	R	H	2B	3B	HR	RBI	SH-SF	HP	BB	SO	SB-CS
Crespo, Felipe	RF-2B-3B	3/5/73	Rio Piedras, P.R.	BB/TR	5-11	195	'96-98	.246	100	207	20	51	12	2	2	24	5–2	5	29	44	5–3
Cruz, Jose	CF-LF	4/19/74	Arroyo, P.R.	BB/TR	6-0	190	'97-	.243	428	1516	240	368	72	11	70	197	3–11	2	220	391	46–15
Dalesandro, Mark	C-3B-DH	5/14/68	Chicago, IL	BR/TR	6-0	185	'98-99	.266	48	94	11	25	5	0	2	15	0–2	1	1	8	1–0
Davis, Bob	C	3/1/52	Pryor, OK	BR/TR	6-0	180	'80	.189	123	307	24	58	13	0	5	27	14–0	2	17	40	0–0
Davis, Dick	LF-DH	9/25/53	Long Beach, CA	BR/TR	6-3	195	'82	.286	3	7	0	2	0	0	0	2	0–1	0	0	1	0–0
Delgado, Carlos	1B-DH-LF	6/25/72	Mayaguez, P.R.	BL/TR	6-3	220	'93-	.282	829	2901	493	818	214	7	190	604	0–32	61	436	728	5–6
DeWillis, Jeff	C	4/13/65	Houston, TX	BR/TR	6-2	170	'87	.120	13	25	2	3	1	0	1	2	1–0	0	2	12	0–0
Diaz, Carlos	C	12/24/64	Elizabeth, NJ	BR/TR	6-3	195	'90	.333	9	3	1	1	0	0	0	0	1–0	0	0	2	0–0
Ducey, Rob	LF-CF-RF	5/24/65	Toronto, ON	BL/TR	6-2	180	'87-92, 2000	.234	188	333	52	77	18	3	2	31	4–4	1	37	95	8–3
Duncan, Mariano	2B	3/13/63	San Pedro de Macoris, D.R.	BR/TR	6-0	185	'97	.228	39	167	20	38	6	0	0	12	0–0	3	6	39	4–2

Jim Eppard

Tom Evans

Sam Ewing

Ron Fairly

Junior Felix

Tony Fernandez

Cecil Fielder

Darrin Fletcher

Brad Fullmer

Carlos Garcia

	Position	Birthdate	Birthplace	Bats/Throws	HT.	WT.	Yrs. With Jays	AVG	G	AB	R	H	2B	3B	HR	RBI	SH-SF	HP	BB	SO	SB-CS
Eppard, Jim	PH	4/27/60	South Bend, IN	BL/TL	6-2	180	'90	.200	6	5	0	1	0	0	0	0	0–0	1	0	2	0–0
Evans, Tom	3B	7/9/74	Kirkland, WA	BR/TR	6-1	200	'97-98	.229	19	48	7	11	2	0	1	2	0–0	1	3	12	0–1
Ewing, Sam	RF-DH	4/9/49	Lewisburg, TN	BL/TR	6-3	200	'77-78	.267	137	300	27	80	8	2	6	43	3–1	0	24	51	1–1
Fairly, Ron	DH-1B-RF	7/12/38	Macon, GA	BL/TL	5-10	181	'77	.279	132	458	60	128	24	2	19	64	8–2	2	58	58	0–4
Felix, Junior	RF-CF	10/3/67	Laguna Salada, D.R.	BB/TR	5-11	165	'89-90	.261	237	878	135	229	37	15	24	111	2–8	5	78	200	31–20
Fernandez, Tony	SS-3B-2B	6/30/62	San Pedro de Macoris, D.R.	BB/TR	6-2	175	'83-90, '93, '98-99	.297	1402	5276	699	1565	287	72	59	601	34–43	47	438	485	172–85
Fielder, Cecil	DH-1B	9/21/63	Los Angeles, CA	BR/TR	6-3	240	'85-88	.243	220	506	67	123	19	2	31	84	0–3	3	46	144	0–2
Fletcher, Darrin	C	10/3/66	Elmhurst, IL	BL/TR	6-1	199	'98-	.298	361	1235	128	368	68	2	47	190	1–15	17	71	131	1–0
Fullmer, Brad	DH	1/17/75	Chatsworth, CA	BL/TR	6-1	185	2000-	.295	133	482	76	142	29	1	32	104	0–6	6	30	68	3–1
Garcia, Carlos	2B	10/15/67	Tachira, Venezuela	BR/TR	6-1	185	'97	.220	103	350	29	77	18	2	3	23	10–4	2	15	60	11–3

Damaso Garcia

Pedro Garcia

Ray Giannelli

Luis Gomez

Rene Gonzales

Alex Gonzalez

Curtis Goodwin

Craig Grebeck

Shawn Green

Charlie Greene

	Position	Birthdate	Birthplace	Bats/Throws	HT.	WT.	Yrs. With Jays	AVG	G	AB	R	H	2B	3B	HR	RBI	SH-SF	HP	BB	SO	SB-CS
Garcia, Damaso	2B	2/7/55	Moca, D.R.	BR/TR	6-0	170	'80-86	.288	902	3572	453	1028	172	26	32	296	27–20	27	110	284	194–86
Garcia, Pedro	2B-DH	4/17/50	Guayama, P.R.	BR/TR	5-10	175	'77	.208	41	130	10	27	10	1	0	9	3–0	3	5	21	0–0
Giannelli, Ray	3B	2/5/66	Brooklyn, NY	BL/TR	6-0	195	'91	.167	9	24	2	4	1	0	0	0	0–0	0	5	9	1–0
Gomez, Luis	SS-3B-2B	8/19/51	Guadalajara, Mexico	BR/TR	5-9	150	'78-79	.227	212	576	50	131	14	3	0	42	21–3	0	40	58	3–10
Gonzales, Rene	SS-3B-2B	9/3/60	Austin, TX	BR/TR	6-3	201	'91	.195	71	118	16	23	3	0	1	6	6–1	4	12	22	0–0
Gonzalez, Alex	SS	4/8/73	Miami, FL	BR/TR	6-0	180	'94-	.243	736	2622	328	637	147	15	66	274	57–13	25	214	609	67–28
Goodwin, Curtis	CF	9/30/72	Oakland, CA	BL/TL	5-11	180	'99	.000	2	8	0	0	0	0	0	0	0–0	0	0	3	0–0
Grebeck, Craig	2B-SS-DH	12/29/64	Johnstown, PA	BR/TR	5-7	148	'98-2000	.289	202	655	89	189	43	2	5	60	12–4	8	69	88	2–2
Green, Shawn	RF	11/10/72	Des Plaines, IL	BL/TL	6-4	190	'93-99	.286	716	2513	402	718	164	15	119	376	2–17	28	206	510	76–25
Greene, Charlie	C	1/23/71	Miami, FL	BR/TR	6-1	170	2000	.111	3	9	0	1	0	0	0	0	0–0	0	0	5	0–0

Todd Greene

Willie Greene

Alfredo Griffin

Kelly Gruber

Jeff Hearron

Rickey Henderson

Pedro Hernandez

Toby Hernandez

Glenallen Hill

Paul Hodgson

	Position	Birthdate	Birthplace	Bats/Throws	HT.	WT.	Yrs. With Jays	AVG	G	AB	R	H	2B	3B	HR	RBI	SH–SF	HP	BB	SO	SB–CS
Greene, Todd	DH-C	5/8/71	Augusta, GA	BR/TR	5-10	195	2000-	.235	34	85	11	20	2	0	5	10	0–0	0	5	18	0–0
Greene, Willie	DH-3B	9/23/71	Milledgeville, GA	BL/TR	5-11	184	'99	.204	81	226	22	46	7	0	12	41	0–2	0	20	56	0–0
Griffin, Alfredo	SS-2B	10/6/57	Santo Domingo, D.R.	BB/TR	5-11	165	'79-84, '92-93	.249	982	3396	382	844	127	50	13	231	74–24	14	146	313	79–73
Gruber, Kelly	3B-IF-OF	2/26/62	Houston, TX	BR/TR	6-0	185	'84-92	.259	921	3094	421	800	145	24	114	434	13–35	35	195	493	80–33
Hearron, Jeff	C	11/19/61	Long Beach, CA	BR/TR	6-1	195	'85-86	.200	16	30	2	6	1	0	0	4	0–0	0	3	9	0–0
Henderson, Rickey	LF	12/25/58	Chicago, IL	BR/TL	5-10	195	'93	.215	44	163	37	35	3	1	4	12	1–2	2	35	19	22–2
Hernandez, Pedro	DH-3B-LF	4/4/59	LaRomana, D.R.	BR/TR	6-1	160	'79'82	.000	11	9	2	0	0	0	0	0	0–0	0	0	3	0–0
Hernandez, Toby	C	11/30/58	Calabozo, Venezuela	BR/TR	6-1	160	'84	.500	3	2	1	1	0	0	0	0	0–0	0	0	0	0–0
Hill, Glenallen	RF-LF-DH	3/22/65	Santa Cruz, CA	BR/TR	6-2	210	'89-91	.243	138	411	65	100	16	5	16	50	0–2	0	28	98	12–6
Hodgson, Paul	LF-DH	4/14/60	Montreal, QC	BR/TR	6-2	190	'80	.220	20	41	5	9	0	1	1	5	2–0	0	3	12	0–1

Dave Hollins

Willie Horton

Roy Howell

Michael Huff

Tommy Hutton

Alex Infante

Garth Iorg

Darrin Jackson

Anthony Johnson

Cliff Johnson

	Position	Birthdate	Birthplace	Bats/Throws	HT.	WT.	Yrs. With Jays	AVG	G	AB	R	H	2B	3B	HR	RBI	SH–SF	HP	BB	SO	SB–CS
Hollins, Dave	DH	5/25/66	Buffalo, NY	BB/TR	6-1	207	'99	.222	27	99	12	22	5	0	2	6	0–0	0	5	22	0–0
Horton, Willie	DH	10/18/42	Arno, VA	BR/TR	5-11	209	'78	.205	33	122	12	25	6	0	3	19	0–1	0	3	29	0–0
Howell, Roy	3B	12/18/53	Lompoc, CA	BL/TR	6-1	190	'77-80	.272	516	1954	219	532	101	17	43	234	12–11	13	178	337	5–6
Huff, Michael	LF-CF-RF	8/11/63	Honolulu, HI	BR/TR	6-1	190	'94-96	.267	152	374	50	100	24	5	4	34	5–6	4	50	53	3–2
Hutton, Tommy	LF-RF-1B	4/20/46	Los Angeles, CA	BL/TL	5-11	180	'78	.254	64	173	19	44	9	0	2	9	5–0	0	19	12	1–2
Infante, Alex	3B-SS-DH	12/4/61	Barquisimeto, Venezuela	BR/TR	5-10	175	'87-89	.185	40	27	8	5	0	0	0	0	1–0	0	2	5	1–0
Iorg, Garth	3B-2B-LF	10/12/54	Arcata, CA	BR/TR	5-11	170	'78, '80-87	.258	931	2450	251	633	125	16	20	238	21–19	11	114	298	22–17
Jackson, Darrin	RF-CF	8/22/62	Los Angeles, CA	BR/TR	6-0	185	'93	.216	46	176	15	38	8	0	5	19	5–0	0	8	53	0–2
Johnson, Anthony	LF-DH	6/23/56	Memphis, TN	BR/TR	6-3	195	'82	.235	70	98	17	23	2	1	3	14	1–1	0	11	26	3–13
Johnson, Cliff	DH	7/22/47	San Antonio, TX	BR/TR	6-4	225	'83-86	.273	400	1175	162	321	58	3	54	202	1–10	12	178	203	0–3

Tim Johnson

Pat D. Kelly

Pat F. Kelly

Jeff Kent

Mickey Klutts

Randy Knorr

Craig Kusick

Tom Lawless

Rick Leach

Manuel Lee

	Position	Birthdate	Birthplace	Bats/Throws	HT.	WT.	Yrs. With Jays	AVG	G	AB	R	H	2B	3B	HR	RBI	SH–SF	HP	BB	SO	SB–CS
Johnson, Tim	SS-2B	7/22/49	Grand Forks, ND	BL/TR	6-1	170	'78-79	.212	110	165	15	35	4	1	0	9	5–1	1	16	31	0–2
Kelly, Pat D.	C	8/27/55	Santa Maria, CA	BR/TR	6-3	210	'80	.286	3	7	0	2	0	0	0	0	0–0	0	0	4	0–0
Kelly, Pat F.	2B	10/14/67	Philadelphia, PA	BR/TR	6-0	182	'99	.267	37	116	17	31	7	0	6	20	1–3	0	10	23	0–1
Kent, Jeff	3B-2B	3/7/68	Bellflower, CA	BR/TR	6-1	185	'92	.240	65	192	36	46	13	1	8	35	0–4	6	20	47	2–1
Klutts, Mickey	3B-DH	9/20/54	Montebello, CA	BR/TR	5-11	189	'83	.256	22	43	3	11	0	0	3	5	0–0	1	1	11	0–1
Knorr, Randy	C	11/12/68	San Gabriel, CA	BR/TR	6-2	215	'91-95	.281	135	377	50	88	13	2	15	57	3–1	1	32	98	0–0
Kusick, Craig	1B	9/30/48	Milwaukee, WI	BR/TR	6-3	232	'79	.204	24	54	3	11	1	0	2	7	0–1	1	7	7	0–0
Lawless, Tom	3B-RF-DH	12/19/56	Erie, PA	BR/TR	5-11	170	'89-90	.207	74	82	21	17	1	0	0	4	1–1	0	7	13	12–3
Leach, Rick	RF-DH-1B	5/4/57	Ann Arbor, MI	BL/TL	6-0	195	'84-88	.283	376	763	95	216	46	6	8	95	0–9	3	67	99	0–2
Lee, Manuel	SS-2B	6/17/65	San Pedro de Macoris, D.R.	BB/TR	5-9	161	'85-92	.254	753	2152	231	547	67	17	16	199	28–17	2	160	426	26–15

Patrick Lennon

Nelson Liriano

Ken Macha

Mike Macha

Mike Maksudian

Candy Maldonado

Fred Manrique

Norberto Martin

Buck Martinez

Dave Martinez

	Position	Birthdate	Birthplace	Bats/Throws	HT.	WT.	Yrs. With Jays	AVG	G	AB	R	H	2B	3B	HR	RBI	SH–SF	HP	BB	SO	SB–CS
Lennon, Patrick	RF-LF	4/27/68	Whiteville, NC	BR/TR	6-2	200	'98-99	.242	11	33	4	8	4	0	1	6	0–0	1	2	12	0–0
Liriano, Nelson	2B	6/3/64	Puerto Plata, D.R.	BB/TR	5-10	172	'87-90	.251	318	1022	132	257	45	9	11	101	18–7	5	96	133	44–19
Macha, Ken	3B-1B	9/29/50	Monroeville, PA	BR/TR	6-2	217	'81	.200	37	85	4	17	2	0	0	6	0–1	0	8	15	1–1
Macha, Mike	3B-C	2/17/54	Victoria, TX	BR/TR	5-11	180	'80	.000	5	8	0	0	0	0	0	0	0–0	0	0	1	0–0
Maksudian, Mike	1B	5/28/66	Belleville, IL	BL/TR	5-11	220	'92	.000	3	3	0	0	0	0	0	0	0–0	0	0	0	0–0
Maldonado, Candy	LF-RF	9/5/60	Humacao, P.R.	BR/TR	6-0	190	'91-92, '95	.272	250	826	112	225	47	4	34	119	2–8	15	107	210	6–3
Manrique, Fred	SS-2B-3B	11/5/61	Edo Bolivar, Venezuela	BR/TR	6-1	175	'81, '84	.189	24	37	1	7	0	0	0	2	0–0	1	0	13	0–1
Martin, Norberto	2B-SS	12/10/66	San Pedro de Macoris, D.R.	BR/TR	5-10	164	'99	.222	9	27	3	6	2	0	0	0	0–0	2	4	4	0–0
Martinez, Buck	C	11/7/48	Redding, CA	BR/TR	5-10	190	'81-86	.222	454	1100	114	244	63	2	35	154	11–23	4	123	175	2–5
Martinez, Dave	RF	9/26/64	New York, NY	BL/TL	5-10	175	2000	.311	47	180	29	56	10	1	2	22	0–1	1	24	28	4–2

Domingo Martinez

Sandy Martinez

Jim Mason

Mike Matheny

Len Matuszek

John Mayberry

Lee Mazzilli

Fred McGriff

Dave McKay

Brian McRae

	Position	Birthdate	Birthplace	Bats/Throws	HT.	WT.	Yrs. With Jays	AVG	G	AB	R	H	2B	3B	HR	RBI	SH-SF	HP	BB	SO	SB-CS
Martinez, Domingo	1B-3B	8/4/67	Santo Domingo, D.R.	BR/TR	6-2	215	'92-93	.409	15	22	4	9	0	0	2	6	0–0	0	1	8	0–0
Martinez, Sandy	C	10/3/72	Villa Mella, D.R.	BL/TR	6-2	200	'95-97	.232	141	422	30	98	21	3	5	43	1–2	5	24	104	0–0
Mason, Jim	SS	8/14/50	Mobile, AL	BL/TR	6-2	190	'77	.165	22	79	10	13	3	0	0	2	2–0	0	7	10	1–1
Matheny, Mike	C	9/22/70	Columbus, OH	BR/TR	6-3	205	'99	.215	57	163	16	35	6	0	3	17	2–1	1	12	37	0–0
Matuszek, Len	DH	9/27/54	Toledo, OH	BL/TR	6-2	195	'85	.212	62	151	23	32	6	2	2	15	0–4	0	11	24	2–1
Mayberry, John	1B-DH	2/18/49	Detroit, MI	BL/TL	6-3	220	'78-82	.256	549	1803	215	461	62	6	92	272	5–16	21	258	248	3–4
Mazzilli, Lee	DH-1B-RF	3/25/55	New York, NY	BB/TR	6-1	185	'89	.227	28	66	12	15	3	0	4	11	0–1	2	17	16	2–0
McGriff, Fred	1B-DH	10/31/63	Tampa, FL	BL/TL	6-3	215	'86-90	.278	578	1944	348	540	99	8	125	305	2–13	11	352	495	21–10
McKay, Dave	2B-3B	3/14/50	Vancouver, BC	BB/TR	6-1	195	'77-79	.223	287	934	96	208	33	11	10	79	24–3	4	34	160	7–6
McRae, Brian	DH-CF	8/27/67	Bradenton, FL	BB/TR	6-0	185	'99	.195	31	82	11	16	3	1	3	11	1–0	2	16	22	0–1

Orlando Merced

Brian Milner

Paul Molitor

Raul Mondesi

Charlie Moore

Mickey Morandini

Lloyd Moseby

Julio Mosquera

Chad Mottola

Rance Mulliniks

	Position	Birthdate	Birthplace	Bats/Throws	HT.	WT.	Yrs. With Jays	AVG	G	AB	R	H	2B	3B	HR	RBI	SH-SF	HP	BB	SO	SB-CS
Merced, Orlando	RF	11/2/66	Hato Rey, P.R.	BB/TR	5-11	170	'97	.266	98	368	45	98	23	2	9	40	0–2	3	47	62	7–3
Milner, Brian	C	11/17/59	Fort Worth, TX	BR/TR	6-2	200	'78	.444	2	9	3	4	0	1	0	2	0–0	0	0	1	0–0
Molitor, Paul	DH-1B	8/22/56	St. Paul, MN	BR/TR	6-0	185	'93-95	.315	405	1615	270	508	98	11	51	246	4–17	9	193	172	54–4
Mondesi, Raul	RF	3/12/71	San Cristobal, D.R.	BR/TR	5-11	202	2000-	.271	96	388	78	105	22	2	24	67	0–3	3	32	73	22–6
Moore, Charlie	C-RF-LF	6/21/53	Birmingham, AL	BR/TR	5-11	180	'87	.215	51	107	15	23	10	1	1	7	4–0	1	13	12	0–0
Morandini, Mickey	2B	4/22/66	Kittanning, PA	BL/TR	5-11	171	2000	.271	35	107	10	29	2	1	0	7	2–0	0	7	23	1–0
Moseby, Lloyd	CF	11/5/59	Portland, AR	BL/TR	6-3	200	'80-89	.257	1392	5124	768	1319	242	60	149	651	38–40	50	547	1015	255–86
Mosquera, Julio	C	1/29/72	Panama City, Panama	BR/TR	6-0	165	'96-97	.233	11	30	2	7	3	0	0	2	0–0	0	0	5	0–1
Mottola, Chad	RF	10/15/71	Augusta, GA	BR/TR	6-3	220	2000	.222	3	9	1	2	0	0	0	2	0–0	1	0	4	0–0
Mulliniks, Rance	3B-DH	1/15/56	Tulare, CA	BL/TR	6-0	170	'82-92	.280	1115	3013	382	843	204	14	68	389	13–24	4	416	465	12–10

Greg Myers

Steve Nicosia

Otis Nixon

Tim Nordbrook

Wayne Nordhagen

Charlie O'Brien

John Olerud

Al Oliver

Jorge Orta

Willis Otanez

	Position	Birthdate	Birthplace	Bats/Throws	HT.	WT.	Yrs. With Jays	AVG	G	AB	R	H	2B	3B	HR	RBI	SH-SF	HP	BB	SO	SB-CS
Myers, Greg	C	4/14/66	Riverside, CA	BL/TR	6-2	205	'87, '89-92	.238	240	673	63	160	37	1	14	72	1–9	0	50	95	0–2
Nicosia, Steve	C	8/6/55	Paterson, NJ	BR/TR	5-10	185	'85	.267	6	15	0	4	0	0	0	1	0–0	0	0	0	0–0
Nixon, Otis	CF	1/9/59	Evergreen, OH	BB/TR	6-2	180	'96-97	.275	226	897	141	247	27	2	2	55	13–5	1	123	122	101–23
Nordbrook, Tim	SS	7/7/49	Baltimore, MD	BR/TR	6-1	180	'77	.175	31	63	10	11	0	1	0	1	1–0	1	4	11	1–0
Nordhagen, Wayne	DH-LF	7/4/48	Thief River Falls, MN	BR/TR	6-2	205	'82	.270	72	185	12	50	6	0	1	20	0–2	0	10	22	0–2
O'Brien, Charlie	C	5/1/60	Tulsa, OK	BR/TR	6-2	190	'96-97	.230	178	549	55	126	32	1	17	71	6–8	28	51	113	0–3
Olerud, John	1B-DH	8/5/68	Seattle, WA	BL/TL	6-5	220	'89-96	.293	920	3103	464	910	213	6	109	468	5–35	32	514	430	3–8
Oliver, Al	DH	10/14/46	Portsmouth, OH	BL/TL	6-0	195	'85	.251	61	187	20	47	6	1	5	23	0–0	1	7	13	0–0
Orta, Jorge	DH-RF-LF	11/26/50	Mazatlan, Mexico	BL/TR	5-10	175	'83	.237	103	245	30	58	6	3	10	38	0–4	0	19	29	1–2
Otanez, Willis	3B-1B-DH	4/19/73	Las Vega Baha, D.R.	BR/TR	6-1	200	'99	.252	42	127	21	32	8	0	5	13	0–0	1	9	30	0–0

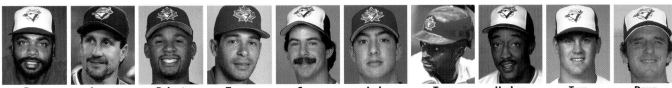

Dave Parker

Lance Parrish

Robert Perez

Tomas Perez

Geno Petralli

Josh Phelps

Tony Phillips

Hosken Powell

Tom Quinlan

Doug Rader

	Position	Birthdate	Birthplace	Bats/Throws	HT.	WT.	Yrs. With Jays	AVG	G	AB	R	H	2B	3B	HR	RBI	SH-SF	HP	BB	SO	SB-CS
Parker, Dave	DH	6/9/51	Grenada, MS	BL/TR	6-5	230	'91	.333	13	36	2	12	4	0	0	3	0–0	0	4	7	0–1
Parrish, Lance	C	6/15/56	Clairton, PA	BR/TR	6-3	220	'95	.202	70	178	15	36	9	0	4	22	6–2	1	15	52	0–0
Perez, Robert	LF-RF	6/4/69	Bolivar, Venezuela	BR/TR	6-3	205	'94-97	.271	144	336	36	91	16	1	5	30	4–1	1	8	39	3–0
Perez, Tomas	2B-SS	12/29/73	Barquisimeto, Venezuela	BB/TR	5-11	165	'95-98	.234	178	525	46	123	19	7	2	36	10–2	2	44	78	2–4
Petralli, Geno	C-3B-DH	9/25/59	Sacramento, CA	BL/TR	6-2	185	'82-84	.314	25	51	3	16	2	0	0	1	1–0	0	5	7	0–0
Phelps, Josh	C	5/12/78	Anchorage, AK	BR/TR	6-3	215	2000-	.000	1	1	0	0	0	0	0	0	0–0	0	0	1	0–0
Phillips, Tony	LF-RF	4/25/59	Atlanta, GA	BB/TR	5-10	175	'98	.354	13	48	9	17	5	0	1	7	0–1	2	9	6	0–0
Powell, Hosken	RF-DH-LF	5/14/55	Selma, AL	BL/TL	6-1	185	'82-83	.250	152	348	49	87	13	4	4	33	0–4	0	17	31	6–4
Quinlan, Tom	3B	3/27/68	St. Paul, MN	BR/TR	6-3	200	'90, '92	.118	14	17	2	2	1	0	0	2	0–0	1	2	10	0–0
Rader, Doug	3B-DH	7/30/44	Chicago, IL	BR/TR	6-3	215	'77	.240	96	313	47	75	18	2	13	40	4–5	3	38	67	2–1

Domingo Ramos

Dave Revering

Leon Roberts

Bob Robertson

Phil Roof

Juan Samuel

Anthony Sanders

Benito Santiago

Dick Schofield

John Scott

	Position	Birthdate	Birthplace	Bats/Throws	HT.	WT.	Yrs. With Jays	AVG	G	AB	R	H	2B	3B	HR	RBI	SH–SF	HP	BB	SO	SB–CS
Ramos, Domingo	2B-SS-DH	3/29/58	Santiago, D.R.	BR/TR	5-10	155	'80	.125	5	16	0	2	0	0	0	0	0–0	0	2	5	0–0
Revering, Dave	DH	2/12/53	Roseville, CA	BL/TR	6-4	210	'82	.215	55	135	15	29	6	0	5	18	0–2	0	22	30	0–3
Roberts, Leon	DH-LF	1/22/51	Vicksburg, MI	BR/TR	6-3	200	'82	.229	40	105	6	24	4	0	1	5	0–1	0	7	16	1–1
Robertson, Bob	1B-DH	10/2/46	Frostburg, MD	BR/TR	6-1	210	'79	.103	15	29	1	3	0	0	1	1	0–0	0	3	9	0–0
Roof, Phil	C	3/5/41	Paducah, KY	BR/TR	6-3	210	'77	.000	3	5	0	0	0	0	0	0	0–0	0	0	1	0–0
Samuel, Juan	DH-RF-IF	12/9/60	San Pedro de Macoris, D.R.	BR/TR	5-11	170	'96-98	.252	157	333	61	84	15	7	12	43	2–1	6	32	106	27–12
Sanders, Anthony	DH-LF	3/2/74	Tucson, AZ	BR/TR	6-2	200	'99	.286	3	7	1	2	1	0	0	2	0–0	0	0	2	0–0
Santiago, Benito	C	3/9/65	Ponce, P.R.	BR/TR	6-1	182	'97-98	.249	112	370	34	92	15	0	13	46	1–5	2	18	86	1–0
Schofield, Dick	SS	11/21/62	Springfield, IL	BR/TR	5-10	178	'93-94	.239	131	435	49	104	15	3	4	37	10–2	4	50	87	10–7
Scott, John	CF-LF	1/24/52	Jackson, MS	BR/TR	6-2	165	'77	.240	79	233	26	56	9	0	2	15	6–0	0	8	39	10–8

David Segui

Mike Sharperson

Ron Shepherd

Ruben Sierra

Cory Snyder

Luis Sojo

Tony Solaita

Ed Sprague

Steve Staggs

Mike Stanley

	Position	Birthdate	Birthplace	Bats/Throws	HT.	WT.	Yrs. With Jays	AVG	G	AB	R	H	2B	3B	HR	RBI	SH–SF	HP	BB	SO	SB–CS
Segui, David	DH-1B	7/19/66	Kansas City, KS	BB/TL	6-1	202	'99	.316	31	95	14	30	5	0	5	13	0–1	0	8	17	0–0
Sharperson, Mike	2B	10/4/61	Orangeburg, SC	BR/TR	6-3	191	'87	.208	32	96	4	20	4	1	0	9	1–0	1	7	15	2–1
Shepherd, Ron	OF-DH	10/27/60	Longview, TX	BR/TR	6-4	175	'84-86	.167	115	108	23	18	6	0	2	5	1–0	0	5	37	3–1
Sierra, Ruben	LF-DH-RF	10/6/65	Rio Piedras, P.R.	BB/TR	6-1	200	'97	.208	14	48	4	10	0	2	1	5	0–1	0	3	13	0–0
Snyder, Cory	RF-IF-DH	11/11/62	Inglewood, CA	BR/TR	6-3	185	'91	.143	21	49	4	7	0	1	0	6	1–1	0	3	19	0–0
Sojo, Luis	2B-SS-LF	1/3/66	Caracas, Venezuela	BR/TR	5-11	174	'90, '93	.205	52	127	19	26	5	0	1	15	2–1	0	4	2	0–0
Solaita, Tony	DH-1B	1/15/47	Nuuuli, Amer. Samoa	bl/tl	6-0	215	'79	.265	36	102	14	27	8	1	2	13	0–2	0	17	16	0–0
Sprague, Ed	3B-1B-C	7/25/67	Castro Valley, CA	BR/TR	6-2	210	'91-98	.245	888	3156	388	773	170	10	113	418	5–28	68	270	647	2–13
Staggs, Steve	2B	5/6/51	Anchorage, AK	BR/TR	5-9	150	'77	.258	72	291	37	75	11	6	2	28	3–1	0	36	38	5–9
Stanley, Mike	DH-1B	6/25/53	Fort Lauderdale, FL	BR/TR	6-1	185	'98	.240	98	341	49	82	13	0	22	47	0–3	5	56	86	2–1

Matt Stark

Shannon Stewart

Dave Stieb

Pat Tabler

Andy Thompson

Lou Thornton

Hector Torres

Willie Upshaw

Otto Velez

Ozzie Virgil

	Position	Birthdate	Birthplace	Bats/Throws	HT.	WT.	Yrs. With Jays	AVG	G	AB	R	H	2B	3B	HR	RBI	SH–SF	HP	BB	SO	SB–CS
Stark, Matt	C	1/21/65	Whittier, CA	BR/TR	6-4	225	'87	.083	5	12	1	0	0	0	0	0	0–0	0	0	0	0–0
Stewart, Shannon	LF-CF	2/25/74	Cincinnati, OH	BR/TR	6-0	175	'95-	.297	488	1930	328	574	114	17	44	216	10–11	34	188	272	121–40
Stieb, Dave	LF	7/22/57	Santa Ana, CA	BR/TR	6-1	195	'79-92, '98	.000	439	2	2	0	0	0	0	0	0–0	0	0	0	0–0
Tabler, Pat	DH-1B-LF	2/2/58	Hamilton, OH	BR/TR	6-2	200	'91-92	.231	131	320	31	74	10	1	1	37	2–6	1	41	35	0–0
Thompson, Andy	LF	10/8/75	Oconomowoc, WI	BR/TR	6-3	210	2000-	.167	2	6	2	1	0	0	0	1	0–0	1	3	2	0–0
Thornton, Lou	LF-RF-DH	4/26/63	Montgomery, AL	BL/TR	6-2	185	'85, '87-88	.237	79	76	24	18	1	1	1	8	0–0	1	3	24	1–1
Torres, Hector	SS-2B	9/16/45	Monterrey, Mexico	BR/TR	6-0	175	'77	.241	91	266	33	64	7	3	5	26	5–4	1	16	33	1–1
Upshaw, Willie	1B-LF	4/27/57	Blanco, TX	BL/TL	6-0	185	'78, '80-87	.265	1115	3710	538	982	177	42	112	478	27–24	21	390	576	76–50
Velez, Otto	DH-OF-1B	11/29/50	Ponce, P.R.	BR/TR	6-0	195	'77-82	.257	522	1531	204	394	76	10	72	243	9–14	11	278	333	6–9
Virgil, Ozzie	DH-C	12/7/56	Mayaguez, P.R.	BR/TR	6-1	205	'89-90	.125	12	16	2	2	1	0	1	2	0–0	0	4	6	0–0

Turner Ward

Mitch Webster

Greg Wells

Vernon Wells

Devon White

Mark Whiten

Dan Whitmer

Ernie Whitt

Ted Wilborn

Kenny Williams

	Position	Birthdate	Birthplace	Bats/Throws	HT.	WT.	Yrs. With Jays	AVG	G	AB	R	H	2B	3B	HR	RBI	SH–SF	HP	BB	SO	SB–CS
Ward, Turner	LF-RF-CF	4/11/65	Orlando, FL	BB/TR	6-2	200	'91-93	.220	98	209	28	46	7	2	5	33	3–4	1	28	32	3–4
Webster, Mitch	CF-LF-DH	5/16/59	Larned, KS	BB/TL	6-1	185	'83-85	.206	41	34	11	7	2	1	0	4	0–0	0	2	8	0–1
Wells, Greg	1B-DH	4/25/54	McIntosh, AL	BR/TR	6-5	218	'81	.247	32	73	7	18	5	0	0	5	0–0	0	5	12	0–2
Wells, Vernon	CF	12/8/78	Shreveport, LA	BR/TR	6-1	195	'99-	.261	27	90	8	23	5	0	1	8	0–0	0	4	18	1–1
White, Devon	CF	12/29/62	Kingston, Jam.	BB/TR	6-2	182	'91-95	.270	656	2711	452	733	155	34	72	274	13–17	29	209	572	126–23
Whiten, Mark	RF	11/25/66	Pensacola, FL	BB/TR	6-3	215	'90-91	.241	79	237	24	57	5	4	4	26	0–4	1	18	49	2–1
Whitmer, Dan	C	11/23/55	Redlands, CA	BR/TR	6-3	195	'81	.111	7	9	0	1	1	0	0	0	0–0	0	1	2	0–0
Whitt, Ernie	C	6/13/52	Detroit, MI	BL/TR	6-2	200	'77-78, '80-89	.253	1218	3514	424	888	164	15	131	518	20–36	4	403	450	22–24
Wilborn, Ted	OF	12/16/58	Waco, TX	BB/TR	6-0	165	'79	.000	22	12	3	0	0	0	0	0	1–0	0	2	7	0–1
Williams, Kenny	OF-DH	4/6/64	Berkeley, CA	BR/TR	6-2	187	'90-91	.198	62	101	18	20	8	1	1	11	0–2	2	11	23	8–2

Mookie Wilson	**Dave Winfield**	**Dewayne Wise**	**Kevin Witt**	**Al Woods**	**Gary Woods**	**Chris Woodward**	**Eddie Zosky**

	Position	Birthdate	Birthplace	Bats/Throws	HT.	WT.	Yrs. With Jays	AVG	G	AB	R	H	2B	3B	HR	RBI	SH–SF	HP	BB	SO	SB–CS
Wilson, Mookie	OF-DH	2/9/56	Bamberg, SC	BB/TR	5-10	170	'89-91	.267	287	1067	139	285	57	9	7	96	11–7	7	42	174	46–8
Winfield, Dave	DH-RF	10/3/51	St. Paul, MN	BR/TR	6-6	220	'92	.290	156	583	92	169	33	3	26	108	1–3	1	82	89	2–3
Wise, Dewayne	LF-RF-CF	2/24/78	Columbia, SC	BL/TL	6-1	180	2000-	.136	28	22	3	3	0	0	0	0	0–0	1	1	5	1–1
Witt, Kevin	DH-1B	1/5/76	High Point, NC	BL/TR	6-4	195	'98-99	.195	20	41	3	8	1	0	1	5	1–0	0	2	12	0–0
Woods, Al	LF-RF-DH	8/8/53	Oakland, CA	BL/TL	6-3	195	'77-82	.270	595	1958	228	529	97	14	33	188	31–15	3	164	176	23–24
Woods, Gary	CF-RF	7/20/54	Santa Barbara, CA	BR/TR	6-2	190	'77-78	.211	68	246	22	52	10	1	0	17	3–0	2	8	39	6–4
Woodward, Chris	SS-3B-IF	6/27/76	Covina, CA	BR/TR	6-0	160	'99-	.192	51	130	17	25	8	0	3	16	1–1	0	12	34	1–0
Zosky, Eddie	SS	2/10/68	Whittier, CA	BR/TR	6-0	175	'91-92	.176	26	34	3	6	1	2	0	3	1–1	0	0	10	0–0

ROSTER ADDITIONS, 2001

Position players

Ryan Freel	**Jeff Frye**	**Luis Lopez**	**Brian Simmons**

	Position	Birthdate	Birthplace	Bats/Throws	HT.	WT.	Yrs. With Jays	AVG	G	AB	R	H	2B	3B	HR	RBI	SH–SF	HP	BB	SO	SB–CS
Freel, Ryan	2B	3/8/76	Jacksonville, FL	BR/TR	5-10	185	2001	–	–	–	–	–	–	–	–	–	–	–	–	–	–
Frye, Jeff	2B	8/31/66	Oakland, CA	BR/TR	5-9	160	2001	–	–	–	–	–	–	–	–	–	–	–	–	–	–
Lopez, Luis	1B-PH	10/5/73	Brooklyn, NY	BR/TR	6-0	205	2001	–	–	–	–	–	–	–	–	–	–	–	–	–	–
Simmons, Brian	LF-CF-PH	9/4/73	Lebanon, PA	BB/TR	6-2	190	2001	–	–	–	–	–	–	–	–	–	–	–	–	–	–

PITCHER BATTING STATISTICS

Since the advent of inter-league play in 1997, 18 Blue Jays pitchers have batted in games played under National League rules.

	Position	Birthdate	Birthplace	Bats/Throws	HT.	WT.	Yrs. With Jays	AVG	G	AB	R	H	2B	3B	HR	RBI	SH–SF	HP	BB	SO	SB–CS
Andrews, Clayton	LHP	5/15/78	Dunedin, FL	BR/TL	6-0	175	2000	.000	8	3	0	0	0	0	0	0	0–0	0	0	2	0–0
Carpenter, Chris	RHP	4/27/75	Exeter, NH	BR/TR	6-6	215	'97-	.000	105	4	0	0	0	0	0	0	0–0	0	1	2	0–0
Castillo, Frank	RHP	4/1/69	El Paso, TX	BR/TR	6-1	190	2000	.143	25	7	0	1	0	0	0	0	0–0	0	0	3	0–0
Clemens, Roger	RHP	8/4/62	Dayton, OH	BR/TR	6-4	220	'97-98	.167	67	6	1	1	1	0	0	0	1–0	0	2	0	0–0
Cubillan, Darwin	RHP	11/15/74	Bobure, Venezuela	BR/TR	6-2	170	2000	.000	7	1	0	0	0	0	0	0	0–0	0	0	0	0–0
Escobar, Kelvim	RHP	4/11/76	LaGuaira, Venezuela	BR/TR	6-1	205	'97-	.000	125	8	0	0	0	0	0	0	0–0	0	0	5	0–0
Guzman, Juan	RHP	10/28/66	Santo Domingo, D.R.	BR/TR	5-11	195	'91-98	.000	195	2	0	0	0	0	0	0	0–0	0	0	0	0–0
Halladay, Roy	RHP	5/14/77	Denver, CO	BR/TR	6-6	205	'98-	.000	57	2	0	0	0	0	0	0	1–0	0	0	2	0–0
Hamilton, Joey	RHP	9/9/70	Statesboro, GA	BR/TR	6-4	220	'99-	.000	28	2	0	0	0	0	0	0	0–0	0	0	1	0–0
Hentgen, Pat	RHP	11/13/68	Detroit, MI	BR/TR	6-2	200	'91-99	.056	252	18	0	1	0	0	0	0	1–0	0	0	8	0–0
Koch, Billy	RHP	12/14/74	Rockville Centre, NY	BR/TR	6-3	218	'99-	.000	124	2	0	0	0	0	0	0	0–0	0	0	2	0–0
Munro, Peter	RHP	6/14/75	Flushing, NY	BR/TR	6-2	200	'99-2000	.000	40	1	0	0	0	0	0	0	0–0	0	0	1	0–0
Myers, Randy	LHP	9/19/62	Vancouver, WA	BL/TL	6-1	215	'98	.000	41	1	0	0	0	0	0	0	0–0	0	0	1	0–0
Person, Robert	RHP	10/6/69	Lowell, MA	BR/TR	5-11	180	'97-99	.000	61	4	0	0	0	0	0	0	0–0	0	1	1	0–0
Quantrill, Paul	RHP	11/3/68	London, ON	BL/TR	6-1	185	'96-	.000	306	1	0	0	0	0	0	0	0–0	0	1	1	0–0
Spoljaric, Paul	LHP	9/24/70	Kelowna, BC	BR/TL	6-3	205	'94, '96-97, '99	.000	104	1	0	0	0	0	0	0	0–0	0	0	0	0–0
Wells, David	LHP	5/20/63	Torrance, CA	BL/TL	6-4	225	'87-92, '99-2000	.083	306	12	0	1	0	0	0	0	1–0	0	0	2	0–0
Williams, Woody	RHP	8/19/66	Houston, TX	BR/TR	6-0	190	'93-98	.375	166	8	0	3	0	0	0	0	0–0	0	0	2	0–0

Jim Acker

Doyle Alexander

Carlos Almanzar

Clayton Andrews

Luis Andujar

Luis Aquino

Bob Bailor

Doug Bair

John Bale

Mike Barlow

	Position	Birthdate	Birthplace	Bats/Throws	HT.	WT.	Yrs. With Jays	W–L	ERA	G	GS	CG	SHO	SV	IP	H	R	ER	HR	HB	BB	SO	WP
Acker, Jim	RHP	9/24/58	Freer, TX	BR/TR	6-2	212	'83-86, '89-91	26–22	4.07	281	17	0	0	14	524.1	535	269	237	49	25	206	273	23
Alexander, Doyle	RHP	9/4/50	Cordova, AB	BR/TR	6-3	205	'83-86	46-26	3.56	106	103	25	3	0	750.0	752	315	297	81	14	172	392	16
Almanzar, Carlos	RHP	11/6/73	Santiago, D.R.	BR/TR	6-2	166	'97-98	2–3	5.06	29	0	0	0	0	32.0	35	19	18	5	1	9	24	0
Andrews, Clayton	LHP	5/15/78	Dunedin, FL	BR/TL	6-0	175	2000	1–2	10.02	8	2	0	0	0	20.2	34	23	23	6	0	9	12	0
Andujar, Luis	RHP	11/22/72	Bani, D.R.	BR/TR	6-2	175	'96-98	1–7	6.43	25	10	0	0	0	70.0	102	59	50	13	1	24	34	4
Aquino, Luis	RHP	5/19/64	Santurce, D.R.	BR/TR	6-1	195	'86	1–1	6.35	7	0	0	0	0	11.1	14	8	8	2	0	3	5	1
Bailor, Bob	RHP	7/10/51	Connellsville, PA	BR/TR	5-11	170	'77-80	0–0	7.71	3	0	0	0	0	2.1	4	2	2	2	0	1	0	0
Bair, Doug	RHP	8/22/49	Defiance, OH	BR/TR	6-0	180	'88	0–0	4.05	10	0	0	0	0	13.1	14	6	6	2	0	3	8	1
Bale, John	LHP	5/22/74	Cheverly, MD	BL/TL	6-4	195	'99-2000	0–0	14.29	3	0	0	0	0	5.2	7	10	9	2	2	5	10	0
Barlow, Mike	RHP	4/30/48	Stamford, NY	BL/TR	6-6	215	'80-81	3–1	4.11	52	1	0	0	5	70.0	79	40	32	5	6	27	24	5

Juan Berenguer

Bud Black

Willie Blair

Brian Bohanon

Mark Bomback

Pedro Borbon

Denis Boucher

Scott Brow

Tom Bruno

DeWayne Buice

	Position	Birthdate	Birthplace	Bats/Throws	HT.	WT.	Yrs. With Jays	W–L	ERA	G	GS	CG	SHO	SV	IP	H	R	ER	HR	HB	BB	SO	WP
Berenguer, Juan	RHP	11/30/54	Aquadulce, Pan	BR/TR	5-11	215	'81	2–9	4.31	12	11	1	0	0	71.0	62	41	34	7	3	35	29	1
Black, Bud	LHP	7/9/32	St. Louis, MO	BR/TR	6-3	197	'90	2–1	4.02	3	2	0	0	0	15.2	10	7	7	2	1	3	3	0
Blair, Willie	RHP	12/18/65	Paintsville, KY	BR/TR	6-1	185	'90	3–5	4.06	27	6	0	0	0	68.2	66	33	31	4	1	28	43	3
Bohanon, Brian	LHP	8/1/68	Denton, TX	BL/TL	6-2	220	'96	0–1	7.77	20	0	0	0	1	22.0	27	19	19	4	2	19	17	2
Bomback, Mark	RHP	4/14/53	Portsmourh, VA	BR/TR	5-11	170	'81-82	6–10	4.74	36	19	0	0	0	150.0	171	86	79	16	4	60	55	9
Borbon, Pedro	LHP	11/15/67	Mao, D.R.	BR/TL	6-1	205	2000-	1–1	6.48	59	0	0	0	1	41.2	45	37	30	5	5	38	29	0
Boucher, Denis	LHP	3/7/68	Montreal, QC	BR/TL	6-1	195	'91	0–3	4.58	7	7	0	0	0	35.1	39	20	18	6	2	16	16	0
Brow, Scott	RHP	3/17/69	Butte, MT	BR/TR	6-3	200	'93-96	2–4	5.81	42	4	0	0	0	85.2	98	67	55	11	2	54	45	2
Bruno, Tom	RHP	1/26/53	Chicago, IL	BR/TR	6-5	210	'77	0–1	7.85	12	0	0	0	0	18.1	30	181	16	4	1	13	9	3
Buice, DeWayne	RHP	8/20/57	Lynwood, CA	BR/TR	6-0	170	'89	1–0	5.82	7	0	0	0	0	17.0	13	12	11	2	0	13	10	1

Tom Buskey

Jeff Byrd

Greg Cadaret

John Candelaria

Tom Candiotti

Chris Carpenter

Giovanni Carrara

Frank Castillo

Tony Castillo

Bill Caudill

	Position	Birthdate	Birthplace	Bats/Throws	HT.	WT.	Yrs. With Jays	W–L	ERA	G	GS	CG	SHO	SV	IP	H	R	ER	HR	HB	BB	SO	WP
Buskey, Tom	RHP	2/20/47	Harrisburg, PA	BR/TR	6-3	220	'78-80	9–12	3.86	85	0	0	0	7	158.2	156	73	68	22	1	55	85	3
Byrd, Jeff	RHP	11/11/56	LaMesa, CA	BR/TR	6-3	195	'77	2–13	6.18	17	17	1	0	0	87.1	98	68	60	5	0	68	40	3
Cadaret, Greg	RHP	2/27/62	Detroit, MI	BL/TL	6-3	214	'94	0–1	5.85	21	0	0	0	0	20.0	24	15	13	4	0	17	15	6
Candelaria, John	LHP	11/6/53	New York, NY	BL/TL	6-7	232	'90	0–3	5.48	13	2	0	0	1	21.1	32	13	13	2	2	11	19	2
Candiotti, Tom	RHP	8/31/57	Walnut Creek, CA	BR/TR	6-2	200	'91	6–7	2.98	19	19	3	0	0	129.2	114	47	43	6	4	45	81	5
Carpenter, Chris	RHP	4/27/75	Exeter, NH	BR/TR	6-6	215	'97-	34–34	5.04	105	88	8	3	0	581.2	666	363	326	71	15	229	410	24
Carrara, Giovanni	RHP	3/4/68	Edo Anzoategui, Venezuela	BR/TR	6-2	210	'95-96	2–5	8.26	23	7	1	0	0	63.2	87	65	58	15	1	37	37	2
Castillo, Frank	RHP	4/1/69	El Paso, TX	BR/TR	6-1	190	2000	10–5	3.59	25	24	0	0	0	138.0	112	58	55	18	5	56	104	0
Castillo, Tony	LHP	3/1/63	Quibor, Venezuela	BL/TL	5-10	188	'88-89, '93-96	13–13	3.49	218	0	0	0	16	296.1	279	125	115	29	9	106	181	6
Caudill, Bill	RHP	7/13/56	Santa Monica, CA	BR/TR	6-1	210	'85-86	6–10	4.09	107	0	0	0	16	105.2	89	51	48	15	4	52	78	0

John Cerutti

Jim Clancy

Bryan Clark

Stan Clarke

Roger Clemens

Pasqual Coco

Joe Coleman

David Cone

Don Cooper

Brad Cornett

	Position	Birthdate	Birthplace	Bats/Throws	HT.	WT.	Yrs. With Jays	W–L	ERA	G	GS	CG	SHO	SV	IP	H	R	ER	HR	HB	BB	SO	WP
Cerutti, John	LHP	4/28/60	Albany, NY	BL/TL	6-2	200	'85-90	46–37	3.87	191	108	7	2	2	772.1	800	378	332	110	16	254	369	30
Clancy, Jim	RHP	12/18/55	Chicago, IL	BR/TR	6-4	220	'77-88	128–140	4.10	352	345	73	11	1	2204.2	2185	1104	1005	219	28	814	1237	82
Clark, Bryan	LHP	7/12/56	Madera, CA	BL/TL	6-2	185	'84	1–2	5.91	20	3	0	0	0	45.2	66	33	30	6	1	22	21	7
Clarke, Stan	LHP	8/9/60	Toledo, OH	BL/TL	6-1	180	'83, '85-86	1–2	6.18	24	0	0	0	0	27.2	31	19	19	7	0	17	18	0
Clemens, Roger	RHP	8/4/62	Dayton, OH	BR/TR	6-4	220	'97-98	41–13	2.33	67	67	14	6	0	498.2	373	143	129	20	19	156	563	10
Coco, Pasqual	RHP	9/8/77	Santo Domingo, D.R.	BR/TR	6-1	185	2000-	0–0	9.00	1	1	0	0	0	4.0	5	4	4	1	1	5	2	1
Coleman, Joe	RHP	2/3/47	Boston, MA	BR/TR	6-3	195	'78	2–0	4.60	31	0	0	0	0	60.2	67	34	31	6	1	30	28	5
Cone, David	RHP	1/2/63	Kansas City, MO	BL/TR	6-1	190	'92, '95	13–9	3.14	25	24	5	2	0	183.1	151	69	64	15	8	70	149	9
Cooper, Don	RHP	1/15/57	New York, NY	BR/TR	6-1	185	'83	0–0	6.75	4	0	0	0	0	5.0	8	4	4	3	0	0	5	0
Cornett, Brad	RHP	2/4/69	Lamesa, TX	BR/TR	6-3	190	'94-95	1–3	7.00	14	4	0	0	0	36.0	49	31	28	14	4	14	26	2

Danny Cox

Tim Crabtree

Victor Cruz

Darwin Cubillan

Steve Cummings

Omar Daal

Mike Darr

Danny Darwin

Tom Davey

Steve Davis

	Position	Birthdate	Birthplace	Bats/Throws	HT.	WT.	Yrs. With Jays	W–L	ERA	G	GS	CG	SHO	SV	IP	H	R	ER	HR	HB	BB	SO	WP
Cox, Danny	RHP	9/21/59	Northampton, Eng.	BR/TR	6-4	235	'93-95	9–10	4.21	78	0	0	0	5	147.1	137	74	69	12	2	69	136	13
Crabtree, Tim	RHP	10/13/69	Jackson, MI	BR/TR	6-4	205	'95-97	8–8	3.99	121	0	0	0	3	140.0	154	74	62	12	7	52	104	9
Cruz, Victor	RHP	12/24/57	Rancho Viejo La Vega, D.R.	BR/TR	5-9	220	'78	7–3	1.71	32	0	0	0	9	47.1	28	10	9	0	1	36	51	3
Cubillan, Darwin	RHP	11/15/74	Bobure, Venezuela	BR/TR	6-2	170	2000	1–0	8.04	7	0	0	0	0	15.2	20	14	14	5	1	11	14	0
Cummings, Steve	RHP	7/15/64	Houston, TX	BB/TR	6-2	200	'89-90	2–0	3.78	11	4	0	0	0	33.1	40	16	14	5	2	16	12	1
Daal, Omar	LHP	3/1/72	Maracaibo, Venezuela	BL/TL	6-3	175	'97	1–1	4.00	9	3	0	0	0	27.0	34	13	12	3	0	6	28	1
Darr, Mike	RHP	3/23/56	Pomona, CA	BR/TR	6-4	190	'77	0–1	33.75	1	1	0	0	0	1.1	3	5	5	1	1	4	1	0
Darwin, Danny	RHP	10/25/55	Bonham, TX	BR/TR	6-3	190	'95	1–8	7.62	13	11	1	0	0	65.0	91	60	55	13	3	24	26	1
Davey, Tom	RHP	9/11/73	Garden City, MI	BR/TR	6-7	215	'99	1–1	4.70	29	0	0	0	1	44.0	40	28	23	5	3	26	42	6
Davis, Steve	LHP	8/4/60	San Antonio, TX	BL/TL	6-1	195	'85-86	2–1	5.12	13	5	0	0	0	31.2	31	21	18	7	0	18	27	1

Ken Dayley

Dennis DeBarr

Matt Dewitt

Butch Edge

Mark Eichhorn

Kelvim Escobar

Nino Espinosa

Leoncio Estrella

Tom Filer

Mike Flanagan

	Position	Birthdate	Birthplace	Bats/Throws	HT.	WT.	Yrs. With Jays	W–L	ERA	G	GS	CG	SHO	SV	IP	H	R	ER	HR	HB	BB	SO	WP
Dayley, Ken	LHP	2/25/59	Jerome, ID	BL/TL	6-0	175	'91-92	0–0	5.40	10	0	0	0	0	5.0	8	5	3	0	1	9	5	2
DeBarr, Dennis	LHP	1/16/53	Cheyenne, WY	BL/TL	6-2	190	'77	0–1	5.91	14	0	0	0	0	21.1	29	14	14	1	0	8	10	2
Dewitt, Matt	RHP	9/4/77	San Bernardino, CA	BR/TR	6-4	220	2000	1–0	8.56	8	0	0	0	0	13.2	20	13	13	4	2	9	6	1
Edge, Butch	RHP	7/18/56	Houston, TX	BR/TR	6-3	203	'79	3–4	5.23	9	9	1	0	0	51.2	60	32	30	6	1	24	19	4
Eichhorn, Mark	RHP	11/21/60	San Jose, CA	BR/TR	6-3	210	'82, '86-88, '92-93	29–19	3.03	279	7	0	0	15	493.0	445	180	166	33	24	167	372	19
Escobar, Kelvim	RHP	4/11/76	LaGuaira, Venezuela	BR/TR	6-1	205	'97-	34–31	5.04	125	64	4	1	16	464.2	489	285	260	51	13	220	379	10
Espinosa, Nino	RHP	8/15/53	Villa Altagracia, D.R.	BR/TR	6-1	192	'81	0–0	9.00	1	0	0	0	0	1.0	4	1	1	0	0	0	0	0
Estrella, Leoncio	RHP	2/20/75	Puerto Plata, D.R.	BR/TR	6-1	185	2000	0–0	5.79	2	0	0	0	0	4.2	9	3	3	1	0	0	3	0
Filer, Tom	RHP	12/1/56	Philadelphia, PA	BR/TR	6-1	198	'85	7–0	3.88	11	9	0	0	0	48.2	38	21	21	6	0	18	24	0
Flanagan, Mike	LHP	12/16/51	Manchester, NH	BL/TL	6-0	195	'87-90	26–27	3.96	76	76	3	1	0	452.1	480	217	198	39	11	150	194	9

Huck Flener

John Frascatore

Willie Fraser

Dave Freisleben

Jerry Garvin

Dave Geisel

Tom Gilles

Gary Glover

Don Gordon

Jim Gott

	Position	Birthdate	Birthplace	Bats/Throws	HT.	WT.	Yrs. With Jays	W–L	ERA	G	GS	CG	SHO	SV	IP	H	R	ER	HR	HB	BB	SO	WP
Flener, Huck	LHP	2/25/69	Austin, TX	BB/TL	5-11	185	'93, '96-97	3–3	5.21	29	12	0	0	0	95.0	108	59	55	12	1	39	53	3
Frascatore, John	RHP	2/4/70	Ozone Park, NY	BR/TR	6-1	200	'99-	9–5	4.25	93	0	0	0	1	110.0	129	67	58	19	8	42	52	8
Fraser, Willie	RHP	5/26/64	New York, NY	BR/TR	6-1	206	'91	0–2	6.15	13	1	0	0	0	26.1	33	20	18	4	3	11	12	2
Freisleben, Dave	RHP	10/31/51	Coraopolis, PA	BR/TR	5-11	200	'79	2–3	4.95	42	2	0	0	3	91.0	101	57	50	5	2	54	35	6
Garvin, Jerry	LHP	10/21/55	Oakland, CA	BL/TL	6-3	195	'77-82	20–41	4.46	196	65	15	1	8	606.0	648	318	300	74	13	219	320	17
Geisel, Dave	LHP	1/18/55	Windber, PA	BL/TL	6-3	210	'82-83	1–4	4.39	63	2	0	0	5	84.0	79	43	41	10	4	48	72	2
Gilles, Tom	RHP	7/2/62	Peoria, IL	BR/TR	6-1	185	'90	1–0	6.75	2	0	0	0	0	1.1	2	1	1	0	0	0	1	0
Glover, Gary	RHP	12/3/76	Cleveland, OH	BR/TR	6-5	200	'99	0–0	0.00	1	0	0	0	0	1.0	0	0	0	0	0	1	0	0
Gordon, Don	RHP	10/10/59	New York, NY	BR/TR	6-1	175	'86-87	0–1	6.06	19	0	0	0	1	32.2	36	25	22	3	1	11	16	0
Gott, Jim	RHP	8/3/59	Hollywood, CA	BR/TR	6-4	220	'82-84	21–30	4.25	99	65	8	3	2	442.1	422	233	209	37	11	183	276	11

Mauro Gozzo

Steve Grilli

Eric Gunderson

Mark Guthrie

Juan Guzman

Darren Hall

Roy Halladay

Joey Hamilton

Erik Hanson

Steve Hargan

	Position	Birthdate	Birthplace	Bats/Throws	HT.	WT.	Yrs. With Jays	W–L	ERA	G	GS	CG	SHO	SV	IP	H	R	ER	HR	HB	BB	SO	WP
Gozzo, Mauro	RHP	3/7/66	New Britain, CT	BR/TR	6-3	212	'89	4–1	4.83	9	3	0	0	0	31.2	35	19	17	1	1	9	10	0
Grilli, Steve	RHP	5/2/49	Brooklyn, NY	BR/TR	6-2	175	'79	0–0	0.00	1	0	0	0	0	2.1	1	0	0	0	0	0	1	0
Gunderson, Eric	LHP	3/29/66	Portland, OR	BR/TL	6-0	195	2000	0–1	7.11	6	0	0	0	0	6.1	15	6	5	0	1	2	2	0
Guthrie, Mark	LHP	9/22/65	Buffalo, NY	BR/TL	6-4	206	2000	0–2	4.79	23	0	0	0	0	20.2	20	12	11	3	1	9	20	2
Guzman, Juan	RHP	1/21/71	Santo Domingo, D.R.	BR/TR	5-11	195	'91-98	76–62	4.07	195	195	15	2	0	1215.2	1099	612	550	115	23	546	1030	88
Hall, Darren	RHP	7/14/64	Marysville, OH	BR/TR	6-3	205	'94-95	2–5	3.75	47	0	0	0	20	48.0	47	21	20	5	1	23	39	1
Halladay, Roy	RHP	5/14/77	Denver, CO	BR/TR	6-6	205	'98-	13–14	5.77	57	33	2	1	1	231.0	272	167	148	35	6	123	139	12
Hamilton, Joey	RHP	9/9/70	Statesboro, GA	BR/TR	6-4	220	'99-	9–9	5.77	28	24	0	0	0	131.0	146	86	84	16	5	51	71	4
Hanson, Erik	RHP	5/18/65	Kinnelon, NJ	BR/TR	6-6	210	'96-98	13–20	5.68	49	45	4	1	0	278.2	331	190	176	39	3	137	195	15
Hargan, Steve	RHP	9/8/42	Fort Wayne, IN	BR/TR	6-3	180	'77	1–3	5.22	6	5	1	0	0	29.1	36	17	17	2	0	14	11	2

Chuck Hartenstein

Tom Henke

Pat Hentgen

Xavier Hernandez

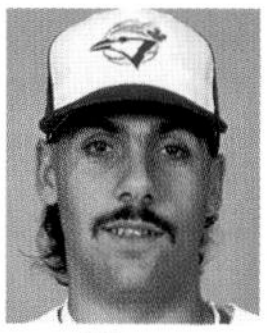
Vince Horsman

John Hudek

Phil Huffman

Edwin Hurtado

Roy Lee Jackson

Marty Janzen

	Position	Birthdate	Birthplace	Bats/Throws	HT.	WT.	Yrs. With Jays	W–L	ERA	G	GS	CG	SHO	SV	IP	H	R	ER	HR	HB	BB	SO	WP
Hartenstein, Chuck	RHP	5/26/42	Seguin, TX	BR/TR	5-11	165	'77	0–2	6.59	13	0	0	0	0	27.1	40	22	20	8	1	6	15	0
Henke, Tom	RHP	12/21/57	Kansas City, MO	BR/TR	6-5	215	'85-92	29–29	2.48	446	0	0	0	217	563.0	411	171	155	48	6	166	644	21
Hentgen, Pat	RHP	11/13/68	Detroit, MI	BR/TR	6-2	200	'91-99	105–76	4.14	252	222	31	9	0	1555.2	1587	783	716	191	37	557	995	55
Hernandez, Xavier	RHP	8/16/65	Port Arthur, TX	BL/TR	6-2	185	'89	1–0	4.76	7	0	0	0	0	22.2	25	15	12	2	1	8	7	1
Horsman, Vince	LHP	3/9/67	Halifax, NS	BR/TL	6-2	180	'91	0–0	0.00	4	0	0	0	0	4.0	2	0	0	0	0	3	2	0
Hudek, John	RHP	8/8/66	Tampa, FL	BB/TR	6-1	200	'99	0–0	12.27	3	0	0	0	0	3.2	8	5	5	1	0	1	2	0
Huffman, Phil	RHP	6/20/58	Freeport, TX	BR/TR	6-2	180	'79	6–18	5.77	31	31	2	1	0	173.0	220	130	111	25	0	68	56	5
Hurtado, Edwin	RHP	2/1/70	Barquisimeto, Venezuela	BR/TR	6-3	215	'95	5–2	5.45	14	10	1	0	0	77.2	81	50	47	11	5	40	33	11
Jackson, Roy Lee	RHP	5/1/54	Opelika, AL	BR/TR	6-2	194	'81-84	24–21	3.50	190	2	0	0	30	337.0	307	148	131	30	7	128	204	10
Janzen, Marty	RHP	5/31/73	Homestead, FL	BR/TR	6-3	197	'96-97	6–7	6.39	27	11	0	0	0	98.2	118	76	70	20	2	51	64	7

Jesse Jefferson

Dane Johnson

Jerry Johnson

Joe Johnson

Ricardo Jordan

Jimmy Key

Paul Kilgus

Don Kirkwood

Billy Koch

Jack Kucek

	Position	Birthdate	Birthplace	Bats/Throws	HT.	WT.	Yrs. With Jays	W–L	ERA	G	GS	CG	SHO	SV	IP	H	R	ER	HR	HB	BB	SO	WP
Jefferson, Jesse	RHP	3/3/49	Midlothian, VA	BR/TR	6-3	195	'77-80	22–56	4.75	127	37	21	4	1	666.1	718	385	352	82	8	266	307	9
Johnson, Dane	RHP	2/10/63	Coral Gables, FL	BR/TR	6-5	205	'96	0–0	3.00	10	0	0	0	0	9.0	5	3	3	0	0	5	7	0
Johnson, Jerry	RHP	12/3/43	Miami, FL	BR/TR	6-3	200	'77	2–4	4.60	43	0	0	0	5	86.0	91	50	44	9	0	54	54	2
Johnson, Joe	RHP	10/30/61	Brookline, MA	BR/TR	6-2	195	'86-87	10–7	4.42	30	29	0	0	0	154.2	171	83	76	13	5	40	66	5
Jordan, Ricardo	LHP	6/27/70	Boynton Beach, FL	BL/TL	5-11	165	'95	1–0	6.60	15	0	0	0	1	15.0	18	11	11	3	2	13	10	1
Key, Jimmy	LHP	4/22/61	Huntsville, AB	BR/TL	6-1	190	'84-92	116–81	3.42	317	250	26	8	10	1695.2	1624	710	645	165	24	404	944	31
Kilgus, Paul	LHP	2/2/62	Bowling Green, KY	BL/TL	6-1	185	'90	0–0	6.06	11	0	0	0	0	16.1	19	11	11	2	1	7	7	0
Kirkwood, Don	RHP	9/24/49	Pontiac, MI	BR/TR	6-3	188	'78	4–5	4.24	16	9	3	0	0	68.0	76	36	32	6	0	25	29	3
Koch, Billy	RHP	12/14/74	Rockville Centre, NY	BR/TR	6-3	218	'99-	9–8	2.97	124	0	0	0	64	142.1	133	54	47	11	5	48	117	1
Kucek, Jack	RHP	6/8/53	Warren, OH	BR/TR	6-2	200	'80	3–8	6.75	23	12	0	0	1	68.0	83	56	51	9	1	41	35	3

Craig Kusick

Dennis Lamp

Gary Lavelle

Rick Leach

Luis Leal

Al Leiter

Dave Lemanczyk

Mark Lemongello

Doug Linton

Graeme Lloyd

	Position	Birthdate	Birthplace	Bats/Throws	HT.	WT.	Yrs. With Jays	W–L	ERA	G	GS	CG	SHO	SV	IP	H	R	ER	HR	HB	BB	SO	WP
Kusick, Craig	RHP	9/30/48	Milwaukee, WI	BR/TR	6-3	232	'79	0–0	4.91	1	0	0	0	0	3.2	3	2	2	1	0	0	0	0
Lamp, Dennis	RHP	9/23/52	Los Angeles, CA	BR/TR	6-3	210	'84-86	21–14	4.20	149	7	0	0	13	263.2	286	145	123	21	1	88	143	9
Lavelle, Gary	LHP	1/3/49	Scranton, PA	BB/TL	6-1	200	'85-87	7–10	3.77	92	0	0	0	9	100.1	90	50	42	7	0	55	67	1
Leach, Rick	LHP	5/4/57	Ann Arbor, MI	BL/TL	6-0	195	'84-88	0–0	27.00	1	0	0	0	0	1.0	2	3	3	1	0	2	0	0
Leal, Luis	RHP	3/21/57	Barquisimeto, Venezuela	BR/TR	6-3	205	'80-85	51–58	4.14	165	151	27	3	1	946.0	958	476	435	101	22	320	491	23
Leiter, Al	LHP	10/23/65	Toms River, NJ	BL/TL	6-3	215	'89-95	26–24	4.20	91	61	4	2	2	415.1	394	209	194	30	12	240	329	24
Lemanczyk, Dave	RHP	8/17/50	Syracuse, NY	BR/TR	6-4	235	'77-80	27–45	4.68	95	82	25	3	0	575.0	632	334	299	52	13	212	240	36
Lemongello, Mark	RHP	7/21/55	Jersey City, NJ	BR/TR	6-1	180	'79	1–9	6.29	18	10	2	0	0	83.0	97	64	58	14	3	34	40	2
Linton, Doug	RHP	2/9/65	Santa Ana, CA	BR/TR	6-1	190	'92-93	1–4	7.97	12	4	0	0	0	35.0	42	31	31	5	1	26	20	2
Lloyd, Graeme	LHP	4/9/67	Victoria, Australia	BL/TL	6-7	234	'99	5–3	3.63	74	0	0	0	3	72.0	68	36	29	11	4	23	47	1

Esteban Loaiza

Eric Ludwick

Steve Luebber

Rick Luecken

Bob MacDonald

Mickey Mahler

Joey McLaughlin

Paul Menhart

Dyar Miller

Paul Mirabella

	Position	Birthdate	Birthplace	Bats/Throws	HT.	WT.	Yrs. With Jays	W–L	ERA	G	GS	CG	SHO	SV	IP	H	R	ER	HR	HB	BB	SO	WP
Loaiza, Esteban	RHP	12/31/71	Tijuana, Mexico	BR/TR	6-4	190	2000-	5–7	3.62	14	14	1	1	0	92.0	95	45	37	8	10	26	62	0
Ludwick, Eric	RHP	12/14/71	Whiteman AFB, MO	BR/TR	6-5	210	'99	0–0	27.00	1	0	0	0	0	1.0	3	3	3	0	0	2	0	0
Luebber, Steve	RHP	7/9/49	Clinton, MO	BR/TR	6-3	195	'79	0–0	INF	1	0	0	0	0	0.0	2	1	1	0	0	1	0	0
Luecken, Rick	RHP	11/15/60	McAllen, TX	BR/TR	6-6	210	'90	0–0	9.00	1	0	0	0	0	1.0	2	1	1	1	0	1	0	0
MacDonald, Bob	LHP	4/27/65	East Orange, NJ	BL/TL	6-3	208	'90-92	4–3	3.48	76	0	0	0	0	103.1	101	43	40	9	1	43	50	1
Mahler, Mickey	LHP	7/30/52	Montgomery, AL	BB/TL	6-3	189	'86	0–0	0.00	2	0	0	0	0	1.0	1	0	0	0	1	0	0	0
McLaughlin, Joey	RHP	7/11/56	Tulsa, OK	BR/TR	6-2	205	'80-84	22–24	3.88	195	10	0	0	31	341.0	343	169	147	36	5	148	207	10
Menhart, Paul	RHP	3/25/69	St. Louis, MO	BR/TR	6-2	190	'95	1–4	4.92	21	9	1	0	0	78.2	72	49	43	9	6	47	50	6
Miller, Dyar	RHP	5/29/46	Batesville, IN	BR/TR	6-1	195	'79	0–0	10.57	10	0	0	0	0	15.1	27	18	18	3	0	5	7	2
Mirabella, Paul	LHP	3/20/54	Belleville, NJ	BL/TL	6-2	196	'80-81	5–12	4.64	41	23	3	1	0	145.1	171	89	75	13	4	73	62	4

Randy Moffitt | **Balor Moore** | **Mike Morgan** | **Jack Morris** | **Peter Munro** | **Tom Murphy** | **Dale Murray** | **Jeff Musselman** | **Ron Musselman** | **Randy Myers**

	Position	Birthdate	Birthplace	Bats/Throws	HT.	WT.	Yrs. With Jays	W–L	ERA	G	GS	CG	SHO	SV	IP	H	R	ER	HR	HB	BB	SO	WP
Moffitt, Randy	RHP	10/13/48	Long Beach, CA	BR/TR	6-3	190	'83	6–2	3.77	45	0	0	0	10	57.1	52	27	24	5	1	24	38	0
Moore, Balor	LHP	1/25/51	Smithville, TX	BL/TL	6-2	184	'78-80	12–17	4.96	102	37	7	0	1	348.1	376	213	192	39	19	164	148	11
Morgan, Mike	RHP	10/8/59	Tulare, CA	BR/TR	6-2	215	'83	0–3	5.16	16	4	0	0	0	45.1	48	26	26	6	0	21	22	3
Morris, Jack	RHP	5/16/55	St. Paul, MN	BR/TR	6-3	200	'92-93	28–18	4.87	61	61	10	2	0	393.1	411	230	213	36	13	145	235	23
Munro, Peter	RHP	6/14/75	Flushing, NY	BR/TR	6-2	200	'99-2000	1–3	6.00	40	5	0	0	0	81.0	108	60	54	7	5	39	54	4
Murphy, Tom	RHP	12/30/45	Cleveland, OH	BR/TR	6-3	185	'77-79	9–12	4.00	79	1	0	0	9	164.1	173	76	73	18	1	63	67	9
Murray, Dale	RHP	2/2/50	Cuero, TX	BR/TR	6-4	205	'81-82	9–7	2.92	67	0	0	0	11	126.1	127	50	41	3	3	37	72	5
Musselman, Jeff	LHP	6/21/63	Doylestown, PA	BL/TL	6-0	180	'86-89	20–11	4.26	94	19	0	0	3	190.1	182	99	90	14	6	98	100	9
Musselman, Ron	RHP	11/11/54	Wilmington, NC	BR/TR	6-2	185	'84-85	5–2	3.79	36	4	0	0	1	73.2	77	35	31	4	0	34	38	3
Myers, Randy	LHP	9/19/62	Vancouver, WA	BL/TL	6-1	215	'98	3–4	4.46	41	0	0	0	28	42.1	44	21	21	4	2	19	32	2

Phil Niekro | **Jose Nunez** | **Lance Painter** | **Robert Person** | **Dan Plesac** | **Paul Quantrill** | **Dave Righetti** | **Bill Risley** | **Ken Robinson** | **Nerio Rodriguez**

	Position	Birthdate	Birthplace	Bats/Throws	HT.	WT.	Yrs. With Jays	W–L	ERA	G	GS	CG	SHO	SV	IP	H	R	ER	HR	HB	BB	SO	WP
Niekro, Phil	RHP	4/1/39	Blaine, OH	BR/TR	6-1	180	'87	0–2	8.25	3	3	0	0	0	12.0	15	11	11	4	0	7	7	1
Nunez, Jose	RHP	1/13/64	Jarabacoa, D.R	BR/TR	6-3	175	'87-89	5–3	4.40	56	12	0	0	0	137.0	127	71	67	15	1	77	131	7
Painter, Lance	LHP	7/21/67	Bedford, Eng.	BL/TL	6-1	195	2000-	2–0	4.73	42	2	0	0	0	66.2	69	37	35	9	2	22	53	4
Person, Robert	RHP	10/6/69	Lowell, MA	BR/TR	5-11	180	'97-99	8–13	6.18	61	22	0	0	8	177.2	179	129	122	29	11	97	142	9
Plesac, Dan	LHP	2/4/62	Gary, IN	BL/TL	6-5	215	'97-99	6–10	4.53	181	0	0	0	5	123.0	116	66	62	16	1	44	142	4
Quantrill, Paul	RHP	11/3/68	London, ON	BL/TR	6-1	185	'96-	19–32	3.79	306	20	0	0	13	434.2	516	205	183	49	12	132	276	4
Righetti, Dave	LHP	11/28/58	San Jose, CA	BL/TL	6-3	198	'94	0–1	6.75	13	0	0	0	0	13.1	9	10	10	2	0	10	10	0
Risley, Bill	RHP	5/29/67	Chicago, IL	BR/TR	6-2	215	'96-98	3–6	4.83	72	0	0	0	0	100.2	88	61	54	16	4	61	73	4
Robinson, Ken	RHP	11/3/69	Barberton, OH	BR/TR	5-7	175	'95, '97	1–2	3.61	24	0	0	0	0	42.1	26	22	17	8	2	23	35	1
Rodriguez, Nerio	RHP	3/22/73	San Pedro de Macoris, D.R.	BR/TR	6-1	195	'98-99	1–1	10.45	9	0	0	0	0	10.1	12	12	12	3	1	10	5	0

Jimmy Rogers | **Mike Romano** | **Mark Ross** | **Randy St. Claire** | **Alex Sanchez** | **Ken Schrom** | **Steve Senteney** | **Jose Silva** | **Steve Sinclair** | **Bill Singer**

	Position	Birthdate	Birthplace	Bats/Throws	HT.	WT.	Yrs. With Jays	W–L	ERA	G	GS	CG	SHO	SV	IP	H	R	ER	HR	HB	BB	SO	WP
Rogers, Jimmy	RHP	1/3/67	Tulsa, OK	BR/TR	6-2	190	'95	2–4	5.70	19	0	0	0	0	23.2	21	15	15	4	0	18	13	0
Romano, Mike	RHP	3/3/72	New Orleans, LA	BR/TR	6-2	195	'99	0–0	11.81	3	0	0	0	0	5.1	8	8	7	1	0	5	3	1
Ross, Mark	RHP	8/8/57	Galveston, TX	BR/TR	6-0	195	'88	0–0	4.91	3	0	0	0	0	7.1	5	6	4	0	0	4	4	0
St. Claire, Randy	LHP	8/23/60	Glens Falls, NY	BR/TR	6-2	190	'94	0–0	9.00	2	0	0	0	0	2.0	4	4	2	0	0	2	2	0
Sanchez, Alex	RHP	4/8/66	Concord, CA	BR/TR	6-2	185	'89	0–1	10.03	4	3	0	0	0	11.2	16	13	13	1	0	14	4	1
Schrom, Ken	RHP	11/23/54	Grangeville, ID	BR/TR	6-2	195	'80, '82	2–0	5.44	23	0	0	0	1	46.1	45	29	28	5	0	34	21	1
Senteney, Steve	RHP	8/7/55	Indianapolis, IN	BR/TR	6-2	205	'82	0–0	4.91	11	0	0	0	0	22.0	23	16	12	5	0	6	20	1
Silva, Jose	RHP	12/19/73	Tijuana, Mexico	BR/TR	6-5	205	'96	0–0	13.50	2	0	0	0	0	2.0	5	3	3	1	0	0	0	0
Sinclair, Steve	LHP	8/2/71	Victoria, BC	BL/TL	6-2	190	'98-99	0–2	6.10	27	0	0	0	0	20.2	20	15	14	4	1	9	11	0
Singer, Bill	RHP	2/24/44	Los Angeles, CA	BR/TR	6-4	200	'77	2–8	6.79	13	12	0	0	0	59.2	71	54	45	5	2	39	33	3

Aaron Small | **Paul Spoljaric** | **Dave Stewart** | **Dave Stieb** | **Todd Stottlemyre** | **Mike Timlin** | **Jackson Todd** | **Steve Trachsel** | **Rick Trlicek** | **Tom Underwood**

	Position	Birthdate	Birthplace	Bats/Throws	HT.	WT.	Yrs. With Jays	W–L	ERA	G	GS	CG	SHO	SV	IP	H	R	ER	HR	HB	BB	SO	WP
Small, Aaron	RHP	11/23/71	Oxnard, CA	BR/TR	6-5	200	'94	0–0	9.00	1	0	0	0	0	2.0	5	2	2	1	0	2	0	0
Spoljaric, Paul	LHP	9/24/70	Kelowna, BC	BR/TL	6-3	205	'94, '96-97, '99	4–8	4.31	104	3	0	0	4	150.1	134	85	72	21	6	81	146	6
Stewart, Dave	RHP	2/19/57	Oakland, CA	BR/TR	6-2	200	'93-94	19–16	5.09	48	48	1	0	0	295.1	297	175	167	49	8	134	207	10
Stieb, Dave	RHP	7/22/57	Santa Ana, CA	BR/TR	6-1	195	'79-92, '98	175–134	3.42	439	408	103	30	3	2873.0	2545	1208	1091	224	129	1020	1658	51
Stottlemyre, Todd	RHP	5/20/65	Sunnyside, WA	BL/TR	6-3	195	'88-94	69–70	4.39	206	175	15	4	1	1139.0	1182	597	555	115	49	414	662	30
Timlin, Mike	RHP	3/10/66	Midland, TX	BR/TR	6-4	210	'91-97	23–22	3.62	305	3	0	0	52	393.1	369	178	158	29	10	167	331	16
Todd, Jackson	RHP	11/20/51	Tulsa, OK	BR/TR	6-2	180	'79-81	7–10	4.27	45	26	7	0	0	215.0	224	117	102	31	7	68	99	9
Trachsel, Steve	RHP	10/31/70	Oxnard, CA	BR/TR	6-4	205	2000	2–5	5.29	11	11	0	0	0	63.0	72	40	37	10	0	25	32	1
Trlicek, Rick	RHP	4/26/69	Houston,TX	BR/TR	6-2	200	'92	0–0	10.80	2	0	0	0	0	1.2	2	2	2	0	0	2	1	0
Underwood, Tom	LHP	12/22/53	Kokomo, IN	BR/TL	5-11	170	'78-79	15–30	3.88	64	62	19	2	0	424.2	414	218	183	46	11	182	267	18

| | Ben Van Ryn | Frank Viola | Pete Vuckovich | Dave Wallace | Duane Ward | Jeff Ware | Dave Weathers | David Wells | Mickey Weston | Mark Wiley |

	Position	Birthdate	Birthplace	Bats/Throws	HT.	WT.	Yrs. With Jays	W–L	ERA	G	GS	CG	SHO	SV	IP	H	R	ER	HR	HB	BB	SO	WP
Van Ryn, Ben	LHP	8/9/71	Fort Wayne, IN	BL/TL	6-5	185	'98	0–1	9.00	10	0	0	0	0	4.0	6	4	4	0	0	2	3	0
Viola, Frank	LHP	4/19/60	Hempstead, NY	BL/TL	6-4	209	'96	1–3	7.71	6	6	0	0	0	30.1	43	28	26	6	2	21	18	1
Vuckovich, Pete	RHP	10/27/52	Johnstown, PA	BR/TR	6-4	220	'77	7–7	3.47	53	8	3	1	8	148.0	143	64	57	13	5	59	123	12
Wallace, Dave	RHP	9/7/47	Waterbury, CT	BR/TR	5-10	185	'78	0–0	3.86	6	0	0	0	0	14.0	12	6	6	1	0	11	7	1
Ward, Duane	RHP	5/28/64	Park View, NM	BR/TR	6-4	210	'86-95	32–36	3.18	452	2	0	0	121	650.2	529	255	230	30	16	278	671	50
Ware, Jeff	RHP	11/11/70	Norfolk, VA	BR/TR	6-3	190	'95-96	3–6	7.47	18	9	0	0	0	59.0	63	52	49	8	3	52	29	8
Weathers, Dave	RHP	9/25/69	Lawrenceburg, TN	BR/TR	6-3	205	'91-92	1–0	5.50	17	0	0	0	0	18.0	20	12	11	2	2	19	16	0
Wells, David	LHP	5/20/63	Torrance, CA	BL/TL	6-4	225	'87-92, '99-2000	84–55	4.06	306	138	18	2	13	1148.2	1171	566	518	126	28	294	784	46
Weston, Mickey	RHP	3/26/61	Flint, MI	BR/TR	6-1	187	'91	0–0	0.00	2	0	0	0	0	2.0	1	0	0	0	0	1	1	0
Wiley, Mark	RHP	2/8/48	National City, CA	BR/TR	6-1	200	'78	0–0	6.75	2	0	0	0	0	2.2	3	2	2	0	0	1	2	0

| | Matt Williams | Woody Williams | Mike Willis | Frank Wills | Shannon Withem |

	Position	Birthdate	Birthplace	Bats/Throws	HT.	WT.	Yrs. With Jays	W–L	ERA	G	GS	CG	SHO	SV	IP	H	R	ER	HR	HB	BB	SO	WP
Williams, Matt	RHP	7/25/59	Houston, TX	BR/TR	6-1	200	'83	1–1	14.63	4	3	0	0	0	8.0	13	13	13	5	1	7	5	0
Williams, Woody	RHP	8/19/66	Houston, TX	BR/TR	6-0	190	'93-98	28–34	4.30	166	76	2	1	0	613.1	589	308	293	88	13	251	439	17
Willis, Mike	LHP	12/26/50	Oklahoma City, OK	BL/TL	6-2	210	'77-81	7–21	4.59	144	6	1	0	15	296.0	312	161	151	36	3	123	149	9
Wills, Frank	RHP	10/26/58	New Orleans, LA	BR/TR	6-2	202	'88-91	9–6	4.65	82	8	0	0	0	195.1	196	105	101	21	3	79	134	6
Withem, Shannon	RHP	9/21/72	Ann Arbor, MI	BR/TR	6-3	185	'98	0–0	3.00	1	0	0	0	0	3.0	3	1	1	0	0	2	2	0

ROSTER ADDITIONS, 2001

Pitchers

| | Kevin Beirne | Bob File | Chris Michalak | Steve Parris |

	Position	Birthdate	Birthplace	Bats/Throws	HT.	WT.	Yrs. With Jays	W–L	ERA	G	GS	CG	SHO	SV	IP	H	R	ER	HR	HB	BB	SO	WP
Beirne, Kevin	RHP	1/1/74	Houston, TX	BL/TR	6-4	210	2001	–	–	–	–	–	–	–	–	–	–	–	–	–	–	–	–
File, Bob	RHP	1/28/77	Philadelphia, PA	BR/TR	6-4	210	2001	–	–	–	–	–	–	–	–	–	–	–	–	–	–	–	–
Michalak, Chris	LHP	1/4/71	Joliet, IL	BL/TL	6-2	195	2001	–	–	–	–	–	–	–	–	–	–	–	–	–	–	–	–
Parris, Steve	RHP	12/17/67	Joliet, IL	BR/TR	6-0	195	2001	–	–	–	–	–	–	–	–	–	–	–	–	–	–	–	–

1977

BATTER Pos.	Avg.	G	AB	R	H	HR	RBI
ASHBY, Alan C	.210	124	396	25	83	2	29
AULT, Doug 1B-DH	.245	129	445	44	109	11	64
BAILOR, Bob IF-OF	.310	122	496	62	154	5	32
BOWLING, Steve OF	.206	89	194	19	40	1	13
CERONE, Rick C	.200	31	100	7	20	1	10
EWING, Sam OF-DH	.287	97	244	24	70	4	34
FAIRLY, Ron DH-1B-OF	.279	132	458	60	128	19	64
GARCIA, Pedro 2B	.208	41	130	10	27	0	9
HOWELL, Roy 3B	.316	96	364	41	115	10	44
MASON, Jim SS	.165	22	79	10	13	0	2
McKAY, Dave IF	.197	95	274	18	54	3	22
NORDBROOK, Tim SS	.175	24	63	9	11	0	1
RADER, Doug 3B-DH	.240	96	313	47	75	13	40
ROOF, Phil C	.000	3	5	0	0	0	0
SCOTT, John OF	.240	79	233	26	56	2	15
STAGGS, Steve 2B	.259	72	290	37	75	2	28
TORRES, Hector IF	.241	91	266	33	64	5	26
VELEZ, Otto OF-DH	.256	120	360	50	92	16	62
WHITT, Ernie C	.171	23	41	4	7	0	6
WOODS, Al OF	.284	122	440	58	125	6	35
WOODS, Gary OF	.216	60	227	21	49	0	17
Designated Hitters	.269	161	583	75	157	22	87
Pinch-Hitters	.280	–	93	10	26	5	23
1977 Totals	**.252**	**161**	**5418**	**605**	**1367**	**100**	**553**

PITCHER	ERA	W-L	SV	G	IP	H	ER	BB	SO
BRUNO, Tom	7.85	0-1	0	12	18.1	30	16	13	9
BYRD, Jeff	6.18	2-13	0	17	87.1	98	60	68	40
CLANCY, Jim	5.05	4-9	0	13	76.2	80	43	47	44
DARR, Mike	33.75	0-1	0	1	1.1	3	5	4	1
DeBARR, Dennis	5.91	0-1	0	14	21.1	29	14	8	10
GARVIN, Jerry	4.19	10-18	0	34	244.2	247	114	85	127
HARGAN, Steve	5.22	1-3	0	6	29.1	36	17	14	11
HARTENSTEIN, Chuck	6.59	0-2	0	13	27.1	40	20	6	15
JEFFERSON, Jesse	4.31	9-17	0	33	217.0	224	104	83	114
JOHNSON, Jerry	4.60	2-4	5	43	86.0	91	44	54	54
LEMANCZYK, Dave	4.25	13-16	0	34	252.0	278	119	87	105
MURPHY, Tom	3.63	2-1	2	19	52.0	63	21	18	26
SINGER, Bill	6.79	2-8	0	13	59.2	71	45	39	33
VUKOVICH, Pete	3.47	7-7	8	53	148.0	143	57	59	123
WILLIS, Mike	3.94	2-6	5	43	107.1	105	47	38	59
1977 Totals	**4.57**	**54-107**	**20**	**161**	**1428.1**	**1538**	**726**	**623**	**771**

1978

BATTER Pos.	Avg.	G	AB	R	H	HR	RBI
ALBERTS, Butch DH	.278	6	18	1	5	0	0
ASHBY, Alan C	.261	81	264	27	69	9	29
AULT, Doug 1B	.240	54	104	10	25	3	7
BAILOR, Bob OF-IF	.264	154	621	74	164	1	52
BOSETTI, Rick OF	.259	136	568	61	147	5	42
CARTY, Rico DH	.284	104	387	51	110	20	68
CERONE, Rick C	.223	88	282	25	63	3	20
EWING, Sam DH-OF	.179	40	56	3	10	2	9
GOMEZ, Luis SS	.223	153	413	39	92	0	32
HORTON, Willie DH	.205	33	122	12	25	3	19
HOWELL, Roy IF	.270	140	551	67	149	8	61
HUTTON, Tommy OF-1B	.254	64	173	19	44	2	9
IORG, Garth 2B	.163	19	49	3	8	0	3
JOHNSON, Tim SS-2B	.241	68	79	9	19	0	3
MAYBERRY, John 1B	.250	152	515	51	129	22	70
McKAY, Dave 2B	.238	145	504	59	120	7	45
MILNER, Brian C	.444	2	9	3	4	0	2
NORDBROOK, Tim SS	.000	7	0	1	0	0	0
UPSHAW, Willie OF-DH	.237	95	224	26	53	1	17
VELEZ, Otto OF	.266	91	248	29	66	9	38
WHITT, Ernie C	.000	2	4	0	0	0	0
WOODS, Al OF	.241	62	220	19	53	3	25
WOODS, Gary OF	.158	8	19	1	3	0	0
Designated Hitters	.250	161	621	75	155	25	96
Pinch-Hitters	.236	–	123	11	29	2	18
1978 Totals	**.250**	**161**	**5430**	**590**	**1358**	**98**	**551**

PITCHER	ERA	W-L	SV	G	IP	H	ER	BB	SO
BUSKEY, Tom	3.38	0-1	0	8	13.1	14	5	5	7
CLANCY, Jim	4.09	10-12	0	31	193.2	199	88	91	106
COLEMAN, Joe	4.60	2-0	0	31	60.2	67	31	30	28
CRUZ, Victor	1.71	7-3	9	32	47.1	28	9	35	51
GARVIN, Jerry	5.54	4-12	0	26	144.2	189	89	48	67
JEFFERSON, Jesse	4.38	7-16	0	31	211.2	214	103	86	97
KIRKWOOD, Don	4.24	4-5	0	16	68.0	76	32	25	29
LEMANCZYK, Dave	6.26	4-14	0	29	136.2	170	95	65	62
MOORE, Balor	4.93	6-9	0	37	144.1	165	79	54	75
MURPHY, Tom	3.93	6-9	7	50	94.0	87	41	37	36
UNDERWOOD, Tom	4.10	6-14	0	31	197.2	201	90	87	139
WALLACE, Dave	3.86	0-0	0	6	14.0	12	6	11	7
WILEY, Mark	6.75	0-0	0	2	2.2	3	2	1	2
WILLIS, Mike	4.56	3-7	7	44	100.2	104	51	39	52
1978 Totals	**4.54**	**59-102**	**23**	**161**	**1429.1**	**1529**	**723**	**614**	**758**

1979

BATTER Pos.	Avg.	G	AB	R	H	HR	RBI
AINGE, Danny 2B	.237	87	308	26	73	2	19
BAILOR, Bob OF-3B	.229	130	414	50	95	1	38
BOSETTI, Rick OF	.260	162	619	59	161	8	65
BROWN, Bobby OF	.000	4	10	1	0	0	0
CANNON, J.J. OF	.211	61	142	14	30	1	5
CARTY, Rico DH	.256	132	461	48	118	12	55
CERONE, Rick C	.239	136	469	47	112	7	61
DAVIS, Bob C	.124	32	89	6	11	1	8
GOMEZ, Luis IF	.239	59	163	11	39	0	11
GRIFFIN, Alfredo SS	.287	153	624	81	179	2	31
HERNANDEZ, Pedro PR	.000	3	0	1	0	0	0
HOWELL, Roy 3B	.247	138	511	60	126	15	72
JOHNSON, Tim IF	.186	43	86	6	16	0	6
KUSICK, Craig 1B	.204	24	54	3	11	2	7
MAYBERRY, John 1B	.274	137	464	61	127	21	74
McKAY, Dave 2B	.218	47	156	19	34	0	12
ROBERTSON, Bob 1B	.103	15	29	1	3	1	1
SOLAITA, Tony DH-1B	.265	36	102	14	27	2	13
VELEZ, Otto OF	.288	99	274	45	79	15	48
WILBORN, Ted OF	.000	22	12	3	0	0	0
WOODS, Al OF	.278	132	436	57	121	5	36
Designated Hitters	.260	162	599	70	156	18	82
Pinch-Hitters	.231	–	52	5	12	4	14
1979 Totals	**.251**	**162**	**5423**	**613**	**1362**	**95**	**562**

PITCHER	ERA	W-L	SV	G	IP	H	ER	BB	SO
BUSKEY, Tom	3.43	6-10	7	44	78.2	74	30	25	44
CLANCY, Jim	5.51	2-7	0	12	63.2	65	39	31	33
EDGE, Butch	5.23	3-4	0	9	51.2	60	30	24	19
FREISLEBEN, Dave	4.95	2-3	3	42	91.0	101	50	53	35
GARVIN, Jerry	2.78	0-1	0	8	22.2	15	7	10	14
GRILLI, Steve	0.00	0-0	0	1	2.1	1	0	0	1
HUFFMAN, Phil	5.77	6-18	0	31	173.0	220	111	68	56
JEFFERSON, Jesse	5.51	2-10	1	34	116.0	150	71	45	43
KUSICK, Craig	4.91	0-0	0	1	3.2	3	2	0	0
LEMANCZYK, Dave	3.71	8-10	0	22	143.0	137	59	45	63
LEMONGELLO, Mark	6.29	1-9	0	18	83.0	97	58	34	40
LUEBBER, Steve	INF	0-0	0	1	0.0	2	1	1	0
MILLER, Dyar	10.57	0-0	0	10	15.1	27	18	5	7
MOORE, Balor	4.84	5-7	0	34	139.1	135	75	79	51
MURPHY, Tom	5.40	1-2	0	10	18.1	23	11	8	6
STIEB, Dave	4.31	8-8	0	18	129.1	139	62	48	52
TODD, Jackson	5.85	0-1	0	12	32.1	40	21	7	14
UNDERWOOD, Tom	3.69	9-16	0	33	227.0	213	93	95	127
WILLIS, Mike	8.44	0-3	0	17	26.2	35	25	16	8
1979 Totals	**4.81**	**53-109**	**11**	**162**	**1417.0**	**1537**	**758**	**594**	**613**

1980

BATTER Pos.	Avg.	G	AB	R	H	HR	RBI
AINGE, Danny OF-IF	.243	38	111	11	27	0	4
AULT, Doug 1B-DH	.194	64	144	12	28	3	15
BAILOR, Bob OF-IF	.236	117	347	44	82	1	16
BONNELL, Barry OF	.268	130	463	55	124	13	56
BOSETTI, Rick OF	.213	53	188	24	40	4	18
BRAUN, Steve PH-DH	.273	37	55	4	15	1	9
CANNON, J.J. PR-OF	.080	70	50	16	4	0	4
DAVIS, Bob C	.216	91	218	18	47	4	19
GARCIA, Damaso 2B	.278	140	543	50	151	4	46
GRIFFIN, Alfredo SS	.254	155	653	63	166	2	41
HODGSON, Paul OF	.220	20	41	5	9	1	5
HOWELL, Roy 3B	.269	142	528	51	142	10	57
IORG, Garth IF	.248	80	222	24	55	2	14
KELLY, Pat C	.286	3	7	0	2	0	0
MACHA, Mike 3B-C	.000	5	8	0	0	0	0
MAYBERRY, John 1B	.248	149	501	62	124	30	82
MOSEBY, Lloyd OF	.229	114	389	44	89	9	46
RAMOS, Domingo IF	.125	5	16	0	2	0	0
STIEB, Dave P-OF	.000	1	1	0	0	0	0
UPSHAW, Willie 1B-DH	.213	34	61	10	13	1	5
VELEZ, Otto DH	.269	104	357	54	96	20	62
WHITT, Ernie C	.237	106	295	23	70	6	34
WOODS, Al OF	.300	109	373	54	112	15	47
Designated Hitters	.229	162	599	73	137	22	84
Pinch-Hitters	.280	–	100	10	28	3	15
1980 Totals	**.251**	**162**	**5571**	**624**	**1398**	**126**	**580**

PITCHER	ERA	W-L	SV	G	IP	H	ER	BB	SO
BAILOR, Bob	7.71	0-0	0	3	2.1	4	2	1	0
BARLOW, Mike	4.09	3-1	5	40	55.0	57	25	21	19
BUSKEY, Tom	4.46	3-1	0	33	66.2	68	33	26	34
CLANCY, Jim	3.30	13-16	0	34	250.2	217	92	128	152
GARVIN, Jerry	2.29	4-7	8	61	82.2	70	21	27	52
JEFFERSON, Jesse	5.47	4-13	0	29	121.2	130	74	52	53
KUCEK, Jack	6.75	3-8	1	23	68.0	83	51	41	35
LEAL, Luis	4.53	3-4	0	13	59.2	72	30	31	26
LEMANCZYK, Dave	5.40	2-5	0	10	43.1	57	26	15	10
McLAUGHLIN, Joey	4.51	6-9	4	55	135.2	159	68	53	70
MIRABELLA, Paul	4.34	5-12	0	33	130.2	151	63	66	53
MOORE, Balor	5.29	1-1	1	31	64.2	76	38	31	22
SCHROM, Ken	5.23	1-0	1	17	31.0	32	18	19	13
STIEB, Dave	3.71	12-15	0	34	242.2	232	100	83	108
TODD, Jackson	4.02	5-2	0	12	85.0	90	38	30	44
WILLIS, Mike	1.71	2-1	3	20	26.1	25	5	11	14
1980 Totals	**4.19**	**67-95**	**23**	**162**	**1466.1**	**1523**	**683**	**635**	**705**

1981

BATTER Pos.	Avg.	G	AB	R	H	HR	RBI
AINGE, Danny 3B	.187	86	246	20	46	0	14
BARFIELD, Jesse OF	.232	25	95	7	22	2	9
BEAMON, Charlie DH-1B	.200	8	15	1	3	0	0
BELL, George OF	.233	60	163	19	38	5	12
BONNELL, Barry OF	.220	66	227	21	50	4	28
BOSETTI, Rick OF	.234	25	47	5	11	0	4
COX, Ted 3B	.300	16	50	6	15	2	9
GARCIA, Damaso 2B	.252	64	250	24	63	1	13
GRIFFIN, Alfredo SS	.209	101	388	30	81	0	21
IORG, Garth 2B-3B	.242	70	215	17	52	0	10
MACHA, Ken 3B-1B	.200	37	85	4	17	0	6
MANRIQUE, Fred IF	.143	14	28	1	4	0	1
MARTINEZ, Buck C	.227	45	128	13	29	4	21
MAYBERRY, John 1B	.248	94	290	34	72	17	43
MOSEBY, Lloyd OF	.233	100	378	36	88	9	43
STIEB, Dave PR	.000	1	0	1	0	0	0
UPSHAW, Willie DH-1B-OF	.171	61	111	15	19	4	10
VELEZ, Otto DH	.213	80	240	32	51	11	28
WELLS, Greg 1B-DH	.247	32	73	7	18	0	5
WHITMER, Dan C	.111	7	9	0	1	0	0
WHITT, Ernie C	.236	74	195	16	46	1	16
WOODS, Al OF	.247	85	288	20	71	1	21
Designated Hitters	.212	106	363	45	77	13	36
Pinch-Hitters	.234	–	77	4	18	1	15
1981 Totals	**.226**	**106**	**3521**	**329**	**797**	**61**	**314**

PITCHER	ERA	W-L	SV	G	IP	H	ER	BB	SO
BARLOW, Mike	4.20	0-0	0	12	15.0	22	7	6	5
BERENGUER, Juan	4.31	2-9	0	12	71.0	62	34	35	29
BOMBACK, Mark	3.89	5-5	0	20	90.1	84	39	35	33
CLANCY, Jim	4.90	6-12	0	22	125.0	126	68	64	56
ESPINOSA, Nino	9.00	0-0	0	1	1.0	4	1	0	0
GARVIN, Jerry	3.40	1-2	0	35	53.0	46	20	23	25
JACKSON, Roy Lee	2.61	1-2	7	39	62.0	65	18	25	27
LEAL, Luis	3.68	7-13	1	29	129.2	127	53	44	71
McLAUGHLIN, Joey	2.85	1-5	10	40	60.0	55	19	21	38
MIRABELLA, Paul	7.36	0-0	0	8	14.2	20	12	7	9
MURRAY, Dale	1.17	1-0	0	11	15.1	12	2	5	12
STIEB, Dave	3.19	11-10	0	25	183.2	148	65	61	89
TODD, Jackson	3.96	2-7	0	21	97.2	94	43	31	41
WILLIS, Mike	5.91	0-4	0	20	35.0	43	23	20	16
1981 Totals	**3.81**	**37-69**	**18**	**106**	**953.1**	**908**	**404**	**377**	**451**

1982

BATTER Pos.	Avg.	G	AB	R	H	HR	RBI
ADAMS, Glenn DH	.258	30	66	2	17	1	11
BAKER, Dave 3B	.250	9	20	3	5	0	2
BARFIELD, Jesse OF	.246	139	394	54	97	18	58
BONNELL, Barry OF	.293	140	437	59	128	6	49
DAVIS, Dick OF-DH	.286	3	7	0	2	0	2
GARCIA, Damaso 2B	.310	147	597	89	185	5	42
GRIFFIN, Alfredo SS	.241	162	539	57	130	1	48
HERNANDEZ, Pedro 3B	.000	8	9	1	0	0	0
IORG, Garth 3B-2B	.285	129	417	45	119	1	36
JOHNSON, Anthony OF-DH	.235	70	98	17	23	3	14
MARTINEZ, Buck C	.242	96	260	26	63	10	37
MAYBERRY, John DH-1B	.273	17	33	7	9	2	3
MOSEBY, Lloyd OF	.236	147	487	51	115	9	52
MULLINIKS, Rance 3B-SS	.244	112	311	32	76	4	35
NORDHAGEN, Wayne DH-OF	.270	72	185	12	50	1	20
PETRALLI, Geno C	.364	16	44	3	16	0	1
POWELL, Hosken OF-DH	.275	112	265	43	73	3	26
REVERING, Dave DH	.215	55	135	15	29	5	18
ROBERTS, Leon OF-DH	.229	40	105	6	24	1	5
UPSHAW, Willie 1B	.267	160	580	77	155	21	75
VELEZ, Otto DH	.192	28	52	4	10	1	5
WHITT, Ernie C	.261	105	284	28	74	11	42
WOODS, Al OF	.234	85	201	20	47	3	24
Designated Hitters	.238	162	596	52	142	8	56
Pinch-Hitters	.271	–	262	24	71	4	53
1982 Totals	**.262**	**162**	**5526**	**651**	**1447**	**106**	**605**

PITCHER	ERA	W-L	SV	G	IP	H	ER	BB	SO
BOMBACK, Mark	6.03	1-5	0	16	59.2	87	40	25	22
CLANCY, Jim	3.71	16-14	0	40	266.2	251	110	77	139
EICHHORN, Mark	5.45	0-3	0	7	38.0	40	23	14	16
GARVIN, Jerry	7.25	1-1	0	32	58.1	81	47	26	35
GEISEL, Dave	3.98	1-1	0	16	31.2	32	14	17	22
GOTT, Jim	4.43	5-10	0	30	136.0	134	67	66	82
JACKSON, Roy Lee	3.06	8-8	6	48	97.0	77	33	31	71
LEAL, Luis	3.93	12-15	0	38	249.2	250	109	79	111
McLAUGHLIN, Joey	3.21	8-6	8	44	70.0	54	25	30	49
MURRAY, Dale	3.16	8-7	11	56	111.0	115	39	32	60
SCHROM, Ken	5.87	1-0	0	6	15.1	13	10	15	8
SENTENEY, Steve	4.91	0-0	0	11	22.0	23	12	6	20
STIEB, Dave	3.25	17-14	0	38	288.1	271	104	75	141
1982 Totals	**3.95**	**78-84**	**25**	**162**	**1443.2**	**1428**	**633**	**493**	**776**

1983

BATTER Pos.	Avg.	G	AB	R	H	HR	RBI
BARFIELD, Jesse OF	.253	128	388	58	98	27	68
BELL, George OF	.268	39	112	5	30	2	17
BONNELL, Barry OF	.318	121	377	49	120	10	54
COLLINS, Dave OF	.271	118	402	55	109	1	34
FERNANDEZ, Tony SS	.265	15	34	5	9	0	2
GARCIA, Damaso 2B	.307	131	525	84	161	3	38
GRIFFIN, Alfredo SS	.250	162	528	62	132	4	47
IORG, Garth 3B-2B	.275	122	375	40	103	2	39
JOHNSON, Cliff DH	.265	142	407	59	108	22	76
KLUTTS, Mickey 3B	.256	22	43	3	11	3	5
MARTINEZ, Buck C	.253	88	221	27	56	10	33
MOSEBY, Lloyd OF	.315	151	539	104	170	18	81
MULLINIKS, Rance 3B-SS	.275	129	364	54	100	10	49
ORTA, Jorge DH-OF	.237	103	245	30	58	10	38
PETRALLI, Geno C	.000	6	4	0	0	0	0
POWELL, Hosken OF	.169	40	83	6	14	1	7
UPSHAW, Willie 1B	.306	160	579	99	177	27	104
WEBSTER, Mitch OF	.182	11	11	2	2	0	0
WHITT, Ernie C	.256	123	344	53	88	17	56
Designated Hitters	.250	162	604	86	151	34	113
Pinch-Hitters	.290	–	200	26	58	5	42
1983 Totals	**.277**	**162**	**5581**	**795**	**1546**	**167**	**748**

PITCHER	ERA	W-L	SV	G	IP	H	ER	BB	SO
ACKER, Jim	4.33	5-1	1	38	97.2	103	47	38	44
ALEXANDER, Doyle	3.93	7-6	0	17	116.2	126	51	26	46
CLANCY, Jim	3.91	15-11	0	34	223.0	238	97	61	99
CLARKE, Stan	3.27	1-1	0	10	11.0	10	4	5	7
COOPER, Don	6.75	0-0	0	4	5.1	8	4	0	5
GEISEL, Dave	4.64	0-3	5	47	52.1	47	27	31	50
GOTT, Jim	4.74	9-14	0	34	176.2	195	93	68	121
JACKSON, Roy Lee	4.50	8-3	7	49	92.0	92	46	41	48
LEAL, Luis	4.31	13-12	0	35	217.1	216	104	65	116
McLAUGHLIN, Joey	4.45	7-4	9	50	64.2	63	32	37	47
MOFFITT, Randy	3.77	6-2	10	45	57.1	52	24	24	38
MORGAN, Mike	5.16	0-3	0	16	45.1	48	26	21	22
STIEB, Dave	3.04	17-12	0	36	278.0	223	94	93	187
WILLIAMS, Matt	14.63	1-1	0	4	8.0	13	13	7	5
1983 Totals	**4.12**	**89-73**	**32**	**162**	**1445.1**	**1434**	**662**	**517**	**835**

1984

BATTER Pos.	Avg.	G	AB	R	H	HR	RBI
AIKENS, Willie DH	.205	93	234	21	48	11	26
BARFIELD, Jesse OF	.284	110	320	51	91	14	49
BELL, George OF	.292	159	606	85	177	26	87
COLLINS, Dave OF	.308	128	441	59	136	2	44
FERNANDEZ, Tony SS	.270	88	233	29	63	3	19
GARCIA, Damaso 2B	.284	152	633	79	180	5	46
GRIFFIN, Alfredo SS-2B	.241	140	419	53	101	4	30
GRUBER, Kelly 3B	.063	15	16	1	1	1	2
HERNANDEZ, Toby C	.500	3	2	1	1	0	0
IORG, Garth 3B	.227	121	247	24	56	1	25
JOHNSON, Cliff DH	.304	127	359	51	109	16	61
LEACH, Rick OF-1B	.261	65	88	11	23	0	7
MANRIQUE, Fred 2B	.333	10	9	0	3	0	1
MARTINEZ, Buck C	.220	102	232	24	51	5	37
MOSEBY, Lloyd OF	.280	158	592	97	166	18	92
MULLINIKS, Rance IF	.324	125	343	41	111	3	42
PETRALLI, Geno C	.000	3	3	0	0	0	0
SHEPHERD, Ron OF	.000	12	4	0	0	0	0
UPSHAW, Willie 1B	.278	152	569	79	158	19	84
WEBSTER, Mitch OF	.227	26	22	9	5	0	4
WHITT, Ernie C	.238	124	315	35	75	15	46
Designated Hitters	.270	163	612	91	165	27	93
Pinch-Hitters	.284	–	215	29	61	6	39
1984 Totals	**.273**	**163**	**5687**	**750**	**1555**	**143**	**702**

PITCHER	ERA	W-L	SV	G	IP	H	ER	BB	SO
ACKER, Jim	4.38	3-5	1	32	72.0	79	35	25	33
ALEXANDER, Doyle	3.13	17-6	0	36	261.2	238	91	59	139
CLANCY, Jim	5.12	13-15	0	36	219.2	249	125	88	118
CLARK, Bryan	5.91	1-2	0	20	45.2	66	30	22	21
GOTT, Jim	4.02	7-6	2	35	109.2	93	49	49	73
JACKSON, Roy Lee	3.56	7-8	10	54	86.0	73	34	31	58
KEY, Jimmy	4.65	4-5	10	63	62.0	70	32	32	44
LAMP, Dennis	4.55	8-8	9	56	85.0	97	43	38	45
LEACH, Rick	27.00	0-0	0	1	1.0	2	3	2	0
LEAL, Luis	3.89	13-8	0	35	222.1	221	96	77	134
McLAUGHLIN, Joey	2.53	0-0	0	6	10.2	12	3	7	3
MUSSELMAN, Ron	2.11	0-2	1	11	21.1	18	5	10	9
STIEB, Dave	2.83	16-8	0	35	267.0	215	84	88	198
1984 Totals	**3.86**	**89-73**	**33**	**162**	**1464.0**	**1433**	**628**	**528**	**875**

1985

BATTER Pos.	Avg.	G	AB	R	H	HR	RBI
AIKENS, Willie DH	.200	12	20	2	4	1	5
ALLENSON, Gary C	.118	14	34	2	4	0	3
BARFIELD, Jesse OF	.289	155	539	94	156	27	84
BELL, George OF	.275	157	607	87	167	28	95
BURROUGHS, Jeff DH	.257	86	191	19	49	6	28
FERNANDEZ, Tony SS	.289	161	564	71	163	2	51
FIELDER, Cecil 1B	.311	30	74	6	23	4	16
GARCIA, Damaso 2B	.282	146	600	70	169	8	65
GRUBER, Kelly 3B	.231	5	13	0	3	0	1
HEARRON, Jeff C	.143	4	7	0	1	0	0
IORG, Garth 3B-2B	.313	131	288	33	90	7	37
JOHNSON, Cliff DH-1B	.274	24	73	4	20	1	10
LEACH, Rick 1B-OF	.200	16	35	2	7	0	1
LEE, Manny IF	.200	64	40	9	8	0	0
MARTINEZ, Buck C	.162	42	99	11	16	4	14
MATUSZEK, Len DH-1B	.212	62	151	23	32	2	15
MOSEBY, Lloyd OF	.259	152	584	92	151	18	70
MULLINIKS, Rance 3B	.295	129	366	55	108	10	57
NICOSIA, Steve C	.267	6	15	0	4	0	1
OLIVER, Al DH	.251	61	187	20	47	5	23
SHEPHERD, Ron OF-DH	.114	38	35	7	4	0	1
THORNTON, Lou OF-DH	.236	56	72	18	17	1	8
UPSHAW, Willie 1B	.275	148	501	79	138	15	65
WEBSTER, Mitch OF-DH	.000	4	1	0	0	0	0
WHITT, Ernie C	.245	139	412	55	101	19	64
Designated Hitters	.247	161	600	77	148	13	78
Pinch-Hitters	.222	–	167	18	37	4	29
1985 Totals	**.269**	**161**	**5508**	**759**	**1482**	**158**	**714**

PITCHER	ERA	W-L	SV	G	IP	H	ER	BB	SO
ACKER, Jim	3.23	7-2	10	61	86.1	86	31	43	42
ALEXANDER, Doyle	3.45	17-10	0	36	260.2	268	100	67	142
CAUDILL, Bill	2.99	4-6	14	67	69.1	53	23	35	46
CERUTTI, John	5.40	0-2	0	4	6.2	10	4	4	5
CLANCY, Jim	3.78	9-6	0	23	128.2	117	54	37	66
CLARKE, Stan	4.50	0-0	0	4	4.0	3	2	2	2
DAVIS, Steve	3.54	2-1	0	10	28.0	23	11	13	22
FILER, Tom	3.88	7-0	0	11	48.2	38	21	18	24
HENKE, Tom	2.03	3-3	13	28	40.0	29	9	8	42
KEY, Jimmy	3.00	14-6	0	35	212.2	188	71	50	85
LAMP, Dennis	3.32	11-0	2	53	105.2	96	39	27	68
LAVELLE, Gary	3.10	5-7	8	69	72.2	54	25	36	50
LEAL, Luis	5.75	3-6	0	15	67.1	82	43	24	33
MUSSELMAN, Ron	4.47	3-0	0	25	52.1	59	26	24	29
STIEB, Dave	2.48	14-13	0	36	265.0	206	73	96	167
1985 Totals	**3.29**	**99-62**	**47**	**161**	**1448.0**	**1312**	**529**	**484**	**823**

1986

BATTER Pos.	Avg.	G	AB	R	H	HR	RBI
BARFIELD, Jesse OF	.289	158	589	107	170	40	108
BELL, George OF	.309	159	641	101	198	31	108
FERNANDEZ, Tony SS	.310	163	687	91	213	10	65
FIELDER, Cecil DH-1B	.157	34	83	7	13	4	13
GARCIA, Damaso 2B	.281	122	424	57	119	6	46
GRUBER, Kelly IF	.196	87	143	20	28	5	15
HEARRON, Jeff C	.217	12	23	2	5	0	4
IORG, Garth 3B-2B	.260	137	327	30	85	3	44
JOHNSON, Cliff DH	.250	107	336	48	84	15	55
LEACH, Rick DH-OF	.309	110	246	35	76	5	39
LEE, Manny 2B-SS	.205	35	78	8	16	1	7
MARTINEZ, Buck C	.181	81	160	13	29	2	12
McGRIFF, Fred 1B-DH	.200	3	5	1	1	0	0
MOSEBY, Lloyd OF	.253	152	589	89	149	21	86
MULLINIKS, Rance 3B	.259	117	348	50	90	11	45
SHEPHERD, Ron OF	.203	65	69	16	14	2	4
UPSHAW, Willie 1B	.251	155	573	85	144	9	60
WHITT, Ernie C	.268	131	395	48	106	16	56
Designated Hitters	.242	162	616	86	149	20	83
Pinch-Hitters	.277	–	155	19	43	4	32
1986 Totals	**.269**	**163**	**5716**	**809**	**1540**	**181**	**767**

PITCHER	ERA	W-L	SV	G	IP	H	ER	BB	SO
ACKER, Jim	4.35	2-4	0	23	60.0	63	29	22	32
ALEXANDER, Doyle	4.46	5-4	0	17	111.0	120	55	20	65
AQUINO, Luis	6.35	1-1	0	7	11.1	14	8	3	5
CAUDILL, Bill	6.19	2-4	2	40	36.1	36	25	17	32
CERUTTI, John	4.15	9-4	1	34	145.1	150	67	47	89
CLANCY, Jim	3.94	14-14	0	34	219.1	202	96	63	126
CLARKE, Stan	9.24	0-1	0	10	12.2	18	13	10	9
DAVIS, Steve	17.18	0-0	0	3	3.2	8	7	5	5
EICHHORN, Mark	1.72	14-6	10	69	157.0	105	30	45	166
GORDON, Don	7.06	0-1	1	14	21.2	28	17	8	13
HENKE, Tom	3.35	9-5	27	63	91.1	63	34	32	118
JOHNSON, Joe	3.89	7-2	0	16	88.0	94	38	22	39
KEY, Jimmy	3.57	14-11	0	36	232.0	222	92	74	141
LAMP, Dennis	5.05	2-6	2	40	73.0	93	41	23	30
MAHLER, Mickey	0.00	0-0	0	2	1.0	1	0	0	0
MUSSELMAN, Jeff	10.13	0-0	0	6	5.1	8	6	5	4
STIEB, Dave	4.74	7-12	1	37	205.0	239	108	87	127
WARD, Duane	13.50	0-1	0	2	2.0	3	3	4	1
1986 Totals	**4.08**	**86-76**	**44**	**163**	**1476.0**	**1467**	**669**	**487**	**1002**

1987

BATTER Pos.	Avg.	G	AB	R	H	HR	RBI
BARFIELD, Jesse OF	.263	159	590	89	155	28	84
BELL, George OF	.308	156	610	111	188	47	134
BENIQUEZ, Juan DH-OF	.284	39	81	6	23	5	21
DEWILLIS, Jeff C	.120	13	25	2	3	1	2
DUCEY, Rob OF	.188	34	48	12	9	1	6
FERNANDEZ, Tony SS	.322	146	578	90	186	5	67
FIELDER, Cecil DH-1B	.269	82	175	30	47	14	32
GRUBER, Kelly 3B-SS	.235	138	341	50	80	12	36
INFANTE, Alexis PR	.000	1	0	0	0	0	0
IORG, Garth 2B-3B	.210	122	310	35	65	4	30
LEACH, Rick OF-DH	.282	98	195	26	55	3	25
LEE, Manny 2B-SS	.256	56	121	14	31	1	11
LIRIANO, Nelson 2B	.241	37	158	29	38	2	10
McGRIFF, Fred DH-1B	.247	107	295	58	73	20	43
MOORE, Charlie C	.215	51	107	15	23	1	7
MOSEBY, Lloyd OF	.282	155	592	106	167	26	96
MULLINIKS, Rance 3B-DH	.310	124	332	37	103	11	44
MYERS, Greg C	.111	7	9	1	1	0	0
SHARPERSON, Mike 2B	.208	32	96	4	20	0	9
STARK, Matt C	.083	5	12	0	1	0	0
THORNTON, Lou DH-OF	.500	12	2	5	1	0	0
UPSHAW, Willie 1B	.244	150	512	68	125	15	58
WHITT, Ernie C	.269	135	446	57	120	19	75
Designated Hitters	.258	162	592	101	153	38	97
Pinch-Hitters	.234	–	167	0	39	3	28
1987 Totals	**.269**	**162**	**5635**	**845**	**1514**	**215**	**790**

PITCHER	ERA	W-L	SV	G	IP	H	ER	BB	SO
CERUTTI, John	4.40	11-4	0	44	151.1	144	74	59	92
CLANCY, Jim	3.54	15-11	0	37	241.1	234	95	80	180
EICHHORN, Mark	3.17	10-6	4	89	127.2	110	45	52	96
FLANAGAN, Mike	2.37	3-2	0	7	49.1	46	13	15	43
GORDON, Don	4.09	0-0	0	5	11.0	8	5	3	3
HENKE, Tom	2.49	0-6	34	72	94.0	62	26	25	128
JOHNSON, Joey	5.13	3-5	0	14	66.2	77	38	18	27
KEY, Jimmy	2.76	17-8	0	36	261.0	210	80	66	161
LAVELLE, Gary	5.53	2-3	1	23	27.2	36	17	19	17
MUSSELMAN, Jeff	4.15	12-5	3	68	89.0	75	41	54	54
NIEKRO, Phil	8.25	0-2	0	3	12.0	15	11	7	7
NUNEZ, Jose	5.01	5-2	0	37	97.0	91	54	58	99
STIEB, Dave	4.09	13-9	0	33	185.0	164	84	87	115
WARD, Duane	6.94	1-0	0	12	11.2	14	9	12	10
WELLS, David	3.99	4-3	1	18	29.1	37	13	12	32
1987 Totals	**3.74**	**96-66**	**43**	**162**	**1454.0**	**1323**	**605**	**567**	**1064**

1988

BATTER Pos.	Avg.	G	AB	R	H	HR	RBI
BARFIELD, Jesse OF	.244	137	468	62	114	18	56
BELL, George OF	.269	156	614	78	165	24	97
BENIQUEZ, Juan DH	.293	27	58	9	17	1	8
BORDERS, Pat C	.273	56	154	15	42	5	21
BUTERA, Sal C	.233	23	60	3	14	1	6
CAMPUSANO, Sil OF	.218	73	142	14	31	2	12
DUCEY, Rob OF	.315	27	54	15	17	0	6
FERNANDEZ, Tony SS	.287	154	648	76	186	5	70
FIELDER, Cecil DH-1B	.230	74	174	24	40	9	23
GRUBER, Kelly 3B	.278	158	569	75	158	16	81
INFANTE, Alexis IF	.200	19	15	7	3	0	0
LEACH, Rick OF	.276	87	199	21	55	0	23
LEE, Manny 2B-SS	.291	116	381	38	111	2	38
LIRIANO, Nelson 2B	.264	99	276	36	73	3	23
McGRIFF, Fred 1B	.282	154	536	100	151	34	82
MOSEBY, Lloyd OF	.239	128	472	77	113	10	42
MULLINIKS, Rance DH	.300	119	337	49	101	12	48
THORNTON, Lou OF	.000	11	2	1	0	0	0
WHITT, Ernie C	.251	127	398	63	100	16	70
Designated Hitters	.288	162	612	90	176	25	95
Pinch-Hitters	.202	–	129	14	26	2	18
1988 Totals	**.268**	**162**	**5557**	**763**	**1491**	**158**	**706**

PITCHER	ERA	W-L	SV	G	IP	H	ER	BB	SO
BAIR, Doug	4.05	0-0	0	10	13.1	14	6	3	8
CASTILLO, Tony	3.00	1-0	0	14	15.0	10	5	2	14
CERUTTI, John	3.13	6-7	1	46	123.2	120	43	42	65
CLANCY, Jim	4.49	11-13	1	36	196.1	207	98	47	118
EICHHORN, Mark	4.19	0-3	1	37	66.2	79	31	27	28
FLANAGAN, Mike	4.18	13-13	0	34	211.0	220	98	80	99
HENKE, Tom	2.91	4-4	25	52	68.0	60	22	24	66
KEY, Jimmy	3.29	12-5	0	21	131.1	127	48	30	65
MUSSELMAN, Jeff	3.18	8-5	0	15	85.0	80	30	30	39
NUNEZ, Jose	3.07	0-1	0	13	29.1	28	10	17	18
ROSS, Mark	4.91	0-0	0	3	7.1	5	4	4	4
STIEB, Dave	3.04	16-8	0	32	207.1	157	70	79	147
STOTTLEMYRE, Todd	5.69	4-8	0	28	98.0	109	62	46	67
WARD, Duane	3.30	9-3	15	64	111.2	101	41	60	91
WELLS, David	4.62	3-5	4	41	64.1	65	33	31	56
WILLS, Frank	5.23	0-0	0	10	20.2	22	12	6	19
1988 Totals	**3.80**	**87-75**	**47**	**162**	**1449.0**	**1404**	**611**	**528**	**904**

1989

BATTER Pos.	Avg.	G	AB	R	H	HR	RBI
BARFIELD, Jesse OF	.200	21	80	8	16	5	11
BATISTE, Kevin OF	.250	6	8	1	2	0	0
BELL, George OF	.297	153	613	88	182	18	104
BORDERS, Pat C-DH	.257	94	241	22	62	3	29
BRENLY, Bob DH-C	.170	48	88	9	15	1	6
CABRERA, Francisco DH	.167	3	12	1	2	0	0
DUCEY, Rob OF	.211	41	76	5	16	0	7
FELIX, Junior OF	.258	110	415	62	107	9	46
FERNANDEZ, Tony SS	.257	140	573	64	147	11	64
GRUBER, Kelly 3B	.290	135	545	83	158	18	73
HILL, Glenallen OF	.288	19	52	4	15	1	7
INFANTE, Alexis IF	.167	20	12	1	2	0	0
LAWLESS, Tom OF-IF	.229	59	70	20	16	0	3
LEE, Manny IF	.260	99	300	27	78	3	34
LIRIANO, Nelson 2B	.263	132	418	51	110	5	53
MAZZILLI, Lee DH-1B	.227	28	66	12	15	4	11
McGRIFF, Fred 1B	.269	161	551	98	148	36	92
MOSEBY, Lloyd OF	.221	135	502	72	111	11	43
MULLINIKS, Rance DH-3B	.238	103	273	25	65	3	29
MYERS, Greg C-DH	.114	17	44	0	5	0	1
OLERUD, John 1B	.375	6	8	2	3	0	0
VIRGIL, Ozzie DH-C	.182	9	11	2	2	1	2
WHITT, Ernie C	.262	129	385	42	101	11	53
WILSON, Mookie OF	.298	54	238	32	71	2	17
Designated Hitters	.216	162	589	66	127	8	55
Pinch-Hitters	.264	–	121	14	32	3	13
1989 Totals	**.260**	**162**	**5581**	**731**	**1449**	**142**	**685**

PITCHER	ERA	W-L	SV	G	IP	H	ER	BB	SO
ACKER, Jim	1.59	2-1	0	14	28.1	24	5	12	24
BUICE, Dewayne	5.82	1-0	0	7	17.0	13	11	13	10
CASTILLO, Tony	6.11	1-1	1	17	17.2	23	12	10	10
CERUTTI, John	3.07	11-11	0	33	205.1	214	70	53	69
CUMMINGS, Steve	3.00	2-0	0	5	21.0	18	7	11	8
FLANAGAN, Mike	3.93	8-10	0	30	171.2	186	75	47	47
GOZZO, Mauro	4.83	4-1	0	9	31.2	35	17	9	10
HENKE, Tom	1.92	8-3	20	64	89.0	66	19	25	116
HERNANDEZ, Xavier	4.76	1-0	0	7	22.2	25	12	8	7
KEY, Jimmy	3.88	13-14	0	33	216.0	226	93	27	118
LEITER, Al	4.05	0-0	0	1	6.2	9	3	2	4
MUSSELMAN, Jeff	10.64	0-1	0	5	11.0	19	13	9	3
NUNEZ, Jose	2.53	0-0	0	6	10.2	8	3	2	14
SANCHEZ, Alex	10.03	0-1	0	4	11.2	16	13	14	4
STIEB, Dave	3.35	17-8	0	33	206.2	164	77	76	101
STOTTLEMYRE, Todd	3.88	7-7	0	27	127.2	137	55	44	63
WARD, Duane	3.77	4-10	15	66	114.2	94	48	58	122
WELLS, David	2.40	7-4	2	54	86.1	66	23	28	78
WILLS, Frank	3.66	3-1	0	24	71.1	65	29	30	41
1989 Totals	**3.58**	**89-73**	**38**	**162**	**1467.0**	**1408**	**584**	**478**	**849**

1990

BATTER Pos.	Avg.	G	AB	R	H	HR	RBI
BELL, George OF-DH	.265	142	562	67	149	21	86
BORDERS, Pat C	.286	125	346	36	99	15	49
DIAZ, Carlos C	.333	9	3	1	1	0	0
DUCEY, Rob OF	.302	19	53	7	16	0	7
EPPARD, Jim PH	.200	6	5	0	1	0	0
FELIX, Junior OF	.263	127	463	73	122	15	65
FERNANDEZ, Tony SS	.276	161	635	84	175	4	66
GRUBER, Kelly 3B	.274	150	592	92	162	31	118
HILL, Glenallen OF-DH	.231	84	260	47	60	12	32
LAWLESS, Tom IF-OF	.083	15	12	1	1	0	1
LEE, Manny 2B	.243	117	391	45	95	6	41
LIRIANO, Nelson 2B	.212	50	170	16	36	1	15
McGRIFF, Fred 1B	.300	153	557	91	167	35	88
MULLINIKS, Rance 3B-DH	.289	57	97	11	28	2	16
MYERS, Greg C	.236	87	250	33	59	5	22
OLERUD, John DH-1B	.265	111	358	43	95	14	48
QUINLAN, Tom 3B	.500	1	2	0	1	0	0
SOJO, Luis IF	.225	33	80	14	18	1	9
VIRGIL, Ozzie C-DH	.000	3	5	0	0	0	0
WHITEN, Mark OF	.273	33	88	12	24	2	7
WILLIAMS, Kenny OF-DH	.194	49	72	13	14	0	8
WILSON, Mookie OF	.265	147	588	81	156	3	51
Designated Hitters	.220	162	604	68	133	14	68
Pinch-Hitters	.216	–	97	4	21	0	14
1990 Totals	**.265**	**162**	**5589**	**767**	**1479**	**167**	**729**

1990 *continued*

PITCHER	ERA	W-L	SV	G	IP	H	ER	BB	SO
ACKER, Jim	3.83	4-4	1	59	91.2	103	39	30	54
BLACK, Bud	4.02	2-1	0	3	15.2	10	7	3	3
BLAIR, Willie	4.06	3-5	0	27	68.2	66	31	28	43
CANDELARIA, John	5.48	0-3	1	13	21.1	32	13	11	19
CERUTTI, John	4.76	9-9	0	30	140.0	162	74	49	49
CUMMINGS. Steve	5.11	0-0	0	6	12.1	22	7	5	4
FLANAGAN, Mike	5.31	2-2	0	5	20.1	28	12	8	5
GILLES, Tom	6.75	1-0	0	2	1.1	2	1	0	1
HENKE, Tom	2.17	2-4	32	61	74.2	58	18	19	75
KEY, Jimmy	4.25	13-7	0	27	154.2	169	73	22	88
KILGUS, Paul	6.06	0-0	0	11	16.1	19	11	7	7
LEITER, Al	0.00	0-0	0	4	6.1	1	0	2	5
LUECKEN, Rick	9.00	0-0	0	1	1.0	2	1	1	0
MacDONALD, Bob	0.00	0-0	0	4	2.1	0	0	2	0
STIEB, Dave	2.93	18-6	0	33	208.2	179	68	64	125
STOTTLEMYRE, Todd	4.34	13-17	0	33	203.0	214	98	69	115
WARD, Duane	3.45	2-8	11	73	127.2	101	49	42	112
WELLS, David	3.14	11-6	3	43	189.0	165	66	45	115
WILLS, Frank	4.73	6-4	0	44	99.0	101	52	38	72
1990 Totals	**3.84**	**86-76**	**48**	**162**	**1454.0**	**1434**	**620**	**445**	**892**

1991

BATTER Pos.	Avg.	G	AB	R	H	HR	RBI
ALOMAR, Roberto 2B	.295	161	637	88	188	9	69
BELL, Derek OF	.143	18	28	5	4	0	1
BORDERS, Pat C	.244	105	291	22	71	5	36
CARTER, Joe OF	.273	162	638	89	174	33	108
DUCEY, Rob OF	.235	39	68	8	16	1	4
GIANNELLI, Ray 3B	.167	9	24	2	4	0	0
GONZALES, Rene IF	.195	71	118	16	23	1	6
GRUBER, Kely 3B	.252	113	429	58	108	20	65
HILL, Glenallen DH-OF	.253	35	99	14	25	3	11
KNORR, Randy C	.000	3	1	0	0	0	0
LEE, Manny SS	.234	138	445	41	104	0	29
MALDONADO, Candy OF	.277	52	177	26	49	7	28
MULLINIKS, Rance DH	.250	97	240	27	60	2	24
MYERS, Greg C	.262	107	309	25	81	8	36
OLERUD, John 1B	.256	139	454	64	116	17	68
PARKER, Dave DH	.333	13	36	2	12	0	3
SNYDER, Cory OF-1B	.143	21	49	4	7	0	6
SPRAGUE, Ed 3B-1B	.275	61	160	17	44	4	20
TABLER, Pat DH-1B	.216	82	185	20	40	1	21
WARD, Turner OF	.308	8	13	1	4	0	2
WHITE, Devon OF	.282	156	642	110	181	17	60
WHITEN, Mark OF	.221	46	149	12	33	2	19
WILLIAMS, Kenny OF	.207	13	29	5	6	1	3
WILSON, Mookie OF-DH	.241	86	241	26	58	2	28
ZOSKY, Eddie SS	.148	18	27	2	4	0	2
Designated Hitters	.252	162	583	70	147	5	56
Pinch Hitters	.236	–	123	13	29	1	21
1991 Totals	**.257**	**162**	**5489**	**684**	**1412**	**133**	**649**

PITCHER	ERA	W-L	SV	G	IP	H	ER	BB	SO
ACKER, Jim	5.20	3-5	1	54	88.1	77	51	36	44
BOUCHER, Denis	4.58	0-3	0	7	35.1	39	18	16	16
CANDIOTTI, Tom	2.98	6-7	0	19	129.2	114	43	45	81
DAYLEY, Ken	6.23	0-0	0	8	4.1	7	3	5	3
FRASER, Willie	6.15	0-2	0	13	26.1	33	18	11	12
GUZMAN, Juan	2.99	10-3	0	23	138.2	98	46	66	123
HENKE, Tom	2.32	0-2	32	49	50.1	33	13	11	53
HENGTEN, Pat	2.45	0-0	0	3	7.1	5	2	3	3
HORSMAN, Vince	0.00	0-0	0	4	4.0	2	0	3	2
KEY, Jimmy	3.05	16-12	0	33	209.1	207	71	44	125
LEITER, Al	27.00	0-0	0	3	1.2	3	5	5	1
MacDONALD, Bob	2.85	3-3	0	45	53.2	51	17	25	24
STIEB, Dave	3.17	4-3	0	9	59.2	52	21	23	29
STOTTLEMYRE, Todd	3.78	15-8	0	34	219.0	194	92	75	116
TIMLIN, Mike	3.16	11-6	3	63	108.1	94	38	50	85
WARD, Duane	2.77	7-6	23	81	107.1	80	33	33	132
WEATHERS, David	4.91	1-0	0	15	14.2	15	8	17	13
WELLS, David	3.72	15-10	1	40	198.1	188	82	49	106
WESTON, Mickey	0.00	0-0	0	2	2.0	1	0	1	1
WILLS, Frank	16.62	0-1	0	4	4.1	8	8	5	2
1991 Totals	**3.50**	**91-71**	**60**	**162**	**1462.2**	**1301**	**569**	**523**	**971**

1992

BATTER Pos.	Avg.	G	AB	R	H	HR	RBI
ALOMAR, Roberto 2B	.310	152	571	105	177	8	76
BELL, Derek OF	.242	61	161	23	39	2	15
BORDERS, Pat C	.242	138	480	47	116	13	53
CARTER, Joe OF-DH	.264	158	622	97	164	34	119
DUCEY, Rob OF-DH	.048	23	21	3	1	0	0
GRIFFIN, Alfredo SS-2B	.233	63	150	21	35	0	10
GRUBER, Kelly 3B	.229	120	446	42	102	11	43
KENT, Jeff IF	.240	65	192	36	46	8	35
KNORR, Randy C	.263	8	19	1	5	1	2
LEE, Manuel SS	.263	128	396	49	104	3	39
MAKSUDIAN, Mike PH	.000	3	3	0	0	0	0
MALDONADO, Candy OF	.272	137	489	64	133	20	66
MARTINEZ, Domingo 1B	.625	7	8	2	5	1	3
MULLINIKS, Rance PH	.500	3	2	1	1	0	0
MYERS, Greg C	.230	22	61	4	14	1	13
OLERUD, John 1B	.284	138	458	68	130	16	66
QUINLAN, Tom 3B	.067	13	15	2	1	0	2
SPRAGUE, Ed C-IF	.234	22	47	6	11	1	7
TABLER, Pat 1B-OF	.252	49	135	11	34	0	16
WARD, Turner OF	.345	18	29	7	10	1	3
WHITE, Devon OF	.248	153	641	98	159	17	60
WINFIELD, Dave DH-OF	.290	156	583	92	169	26	108
ZOSKY, Eddie SS	.286	8	7	1	2	0	1
Designated Hitters	.267	162	619	95	165	29	112
Pinch Hitters	.273	–	55	8	15	0	9
1992 Totals	**.263**	**162**	**5536**	**780**	**1458**	**163**	**737**

PITCHER	ERA	W-L	SV	G	IP	H	ER	BB	SO
CONE, David	2.55	4-3	0	8	53.0	39	15	29	47
EICHHORN, Mark	4.35	2-0	0	23	31.0	35	15	7	19
GUZMAN, Juan	2.64	16-5	0	28	180.2	135	53	72	165
HENKE, Tom	2.26	3-2	34	57	55.2	40	14	22	46
HENGTEN, Pat	5.36	5-2	0	28	50.1	49	30	32	39
KEY, Jimmy	3.53	13-13	0	33	216.2	205	85	59	117
LEITER, Al	9.00	0-0	0	1	1.0	1	1	2	0
LINTON, Doug	8.63	1-3	0	8	24.0	31	23	17	16
MacDONALD, Bob	4.37	1-0	0	27	47.1	50	23	16	26
MORRIS, Jack	4.04	21-6	0	34	240.2	222	108	80	132
STIEB, Dave	5.04	4-6	0	21	96.1	98	54	43	45
STOTTLEMYRE, Todd	4.50	12-11	0	28	174.0	175	87	63	98
TIMLIN, Mike	4.12	0-2	1	26	43.2	45	20	20	35
TRLICEK, Ricky	10.80	0-0	0	2	1.2	2	2	2	1
WARD, Duane	1.95	7-4	12	79	101.1	76	22	39	103
WEATHERS, David	8.10	0-0	0	2	3.1	5	3	2	3
WELLS, David	5.40	7-9	2	41	120.0	138	72	36	62
1992 Totals	**3.91**	**96-66**	**49**	**162**	**1440.2**	**1346**	**626**	**541**	**954**

1993

BATTER Pos.	Avg.	G	AB	R	H	HR	RBI
ALOMAR, Roberto 2B	.326	153	589	109	192	17	93
BORDERS, Pat C	.254	138	488	38	124	9	55
BUTLER, Rob OF	.271	17	48	8	13	0	2
CANATE, WIllie OF	.213	38	47	12	10	1	3
CARTER, Joe OF	.254	155	603	92	153	33	121
CEDENO, Domingo SS-2B	.174	15	46	5	8	0	7
COLES, Darnell OF-3B	.253	64	194	26	49	4	26
DELGADO, Carlos C	.000	2	1	0	0	0	0
FERNANDEZ, Tony SS	.306	94	353	45	108	4	50
GREEN, Shawn OF	.000	3	6	0	0	0	0
GRIFFIN, Alfredo IF	.211	46	95	15	20	0	3
HENDERSON, Rickey OF	.215	44	163	37	35	4	12
JACKSON, Darrin OF	.216	46	176	15	38	5	19
KNORR, Randy C	.248	39	101	11	25	4	20
MARTINEZ, Domingo 1B	.286	8	14	2	4	1	3
MOLITOR, Paul DH-1B	.332	160	636	121	211	22	111
OLERUD, John 1B-DH	.363	158	551	109	200	24	107
SCHOFIELD, Dick SS	.191	36	110	11	21	0	5
SOJO, Luis IF	.170	19	47	5	8	0	6
SPRAGUE, Ed 3B	.260	150	546	50	142	12	73
WARD, Turner OF	.192	72	167	20	32	4	28
WHITE, Devon OF	.273	146	598	116	163	15	52
Designated Hitters	.308	162	639	116	197	20	101
Pinch Hitters	.185	–	27	1	5	1	5
1993 Totals	**.279**	**162**	**5579**	**847**	**1556**	**159**	**796**

PITCHER	ERA	W-L	SV	G	IP	H	ER	BB	SO
BROW, Scott	6.00	1-1	0	6	18.0	19	12	10	7
CASTILLO, Tony	3.38	3-2	0	51	50.2	44	19	22	28
COX, Danny	3.12	7-6	2	44	83.2	73	29	29	84
DAYLEY, Ken	0.00	0-0	0	2	0.2	1	0	4	2
EICHHORN, Mark	2.72	3-1	0	54	72.2	76	22	22	47
FLENER, Huck	4.05	0-0	0	6	6.2	7	3	4	2
GUZMAN, Juan	3.99	14-3	0	33	221.0	211	98	110	194
HENTGEN, Pat	3.87	19-9	0	34	216.1	215	93	74	122
LEITER, Al	4.11	9-6	2	34	105.0	93	48	56	66
LINTON, Doug	6.55	0-1	0	4	11.0	11	8	9	4
MORRIS, Jack	6.19	7-12	0	27	152.2	189	105	65	103
STEWART, Dave	4.44	12-8	0	26	162.0	146	80	72	96
STOTTLEMYRE, Todd	4.84	11-12	0	30	176.2	204	95	69	98
TIMLIN, Mike	4.69	4-2	1	54	55.2	63	29	27	49
WARD, Duane	2.13	2-3	45	71	71.2	49	17	25	97
WILLIAMS, Woody	4.38	3-1	0	30	37.0	40	18	22	24
1993 Totals	**4.21**	**95-67**	**50**	**162**	**1441.1**	**1441**	**674**	**620**	**1023**

1994

BATTER Pos.	Avg.	G	AB	R	H	HR	RBI
ALOMAR, Roberto 2B	.306	107	392	78	120	8	38
BORDERS, Pat C	.247	85	295	24	73	3	26
BUTLER, Rob OF	.176	41	74	13	13	0	5
CARTER, Joe OF	.271	111	435	70	118	27	103
CEDENO, Domingo 2B-SS	.196	47	97	14	19	0	10
COLES, Darnell OF-1B	.210	48	143	15	30	4	15
DELGADO, Carlos OF	.215	43	130	17	28	9	24
GONZALEZ, Alex SS	.151	15	53	7	8	0	1
GREEN, Shawn OF	.091	14	33	1	3	0	1
HUFF, Mike OF	.304	80	207	31	63	3	25
KNORR, Randy C	.242	40	124	20	30	7	19
MOLITOR, Paul DH	.341	115	454	86	155	14	75
OLERUD, John 1B	.297	108	384	47	114	12	67
PEREZ, Robert OF	.125	4	8	0	1	0	0
SCHOFIELD, Dick SS	.255	95	325	38	83	4	32
SPRAGUE, Ed 3B	.240	109	405	38	97	11	44
WHITE, Devon OF	.270	100	403	67	109	13	49
Designated Hitters	.333	115	457	84	152	14	75
Pinch Hitters	.125	–	32	4	4	1	4
1994 Totals	**.269**	**115**	**3962**	**566**	**1064**	**115**	**534**

PITCHER	ERA	W-L	SV	G	IP	H	ER	BB	SO
BROW, Scott	5.90	0-3	2	18	29.0	34	19	19	15
CADARET, Greg	5.85	0-1	0	21	20.0	24	13	17	15
CASTILLO, Tony	2.51	5-2	1	41	68.0	66	19	28	43
CORNETT, Brad	6.68	1-3	0	9	31.0	40	23	11	22
COX, Danny	1.45	1-1	3	10	18.2	7	3	7	14
GUZMAN, Juan	5.68	12-11	0	25	147.1	165	93	76	124
HALL, Darren	3.41	2-3	17	30	31.2	26	12	14	28
HENTGEN, Pat	3.40	13-8	0	24	174.2	158	66	59	147
LEITER, Al	5.08	6-7	0	20	111.2	125	63	65	100
RIGHETTI, Dave	6.75	0-1	0	13	13.1	9	10	10	10
ST. CLAIRE, Randy	9.00	0-0	0	2	2.0	4	2	2	2
SMALL, Aaron	9.00	0-0	0	1	2.0	5	2	2	0
SPOLJARIC, Paul	38.57	0-1	0	2	2.1	5	10	9	2
STEWART, Dave	5.87	7-8	0	22	133.1	151	87	62	111
STOTTLEMYRE, Todd	4.22	7-7	1	26	140.2	149	66	48	105
TIMLIN, Mike	5.18	0-1	2	34	40.0	41	23	20	38
WILLIAMS, Woody	3.64	1-3	0	38	59.1	44	24	33	56
1994 Totals	**4.70**	**55-60**	**26**	**115**	**1025.0**	**1053**	**535**	**482**	**832**

1995

BATTER Pos.	Avg.	G	AB	R	H	HR	RBI
ALOMAR, Roberto 2B	.300	130	517	71	155	13	66
BATTLE, Howard 3B	.200	9	15	3	3	0	0
CARTER, Joe OF	.253	139	558	70	141	25	76
CEDENO, Domingo SS-2B	.236	51	161	18	38	4	14
DELGADO, Carlos OF-DH-1B	.165	37	91	7	15	3	11
GONZALEZ, Alex SS	.243	111	367	51	89	10	42
GREEN, Shawn OF	.288	121	379	52	109	15	54
HUFF, Michael OF	.232	61	138	14	32	1	9
KNORR, Randy C	.212	45	132	18	28	3	16
MALDONADO, Candy OF	.269	61	160	22	43	7	25
MARTINEZ, Sandy C	.241	62	191	12	46	2	25
MOLITOR, Paul DH	.270	130	525	63	142	15	60
OLERUD, John 1B	.291	135	492	72	143	8	54
PARRISH, Lance C	.202	70	178	15	36	4	22
PEREZ, Robert OF	.188	17	48	2	9	1	3
PEREZ, Tomas SS-2B	.245	41	98	12	24	1	8
SPRAGUE, Ed 3B	.244	144	521	77	127	18	74
STEWART, Shannon OF	.211	12	38	2	8	0	1
WHITE, Devon OF	.283	101	427	61	121	10	53
Designated Hitters	.262	144	584	68	153	16	69
Pinch Hitters	.192	–	73	6	14	1	8
1995 Totals	**.260**	**144**	**5036**	**642**	**1309**	**140**	**613**

PITCHER	ERA	W-L	SV	G	IP	H	ER	BB	SO
CARRARA, Giovanni	7.21	2-4	0	12	48.2	64	39	25	27
CASTILLO, Tony	3.22	1-5	13	55	72.2	64	26	24	38
CONE, David	3.38	9-6	0	17	130.1	113	49	41	102
CORNETT, Brad	9.00	0-0	0	5	5.0	9	5	3	4
COX, Danny	7.40	1-3	0	24	45.0	57	37	33	38
CRABTREE, Tim	3.09	0-2	0	31	32.0	30	11	13	21
DARWIN, Danny	7.62	1-8	0	13	65.0	91	55	24	36
GUZMAN, Juan	6.32	4-14	0	24	135.1	151	95	73	94
HALL, Darren	4.41	0-2	3	17	16.1	21	8	9	11
HENTGEN, Pat	5.11	10-14	0	30	200.2	236	114	90	135
HURTADO, Edwin	5.45	5-2	0	14	77.2	81	47	40	33
JORDAN, Ricardo	6.60	1-0	1	15	15.0	18	11	13	10
LEITER, Al	3.64	11-11	0	28	183.0	162	74	108	153
MENHART, Paul	4.92	1-4	0	21	78.2	72	43	47	50
ROBINSON, Ken	3.69	1-2	0	21	39.0	25	16	22	31
ROGERS, Jimmy	5.70	2-4	0	19	23.2	21	15	18	13
TIMLIN, Mike	2.14	4-3	5	31	42.0	38	10	17	36
WARD, Duane	27.00	0-1	0	4	2.2	11	8	5	3
WARE, Jeff	5.47	2-1	0	5	26.1	28	16	21	18
WILLIAMS, Woody	3.69	1-2	0	23	53.2	44	22	28	41
1995 Totals	**4.88**	**56-88**	**22**	**144**	**1292.2**	**1336**	**701**	**654**	**894**

1996

BATTER Pos.	Avg.	G	AB	R	H	HR	RBI
BRITO, Tilson 2B-SS	.238	26	80	10	19	1	7
BRUMFIELD, Jacob OF-DH	.256	90	308	52	79	12	52
CAIRO, Miguel 2B	.222	9	27	5	6	0	1
CARTER, Joe OF-1B-DH	.253	157	625	84	158	30	107
CEDENO, Domingo 2B-SS	.280	77	282	44	79	2	17
CRESPO, Felipe IF	.184	22	49	6	9	0	4
DELGADO, Carlos 1B-DH	.270	138	488	68	132	25	92
GONZALEZ, Alex SS	.235	147	527	64	124	14	64
GREEN, Shawn OF	.280	132	422	52	118	11	45
HUFF, Mike OF-3B	.172	11	29	5	5	0	0
MARTINEZ, Sandy C	.227	76	229	17	52	3	18
MOSQUERA, Julio C	.227	8	22	2	5	0	2
NIXON, Otis OF	.286	125	496	87	142	1	29
O'BRIEN, Charlie C	.238	109	324	33	77	13	44
OLERUD, John 1B-DH	.274	125	398	59	109	18	61
PEREZ, Robert OF-DH	.327	86	202	30	66	2	21
PEREZ, Tomas IF	.251	91	295	24	74	1	19
SAMUEL, Juan DH-OF-1B	.255	69	188	34	48	8	26
SPRAGUE, Ed 3B-DH	.247	159	591	88	146	36	101
STEWART, Shannon OF	.176	7	17	2	3	0	2
Designated Hitters	.260	162	628	95	163	32	109
Pinch Hitters	.204	–	113	15	23	2	14
1996 Totals	**.259**	**162**	**5599**	**766**	**1451**	**177**	**712**

PITCHER	ERA	W-L	SV	G	IP	H	ER	BB	SO
ANDUJAR, Luis	5.02	1-1	0	3	14.1	14	8	1	5
BOHANON, Brian	7.77	0-1	1	20	22.0	27	19	19	17
BROW, Scott	5.59	1-0	0	18	38.2	45	24	25	23
CARRARA, Giovanni	11.40	0-1	0	11	15.0	23	19	12	10
CASTILLO, Tony	4.23	2-3	1	40	72.1	72	34	20	48
CRABTREE, Tim	2.54	5-3	1	53	67.1	59	19	22	57
FLENER, Huck	4.58	3-2	0	15	70.2	68	36	33	44
GUZMAN, Juan	2.93	11-8	0	27	187.2	158	61	53	165
HANSON, Eric	5.41	13-17	0	35	214.2	243	129	102	156
HENTGEN, Pat	3.22	20-10	0	35	265.2	238	95	94	177
JANZEN, Marty	7.33	4-6	0	15	73.2	95	60	38	47
JOHNSON, Dane	3.00	0-0	0	10	9.0	5	3	5	7
QUANTRILL, Paul	5.43	5-14	0	38	134.1	172	81	51	86
RISLEY, Bill	3.89	0-1	0	25	41.2	33	18	25	29
SILVA, Jose	13.50	0-0	0	2	2.0	5	3	0	0
SPOLJARIC, Paul	3.08	2-2	1	28	38.0	30	13	19	38
TIMLIN, Mike	3.65	1-6	31	59	56.2	47	23	18	52
VIOLA, Frank	7.71	1-3	0	6	30.1	43	26	21	18
WARE, Jeff	9.09	1-5	0	13	32.2	35	33	31	11
WILLIAMS, Woody	4.73	4-5	0	12	59.0	64	31	21	43
1996 Totals	**4.57**	**74-88**	**35**	**162**	**1445.2**	**1476**	**734**	**610**	**1033**

1997

BATTER Pos.	Avg.	G	AB	R	H	HR	RBI
BRITO, Tilson IF	.222	49	126	9	28	0	8
BRUMFIELD, Jacob OF	.207	58	174	22	36	2	20
BUTLER, Rob OF-DH	.286	7	14	3	4	0	2
CARTER, Joe DH-OF-1B	.234	157	612	76	143	21	102
CRESPO, Felipe 3B-DH-2B	.286	12	28	3	8	1	5
CRUZ Jr., Jose OF	.231	55	212	31	49	14	34
DELGADO, Carlos 1B-DH	.262	153	519	79	136	30	91
DUNCAN, Mariano 2B	.228	39	167	20	38	0	12
EVANS, Tom 3B	.289	12	38	7	11	1	2
GARCIA, Carlos 2B	.220	103	350	29	77	3	23
GONZALEZ, Alex SS	.239	126	426	46	102	12	35
GREEN, Shawn OF-DH	.287	135	429	57	123	16	53
MARTINEZ, Sandy C	.000	3	2	1	0	0	0
MERCED, Orlando OF	.266	98	368	45	98	9	40
MOSQUERA, Julio C	.250	3	8	0	2	0	0
NIXON, Otis OF	.262	103	401	54	105	1	26
O'BRIEN, Charlie C	.218	69	225	22	49	4	27
PEREZ, Robert OF-DH	.192	37	78	4	15	2	6
PEREZ, Tomas SS-2B	.195	40	123	9	24	0	9
SAMUEL, Juan DH-1B-OF	.284	45	95	13	27	3	15
SANTIAGO, Benito C	.243	97	341	31	83	13	42
SIERRA, Ruben OF-DH	.208	14	48	4	10	1	5
SPRAGUE, Ed 3B	.228	138	504	63	115	14	48
STEWART, Shannon OF	.286	44	168	25	48	0	22
Designated Hitters	.237	156	598	71	142	25	95
Pinch Hitters	.127	–	63	8	8	1	8
Pitchers	.118	162	17	1	2	0	0
1997 Totals	**.244**	**162**	**5473**	**654**	**1333**	**147**	**627**

1997 *continued*

PITCHER	ERA	W-L	SV	G	IP	H	ER	BB	SO
ALMANZAR, Carlos	2.70	0-1	0	4	3.1	1	1	1	4
ANDUJAR, Luis	6.48	0-6	0	17	50.0	76	36	21	28
CARPENTER, Chris	5.09	3-7	0	14	81.1	108	46	37	55
CLEMENS, Roger	2.05	21-7	0	34	264.0	204	60	68	292
CRABTREE, Tim	7.08	3-3	2	37	40.2	65	32	17	26
DAAL, Omar	4.00	1-1	0	9	27.0	34	12	6	28
ESCOBAR, Kelvim	2.90	3-2	14	27	31.0	28	10	19	36
FLENER, Huck	9.87	0-1	0	8	17.1	40	19	6	9
GUZMAN, Juan	4.95	3-6	0	13	60.0	48	33	31	52
HANSON, Eric	7.80	0-0	0	3	15.0	15	13	6	18
HENTGEN, Pat	3.68	15-10	0	35	264.0	253	108	71	160
JANZEN, Marty	3.60	2-1	0	12	25.0	23	10	13	17
PERSON, Robert	5.61	5-10	0	23	128.1	125	80	60	99
PLESAC, Dan	3.58	2-4	1	73	50.1	47	20	19	61
QUANTRILL, Paul	1.94	6-7	5	77	88.0	103	19	17	56
RISLEY, Bill	8.31	0-1	0	3	4.1	3	4	2	2
ROBINSON, Ken	2.70	0-0	0	3	3.1	1	1	1	4
SPOLJARIC, Paul	3.19	0-3	3	37	48.0	37	17	36	70
TIMLIN, Mike	2.87	3-2	9	38	47.0	41	15	15	36
WILLIAMS, Woody	4.35	9-14	0	31	194.2	201	94	66	124
1997 Totals	**3.92**	**76-86**	**34**	**162**	**1442.2**	**1453**	**628**	**497**	**1150**

1998

BATTER Pos.	Avg.	G	AB	R	H	HR	RBI
BROWN, Kevin C	.264	52	110	17	29	2	15
CANSECO, Jose DH-OF	.237	151	583	98	138	46	107
CRESPO, Felipe OF-IF	.262	66	130	11	34	1	15
CRUZ Jr., Jose OF	.253	105	352	55	89	11	42
DALESANDRO, Mark C-3B-1B	.299	32	67	8	20	2	14
DELGADO, Carlos 1B	.292	142	530	94	155	38	115
EVANS, Tom 3B	.000	7	10	0	0	0	0
FERNANDEZ, Tony 2B-3B	.321	138	486	71	156	9	72
FLETCHER, Darrin C	.283	124	407	37	115	9	52
GONZALEZ, Alex SS	.239	158	568	70	136	13	51
GREBECK, Craig IF	.256	102	301	33	77	2	27
GREEN, Shawn OF	.278	158	630	106	175	35	100
LENNON, Patrick OF	.500	2	4	1	2	0	0
PEREZ, Tomas SS-2B	.111	6	9	1	1	0	0
PHILLIPS, Tony OF	.354	13	48	9	17	1	7
SAMUEL, Juan DH-OF	.180	43	50	14	9	1	2
SANTIAGO, Benito C	.310	15	29	3	9	0	4
SPRAGUE, Ed 3B	.238	105	382	49	91	17	51
STANLEY, Mike DH-1B	.240	98	341	49	82	22	47
STEWART, Shannon OF	.279	144	516	90	144	12	55
WITT, Kevin 1B	.143	5	7	0	1	0	0
Designated Hitters	.228	155	597	94	136	43	101
Pinch Hitters	.204	–	54	4	11	1	5
Pitchers	.100	163	20	0	2	0	0
1998 Totals	**.266**	**163**	**5580**	**816**	**1482**	**221**	**776**

PITCHER	ERA	W-L	SV	G	IP	H	ER	BB	SO
ALMANZAR, Carlos	5.34	2-2	0	25	28.2	34	17	8	20
ANDUJAR, Luis	9.53	0-0	0	5	5.2	12	6	2	1
CARPENTER, Chris	4.37	12-7	0	33	175	177	85	61	136
CLEMENS, Roger	2.65	20-6	0	33	234.2	169	69	88	271
ESCOBAR, Kelvim	3.73	7-3	0	22	79.2	72	33	35	72
GUZMAN, Juan	4.41	6-12	0	22	145.0	133	71	65	113
HALLADAY, Roy	1.93	1-0	0	2	14.0	9	3	2	13
HANSON, Eric	6.24	0-3	0	11	49.0	73	34	29	21
HENTGEN, Pat	5.17	12-11	0	29	177.0	208	102	69	94
MYERS, Randy	4.46	3-4	28	41	42.1	44	21	19	32
PERSON, Robert	7.04	3-1	6	27	38.1	45	30	22	31
PLESAC, Dan	3.78	4-3	4	78	50.0	41	21	16	55
QUANTRILL, Paul	2.59	3-4	7	82	80.0	88	23	22	59
RISLEY, Bill	5.27	3-4	0	44	54.2	52	32	34	42
RODRIGUEZ, Nerio	9.72	1-0	0	7	8.1	10	9	8	3
SINCLAIR, Steve	3.60	0-2	0	24	15.0	13	6	5	8
STIEB, Dave	4.83	1-2	2	19	50.1	58	27	17	27
VAN RYN, Ben	9.00	0-1	0	10	4.0	6	4	2	3
WILLIAMS, Woody	4.46	10-9	0	32	209.2	196	104	81	151
WITHEM, Shannon	3.00	0-0	0	1	3.0	3	1	2	2
1998 Totals	**4.28**	**88-74**	**47**	**163**	**1465.0**	**1443**	**697**	**587**	**1154**

1999

BATTER Pos.	Avg.	G	AB	R	H	HR	RBI
BATISTA, Tony SS	.285	98	375	61	107	26	79
BERROA, Geronimo DH-PH	.194	22	62	11	12	1	6
BLAKE, Casey 3B	.256	14	39	6	10	1	1
BORDERS, Pat C-DH	.214	6	14	1	3	1	3
BROWN, Kevin C	.444	2	9	1	4	0	1
BRUMFIELD, Jacob OF	.235	62	170	25	40	2	19
BUSH, Homer 2B-SS	.320	128	485	69	155	5	55
BUTLER, Rich DH-OF	.143	8	7	1	1	0	1
CRUZ Jr., Jose OF	.241	106	349	63	84	14	45
DALESANDRO, Mark C-DH-3B	.185	16	27	3	5	0	1
DELGADO, Carlos 1B	.272	152	573	113	156	44	134
FERNANDEZ, Tony 3B	.328	142	485	73	159	6	75
FLETCHER, Darrin C	.291	115	412	48	120	18	80
GONZALEZ, Alex SS	.292	38	154	22	45	2	12
GOODWIN, Curtis OF	.000	2	8	0	0	0	0
GREBECK, Craig IF-DH	.363	34	113	18	41	0	10
GREEN, Shawn OF	.309	153	614	134	190	42	123
GREENE, Willie DH-3B-OF	.204	81	226	22	46	12	41
HOLLINS, Dave DH	.222	27	99	12	22	2	6
KELLY, Pat 2B	.267	37	116	17	31	6	20
LENNON, Patrick OF	.207	9	29	3	6	1	6
MARTIN, Noberto 2B	.222	9	27	3	6	0	0
MATHENY, Mike C	.215	57	163	16	35	3	17
McRAE, Brian DH-OF	.195	31	82	11	16	3	11
OTANEZ, Willis 3B-1B	.252	42	127	21	32	5	13
SANDERS, Anthony DH-OF	.286	3	7	1	2	0	2
SEGUI, David DH-1B	.316	31	95	14	30	5	13
STEWART, Shannon OF	.304	145	608	102	185	11	67
WELLS, Vernon OF	.261	24	88	8	23	1	8
WITT, Kevin DH-PH	.206	15	34	3	7	1	5
WOODWARD, Chris SS	.231	14	26	1	6	0	2
Designated Hitters	.250	153	608	80	152	24	81
Pinch Hitters	.238	–	84	9	20	4	13
Pitchers	.053	162	19	0	1	0	0
1999 Totals	**.280**	**162**	**5642**	**883**	**1580**	**212**	**856**

PITCHER	ERA	W-L	SV	G	IP	H	ER	BB	SO
BALE, John	13.50	0-0	0	1	2.0	2	3	2	4
CARPENTER, Chris	4.38	9-8	0	24	150.0	177	73	48	106
DAVEY, Tom	4.70	1-1	1	29	44.0	40	23	26	42
ESCOBAR, Kelvim	5.69	14-11	0	33	174.0	203	110	81	129
FRASCATORE, John	3.41	7-1	1	33	37.0	42	14	9	22
GLOVER, Gary	0.00	0-0	0	1	0.0	0	0	1	0
HALLADAY, Roy	3.92	8-7	1	36	149.1	156	65	79	82
HAMILTON, Joey	6.52	7-8	0	22	98.0	118	71	39	56
HENTGEN, Pat	4.79	11-12	0	34	199.0	225	106	65	118
HUDEK, John	12.27	0-0	0	3	3.2	8	5	1	2
KOCH, Billy	3.39	0-5	31	56	63.2	55	24	30	57
LLOYD, Graeme	3.63	5-3	3	74	72.0	68	29	23	47
LUDWICK, Eric	27.00	0-0	0	1	1.0	3	3	2	0
MUNRO, Peter	6.02	0-2	0	31	55.1	70	37	23	38
PERSON, Robert	9.82	0-2	2	11	11.0	9	12	15	12
PLESAC, Dan	8.34	0-3	0	30	22.2	28	21	9	26
QUANTRILL, Paul	3.33	3-2	0	41	48.2	53	18	17	28
RODRIGUEZ, Nerio	13.50	0-1	0	2	2.0	2	3	2	2
ROMANO, Mike	11.81	0-0	0	3	5.1	8	7	5	3
SINCLAIR, Steve	12.71	0-0	0	3	5.2	7	8	4	3
SPOLJARIC, Paul	4.65	2-2	0	37	62.0	62	32	32	63
WELLS, David	4.82	17-10	0	34	231.2	246	124	62	169
1999 Totals	**4.93**	**84-78**	**39**	**162**	**1439.0**	**1582**	**788**	**575**	**1009**

2000

BATTER Pos.	Avg.	G	AB	R	H	HR	RBI
BATISTA, Tony 3B	.263	154	620	96	163	41	114
BUSH, Homer 2B	.215	76	297	38	64	1	18
CASTILLO, Alberto C	.211	66	185	14	39	1	16
CORDOVA, Marty OF-DH	.245	62	200	23	49	4	18
CRUZ Jr., Jose OF	.242	162	603	91	146	31	76
DELGADO, Carlos 1B	.344	162	569	115	196	41	137
DUCEY, Rob OF	.154	5	13	2	2	0	1
FLETCHER, Darrin C	.320	122	416	43	133	20	58
FULLMER, Brad DH	.295	133	482	76	142	32	104
GONZALEZ, Alex SS	.252	141	527	68	133	15	69
GREBECK, Craig 2B-SS	.295	66	241	38	71	3	23
GREENE, Charlie C	.111	3	9	0	1	0	0
GREENE, Todd DH-PH	.235	34	85	11	20	5	10
MARTINEZ, Dave OF	.311	47	180	29	56	2	22
MONDESI, Raul OF	.271	96	388	78	105	24	67
MORANDINI, Mickey 2B	.271	35	107	10	29	0	7
MOTTOLA, Chad OF	.222	3	9	1	2	0	2
PHELPS, Josh C	.000	1	1	0	0	0	0
STEWART, Shannon OF	.319	136	583	107	186	21	69
THOMPSON, Andy OF	.167	2	6	2	1	0	1
WELLS, Vernon OF	.000	3	2	0	0	0	0
WISE, Dewayne OF	.136	28	22	3	3	0	0
WOODWARD, Chris IF	.183	37	104	16	19	3	14
Pitchers	.107	162	28	3	3	0	0
Designated Hitters	.285	153	606	92	173	39	120
Pinch Hitters	.333	–	51	6	17	0	8
2000 Totals	**.275**	**162**	**5677**	**861**	**1562**	**244**	**826**

PITCHER	ERA	W-L	SV	G	IP	H	ER	BB	SO
ANDREWS, Clayton	10.02	1-2	0	8	20.2	34	23	9	12
BALE, John	14.73	0-0	0	2	3.2	5	6	3	6
BORBON, Pedro	6.48	1-1	1	59	41.2	45	30	38	29
CARPENTER, Chris	6.26	10-12	0	34	175.1	204	122	83	113
CASTILLO, Frank	3.59	10-5	0	25	138.0	112	55	56	104
COCO, Pasqual	9.00	0-0	0	1	4.0	5	4	5	2
CUBILLAN, Darwin	8.04	1-0	0	7	15.2	20	14	11	14
DeWITT, Matt	8.56	1-0	0	8	13.2	20	13	9	6
ESCOBAR, Kelvim	5.35	10-15	2	43	180.0	186	107	85	142
ESTRELLA, Leoncio	5.79	0-0	0	2	4.2	9	3	0	3
FRASCATORE, John	5.42	2-4	0	60	73.0	87	44	33	30
GUNDERSON, Eric	7.11	0-1	0	6	6.1	15	5	2	2
GUTHRIE, Mark	4.79	0-2	0	23	20.2	20	11	9	20
HALLADAY, Roy	10.64	4-7	0	19	67.2	107	80	42	44
HAMILTON, Joey	3.55	2-1	0	6	33.0	28	13	12	15
KOCH, Billy	2.63	9-3	33	68	78.2	78	23	18	60
LOAIZA, Esteban	3.62	5-7	0	14	92.0	95	37	26	62
MUNRO, Pete	5.96	1-1	0	9	25.2	38	17	16	16
PAINTER, Lance	4.73	2-0	0	42	66.2	69	35	22	53
QUANTRILL, Paul	4.52	2-5	1	68	83.2	100	42	25	47
TRACHSEL, Steve	5.29	2-5	0	11	63.0	72	37	25	32
WELLS, David	4.11	20-8	0	35	229.2	266	105	31	166
2000 Totals	**5.14**	**83-79**	**37**	**162**	**1437.1**	**1615**	**821**	**560**	**978**

Average (350 AB)

BATTER	AVG
MOLITOR	.315
ALOMAR	.307
FLETCHER	.298
FERNANDEZ	.297
STEWART, S	.297
FULLMER	.295
OLERUD	.293
COLLINS	.291
WINFIELD	.290
BUSH	.289
GREBECK	.289
GARCIA, D	.288
BELL, G	.286
GREEN	.286
LEACH	.283
DELGADO	.282
BONNELL	.281
KNORR	.281
MULLINIKS	.280
FAIRLY	.279
McGRIFF	.278
NIXON	.275
JOHNSON, C	.273
HOWELL	.272

Games

BATTER	G
FERNANDEZ	1402
MOSEBY	1392
WHITT	1218
BELL, G	1181
MULLINIKS	1115
UPSHAW	1115
CARTER	1039
BARFIELD	1032
GRIFFIN	982
IORG	931
GRUBER	921
OLERUD	920
GARCIA, D	902
SPRAGUE	888
DELGADO	829
LEE	753
BORDERS	747
GONZALEZ	736
GREEN	716
ALOMAR	703
WHITE	656
WOODS, A	595
McGRIFF	578
MAYBERRY	549

At Bats

BATTER	AB
FERNANDEZ	5276
MOSEBY	5124
BELL, G	4528
CARTER	4093
UPSHAW	3710
GARCIA, D	3572
WHITT	3514
BARFIELD	3463
GRIFFIN	3396
SPRAGUE	3156
OLERUD	3103
GRUBER	3094
MULLINIKS	3013
DELGADO	2901
WHITE	2711
ALOMAR	2706
GONZALEZ	2622
GREEN	2513
IORG	2450
BORDERS	2309
LEE	2152
WOODS, A	1958
HOWELL	1954
McGRIFF	1944

Runs

BATTER	R
MOSEBY	768
FERNANDEZ	699
BELL, G	641
CARTER	578
UPSHAW	538
BARFIELD	530
DELGADO	493
OLERUD	464
GARCIA, D	453
WHITE	452
ALOMAR	451
WHITT	424
GRUBER	421
GREEN	402
SPRAGUE	388
GRIFFIN	382
MULLINIKS	382
McGRIFF	348
GONZALEZ	328
STEWART, S	328
MOLITOR	270
IORG	251
CRUZ Jr.	240
LEE	231

Hits

BATTER	H
FERNANDEZ	1565
MOSEBY	1319
BELL, G	1294
CARTER	1051
GARCIA, D	1028
UPSHAW	982
BARFIELD	919
OLERUD	910
WHITT	888
GRIFFIN	844
MULLINIKS	843
ALOMAR	832
DELGADO	818
GRUBER	800
SPRAGUE	773
WHITE	733
GREEN	718
GONZALEZ	637
IORG	633
BORDERS	590
STEWART, S	574
LEE	547
McGRIFF	540
HOWELL	532

Doubles

BATTER	2B
FERNANDEZ	287
MOSEBY	242
BELL, G	237
CARTER	218
DELGADO	214
OLERUD	213
MULLINIKS	204
UPSHAW	177
GARCIA, D	172
SPRAGUE	170
WHITT	164
GREEN	164
BARFIELD	162
WHITE	155
ALOMAR	152
GONZALEZ	147
GRUBER	145
GRIFFIN	127
BORDERS	127
IORG	125
STEWART, S	114
HOWELL	101
McGRIFF	99
MOLITOR	98

Triples

BATTER	3B
FERNANDEZ	72
MOSEBY	60
GRIFFIN	50
UPSHAW	42
ALOMAR	36
WHITE	34
BELL, G	32
CARTER	28
BARFIELD	27
GARCIA, D	26
GRUBER	24
BAILOR	19
COLLINS	19
STEWART, S	17
HOWELL	17
LEE	17
IORG	16
WHITT	15
GREEN	15
GONZALEZ	15
FELIX	15
MULLINIKS	14
WOODS, A	14
BONNELL	14

Home Runs

BATTER	HR
CARTER	203
BELL, G	202
DELGADO	190
BARFIELD	179
MOSEBY	149
WHITT	131
McGRIFF	125
GREEN	119
GRUBER	114
SPRAGUE	113
UPSHAW	112
OLERUD	109
MAYBERRY	92
WHITE	72
VELEZ	72
CRUZ Jr.	70
MULLINIKS	68
BATISTA	67
GONZALEZ	66
FERNANDEZ	59
ALOMAR	55
BORDERS	54
JOHNSON, C	54
MOLITOR	51

RBIs

BATTER	RBI
BELL, G	740
CARTER	736
MOSEBY	651
DELGADO	604
FERNANDEZ	601
BARFIELD	527
WHITT	518
UPSHAW	478
OLERUD	468
GRUBER	434
SPRAGUE	418
MULLINIKS	389
GREEN	376
ALOMAR	342
McGRIFF	305
GARCIA, D	296
WHITE	274
GONZALEZ	274
MAYBERRY	272
BORDERS	272
MOLITOR	246
VELEZ	243
IORG	238
HOWELL	234

Walks

BATTER	BB
MOSEBY	547
OLERUD	514
FERNANDEZ	438
DELGADO	436
MULLINIKS	416
WHITT	403
UPSHAW	390
McGRIFF	352
BARFIELD	342
ALOMAR	322
CARTER	286
VELEZ	278
SPRAGUE	270
MAYBERRY	258
BELL, G	255
CRUZ Jr.	220
GONZALEZ	214
WHITE	209
GREEN	206
GRUBER	195
MOLITOR	193
STEWART, S	188
HOWELL	178
JOHNSON, C	178

Strikeouts

BATTER	SO
MOSEBY	1015
BARFIELD	855
DELGADO	728
CARTER	696
SPRAGUE	647
GONZALEZ	609
UPSHAW	576
WHITE	572
BELL, G	563
GREEN	510
McGRIFF	495
GRUBER	493
FERNANDEZ	485
MULLINIKS	465
WHITT	450
OLERUD	430
LEE	426
CRUZ Jr.	391
BORDERS	364
HOWELL	337
VELEZ	333
GRIFFIN	313
IORG	298
ALOMAR	291

Stolen Bases

BATTER	SB
MOSEBY	255
ALOMAR	206
GARCIA, D	194
FERNANDEZ	172
WHITE	126
STEWART, S	121
NIXON	101
COLLINS	91
GRUBER	80
GRIFFIN	79
CARTER	78
UPSHAW	76
GREEN	76
GONZALEZ	67
BELL, G	59
BARFIELD	55
MOLITOR	54
WILSON	46
BAILOR	46
CRUZ Jr.	46
LIRIANO	44
BUSH	41
FELIX	31
BONNELL	31

Hit By Pitch

BATTER	HBP
SPRAGUE	68
DELGADO	61
MOSEBY	50
CARTER	49
FERNANDEZ	47
BELL, G	35
GRUBER	35
STEWART, S	34
OLERUD	32
WHITE	29
GREEN	28
O'BRIEN	28
BARFIELD	27
GARCIA, D	27
GONZALEZ	25
MAYBERRY	21
UPSHAW	21
FLETCHER	17
ALOMAR	16
BAILOR	15
MALDONADO	15
GRIFFIN	14
HOWELL	13
JOHNSON, C	12
BUSH	11

Sacrifice Hits

BATTER	SH
GRIFFIN	74
GONZALEZ	57
ALOMAR	39
MOSEBY	38
FERNANDEZ	34
WOODS, A	31
LEE	28
GARCIA, D	27
UPSHAW	27
McKAY	24
GOMEZ	21
BAILOR	21
IORG	21
WHITT	20
BORDERS	19
LIRIANO	18
DAVIS, B	14
ASHBY	14
CEDENO	13
NIXON	13
BOSETTI	13
WHITE	13
MULLINIKS	13
GRUBER	13
BARFIELD	13

Sacrifice Flies

BATTER	SF
CARTER	65
BELL, G	59
FERNANDEZ	43
MOSEBY	40
WHITT	36
GRUBER	35
OLERUD	35
DELGADO	32
SPRAGUE	28
MULLINIKS	24
GRIFFIN	24
BARFIELD	24
UPSHAW	24
MARTINEZ, B	23
ALOMAR	22
GARCIA, D	20
IORG	19
MOLITOR	17
LEE	17
BORDERS	17
GREEN	17
WHITE	17
MAYBERRY	16
FLETCHER	15
WOODS, A	15

Total Bases

BATTER	TB
BELL, G	2201
FERNANDEZ	2173
MOSEBY	2128
CARTER	1934
BARFIELD	1672
DELGADO	1616
UPSHAW	1579
WHITT	1475
OLERUD	1462
GARCIA, D	1348
GRUBER	1335
SPRAGUE	1302
MULLINIKS	1279
GREEN	1269
ALOMAR	1221
WHITE	1172
GRIFFIN	1110
McGRIFF	1030
GONZALEZ	1012
BORDERS	897
STEWART, S	854
IORG	850
MAYBERRY	811
HOWELL	796
MOLITOR	781

On-Base Pct. (350 AB)

BATTER	OBP
OLERUD	.395
McGRIFF	.389
MOLITOR	.387
DELGADO	.383
ALOMAR	.382
WINFIELD	.377
VELEZ	.372
JOHNSON, C	.372
STEWART, S	.368
MULLINIKS	.365
MALDONADO	.363
NIXON	.362
FAIRLY	.362
GREBECK	.361
COLLINS	.355
HUFF	.355
FERNANDEZ	.353
MAYBERRY	.353
MERCED	.352
GREEN	.344
FLETCHER	.341
FULLMER	.340
LEACH	.340
CRUZ Jr.	.337
UPSHAW	.336

Slugging Pct. (350 AB)

BATTER	SLG
FULLMER	.558
DELGADO	.557
BATISTA	.537
McGRIFF	.530
MONDESI	.523
CANSECO	.518
GREEN	.505
WINFIELD	.491
BELL, G	.486
MOLITOR	.484
BARFIELD	.483
CARTER	.473
FIELDER	.472
OLERUD	.471
FLETCHER	.470
JOHNSON, C	.466
FAIRLY	.465
MALDONADO	.462
VELEZ	.461
ALOMAR	.451
MAYBERRY	.450
CRUZ Jr.	.443
STEWART, S	.442
WHITE	.432
CARTY	.432

Wins

PITCHER	W
STIEB	175
CLANCY	128
KEY	116
HENTGEN	105
WELLS, D	84
GUZMAN	76
STOTTLEMYRE	69
LEAL	51
ALEXANDER	46
CERUTTI	46
CLEMENS	41
CARPENTER	34
ESCOBAR	34
WARD, D	32
EICHHORN	29
HENKE	29
MORRIS	28
WILLIAMS, W	28
LEMANCZYK	27
ACKER	26
FLANAGAN	26
LEITER	26
JACKSON, RL	24
TIMLIN	23
JEFFERSON	22
McLAUGHLIN	22

Losses

PITCHER	L
CLANCY	140
STIEB	134
KEY	81
HENTGEN	76
STOTTLEMYRE	70
GUZMAN	62
LEAL	58
JEFFERSON	56
WELLS, D	55
LEMANCZYK	45
GARVIN	41
CERUTTI	37
WARD, D	36
CARPENTER	34
WILLIAMS, W	34
QUANTRILL	32
ESCOBAR	31
GOTT	30
UNDERWOOD	30
HENKE	29
FLANAGAN	27
ALEXANDER	26
LEITER	24
McLAUGHLIN	24
ACKER	22
TIMLIN	22

ERA (162 IP)

PITCHER	ERA
CLEMENS	2.33
HENKE	2.48
EICHHORN	3.03
CONE	3.14
WARD, D	3.18
STIEB	3.42
KEY	3.42
CASTILLO, T	3.49
JACKSON, RL	3.50
ALEXANDER	3.56
TIMLIN	3.62
QUANTRILL	3.79
CERUTTI	3.87
UNDERWOOD	3.88
McLAUGHLIN	3.88
FLANAGAN	3.96
MURPHY	4.00
WELLS, D	4.06
GUZMAN	4.07
ACKER	4.07
CLANCY	4.10
HENTGEN	4.14
LEAL	4.14
LEITER	4.20
LAMP	4.20

Games

PITCHER	G
WARD, D	452
HENKE	446
STIEB	439
CLANCY	352
KEY	317
QUANTRILL	306
WELLS, D	306
TIMLIN	305
ACKER	281
EICHHORN	279
HENTGEN	252
CASTILLO, T	218
STOTTLEMYRE	206
GARVIN	196
GUZMAN	195
McLAUGHLIN	195
CERUTTI	191
JACKSON, RL	190
PLESAC	181
WILLIAMS, W	166
LEAL	165
LAMP	149
WILLIS	144
JEFFERSON	127
ESCOBAR	125

Games Started

PITCHER	GS
STIEB	408
CLANCY	345
KEY	250
HENTGEN	222
GUZMAN	195
STOTTLEMYRE	175
LEAL	151
WELLS, D	138
CERUTTI	108
ALEXANDER	103
CARPENTER	88
LEMANCZYK	82
FLANAGAN	76
WILLIAMS, W	76
CLEMENS	67
GARVIN	65
GOTT	65
ESCOBAR	64
UNDERWOOD	62
LEITER	61
MORRIS	61
STEWART, D	48
HANSON	45
JEFFERSON	37
MOORE, B	37

Complete Games

PITCHER	CG
STIEB	103
CLANCY	73
HENTGEN	31
LEAL	27
KEY	26
LEMANCZYK	25
ALEXANDER	25
JEFFERSON	21
UNDERWOOD	19
WELLS, D	18
GARVIN	15
STOTTLEMYRE	15
GUZMAN	15
CLEMENS	14
MORRIS	10
GOTT	8
CARPENTER	8
TODD	7
MOORE, B	7
CERUTTI	7
CONE	5
HANSON	4
LEITER	4
ESCOBAR	4
Several Tied with	3

Shutouts

PITCHER	SHO
STIEB	30
CLANCY	11
HENTGEN	9
KEY	8
CLEMENS	6
JEFFERSON	4
STOTTLEMYRE	4
GOTT	3
LEMANCZYK	3
CARPENTER	3
ALEXANDER	3
LEAL	3
CONE	2
MORRIS	2
LEITER	2
UNDERWOOD	2
CERUTTI	2
WELLS, D	2
GUZMAN	2
Several Tied with	1

Saves

PITCHER	SV
HENKE	217
WARD, D	121
KOCH	64
TIMLIN	52
McLAUGHLIN	31
JACKSON, RL	30
MYERS	28
HALL	20
ESCOBAR	16
CAUDILL	16
CASTILLO, T	16
WILLIS	15
EICHHORN	15
ACKER	14
LAMP	13
WELLS, D	13
QUANTRILL	13
MURRAY	11
MOFFITT	10
KEY	10
CRUZ	9
MURPHY	9
LAVELLE	9
PERSON	8
VUCKOVICH	8
GARVIN	8

Innings Pitched

PITCHER	IP
STIEB	2873.0
CLANCY	2204.2
KEY	1695.2
HENTGEN	1555.2
GUZMAN	1215.2
WELLS, D	1148.2
STOTTLEMYRE	1139.0
LEAL	946.0
CERUTTI	772.1
ALEXANDER	750.0
JEFFERSON	666.1
WARD, D	650.2
WILLIAMS, W	613.1
GARVIN	606.0
CARPENTER	581.2
LEMANCZYK	575.0
HENKE	563.0
ACKER	524.1
CLEMENS	498.2
EICHHORN	493.0
ESCOBAR	464.2
FLANAGAN	452.1
GOTT	442.1
QUANTRILL	434.2
UNDERWOOD	424.2

HR/9 IP (162 IP)

PITCHER	HR/9
CLEMENS	0.36
WARD, D	0.41
EICHHORN	0.60
LEITER	0.65
MUSSELMAN, J	0.66
TIMLIN	0.66
STIEB	0.70
LAMP	0.72
CONE	0.74
GOTT	0.75
HENKE	0.77
FLANAGAN	0.78
JACKSON, RL	0.80
LEMANCZYK	0.81
MORRIS	0.82
ACKER	0.84
GUZMAN	0.85
KEY	0.88
CASTILLO, T	0.88
CLANCY	0.89
STOTTLEMYRE	0.91
McLAUGHLIN	0.95
LEAL	0.96
WILLS	0.97
ALEXANDER	0.97
UNDERWOOD	0.97

Hits/9 IP (162 IP)

PITCHER	H/9
HENKE	6.57
CLEMENS	6.73
WARD, D	7.32
CONE	7.41
STIEB	7.97
EICHHORN	8.12
GUZMAN	8.14
JACKSON, RL	8.20
TIMLIN	8.44
CASTILLO, T	8.47
LEITER	8.54
GOTT	8.59
MUSSELMAN, J	8.61
KEY	8.62
WILLIAMS, W	8.64
UNDERWOOD	8.77
CLANCY	8.92
ALEXANDER	9.02
WILLS	9.03
STEWART, D	9.05
McLAUGHLIN	9.05
PERSON	9.07
LEAL	9.11
WELLS, D	9.17
HENTGEN	9.18
ACKER	9.18

Walks/9 IP (162 IP)

PITCHER	BB/9
ALEXANDER	2.06
KEY	2.14
WELLS, D	2.30
HENKE	2.65
QUANTRILL	2.73
CLEMENS	2.82
TODD	2.85
CERUTTI	2.96
FLANAGAN	2.98
LAMP	3.00
LEAL	3.04
EICHHORN	3.05
STIEB	3.20
CASTILLO, T	3.22
HENTGEN	3.22
GARVIN	3.25
STOTTLEMYRE	3.27
MORRIS	3.32
LEMANCZYK	3.32
CLANCY	3.32
JACKSON, RL	3.42
CONE	3.44
MURPHY	3.45
ACKER	3.54
HUFFMAN	3.54
CARPENTER	3.54

Winning Pct. (15 decisions)

PITCHER	W-L %
CLEMENS	.759
CASTILLO, F	.667
MUSSELMAN, J	.645
ALEXANDER	.639
MORRIS	.609
WELLS, D	.604
EICHHORN	.604
LAMP	.600
WILLS	.600
CONE	.591
KEY	.589
JOHNSON, Jo	.588
HENTGEN	.580
STIEB	.566
MURRAY	.563
CERUTTI	.554
GUZMAN	.551
STEWART, D	.543
ACKER	.542
JACKSON, RL	.533
KOCH	.529
ESCOBAR	.523
LEITER	.520
TIMLIN	.511
Several Tied at	.500

Strikeouts

PITCHER	K
STIEB	1658
CLANCY	1237
GUZMAN	1030
HENTGEN	995
KEY	944
WELLS, D	784
WARD, D	671
STOTTLEMYRE	662
HENKE	644
CLEMENS	563
LEAL	491
WILLIAMS, W	439
CARPENTER	410
ALEXANDER	392
ESCOBAR	379
EICHHORN	372
CERUTTI	369
TIMLIN	331
LEITER	329
GARVIN	320
JEFFERSON	307
QUANTRILL	276
GOTT	276
ACKER	273
UNDERWOOD	267

Strikeouts/9 IP (162 IP)

PITCHER	K/9 INN
HENKE	10.29
CLEMENS	10.16
WARD, D	9.28
GUZMAN	7.63
TIMLIN	7.57
ESCOBAR	7.34
CONE	7.31
PERSON	7.19
LEITER	7.13
EICHHORN	6.79
WILLIAMS, W	6.44
CARPENTER	6.34
STEWART, D	6.31
HANSON	6.30
WILLS	6.17
WELLS, D	6.14
HENTGEN	5.76
QUANTRILL	5.71
UNDERWOOD	5.66
GOTT	5.62
CASTILLO, T	5.50
McLAUGHLIN	5.46
JACKSON, RL	5.45
HALLADAY	5.42
MORRIS	5.38

Runs Allowed

PITCHER	R
STIEB	1208
CLANCY	1104
HENTGEN	783
KEY	710
GUZMAN	612
STOTTLEMYRE	597
WELLS, D	566
LEAL	476
JEFFERSON	385
CERUTTI	378
CARPENTER	363
LEMANCZYK	334
GARVIN	318
ALEXANDER	315
WILLIAMS, W	308
ESCOBAR	285
ACKER	269
WARD, D	255
GOTT	233
MORRIS	230
UNDERWOOD	218
FLANAGAN	217
MOORE, B	213
LEITER	209
QUANTRILL	205

Hit Batsmen

PITCHER	HB
STIEB	129
STOTTLEMYRE	49
HENTGEN	37
CLANCY	28
WELLS, D	28
ACKER	25
KEY	24
EICHHORN	24
GUZMAN	23
LEAL	22
CLEMENS	19
MOORE, B	19
CERUTTI	16
WARD, D	16
CARPENTER	15
ALEXANDER	14
WILLIAMS, W	13
GARVIN	13
LEMANCZYK	13
ESCOBAR	13
MORRIS	13
QUANTRILL	12
LEITER	12
Several Tied with	11

Wild Pitches

PITCHER	WP
GUZMAN	88
CLANCY	82
HENTGEN	55
STIEB	51
WARD, D	50
WELLS, D	46
LEMANCZYK	36
KEY	31
STOTTLEMYRE	30
CERUTTI	30
CARPENTER	24
LEITER	24
LEAL	23
ACKER	23
MORRIS	23
HENKE	21
EICHHORN	19
UNDERWOOD	18
WILLIAMS, W	17
GARVIN	17
ALEXANDER	16
TIMLIN	16
HANSON	15
COX	13
HALLADAY	12
VUCKOVICH	12

Credits

CP Picture Archive:
Elise Amendola 136 (bottom left); Robert Borea 150 (left); Hans Deryk 138 (top inset); Kevin Frayer 145, 146, 160 (top), 163, 164 (bottom right); Frank Gunn 130, 136 (bottom right), 144 (left), 153 (right); Aaron Harris 159; Bill Janscha 157 (right); Rene Johnston 153, 154 (top), 156, 158; Jim Rogash 147; Phil Snell 120 (bottom), 121 (bottom left), 136 (top right).

Globe and Mail:
Barrie Davis 17; Hans Deryk 57 (bottom), 58, 62 (top); Tibor Kolley 14 (bottom right), 57 (top), 63, 90 (right), 140 (top left); Fred Lum 111; John Maiola 29 (right), 33 (top); John McNeill 31; Edward Regan 15 (top), 88 (bottom); Dennis Robinson 10, 16 (top); Thomas Szlukovenyi 47, 59 (bottom), 89 (top), 166; Jeff Wasserman 62 (bottom), 71 (top).

Oakland Tribune:
Ron Reisterer 89 (bottom).

Rich Pilling/Major League Baseball Photos:
164 (bottom left).

Seattle Times:
Greg Gilbert 103.

Toronto Blue Jays Archives:
endpapers, 2–4, 6–10, 13, 14 (top left, bottom left), 15 (bottom), 16 (bottom), 18, 20, 22 (bottom), 24 (bottom), 26–28, 29 (bottom), 30, 32, 33 (bottom), 34, 36–43, 46, 48, 49, 50 (top), 51, 52, 54, 59 (top), 65, 66, 68, 69 (bottom), 70, 76, 78, 82, 83, 84 (bottom), 85–87, 91, 92 (top), 93, 94, 96 (top, inset), 97, 98, 102 (bottom), 104 (bottom), 105, 107 (right), 109, 110 (right), 112, 113, 115, 116 (right), 117 (right), 118, 119 (inserts), 120 (top), 122–124, 126–129, 131–133, 135, 136 (top left) 137–139, 140 (right, bottom), 141–143, 144 (right), 148, 150 (right), 151 (left), 152 (left), 154 (bottom), 155, 157 (left), 160 (bottom) 161, 162, 164 (top), 167–169, 171, 173, 175–177, 179–183, 185–188, 190–198, 200, 201, 203–216.

Toronto Star:
(David Bebee, Graham Bezant, Tony Bock, Ron Bull, David Cooper, Al Dunlop, Jeff Goode, Doug Griffin, Richard Lautens, Frank Lennon, Dick Loek, Mike Slaughter, Boris Spremo C.M., Michael Stuparyk, Jim Wilkes) 14 (top right), 19, 21, 22 (top), 23, 24 (top left), 29 (top), 45, 50 (bottom), 55, 56, 64 (top), 75 (top), 79, 80, 102 (top), 104 (top), 106, 125, 149, 151 (right).

Toronto Sun:
117 (left); Carlo Allegri 107 (left); Stan Behal 67, 73, 74, 90 (left), 99 (top), 108 (top), 111 (insert), 114 (left), 116 (left) 119, 121 (top left); Norm Betts 75 (bottom), 99 (bottom); Mike Cassese 71 (bottom), 77, 81,100–101, Jack Cusano 53; Hans Deryk 44; Barry Gray 25; Veronica Henri 110 (left); Paul Henry 88 (top); Ken Kerr 72, 96 (bottom); Tim McKenna 84 (top); Michael Peake 35; Greig Reekie 114 (right); Craig Robertson 92 (bottom), 108 (bottom); Bill Sanford 69 (top); Fred Thornhill 60, 61, 95, 121 (bottom right), 134, 136 (top right), 138 (bottom inset); Alex Urosevic 121 (top right).

Stephen Zweig:
170.

Contributing photographers, Toronto Blue Jays Archives:
Terry Hancey, Roger Luce, Major League Baseball Photos (Paul Cunningham, Rich Pilling, Jerry Wachter), Al Messerschmidt, Miles Nadel, Fred Thornhill.

Baseball cards courtesy of Ralph Dinger.
Blue Jays memorabilia courtesy of the Zweig family.

Special Thanks...

In addition to the players, coaches and managers that have worn the Blue Jays uniform from 1977 to 2001, many people have contributed to the organization's success. Special thanks to the club's many fans and to everyone who has worked for the Blue Jays including scouts, in-stadium personnel, trainers and clubhouse staff, ticketing and group sales, groundskeepers, baseball operations, media relations, marketing, finance, information systems, merchandising, broadcasting, team doctors as well as minor league players, coaches and staff.